D0144996

Is it true, as the textbooks tell us, that Darwinism basically encouraged war and racist imperialism, that it generated violent images of 'man the fighting animal' – perceptions that paved the way for the holocaust of 1914–18? Or was there an alternative legacy from Darwin that legitimised peace and mutual aid, rather than bloody struggle, human freedom rather than biological determinism? This book examines these issues, tracing the historical debate that raged over the biological causes and effects of war between the publication of Darwin's *Origin of Species* in 1859 and World War I. It reconstructs the theories of war and human pugnacity of thinkers such as Charles Darwin, Herbert Spencer, Walter Bagehot, Alfred Wallace, T. H. Huxley, Karl Pearson, Peter Kropotkin, Jacques Novicow, William McDougall, Peter Chalmers Mitchell and a host of now-forgotten naturalists, biometricians, geneticists, eugenists, physicians, psychologists, professionals and minor savants of the time. It explores the use, and misuse, of analogies drawn from biology and applied to society. Paul Crook concludes that historians have undervalued the discourse of 'peace biology' that stemmed from Darwin's holistic ecology; a discourse that was in significant ways more amenable to traditional moral culture than was unpleasantly ruthless militarism. Peace biology proved to be versatile and resilient, although bedevilled by internal dissonances. Its liberal vision of an autonomous humanity survived even the challenge of the 'new genetics' and the shock of the First World War, when instinctivist theories promoted a reductionist image of a belligerent and territorial humankind, reminiscent of present-day sociobiology.

Darwinism, war and history

*The debate over the biology of war from the
'Origin of Species' to the First World War*

Paul Crook

The University of Queensland

BF
575
.A3
C76
1994

Indiana University
Library
Northwest

CAMBRIDGE
UNIVERSITY PRESS

Published by the Press Syndicate of the University of Cambridge
The Pitt Building, Trumpington Street, Cambridge, CB2 1RP
40 West 20th Street, New York, NY 10011-4211, USA
10 Stamford Road, Oakleigh, Melbourne 3166, Australia

© Cambridge University Press 1994

First published 1994

Printed in Great Britain at the University Press, Cambridge

A catalogue record for this book is available from the British Library

Library of Congress cataloguing in publication data

Crook, D. P. (David Paul)
Darwinism, war and history: the debate over the biology of war from the
Origin of Species to the First World War/by Paul Crook.
  p. cm.
Includes bibliographical references.
ISBN 0 521 444659 (hc)
1. Aggressiveness (Psychology) – History. 2. Darwin, Charles
1809–1882 – Influence. 3. Social Darwinism – History. 4. Biopolitics –
History. 5. World War 1914–1918 – Causes. 6. War – Psychological
aspects – History. 7. Peace – Psychological aspects – History. I. Title.
BF575.A3C76 1994
303.6′6–dc20 93-11156 CIP

ISBN 0 521 44465 9 hardback

ISBN 0 521 46645 8 paperback

TAG

In memory of
Gordon Greenwood and Damodar Singhal

Contents

Acknowledgements

I cannot here thank all of the institutions and people who over the years have helped to sustain my research. They are too numerous to list. My heartfelt gratitude goes out to them all, but in particular I must express my indebtedness to the following: for funding, to the Australian Research Commission and the University of Queensland; for library assistance to a host of bodies, but in particular to the University of Queensland Library, especially to the overworked inter-library loan staff and to my old friend Spencer Routh, all-knowing and all-modest, and also to the Cambridge University Library; for research assistance, at various times, to Alexia Strong, Dushen Salecich, Dan O'Donnell, Lyn Gasteen, Mary Kooyman, Bernadette Turner, and especial thanks to Margaret Lee, not least for her work in helping to correct the manuscript and prepare the bibliography. A number of friends and colleagues read parts of the manuscript, and offered amiable criticism, interest and moral support. They include Bob Bannister, Tony Barnett, John Halliday and Ann Wallin. I would also propose a vote of thanks to friends in the History Department of the University of Queensland, my extended family so to speak, and to Geoffrey Bolton, who as head of department has been unfailingly supportive of scholarly endeavour. Richard Fisher, my editor at Cambridge University Press, has also been a rock of encouragement over the years. A good deal of the research for this book was done in the congenial atmosphere of Cambridge during periods of study leave generously granted to me by my university. I particularly benefited from a Visiting Fellowship bestowed upon me by Clare Hall in 1992. Finally, I dedicate this book to the memory of two great men, Gordon Greenwood and Damodar Singhal, who were mentors to me as a young scholar and whose intellectual and human influence upon me has been incalculable.

The journals below have kindly granted permission to incorporate material that first appeared in the following articles of mine: 'Darwinism – The Political Implications', *History of European Ideas*, 2, 1 (1981), 19–34 (reprinted by permission of Kluwer Academic Publishers); 'Darwin on War and Aggression', *Australian Journal of Politics and History*, 29, 2

(1983), 344–53; 'Nature's Pruning Hook', *Australian Journal of Politics and History*, 33, 3 (1987), 237–52; 'Peter Chalmers Mitchell and Anti-War Evolutionism in Britain During the Great War', *Journal of the History of Biology*, 22, 2 (1989), 325–56; 'Man the Fighting Animal: Belligerent Images of Humankind in the Anglo-American World, 1914–18', *Australian Journal of American Studies*, 8, 2 (1989), 25–39; 'War as a Genetic Disaster? The World War I Debate over the Eugenics of Warfare', *War and Society*, 8, 1 (1990), 47–70.

David Paul Crook
Brisbane, Australia

Introduction

At a Washington science conference in the early summer of 1918, as the First World War was drawing towards its finale, the noted American biologist Raymond Pearl rebuked his fellow naturalists for failing to conceive of war as a biological event, 'a gigantic experiment in human evolution'. Reluctantly he traced the war back to his hero, 'that gentlest and kindest of souls', Charles Darwin: 'I believe it to be literally true that the one event in the history of Western Europe which more than any other single one laid the foundation for the situation in which Western Europe finds itself today, was the publication of a book called *The Origin of Species*.' Pearl exemplified the schizoid tendencies that often prevailed in western thought about the connection between Darwinism and war. On the one hand, he blamed 'the frightful welter of blood' on the 'gross perversion' of Darwin's views by German biologists, who ignored the mental and moral qualities of humankind. On the other hand, Pearl himself saw humans as innately pugnacious and war an adaptive response to long-term evolutionary pressures.[1] In this he anticipated the neo-Darwinist doctrine of modern sociobiology. In fact the ancestors of sociobiology on war and human aggression are to be discovered in the era from 1880 to 1919.

World War I seemed to validate images of violent simian humanity, while Allied propaganda magnified the demonic role of Prussianised Social Darwinism in causing the war. Perhaps for these reasons, an imaginative version or mythology of Darwinism as bellicose has been perpetuated in the historical literature of this era to the virtual exclusion of alternative readings of Darwinism that legitimised civilised non-violence.[2] This historiography reconstructs and misrepresents things as they were. It is remembered past more than real past.

This book will examine the debate over the 'biology of war' – that is, over the supposedly biological causes and effects of war – that took place between 1859 and 1919, with especial attention to the legacy of Darwinism for theories of war and human aggression. Darwinism, one of the great scientific revolutions of modern times, conditioned western attitudes of

1

racial and cultural superiority that translated into imperial and militarist doctrines, and this will be explored. However, this study is more concerned to investigate the alternative tradition of 'peace biology' that grew out of co-operationist interpretations of biological theory. 'Peace biology' is defined as a matrix of biological arguments and vocabularies that could be used ideologically to foster peace causes. A sub-genre of 'anti-war evolutionism' employed specifically evolutionary, and especially Darwinian, discourse to counter the war school's use of struggle-based analogies from nature. Peace biology expounded an optimistic world-view based upon Darwin's holistic ecology, and used new disciplines such as eugenics to demonstrate that war was a biological disaster for humankind. A very powerful tradition was built upon this foundation during the post-Darwinian years, and it survived even the shock of the First World War.

This topic has been strangely neglected. There has of course been intense interest in the social and political ramifications of Darwin's paradigm, and much polemic. The historiography of 'Social Darwinism' is now a rich field, and much has been said on the connection between biological science – or pseudo-science – and subjects such as religion, ethics, class, eugenics, race and empire. There has been much less systematic investigation, however, of the nexus between Darwinism and theories of war. In what ways, for example, did Darwinist ideas of 'survival of the fittest', or alternatively, of nature as a web of interdependence, affect prevailing concepts of war's desirability or otherwise? To what extent did the languages of war theory and biology interact, and resonate voices of specific cultures and the cultural anxieties of the pre-1914 era? In what way did the changing facts of modern warfare, or war-linked social data, affect bio-social or bio-political analysis and rhetoric? How did – and how does – supposedly 'hard science' translate into dangerously reductionist, determinist and authoritarian cultural and political dogma or, to be optimistic, translate into more open and liberal categories cherishing peace and free will? Or were these polarities, on closer inspection, less clear-cut than we might imagine? The issues here, as in other areas of Social Darwinism, are complex and ambiguous. But answers are required if we are to resolve the larger question of the exact role of the Darwinist model in the value systems of particular cultures at particular times in history.

The intention is to focus upon the interactions between biological and social theory, to witness the extent to which nineteenth-century biology was both culturally regulated by, and pressed into the service of, social values associated with violence and war – and their opposites. Both militarist and pacifist speculation used naturalistic analogy and readings of human behaviour based upon supposedly universal and inescapable biological laws. Offsetting this in the debate were less strident, but persistent, themes against biological determinism. These may be traced back to Darwin, who was no determinist, even though his work set a fashion for arguing from nature to society, for finding an organic basis for culture and factors such as class and race. It was highly problematic for people to read into Darwin a necessary belief in a system of ethics chained to the empirical contours of nature, especially since his theory of cultural evolution stressed the human capacity to control nature and transcend natural selection. A. R. Wallace and T. H. Huxley became key figures who denied the 'imperial' right of biology to have free access into the world of human behaviour and values. Such dissent amplified protests against evolutionary ethics that were being made in philosophical and other circles.

This style of thought, sceptical of analogy and determinism, proved of major benefit to the peace tradition. Its talk was of humans being able to escape the thralls of a violent nature, being able to construct an independent culture and morality based upon peace. The champions of non-violence effectively censured their militaristic enemies for 'distorting' Darwinism, and illicitly universalising data from nature. At the same time, they themselves frequently used Darwinian science and animal comparisons to legitimise cooperative models for humanity. Surprisingly, this double-dealing was rarely noticed, or criticised. Why? I suggest this was largely because Anglo-American peace theorists grabbed the middle ground of ethics from their rivals. Peace biology benefited immensely because its value system was more congruent with entrenched moral culture than was that of the less conventional, unpleasantly ruthless, militarist school. This was the fatal flaw in nineteenth-century militarism, and helps to explain why – even in Wilhelmine Germany, whose *Kultur* was notably amenable to philosophies of might – rhetorics of war as biological necessity were subsidiary in militarist propaganda to more central concerns of national identity and interest. These could be embraced more readily by those with sensitive consciences.

A word about scope and limits. This study will deal not only with Darwinism, but with a range of biological speculations that include Lamarckism, a broad gamut of biologically based readings of history, and more historically oriented accounts of social evolution. Regard will be had to context, especially biographical context. A great deal of nonsense has been written in Social Darwinist discourse precisely because context has been ignored, because ideas have been wrenched from their proper settings and simplistically deployed as polemics. The best antidote is to return to the original thinkers, texts and ambience. Certainly the debate over war requires considerable explanatory information before it becomes fully meaningful. Inevitably that debate became enmeshed with larger issues: with questions such as man's place in nature, instinct versus culture, perceptions of social evolution, the role of analogy, the case for and against naturalistic ethics, science's claim to pronounce on history and policy, theories of determinism, teleology and reductionism. These issues rightly claim their due of literary space. Although European and American thought is treated when appropriate, the primary focus is upon Britain.

The following chapters concentrate upon war/peace biology as discourse. It is beyond the scope of this enterprise to judge the complex specificities of issues such as the institutional and political influence of this discourse. I do not frontally address certain problems: to what extent was peace biology an organised movement? What was its sociology? How does peace/war biology figure precisely in any analysis of the causes of World War I? To elucidate such issues would require an entirely new research programme. Massive research would be needed into official archives and the private papers of participants and political decision-makers. I offer a preliminary reconnaissance of the field. Hopefully the heavier battalions will move in later.

Many of the people discussed below are now forgotten; naturalists, physicians, eugenists, psychologists, socialists, professionals and various experts, minor savants of their time. Their interest in the biological dimensions of war may possibly be explained in Foucault's terms of empowerment. Geneticists, biometricians and physiologists may have been motivated by ambitions, conscious or unconscious, to establish status and a locus of power for their professions in a world dominated by traditional elites and business groups. Certainly the historians of eugenics (especially American eugenics) have embraced such interpretations.[3] If war (and other massive human phenomena) could be understood in essentially biological terms, the disciplines and practitioners of biology, bio-medicine and bio-psychology might expect to play a vital role in future human affairs, both in mediating knowledge and in orchestrating political planning and control. However, any purely instrumental account of biological war theory seems unsatisfactory. There are other dimensions. There is the broader possibility that the war debate represented, at one level, a psychological resolution or adjustment to pervading cultural anxieties in western civilisation. War could be comfortably conceived either as fatalistic necessity, or as controllable by means of culture. At another level, the 'biologisation of war' might represent a legitimate aspiration to explore the internal logic and dynamics of a new, exciting scientific paradigm. During the nineteenth century the language of Darwinism, then genetics, infiltrated many human fields. The biologising of social thought was much remarked on. War biology was part of a widely shared language of the age. Nobody denies that this discourse absorbed a disconcerting share of scientific quackery, of ideologically conditioned and self-serving biology. But it would be over-cynical to deny that it also reflected concern for human welfare and a genuine intellectual quest for knowledge.

1 The Darwinian legacy

The general debate

Darwinism has often been blamed for encouraging the idea that humankind is essentially pugnacious and competitive, and that war is therefore a normal part of the human condition. The logic of this argument varies, but it is possible to analyse within it certain recurring constructs, most notably those referring to Darwin's 'conflict paradigm' and the theme of 'animal reductionism'. The conflict paradigm is said to underlie Darwinism. The concept of natural selection, however it was derived – we shall look at its historical derivation soon – emphasised the relentless struggle of superfecund populations for limited resources. This was the precondition for evolutionary change and adaptation, for 'survival of the fittest' (in Herbert Spencer's evocative, if dangerously evaluative, term). Struggle and competition, violence, bloodshed and cruelty were the filtering mechanisms, crude, chancy, wasteful, by which species change and natural progress occurred. It was this side of natural selection that allegedly struck the nineteenth-century imagination, the idea of Nature 'red in tooth and claw' (although Tennyson's line predated *The Origin of Species* by almost a decade). The 'law of the jungle' was offered as the harsh ruling principle governing not only animals in their habitat but humans in their cities and societies. This law became (it is said) a vivid justification for rampant capitalism and uncontrolled individualism, doctrines praising survivors and victors and damning the unfit. T. H. Huxley condemned it as 'the gladiatorial theory of existence', embodying a naturalistic ethic that was a form of 'reasoned savagery'.[1] Moralists pointed out that Darwinism not only gave evolutionary explanations for ethics, but – a logically separate step – helped create a fashion for judging right action by criteria derived from a brutal natural world, such as survival or domination. Taken to extremes, Darwinist discourse conferred approval on a range of doctrines glorifying power, status, elitism, conquest and repression. Differences between cultures, genders, classes and races were reduced to fixed biological differences, imprinted in humans during eons of selective struggle. Darwin's conflict model generated militarist and racist extrapolations that conferred approval on war and imperial struggle as 'biological necessities'.

The theme of 'animal reductionism' came out of Darwin's hypothesis of transformism, which argued that *Homo sapiens* had derived from animal ancestors according to the laws of species change, via natural selection, isolation, sexual selection and hereditary transmission. Humans were animals, part of the animal world, subject to the same laws of nature. While Darwin in *The Descent of Man* (1871) acknowledged man's 'noble qualities', 'exalted powers' and social sympathy, 'his godlike intellect which has penetrated into the movements and constitution of the solar system', he also insisted that humans still bore the indelible stamp of their lowly origins. The insistence became even stronger in *The Expression of the Emotions in Man and Animals* (1872). From such an observation, not new with Darwin but given a terrible new impetus by him, could spring reductionist doctrines of all sorts. Human beings, or classes or races of human beings, were seen to be little better than the animals, which were assumed to be unreasoning and motivated by simple primal instincts, aggressive and territorial.

From such assumptions a variety of unpleasant consequences could be derived (not always logically). Popularisers from the 1880s on wrote about man as fighting ape (or, more recently and flatteringly, as 'imperial animal').[2] If pugnacity is rooted in human, as in animal, nature, an ineradicable instinct, the product of genetically programmed behaviour patterns that are relatively immune to cultural influences or 'nurture', then violence is a constant human potential, war is not aberrant and may even be commended as a biological necessity. War is rationalised and opposition to it eroded by the spread of pessimistic and quietist sentiments. As Frederick Wertham has argued, if violence 'is all in human nature, and if we are all guilty, then nobody is guilty. And if we are all responsible, no man is responsible'.[3] The alternative view that violence is socially caused, and socially preventable, is laughed out of court. Major elements of the above agenda appear in modern sociobiology, especially in the work of its founder E. O. Wilson, although in the nuclear age there is little temptation to speak of war as a biological necessity.

In the above there is also much potential for manipulative and authoritarian politics. We all live in a 'human zoo' and zoos require zookeepers. Discipline, conditioning and culling will be necessary. Humans are seen as 'nothing but' animals. When, as the organismic biologist Ludwig Von Bertalanffy said, thinkers and leaders see in man, not just an analogue to a rat, but nothing but an overgrown rat, then it is time to be alarmed. What Arthur Koestler condemned as 'ratomorphic philosophy' has become pervasive in the twentieth century: systematic depreciation of the human spirit, people turned into automata of consumption or marionettes of political power, dehumanised by a sophisticated psychological technology.[4]

Zoological reductionism caught on in the nineteenth century for a variety of reasons. Discourse about animals was a way by which humans expressed assumptions about themselves and their society. Enterprises such as hunting and zookeeping paralleled and justified imperial enterprise. English elites felt a sense of domination over animals, who became a metaphor for the lesser imperial breeds, or lesser social classes, over whom they ruled.[5]

Judeo-Christian tradition also equated sin and bestiality, seeing animals as vicious, and human vengeance and war as a reversion to an animal world of chaos. Scholars explain this dark vision of animality in terms of early monotheistic efforts to counter beast-worship. Animals became scapegoats to shoulder guilt about humans' own patently ferocious behaviour to their own and other species. Religious tradition also fostered a view of the animal world as a field for exploitation, God's gift for humankind's exclusive use, a tradition reinforced in the nineteenth century by the prevailing scientific world-view. In contrast to Christian thought, which at least theoretically blamed sin on man's own fallen nature, classical tradition perpetuated Plato's imagery of 'the wild beast within us', the incarnation of rampant carnality, violence, treachery, the source of ignobility in humans.[6]

The myth of the Beast Within intensified in the later nineteenth century. We find it in Social Darwinist discourse, in Nietzsche, Robert Louis Stevenson's *Dr Jekyll and Mr Hyde*, in H. G. Wells's *The Island of Dr Moreau* (warning against the perils of bestiality and science), and in much of the widespread literature on 'degeneration'. In such soil doctrines of despair and nihilism flourished and with them, one may argue, the potential for totalitarian and warmongering politics. The First World War – as we shall see – was portrayed as the final vindication of the mythology of bestiality, encoded anew in terms of neo-Darwinian genetics and instinct theory.

I cannot dwell here on the more general accusations made against Darwinism as depreciating human dignity. There was religious disquiet that Darwin had destroyed Christian teleology in the tradition of William Paley, and had expelled man from the centre of God's creation and concern. There was philosophical disquiet that Darwin had replaced a purposeful and benevolent world by a purposeless and violent one. As John Burrow has said: 'Nature, according to Darwin, was the product of blind chance and a blind struggle, and man a lonely, intelligent mutation, scrambling with the brutes for his sustenance ... Darwinian nature held no clues for human conduct, no answers to human moral dilemmas.'[7] Darwinism has been widely viewed as one of those potent intellectual forces that helped erode the west's traditional moral order in the later nineteenth century. By undermining ideas of absolute morality, by emphasising man's animality, it is said to have weakened the Christian association of war with sin (the basis of much pacifism), and contributed to a growing 'cult of violence', a cult that romanticised force as exciting, liberating, 'instinctive and elemental'.[8]

Biological militarism drew upon all of the above notions. Peace biology, however, appealed to other connotations of Darwinism. It challenged the conflict model and its political ramifications, a challenge that – as we shall shortly see – is consistent with recent revisionist historiography on Social Darwinism. It was always possible to see in Darwinian biology more than conflict theory, to see it as an holistic ecology that postulated a web of coexistence linking organisms. This holistic concept gave sustenance to social doctrines leading in reform-collectivist and 'new liberal' directions; and it encouraged optimistic assumptions about human nature and the possibilities of a peaceful human future. The conflict model could be replaced by a cooperationist model.

Animal reductionism also became more complex on analysis. Naturalising, or 'lowering', man could also involve humanising or 'raising' animals and puncturing myths of animal violence. The obverse of the thesis about man's brutal stamp, for Darwin and Huxley, was a case about animal skill and 'consciousness'.[9] It has been suggested that generations of middle-class stories about animal sagacity and character influenced Darwin's closing of the gap between man and animals, the case for a common ancestor and differences of degree only in mental capacity between humans and apes.[10] The dark vision of an animal world of chaos could be replaced by a brighter vision; one that took account of the considerable evidence of structural, social behaviour in animals. Within animal groups cooperative behaviour was marked, environmental interdependence undeniable. Darwin made this point, and it was expanded in Peter Kropotkin's *Mutual Aid* (1902).

Naturalists pointed out that murder and war were virtually unknown among non-human primates and most other species (except for warfare among social insects such as ants). Killing was largely predation directed at species other than one's own. Within species killing tended to be curbed by instinctive controls. Such observations diminished the militaristic analogy from nature. But they were less reassuring about humanity itself, pointing up the warlikeness and general unpleasantness of the human species by comparison with the rest. As modern commentators have often remarked, man was a killer, 'the greatest predator the world has ever known – the only mammal to slay other members of his species in vast numbers'.[11] Angst about man's uniquely fallen condition is now conceived biologically rather than religiously.

More optimistically, Darwin's *Descent* broke down the traditional demarcation between humans as persons and animals as things. Darwin sought out in the lower animals incipient senses and intuitions, emotions and faculties (such as love, memory, curiosity, imitation, reason) akin to those of humans. Ultimately this sustained what the American biologist Liberty Hyde Bailey called a 'biocentric', rather than man-centred, view of the living creation.[12] The social evolutionist Benjamin Kidd predicted that the concept of brotherhood would be extended 'outside the limits of race and beyond all political barriers', while a sense of human responsibility would extend 'first of all to fellow creatures and then to life itself'.[13] In *Prolegomena to Ethics* (1883), the Oxford Idealist T. H. Green similarly applied the idea of neighbourship to the whole sentient universe. A style of opinion and alternative politics grew up that was sympathetic towards environment, tolerant towards all living creatures, and impatient of mindless destruction of natural resources. It was to be a force for peace in the twentieth century.

Animal reductionism was counterbalanced by teleological and ortho-genic doctrines associated with Darwinism. Strictly speaking they were illicitly associated with it. Darwin denied that evolutionary change worked purposefully towards a long-term goal (teleology) or that it proceeded in a single direction (orthogenesis). He warned himself not to use terms such as 'higher' or 'lower' (implying progress up or down an evolutionary ladder), and warned his readers that evolution often led into dead ends. Never-theless elements of natural theology (which was teleological) persisted in his thought, and much of his language was reminiscent of the Victorian 'doctrine of progress'.

While animal reductionism implied that man's origins were all, the opposite 'elevationist' view was more respectful of human dignity and potential. To that degree it nourished liberal politics concerned with individual growth, freedom, creativity and choice. True, humanity was subject to evolutionary laws, a proper subject of scientific scrutiny, no longer projected above nature by metaphysical discourse. Man's animal nature was not in question (not by evolutionists anyway). However, evolution dealt not only in origins, but in historical change and development. It was prospective as well as retrospective. If humans were barely domesticated brutes to the reductionists, to others they were the splendidly endowed end product of evolution, creators of civilisation and culture. Through their tool-making, language and learning skills, humans had made a quantum leap in evolutionary history. Intelligence had developed to the stage where the human race had not only adapted to, but had mastered its natural environment.

The optimistic alternative to reductionist pessimism postulated – in a curious parallel to earlier theistic thought – the qualitative difference between humans and the lower animals. Man's superior reason, capacity for social sympathy and mutualist endeavour, ethical sense, aesthetic and creative abilities raised hopes – often utopian – of a future in which the politics of violence could be supplanted by that of civilised co-operation and liberal tolerance. Such hopes flourished particularly in liberal and socialist camps in the generation preceding World War I. The war did much to restore the idea of primal recidivism. However elevationist ideals and anti-war evolutionism proved to be highly durable, even under that grave challenge.

One would not wish, of course, to claim that orthogenic or teleological doctrines invariably produced liberal or non-violent politics. It will suffice here to mention that such doctrines could also be associated with historical determinism of various sorts, and with potentially authoritarian movements like eugenics. Nor were teleology or orthogenesis necessary elements of the 'elevationist' position. Indeed they might be more fairly described as heresies from Darwinian orthodoxy that intruded surprisingly often into bio-sociology. The broader 'elevationist' tradition included those who emphasised cultural as opposed to organic evolution as a determinant of human behaviour; those who spoke less of heredity than of nurture, more of human plasticity and malleability than of innate limits to behaviour. Generally they were sceptical that aggression was rooted in human nature, readier to believe that it was socially determined and preventable. I shall try to show that peace biology was centrally located in elevationist thought. However, mainly because of the emerging significance of peace eugenics in the pre-war generation, a discursive tension arose within peace discourse between the culturalists and the hereditarians.

On a more general and philosophical level, spirited defences were made against the charge that Darwinism depreciated the human spirit. Defenders argued, briefly, that Darwinism expanded human self-knowledge rather than circumscribing our self-image; that evolution opened the way for a new 'science of society' in a range of disciplines, offering exciting possibilities for self-realisation and self-expansion;[14] that Darwinism emancipated humankind from the trammels of superstition and obscurantist religion. Humanist and existential thinkers denied that belief in God or a purposeful universe was necessary for the development of authentic, human-centred philosophies.

As I suggested above, the historiography of Social Darwinism is relevant to the war/peace debate, especially since it has questioned the dimensions and nature of the conflict model that underpinned much militaristic thought. Recent scholarship, recognising the complex links between science and social thought, has viewed Darwinism as a multiplex phenomenon translatable into many social and ideological idioms. Social Darwinism, once conceived as a culturally radical ideology that legitimised a free-scrambling capitalism, has been reconstituted as an essentially accommodating force, seeking to reconcile science with traditional theodicies and culture, but also capable of generating liberal-reformist values. The conventional wisdom now is that the Darwinian paradigm had less than revolutionary religious and political effects.

Darwin's more threatening ideas – his bleak image of a purposeless, violent universe which relegated God to remote first cause or unnecessary hypothesis, his philosophical materialism and rejection of theology as non-cognitive – were camouflaged by Darwin's own defensive strategy of subsuming into his theory earlier cultural forms and grammar, especially those of Paley's natural theology and Scots common sense philosophy. Later apostles and users of Darwinism – and this includes the school of peace biology – prudently distanced themselves from the harsher implications of natural selection, and ingeniously reworked Darwinian theory to fashion more acceptable and/or progressive epistemes. Naked theories of survival, power, struggle, exploitation and domination were contained within a safer political and ethical tradition. Revisionism is open to the criticism that it underestimates the potential of Darwinism to disturb, to alter the rules of the game, to induce new ideas and prejudices, especially in areas such as race theory or changing biological images of humankind; or that it exaggerates the acceptable face of traditional discourse, and maximises the elements of order and over-arching harmony in the dogmas of Malthusianism or utilitarianism. The assimilationists reply by pointing to the major elements of order in the Darwinian world-view: in its stress on history, on slow change over eons of time, in the uniformitarianism it inherited from Hutton and Lyell – all useful ammunition for gradualism against the ideological radicalism of capitalism, Marxism or militarism. Revisionists also defend the vitality and pliability of Victorian culture, highly capable of absorbing dangerous ideas into a pragmatic national tradition. (For further discussion, see Appendix.)

'One great slaughter-house the warring world'

In order to comprehend the Darwinian theory of war, we need to situate historically Darwin's notion of struggle. Darwinism itself can be regarded as a quintessential product of centuries of fast-running change in western history, change that disturbed 'the seemingly static equilibrium that had existed between people and land, peasant and lord, lord and king, work and rest, production and consumption'.[15] Values were revolutionised. Older concepts of fixed or ideal types were displaced in scientific and social theory by developmental values. Darwinism focused upon origin and transition, no longer signs of defect and unreality. As the American philosopher John Dewey observed in 1909: 'In laying hands upon the sacred ark of absolute permanency ... the *Origin of Species* introduced a mode of thinking that in the end was bound to transform the logic of knowledge, and hence the treatment of morals, politics and religion'.[16]

Robert Young has claimed that 'biological ideas have to be seen as constituted by, evoked by, and following an agenda set by, larger social forces that determine the tempo, the mode, the mood, and the meaning of nature'.[17] The Darwinian debate over man's place in nature occurred (he says) within the context of a competitive Victorian ethos, growing secularisation, and the development of a scientific method that encouraged the naturalisation of value systems. A mobile, urban industrialised society was a more likely seed-bed for change-based, historicist Darwinism than was 'the rural pastoral order that suited a deistic age of fixed, classified social stasis – the age of Paley'. Certainly evolutionary science was suffused by the language and imagery of the Victorian age. The *Origin*'s 'message of competition, its vision of conflict, struggle, its images of war and destruction were peculiarly Victorian'.[18]

Karl Marx identified Darwinism specifically with English capitalism. It was remarkable, he thought, 'how Darwin recognizes among beasts and plants his English society with its division of labour, competition opening up of new markets, invention, and the Malthusian "struggle for existence"'. Engels complained that the Darwinists simply transferred from society to nature Hobbes's doctrine of the war of all against all, 'of the bourgeois-economic doctrine of competition, together with Malthus's theory of population', then in a 'conjuror's trick' transferred the same theories from organic nature into history, claiming them valid as eternal laws: 'The puerility of this procedure is so obvious that not a word need be said about it.'[19] Others also saw the class conflict of the early industrial revolution refracted within Darwinism. The German historian-philosopher Oswald Spengler described the *Origin* as the application of economics to biology, and said that it reeked of the English factory. Benjamin Kidd saw natural selection as analogous to the acquisitive ethic of *laissez-faire* capitalism. Both concepts pictured life as a self-centred struggle of individuals pursuing their own interests, yet at the same time achieving overall progress.[20]

Darwin was no unread provincial, but a cultivated Victorian intellectual with a sharp interest in the great changes and great ideas of his age, reading widely in anthropology, sociology, demography, philosophy, and notably political economy.[21] His biology was permeated with concepts and images taken from classical economics. The centrepoint of his theory, natural selection, owed much to a perception gleaned from Thomas Malthus. The key idea of divergence was modelled after the ideas of the Scottish economists, especially Adam Smith and James Steuart, with their concepts of division of labour, and a self-regulating, open and progressive market. (Silvan Schweber makes the point that the *Origin* embodied the great Edinburgh and Cambridge traditions in Darwin's upbringing. Divergence came from the Edinburgh economists and philosophers, while Malthusian population principles reflected a deterministic, quantitative, mechanistic Newtonianism that came from Cambridge.)[22] Darwin used metaphors drawn from business, banking, industry and imperialism to depict animal behaviour. He spoke of profit and loss, increments, diligence, inheritance, saving, utility, success, progress through competition: 'the common coin, the small change of Victorian social and economic discourse'.[23] Darwin referred to workshops and work-stations in nature (areas of large animal populations and intense population), and he compared ecological niches or places to 'colonizing enterprises'.

Darwin's key term 'struggle for existence' was a culturally loaded term, rich in connotations for his readers. As Gillian Beer has aptly said: 'The unused, or uncontrolled, elements in metaphors such as "the struggle for existence" take on a life of their own. They surpass their status in the text and generate further ideas and ideologies.'[24] Many of Darwin's interpreters leapt at the obvious, stressing physical conflict and ubiquitous violence in nature. In their turn, ecologically and peace-minded commentators seized upon Darwin's explanation of 'struggle' in terms of environmental dependence.

Darwin thought of using Hobbes's phrase 'war of nature' as a heading to his chapter on struggle in his projected 'big book' *Natural Selection*.[25] He was acquainted with Linnaeus's description 'one great slaughter-house the warring world', and was impressed by the botanist Augustin de Candolle's similar view of the plant world (1820). Naturalist texts of the time were replete with the language of 'struggle for existence'. Darwin encountered the phrase in works ranging from von Wrangel's *Expedition to the Polar Sea* (2nd edn, 1844) and Edward Blyth's 'Attempt to Classify Varieties' (1835) to Malthus's *Essay on Population* (6th edn, 1826) and Charles Lyell's milder, equilibristic statement in *Principles of Geology* (vol. II, 1832). However, images of conflict used by naturalists before Darwin were almost invariably presented within a context that assumed 'the idea of a basically harmonious, ordered, economical and plenitudinous nature, with its implications of an intelligent, beneficent God'.[26] To the extent that Darwin freed himself from this paradigm (and there is much debate on this point), he was able to present the image of a 'warring' nature without inhibition, since the link was cut with God's purposes, with notions of either benign or malign order.[27]

In famous passages Darwin insisted upon the violent reality that lay behind 'the contented face of a bright landscape or a tropical forest glowing with life ... the doctrine that all nature is at war is most true. The struggle very often falls on the seed and egg, or on the seedling, larva and young; but fall it must sometime in the life of each individual, or more commonly at intervals on successive generations and then with extreme severity.'[28] Darwin transferred metaphors taken from European military and imperial experience directly to nature. He spoke of creatures 'overmastering' one another: 'through his continual use of highly dramatic language representing the life of organisms in nature as some heroic war, with attendant battles, victories, famine, dearth, and destruction, Darwin creates the image of a great literal struggle for existence – an image which pervades the *Origin*'.[29] An ecological historian even sees Darwin as the chief architect of an 'anti-arcadian' outlook on nature, influenced by post-Romantic visions of 'an antagonistic, malignant nature', and by his own temperament: 'Violent encounter was the dominant theme in Darwin's personal makeup: now fear of it, now relish'.[30]

What must not be forgotten, however, was the subtlety of Darwin's mature view of struggle. In fact he found the word distinctly inadequate. His meanings included not only direct struggle to the death, or for dominance, between individual organisms; but more complex 'struggles' between individuals of the same or different species for finite resources or environmental leverage in a context of constantly expanding populations; and also 'struggles' of animals and plants against environment, a struggle to survive and reproduce. The setting was ecological. The success stories – and failure stories – were intricately plotted, the result, often unpredictable, of innumerable pressures, adaptations and selections.

Darwin insisted that he used the expression 'struggle for existence' in a large metaphorical sense. In his 'big book' he carefully distinguished types of struggle: 'Carnivorous animals prowling for their prey in a time of dearth may be truly said to be struggling for existence.' So also when seeds sown thickly together strove to grow, they struggled 'though not voluntarily' against each other. Struggle was related to the idea of dependency, for instance when a multitude of animals depended on other animals and plants, and plants on the nature of the station inhabited by them. Then, 'a plant on the edge of a desert is often said to struggle for existence; this struggle consisting in the chance of a seed alighting in a somewhat damper spot, and then being just able to live'. Again, 'it may metaphorically be called a struggle which individual plant of the species shall produce most seed, and so have the best chance of leaving descendants; and again it may be called a struggle whether the plant or the bird (or insect) which feeds on its seeds gets the upper hand'. Lyell had used the term 'equilibrium in the number of species' to cover such cases, but Darwin thought the phrase too quiescent: 'Hence I shall use the word struggle ... including in this term several ideas primarily distinct, but graduating into each other, as the dependency of one organic being on another – the agency whether organic or inorganic of what may be called chance ... and lastly what may be more strictly called a struggle, whether voluntarily as in animals or involuntary as in plants.'[31]

Darwin's concept of struggle is thus resolvable into related senses of conflict, dependence and chance, into possibilities not only of victory or dominance but of coadaptation and coexistence.[32] Gillian Beer makes the point about Darwin that 'the deliberately guarded and consciously metaphoric status that he gives to the phrase "struggle for existence" ... expresses his unwillingness to give dominance to a militant or combative order of nature. He interprets it as an interdependence or endurance as much as battle'.[33] Darwin was proposing a dynamic new ecological model that would supplant that of the more static 'chain of being' (or *Scala Naturae*). In Darwin's model there was constant flux, challenge, environmental coups and displacements – but all taking place within an integrated total system, a grand historical system grouping together 'all living and extinct forms'.

Thus he used metaphors such as the web of nature, the tree of life and the 'tangled bank' to represent the holistic interdependence of biological systems: 'Plants and animals, most remote in the scale of nature, are bound together [he said] by a web of complex relations.' He spoke of the 'inextricable web of affinities' that linked members of a class, a pattern of 'most complex and radiating lines of affinities'. The web metaphor was a striking one, suggesting not only a spider's web, and the more common Victorian connotation of woven fabric, but also family relatedness. Images of thread, cloth and tissue (including human tissue) evoked contiguity, the ordering of life, the interconnectedness of society.[34]

The branching tree model used to illustrate the genealogical continuity between species living and dead freed Darwin from the problems of the old, inflexible *Scala Naturae* model, enabling him to place humanity more firmly within nature.[35] This metaphor has been dubbed a typically Romantic one, 'intended to illustrate that the whole of nature is an organic unity, developing from a single set of roots and diversifying in interconnected branches with no more conflict or competition than that exhibited by the organs of the body'.[36] Finally, in Darwin's famous 'tangled bank' metaphor at the end of the *Origin*, 'profusion and harmonious contiguity replace conflict', with the emphasis on 'the delicate richness and variety of life, on complex interdependency, ecological interpretation, weaving together an aesthetic fullness'.[37]

Thomas Malthus, the 'dismal parson', has been much blamed for bequeathing to Darwinism a bleakly capitalistic theory of crowding and struggle, that eventually found its way into militaristic Social Darwinism. While partly true, this rather ignores the complexities of the Malthusian discourse, and the considerable disjunctures between it and Darwinism.

Darwin certainly derived some concept of struggle from Malthus, although not necessarily the Hobbesian and supposedly capitalistic image of a disordered world based on the war of all against all. Malthus focused on one of what were to be the many meanings of struggle in Darwin: the idea of struggle against environment. Even before his seminal reading of Malthus's *Essay on the Principle of Population* in September 1838, Darwin had seized upon the key concept of variability of species, and had a 'just idea' of the power of selection from his study of domestic breeding. He was also, as he recalled in 1868, 'prepared to appreciate the struggle for existence by having long studied the habits of animals'.[38] However, as Darwin recorded in his notebook of September 1838, Malthus gave him a deeper meaning of the 'warring of the species':

increase of brutes must be prevented solely by positive checks... in nature production does not increase, while no check prevail, but the positive check of famine and consequently death ... One may say that there is a force like a hundred thousand wedges trying [to] force every kind of adapted structure into the gaps in the oeconomy of nature, or rather forming gaps by thrusting out weaker ones.[39]

It is now widely accepted that this insight helped Darwin catalyse his theory of natural selection. Malthus concentrated his mind upon 'the competitive edges to nature – predation, famine, natural disaster – as they played upon the individual differences of members of the same group'.[40] Malthus showed what terrible pruning was exercised on the individuals of a species by crowding, the competition for food, space and resources, the struggle to survive, leading Darwin on to the extended concept (well beyond Malthus) of 'survival of the fittest': the result of the differential survival or reproduction caused within populations by the incessant pressure of numbers on resources.

Malthus argued that human population growth, if unchecked, tended to expand in geometrical progression, while food supply expanded, at best, in arithmetical progression. Population was in practice constantly checked by

Malthus's deadly factors, or 'positive checks': famine, disease, poverty and war. There were also 'preventive checks' on births, either the immoral checks of abortion, homosexuality or promiscuous sexuality (with precautions against conception); or else 'moral restraint': continence before marriage, later marriages and smaller families.

Malthus and Darwin were engaged in separate intellectual enterprises. Darwin sought scientific explanations for species change, a global biological theory applicable to all organisms. Malthus combined an essentially modern social science investigation of human behaviour (demographic and economic) with a traditionally religious purpose. He was a natural theologian as well as an embryonic sociologist, placing behaviour into moral categories, showing a benevolent divine purpose at work even behind the misery and vice that were the usual lot for humankind. Darwin, by contrast, used the rhetoric of natural theology to reduce opposition to his theory, but was ultimately more ruthless in abandoning ideas of design.

The more pessimistic side of Malthus's social theory connects with his political aim of refuting the utopian radicalism of Condorcet, Godwin and his own father, and with his economic aim of justifying a capitalistic work ethic. The optimistic radicals of the Enlightenment pictured humankind as perfectible and foretold a golden future based upon reason, mutual aid and world peace. (Even sordid functions such as sex and reproduction would wither away, according to Godwin. Interestingly, similar ideas were to resurface with Herbert Spencer.)[41] Malthus insisted that the real world was plagued by intractable problems such as the population explosion, and a constant struggle for food. In the more pessimistic first edition of the *Essay* on population (1798) he saw the responses to the crowding crisis as mainly 'vice and misery'. The distress of the lower classes was 'an evil so deeply seated that no human ingenuity can reach it ... palliatives are all that the nature of the case will admit' (1*st Essay*, ch. 5). However, without the spur of harsh conditions, man would have remained, as he naturally was, 'inert, sluggish and averse from labour'. If nature were eternally bountiful and benign, with no punishments dealt out for dereliction of effort, then there would be no progress of civilisation or wealth, creativity or invention, no implementation of God's 'mighty process for the creation and formation of mind' (1*st Essay*, ch. 18). Economically, this translated into a need for *laissez-faire*. As Malthus said, the English middle class would never have prospered 'if no man could hope to rise or fear to fail, in society, if industry did not bring with it its reward and idleness its punishment' (ch. 18).

Malthus illustrates the gap between Darwinism, with its purposeless universe, and the discourses of natural theology and classical economics – personified by Malthus – with their mystic faith that God, or the market, were working towards a benevolent telos for humankind. Malthus, as moralist, would not accept the idea of a disordered universe. As economist, he believed that unfettered competition between individuals pursuing their self-interest would lead not to a bloody struggle of all against all, or to elimination of the unfit, but to a 'natural equilibrium', a harmony of social and economic interests in the body politic. Despite the pain, the harsh natural laws, human irrationality and immorality, the system was ultimately productive of good. Malthus and most of the classical economists did not conceive of *laissez-faire* society as amoral. Malthus said that people should be free to pursue their own interests in their own way, but only so long as they adhered to 'the rules of justice'. Thus he, and his fellow economists, rejected 'naturalistic ethics', the 'law of the jungle', etc. often seen as the hallmark of later Social Darwinism.[42] In fact it may be that Malthus's theodicy – because it was more than just a survivor ethic – was better than Darwinism in fulfilling the political function of validating an inegalitarian industrial capitalism, and of discouraging activist protest against the status quo.[43]

Revisionist scholarship has suggested another view of Malthus, namely that he conceived of war and human violence in the context of primitive societies, not of modern capitalism.[44] Significantly, of the 'positive checks' that Malthus listed as curbing population growth – famine, epidemics, poverty and war, all classed as misery and thus undesirable – only war involved direct physical violence between humans. Also important, Darwin read Malthus's *Essay* in 1838 in the sixth edition. This had an extended treatment of primitive warfare that may well have crystallised Darwin's thinking about natural selection. Here Malthus discussed how, with shepherd tribes of Asia or the American Indians, overpopulation led to expansionist threats and territorial battles, where 'death was the punishment for defeat and life the prize of victory'. Since primitives were deemed to be closer than civilised peoples to animals in nature, Darwin (in this reading) seized upon savage warfare, rather than capitalism, as a key to conflict and thus selection within species. Malthus generally did not conceive of modern society as based upon intra-species struggle.[45]

I have said that the Malthusian paradigm – based on natural theology and 'natural harmony' economics – differed from the Darwinian paradigm in significant respects. However, the contrast is not black and white. For one thing, Darwin himself was slow to abandon natural theology, especially the idea of design in nature and the perfect adaptation of organisms, in favour of the more astringent concept of natural selection based on chance, struggle and imperfect adaptation. Darwin possibly retained a type of Malthusian theodicy until the *Origin*, still conceiving of purposive and good general laws in nature masterminded by God ('a First

Cause having an intelligent mind in some degree analogous to that of man') rather than by 'blind chance or necessity'.[46]

Again, one may argue that both Malthus and Darwin moved away from a depressing view of nature governed by iron laws of struggle by allowing for some degree of human control of events. The later editions of Malthus's *Essay* – in reality a different book from the first edition – envisaged a more optimistic future for humankind. This was based upon 'moral restraint', the only preventive check that was ethical. Malthus was heartened by his demographic study of modern European countries. There seemed to be a correlation between rising living standards and the use of prudential checks on fertility, for example through later marriages. He began to favour a mild improvement in people's living standards and national education promoting industry and 'moral restraint'. The book ended with almost rosy predictions of a stable and enlightened society, in which a key role was to be played by 'the science of moral and political philosophy'. Malthus thus foreshadowed the positivist and Fabian ideal of social engineering, with a group of experts, the economists, social scientists, Saint-Simon's 'savants' or H. G. Wells's 'new republicans', using human reason to control violent natural forces. There was a parallel here with Darwin too. As we shall now see, his later theory of human evolution increasingly favoured social co-operation and the human use of reason, rather than individualistic struggle, as the means by which groups achieved mastery over their habitat, and thus environmental success.

Darwin on war and aggression

When militarists used Darwinian rationalisations for war, they relished phrases such as 'survival of the fittest', but rarely examined Darwin's actual words on human pugnacity and war. There were good reasons for this, since Darwin did not talk in terms of instinctive pugnacity in humans, warned that modern warfare was dysgenic, and hoped for a peaceful and mutualistic human culture in the future. True, he recognised that endemic warfare and genetic usurpation had been important selective forces in human history. (E. O. Wilson says that the *Descent of Man* was, in this respect, 'a remarkable model that foreshadowed many of the elements of modern group selection theory'.)[47] However Darwin viewed violence and altruism as dancing a complex tango in human evolution, and he saw evidence that the cruder forms of human conflict were steadily giving way to a wider sense of sympathy.

During the voyage of the *Beagle* Darwin hinted that primitive peoples could be ranged on a scale with respect to traits such as aggression (for example, Maoris were more bellicose than Tahitians). However, overall, the early notebooks attributed such differences to history and culture. In his first notebook on transmutation of species (1837) Darwin denied that humans had instinctive urges, or 'hereditary prejudices' to conquer each other.[48] Darwin did allow that 'habits' (a rather vague term) might become hereditary through natural or sexual selection in animals. This was less likely to happen with humans, although they were probably still affected at times by instincts inherited from the primal past. Thus Darwin wrote in his *Beagle* diary (1836) that 'the love of the chase is an inherited delight in man – a relic of an instinctive passion'. In later works Darwin, like his generation, often applied the term 'instinct' loosely to humans, applying it not only to drives like hunger, sex and self-preservation, but also to 'vengeance'. In general, though, Darwin had an essentially modern and open concept of instinct. His concept of instinct allowed for interaction between inherited structure and environment, even when the organism study was low on the scale of nature. Darwin's theory indeed demanded such a flexible concept, for if behaviour was rigidly pre-determined by structure, there would be little scope for selective pressures from the environment to induce adaptive change in species.[49] As humans stood atop the evolutionary tree, they enjoyed a maximum of reason and a minimum of instinct: 'man as he now exists, has few special instincts'.[50]

The Descent of Man gives Darwin's fullest account of war and human instincts, and it borrowed more frankly than the *Origin* from current social theory (the anthropology of Maine and Lubbock, the social psychology of Spencer, Galton, W. R. Greg and Bagehot).[51] In the *Descent* he finally tackled what had been a sub-text in his earlier writings, the claim 'that man is the co-descendent with other species of some ancient, lower and extinct form' (p. 4). (It was not, one critic thought, the safest idea to propagate 'when the sky of Paris was red from the incendiary flames of the Commune', but it was an idea that he had long held.) As a young man he had declared: 'Man in his arrogance thinks himself a great work worthy the interposition of a deity. More humble and I believe truer [is] to consider him created from animals.'[52] The book tried to document the evolutionary continuity between humans and the lower animals, in bodily affinities and in mental and moral faculties. Darwin searched for rudimentary signs of human-style consciousness, reasoning, a sense of beauty or morality in creatures supposedly lower down the evolutionary scale, in 'barbarians', 'savages', children, the lower primates. He also sought for animal senses, habits and 'some few instincts' in humankind.

Darwin was more inclined to speak of sociability, rather than pugnacity, as a human instinct – an open rather than fixed instinct. His fascination with the 'social instincts' of man and animals is understandable, given his strong desire to give a naturalistic explanation for man's supposedly unique moral sense or conscience. Sociability and cooperative behaviour were commonly observed in the animal world (although usually confined to small groups and not species-wide) and this (Darwin felt) led to the development of moral sense. Social sympathy was strengthened by habit and the desire to win approval, or avoid the censure, of fellow creatures. As the organic scale was ascended, as linguistic and mental powers expanded, conscience and a sense of shame or guilt developed, especially when individuals yielded to passing instinctive desires that breached 'the enduring and always present social instinct' that harmed the community.

Cooperative behaviour persisted in the higher animals because of its selective value. Herds and troops were organised to provide mutual defence against enemies and predators. Solitary animals tended to perish in greater numbers (in many species), so natural selection favoured the group by preserving individuals with social instincts. Darwin also allowed the Lamarckian possibility of inheritance of behaviour patterns of sociability acquired through persistent habit. Social patterns of behaviour applied to defence, to mutual service (such as grooming), and to predation (hunting in packs, fishing in concert), generally requiring fidelity between group-fellows and obedience to a leader.

Altruism became more complex and self-conscious in humans, since they themselves were more self-conscious: 'Man, from the activity of his mental faculties, cannot avoid reflection: past impressions and images are incessantly and clearly passing through his mind' (p. 171). Altruism was reinforced by selfishness, experience and imitation. On selfishness, Darwin noted: 'we are led by the hope of receiving good in return to perform acts of sympathetic kindness to others; and sympathy is much strengthened by habit' (an idea of 'reciprocal altruism' that has been much discussed recently in sociobiology). Again, selective pressures counted with human sociality, 'for those communities, which included the greatest number of the most sympathetic members, would flourish best, and rear the greatest number of offspring' (p. 163).

Darwin observed that ape-man and savage man were both social and endemically warlike. The social instincts applied to groups, making them cohesive, but did not extend to the whole species *Homo sapiens*. Tribes were constantly at war with their neighbours. There was a never-ending fight for survival. The nobler sides of humanity, the moral faculties and social sympathies, had their darker side, for they were used to improve fighting and warfare. (Darwin was indebted to Walter Bagehot on this issue: see chapter 2.) Social co-operation went with military and imperial efficiency, while warfare had its social benefits and biological justifications.

Darwin showed that man's success in predation and fighting was not a simple matter of innate urges. It was intricately connected with human intelligence and the key role of cultural evolution. With the ascent of man, organic evolution faded in favour of mental and social evolution, the path to a new malleability and selective advantage. Skill in hunting and fighting was a critical factor in this cultural progression:

We see that in the rudest state of society, the individuals who were the most sagacious, who invented and used the best weapons or traps, and who were best able to defend themselves, would rear the greatest number of offspring. The tribes, which included the largest number of men thus endowed, would increase in number and supplant other tribes (p. 196).

From the remotest times tribes that were not only robust, but socially cohesive, skilled in organisation, technology and weaponry (Darwin called this 'superiority in the arts'), tribes that included 'a great number of courageous, sympathetic and faithful members, who were always ready to warn each other of danger, to aid and defend each other', had genetically usurped other tribes (p. 199). As peoples highly endowed with social, but also military discipline, triumphed over others, 'the social and moral qualities would tend slowly to advance and be diffused throughout the world' (p. 200).

This raised a perplexing dilemma, and a persistent one in subsequent debate. As humans advanced socially, would their warlike propensities disappear, or would they prove to be almost ineradicable? Like many Victorians, Darwin had his ambivalent moments on the issue of human progress, but generally he was a cautious optimist. For one thing he was not inclined to view human pugnacity (or the social instincts for that matter) as a fixed pattern of behaviour immune to cultural modification. It is often forgotten that Darwin allowed full play within his theory for factors of education and conditioning. He predicted that ethical values would spread 'through instruction and example to the young', and become an integral part of human culture (p. 188). Altruism would become habitual and general under the influence of reason and conscience. Ultimately our moral sense 'becomes a highly complex sentiment – originating in the social instincts, largely guided by the approbation of our fellow-men, ruled by reason, self-interest, and in later times by deep religious feelings, and confirmed by instruction and habit' (p. 203). As early as 1838, in the M notebook on 'Man, Mind and Materialism', Darwin had speculated that 'instincts' such as 'revenge and anger' – 'which experience shows it must be for [man's] happiness to check' – were being softened by the conditioning of external circumstances: 'with lesser intellect they might be necessary & no doubt were preservative, & are now, like all other structures slowly vanishing ... – Our descent, then, is the origin of our evil passions!! – The Devil under form of Baboon is our grandfather!'[53]

Darwin indicated that through conflict – of tribes, then nations and empires – had come, and would come, higher ethics and broader sympathy, that would ultimately render war and similar crudities obsolete. However, he made at least two qualifications to his position: (1) he accepted that a continuing struggle for existence was necessary for human development; and (2) he allowed for the possibility of retrogression, or even a dead end, for human evolution.

On the first issue he wrote that 'as man suffers from the same physical evils as the lower animals, he has no right to expect immunity from the evils consequent on the struggle for existence. Had he not been subjected during primeval times to natural selection, assuredly he would never have attained to his present rank' (p. 219). Natural selection required population pressure, even though it resulted in evils such as infanticide in barbarous tribes, poverty and celibacy in civilised nations. Darwin raised the alarm, taken up later by eugenists and degenerationists, that advanced societies risked decay because they over-protected the weak and poor, building asylums for the imbecile and sick, keeping alive those with poor constitutions through better medicine and vaccination: 'Thus the weak members of civilised societies propagate their kind. No one who has attended to the breeding of domestic animals will doubt that this must be highly injurious to the race of man' (p. 206).

On the other hand, Darwin thought that the threat of degeneracy was offset by other trends: the antisocial were imprisoned or executed, the melancholic and insane committed suicide, violent men came to bloody ends. Overall Darwin accepted the need for humanitarianism. It was part of the 'instinct of sympathy', the 'noblest part of our nature'. Nor did he advocate war as a selective method. He warned that modern warfare at least was dysgenic, a warning conveniently forgotten by militarists. In countries with large standing armies, the finest young men were conscripted or enlisted:

They are thus exposed to early death during war, and are often tempted into vice [VD was much higher in the armed forces], and are prevented from marrying during the prime of life. On the other hand, the shorter and feebler men, with poor constitutions, are left at home, and consequently have a much better chance of marrying and propagating their kind (p. 207).

On the second issue, natural selection was a theory of perennial adaptation to specific conditions. The pure doctrine did not entail progress or perfectibility. Darwin in fact was less than consistent on human progress, saying at different times that progress was 'no invariable rule', that history refuted the idea that progress was normal in human society, but also that it had been 'much more general than retrogression' (pp. 204, 216, 224). History (he suggested) was full of the extinction of highly able peoples, such as the ancient Greeks 'who stood some grades higher in the intellect than any race that has ever existed [he took this from his cousin Francis Galton's *Hereditary Genius*, 1869], and who ought, if the power of natural selection were real, to have risen still higher in the scale, increased in number, and stocked the whole of Europe' (p. 216). But success depended upon circumstances: 'Natural selection acts only tentatively. Individuals and races may have acquired certain indisputable advantages, and yet have perished from failing in other characters' (p. 217). He blamed the fall of Greek civilisation on historical, geographical and moral factors: 'from a want of coherence between many small states, from the small size of their whole country, from the practice of slavery, or from extreme sensuality' (p. 217).[54]

Extinction might even overtake the western nations of Europe 'who now so immeasurably surpass their former savage progenitors, and stand at the summit of civilisation' (p. 217). However Darwin privately was convinced that white Europeans would be top dogs for some considerable time. He wrote to a friend a year before his death:

Remember what risk the nations of Europe ran not so many centuries ago of being overwhelmed by the Turks, and how ridiculous such an idea now is! The more civilised so-called Caucasian races have beaten the Turkish hollow in the struggle for existence. Looking to the world at no very distant date, what an endless number of the lower races will have been eliminated by the higher civilised races throughout the world.[55]

Darwin's contribution to racism has been much debated. As with other areas, any number of readings of history and human destiny could be made from Darwinism: from racist and survivalist to cosmopolitan and cooperative ones. Although white racism predated Darwinism in quite virulent forms, and humans were classified by racial type well before the theory of natural selection, it could be urged that evolutionary ideas acted as a catalyst to give new forms to old prejudices. From Darwin's conflict and developmental models of evolution came a number of racist and militaristic extrapolations that justified conquest and repression of subject peoples, that drew up evolutionary ladders which placed at the top peoples supreme in war and trade, while relegating others to the lower rungs. Primitives were commonly seen as over-endowed with primal animalistic instincts. Believing that individual development in humans repeated the evolutionary history of the species, recapitulation theorists such as Ernst Haeckel, Herbert Spencer and D. G. Brinton urged that primitive peoples were arrested at a childlike stage in evolution.[56]

On the other hand, Darwin conceived of humans as basically one species, probably descended from a common ancestor. Typically he was cautious, and did not entirely rule out the possibility of multiple evolution from a number of types and regions. Overall he and Huxley tried to get away from the earlier mono-polygenesis debate, which they saw as pseudo-scientific and too political.[57] Racial differences were best explained in the usual Darwinian terms of adaptation, selection, divergence and geographical isolation. Darwin opposed rigid taxonomies (although this did not stop late-Victorian scientists, influenced by anthropometry and Galtonian statistics, still thinking in terms of racial typologies).[58] There was also some antidote to western hubris in Darwin's theoretical denial of teleology. Evolution was, in strict terms, non-directive. Human history might be heading up a blind alley, and there was no guarantee that top dog races would stay there for ever.

Darwin himself shared the ambivalences of his age on race, wavering between the standard Victorian stereotypes, a scientific perceptiveness, and a quiet cynicism about colour and cultural superiority. He was relatively liberal in politics, passionately anti-slavery, supported the North in the American Civil War, and opposed Governor Eyre in the controversy over Eyre's bloody suppression of the Morant rising in Jamaica in 1865. He was uneasy over the general prospect of white genocide against 'lower races' in the name of progress. He once commented sarcastically that 'the white man is "improving off the face of the earth" even races nearly his equal'. True, Darwin exhibited culture shock on encountering strange savages, such as the Patagonians he met in 1832 on his *Beagle* voyage: 'Viewing such men, one can hardly make oneself believe that they are fellow-creatures and inhabitants of the same world.' But his more usual reaction was a natural history curiosity about, and respect for, native peoples and their culture. He expressed admiration for 'noble savages', such as the heroic Indians who fought to the last against the Spaniards in South America. Gillian Beer has shown that Darwin was deeply interested in the question of 'intrusion' by conquerors into the habitat of 'native inhabitants', a condition of competition that constantly occurred in nature. As the case of the Spaniards and Indians illustrated, the conquest of indigenes commonly resulted in their loss of adaptability and fitness to survive. (Darwin was much impressed by William H. Prescott's *History of the Conquest of Mexico*, 1843, sympathetic to Aztec culture, and Beer thinks that this may well have influenced his concept of artificial selection.) Although Darwin allowed the possibility of 'improvement' through invasion by 'foreigners', he also scrutinised possible strategies of native resistance to intrusion and exploitation.[59]

Darwin was bafflingly vague when it came to explaining the alleged superiority of 'the higher civilised races'. Sometimes he stressed cultural evolution, at other times he reverted to natural selection. In civilised man (he said) bodily evolution had become secondary to mental and moral evolution. (Darwin was influenced here by Wallace, who in 1864 gave a paper to the Anthropological Society that depicted humankind gradually emancipating itself from natural selection.)[60] Also, 'with highly civilised nations continued progress depends in a subordinate degree on natural selection; for such nations do not supplant and exterminate one another as do savage tribes' (p. 220). This statement reflected mid-Victorian optimism, especially the hopes of the Enlightenment and Manchester School free trade, and it was to become a staple of peace biology, which dismissed genocide as a selective factor in modern history. Darwin seemed to open the way for cultural evolution as the key to future human evolution.

However, in the same passage he suggested a genetic factor at work: 'Nevertheless the more intelligent members within the same community will succeed better in the long run than the inferior, and leave a more numerous progeny, and this is a form of natural selection' (p. 220). Presumably individual mental and moral faculties were passed on genetically to progeny, were selected because of their survival power in a context of crowding and social competition. At the same time, he had already contended that social and other faculties were not fixed, but were modifiable under environmental change. How these traits were passed on was not clearly explained, but he suggested loosely that this happened either through natural selection, or through a Lamarckian process of inheritance of acquired characteristics. Whether legitimately or not, sociocultural factors were permitted into any account of higher evolution. Darwin said for example that 'the more efficient causes of progress seem to consist of a good education during youth whilst the brain is impressible, and a high standard of excellence, inculcated by the ablest and best men, embodied in the laws, customs and traditions of the nation, and enforced by public opinion' (p. 220). This was hardly biological determinism. Inherent natural differences could not alone dictate racial destiny. This fitted Darwin's personal philosophy, which was opposed to determinism. He saw specific events as determined, but not the totality of events, and no prediction was possible.[61]

Darwin saw history and culture as complex and perplexing factors that could aid or hinder biological progress. He followed Galton, for instance, in condemning celibacy in Catholic countries for preventing able, scholarly and gentle individuals from reproducing. He noted indignantly that the Inquisition 'selected with extreme care the freest and boldest men in order to burn or imprison them. In Spain alone some of the best men – those who doubted, and without doubting there can be no progress – were eliminated during three centuries at the rate of a thousand a year' (pp. 217–18). Social policy could thus directly shape the genetic stock, the key to human progress: 'Obscure as is the problem of the advance of civilisation, we can at least see that a nation which produced during a lengthened period the greatest number of highly intellectual, energetic, brave, patriotic, and benevolent men, would generally prevail over less favoured nations' (p. 219). His discussion was couched in terms of a continuing interaction between genetic and environmental influences. Progress was a matter not just of heritable particles or innate instincts, but also of culture, nurture and history.

Darwin's speculative bio-history of humanity, although dark and violent in its account of genesis and tribal warfare, was ultimately predicated within a language of social optimism. As small tribes had been absorbed into larger and larger communities through war and genocide, people's sympathies became broader: 'The simplest reason would tell each individual that he ought to extend his social instincts and sympathies to all the members of the same nation ... This point being once reached, there is only an artificial barrier to prevent his sympathies extending to the men of all nations and races' (p. 188). Naturally, there would be many problems before this consummation was achieved. Experience showed that it took a long time for people separated by 'great differences in appearance and habits' to regard each other as fellow creatures. But that time would come. The virtue of sympathy, 'one of the noblest with which man is endowed', would eventually be extended 'to all sentient things' (p. 188).

Darwin was not inclined to take a 'pitiably low view of human nature', although reductionists and determinists speaking in his name have subsequently done so (and our own bloodstained age has lent credence to their claims). Darwin preferred the more cheerful view – reflecting the ethos of his age – 'that man has risen, though by slow and interrupted steps, from a lowly condition to the highest standard as yet attained by him in knowledge, morals and religion' (p. 224).

2   The age of Spencer and Huxley

Conflict theory

Just as Darwinism was not linked indissolubly with conflict theory, conflict theory could, and did, exist independently of Darwin. Nor was conflict theory necessarily linked with militarism, although that linkage was readily available. Definitions and interpretations of 'conflict', 'struggle' and 'competition' varied widely, especially when applied to individuals, groups and nations. Even those like Herbert Spencer and W. G. Sumner who took a hard-bitten, free-scrambling competitionist stance on domestic social policy – not necessarily Darwinian – drew the line at international warfare. Indeed Spencer and Andrew Carnegie – the fiercest of Social Darwinists in popular mythology, if not in fact – were notorious pacifists, while apostles of social co-operation like Lester Ward and Karl Pearson (an outspoken socialist) endorsed racial and global violence as the outcome of cosmic laws. Capitalism, in the eyes of the left a system of unbridled aggression, produced a string of cosmopolitan peace models, of which the most famous was that of the Manchester School of economics. Paradox abounded. Much depended upon context.

During the middle and late nineteenth century doctrines of biological militarism manifested themselves in western history, but encountered crucial opposition in the more liberal political cultures because such stark doctrines breached commonly held values based on conventional morality, order and legitimacy. For such reasons Anglo-American militarism, a by no means negligible phenomenon, tended to be couched less in aggressive Darwinian terms than in those of racial and imperial service and paternalism. Where militaristic systems and ideologies were of obvious historical significance, as in Bismarckian Germany, it is contendable that they were less dependent upon biological than upon nationalistic and realpolitical justifications. This would not be surprising, given the disparity between Darwin's empiricism and the romantic, *volkisch* element in German chauvinism. It remains completely open to the historian, of course, to argue that changing biological images of humankind, most notably those relating to race and pugnacity, were important in contributing to the growth of nationalistic rivalries and human enmities that led to World War I.

The linkage of Darwinism with militarism and imperialism was probably closest in Germany, but even here the interaction was complex. Economic imperialists and early *Lebensraum* theorists certainly appealed to Darwin, but it was not until the turn of the century that a warlike and expansionist umbrella ideology was fashioned that offered consensus appeal, combining the prestige of Darwinian science with the powerful *Staatsräson* tradition.[1] When the *Origin* first entered the German states, still disunified, its reception was conditioned by widely divergent values in the culture complex of German science. Darwinism quickly became embroiled in ideological rivalries, especially between doctrines of national unification and liberal individualism.

A basically empirical English biology was mediated to German, and wider European, audiences via Ernst Haeckel's more polemical and mystical monist theory, emanating from the University of Jena in Saxe-Weimar, a proselytising centre for German unity and *volkisch* culture. Haeckel's cell theory and embryology reinforced his monist faith in the unity of man and nature, and was deployed politically in a variety of causes, from anti-clericalism and radical popular Darwinism to authoritarian and expansionist movements of folk unity. Haeckel in the 1860s and 1870s used his evolutionary biology in liberal causes, attacking the militaristic Prussian nobility and reactionary Catholic establishment. He said that man, in terms of natural and sexual selection, had moved from an era of bodily struggle, waged with the weapons of murder, to one increasingly of intellectual and aesthetic competition, to the perfection of culture and freedom. He followed Darwin in denouncing modern militarism as a type of damaging artificial selection. However there was a rightward shift in Haeckel's thought from the 1870s which mirrored the career of German liberalism at large.[2]

There was an anti-capitalist (or anti-*Manchestertum*) thread in Haeckel's thought, which used organismic and holistic models derived from nature. He accepted the role of struggle in selection theory, a precondition to progress, but he used physiological parallels to underline the nationalistic principles of integration and mutual dependence in social evolution. (Ironically he took some of his parallels from the arch proponent of *laissez-faire* Herbert Spencer in the 1860s.) By contrast the medical scientist Rudolph Virchow feared that Haeckelian Darwinism might lead to the ogre of socialism rather than a powerful fatherland, and he insisted that organisms were federal rather than centralised unities. The clash between Virchow's and Haeckel's cell theories reflected the divisions between

Virchow's Progressive Liberal Party and the pro-Bismarck National Liberals.[3]

Recent detailed study of German Social Darwinism has rejected any simple identification of Darwinism with either bourgeois or bellicose state ideology. The cultural malleability of Darwinism made it available for a surprising diversity of users: 'Feminists and anti-feminists, revolutionaries and revisionists, socialists, liberals and conservatives, imperialists and internationalists: all, or almost all, seemed to find something in Darwinism, and the idea of evolution which benefitted their cases.'[4] In the early years the rich genre of popular Darwinism seems to have been mainly influential on the left half of the political and cultural spectrum. Liberal bourgeois reformers saw it as reinforcing the radical, secular and materialist tradition of the Enlightenment, a cultural extension of the cosmopolitan democratic spirit of 1848: 'a spirit that was suppressed in the political arena but could live on in less threateningly nonpolitical guises'.[5]

Conservative German universities, like Berlin and Munich, resisted evolutionary science, as did traditionalist opinion generally, alarmed at the modernist and materialist implications of Darwinism. It appeared to be religiously erosive and politically dangerous, especially to agrarian and gentry groups who were under economic siege or felt threatened by industrial change. There is little evidence that Darwin's struggle theorem was used in the early Bismarckian years to validate emerging capitalism through sustained 'Social Darwinist' paradigms. Revisionist scholarship suggests that until the 1880s or 1890s most Social Darwinism was moderate, typified by the best-selling Wilhelm Bolsche. German anthropology, founded in the 1860s and 1870s, at first repudiated Aryan racial theories. However, as liberalism weakened, there came to the fore an organicist and authoritarian type of biology supporting hierarchical nationalism.[6] On the left, working-class Darwinism expressed 'popular Marxism in disguise', endorsing historicist change and attacking ruling elites as unfit. After the 1890s there appeared more radical phases of Social Darwinism marked by eugenic proposals to save the nation or race. German fear of ethnic swamping from the Slavic east created the conditions for the racialisation of Social Darwinism, with Arthur Gobineau's race theories penetrating Germany from France.[7]

It no longer appears that key figures in the mythology of a militaristic Social Darwinism actually deserve their star billing. Ludwig Gumplowicz, the founder of conflict sociology, has been relocated as a moderate Social Darwinist, leaning towards liberal humanism, opposed to making analogies between human and natural struggle. Albert Schäffle did not share Friedrich Hellwand's bellicose reading of human history, but opposed unbridled capitalism and thought that physical struggle was being steadily transmuted into a struggle of ideas. Glorification of war by Count von Moltke, Heinrich von Treitschke and other nationalists was only superficially Darwinian, restating old 'might makes right' axioms. (In fact Treitschke was suspicious of Darwinism, and blamed it for the assassination attempt on the Kaiser in 1878.) Even Friedrich von Bernhardi – targeted by Anglo-American propagandists during World War I as the evil genius behind biological militarism – used Darwinism not as a major inspiration but as a useful adjunct to his main ideas for German hegemony. (We shall return to Bernhardi in a later chapter.) As Alfred Kelly observes: 'Many old-fashioned militarists, nationalists, and imperialists have been tagged with the label "Social Darwinist" solely by virtue of the fact that their bellicose utterances succeeded the publication of Darwin's *Origin*. (We might dub this the fallacy of "Post Darwin, ergo propter Darwin".)'[8]

The real mentors of German conflict sociology were the Prussian historians Friedrich Hegel, Leopold von Ranke and Heinrich von Treitschke, with their pre-Darwinian rationalisations of state violence, and their preoccupation with the dynamics of power. While Hegel hoped that war's evils might eventually be transcended within a higher system of reason and ethics, he commended war's energising effects: 'Just as the blowing of the winds preserves the sea from the foulness which would be the result of a prolonged calm, so also corruption in nations would be the product of prolonged, let alone "perpetual" peace.' Ranke rejected contract and other liberal theories of the origin of the state, claiming that the state arose out of war, 'the father of all things', the catalyst of progress, part of God's mysterious purpose. Treitschke succeeded Ranke in the history chair at Berlin University in 1874, 'and there for twenty-two years as an unabashed propagandist for pan-Germanism and anti-Semitism, he excited a complete generation of budding civil servants and military officers'.[9]

The conflict theorists Ludwig Gumplowicz and Franz Oppenheimer absorbed the *realpolitik* atmosphere of the universities of Cracow, Vienna, Berlin and Frankfurt – indeed the whole pessimistic discourse of struggle sociology needs to be situated within the disturbed and nihilistic historical milieu of central Europe in the mid nineteenth century.[10] Gumplowicz was a Polish Jew who became a minor academic in the Habsburg Empire and suffered the slings and arrows directed at oppressed minorities during the Bismarckian era. Understandably he gave a key role to ethnic/group struggle in his theory of social evolution. In *Der Rassenkampf* (1883) he depicted individual values as mere reflexes of the social milieu; ethics were the code of the hegemonic classes, and the heroes of history were 'only marionettes who carry out the will of the group'.

The ideas of Gumplowicz and his friend Gustav Ratzenhofer were to have considerable currency in war theory, and also influenced American sociology (through Albion Small, Lester Ward, Robert Park and Arthur Bentley). Gumplowicz anticipated crowd theory, popular in the pre-1914 generation, when he detected the genesis of society, class and the state in the primal conflicts of primitive hordes governed by simple animal impulses, sexual and territorial, and bonded together by intense feelings of kinship and instinctive pugnacity against aliens and rival hordes. The American sociologist William Graham Sumner explored this theme of group solidarity in Gumplowicz, Ratzenhofer and Walter Bagehot's *Physics and Politics*. He concluded that, since the competition of life arose between groups, 'it is the competition of life that makes war, and that is why war has always existed and always will'.[11] In the 1890s the Russian–French peace biologist Jacques Novicow singled out Gumplowicz as an arch exponent of militaristic *Darwinisme social*, a verdict that had considerable impact in the historiography of Social Darwinism but now seems strained, given the relatively minor interest of struggle sociology in pure biology, its greater intellectual and emotional debt to folk and *realpolitik* traditions.[12]

Gumplowicz's sexual anthropology pointed the way to J. J. Atkinson and Sigmund Freud. Yet it is symptomatic of his limited biological perspective that he showed no interest in converting his sexual theory of war and society into terms of differential reproduction or selective advantage. He postulated a ubiquitous and dominating sex drive in humans. Following the Victorian anthropologist John McLennan, Gumplowicz held that the simplest and earliest system of human relations was a free-ranging, promiscuous one. Fathers were unknown and unacknowledged in the horde, while unifying kinship bonds were forged through the mother, resulting in a system of 'mother-rule' and 'mother-rights'. This 'gynaecocratic' or matriarchal structure was ultimately broken down by the practice of woman-stealing from other hordes.[13] Exogamy (forbidding cohabitation within the group) enhanced male privilege. Foreign women served as slave property and economic assets ('more valuable than cattle'), 'and a new ethico-legal institution prevailed: father-hood, father-family, father-right'. Sexual expansionism had momentous results, ranging from ethnic intermingling that fostered 'an endless number of differentiated social unities', to imperial conquests and territorial aggrandisements that laid the foundation for the growth of civilisation. Gumplowicz found the origins of the state, property and class in the subjection of less efficient social groups by those with mental and military superiority. He conceived of the state as essentially an agency of ethnic culture and oppression (anticipating some recent debates over the role of ethnicity in nationalism). The function of the state was to deliver safety and favourable living conditions for the dominant kinship group or class, both against outside rivals, and against subject clans or labour forces within the state ('there are always ethnic differences between the ruling class and the ruled'). War and subjection were the agencies by which ethnicity had become entrenched as a principle of human solidarity in history.[14]

For Gumplowicz it was normal for disruptive factors such as war, revolution or *anomie* to cause rapid cultural change. He thought this to be more realistic than the equilibristic functionalism of Spencer and his followers. Thus his focus was upon the rise, maturation and decay of cultures, rather than upon the liberal-rationalist picture of perennial progress.[15] He was a forerunner of the 'degenerationist' thinkers of the late nineteenth century, with their despair about progress and dire warnings about the imminent decline of the west. As a Jew he was also suspicious of attempts to validate from biology and anthropology the 'progressive' German philosophies of the day, since they were founded upon anti-Semitism and fevered Bismarckian nationalism. He inclined towards a fatalistic determinism, and doubted that human intellect could achieve social progress. In 1903, however, a visit by the American reform Darwinist Lester Ward to Gumplowicz caused him to look more kindly upon 'humanity-tinkerers'.[16] A recent monograph portrays him as finally backing away from 'crude Social Darwinism'. He accepted that a 'natural' competitive system could itself generate radical social movements intent on reform: 'In Darwinian terms, this impulse might be expressed as a drive to convert fierce group struggle into refined individual competition.'[17]

Ratzenhofer was more of an optimist about racial squabbles and global control of war than Gumplowicz. The son of a Viennese watchmaker, largely self-educated, Ratzenhofer had raised himself from penury to the rank of field-marshal in the Austrian army, working in military archives and tribunals. In retirement he became a pioneering theorist of sociology, surely the only field-marshal to make a mark in the social sciences. His theory of interests was profoundly to influence Albion Small, leader of the Chicago school of sociology, and Small vigorously disseminated the Austrian's subtle ideas within American sociology. (In fact Ratzenhofer's main writings were only available in English through Small's *General Sociology* (1905), which contained over 200 pages of translation and exegesis.)

Appropriately Ratzenhofer projected sociology as an all-encompassing queen of the 'psychical sciences', capable of demonstrating all social regularities. He justified this philosophically with a curious blending of Comtean positivism and German monism. Hopefully problems such as war could be solved when humans learnt to raise politics 'to a scientific discipline upon the basis of sociological intelligence'. Ratzenhofer was an

ethical idealist, less committed to group conflict and power theory than
Gumplowicz. Nevertheless he still viewed selective struggle as a key to
evolution, and regarded war as entrenched in the human condition: 'it is
more and more evident that wars are the consequences of social
development; that is, (a) of the increase of population in reaction upon the
life-conditions, and (b) of racial antitheses'.[18]

Ratzenhofer denied that sociology could be derived from biology, but
his theory of drives and interests was strongly biological. Racial antipathies, tribal and national warfares reflected the properties of life itself as
well as social structures. These properties included 'propagation, avoid-
ance of alien conditions; a tendency towards individualization'.[19] Sustaining all life was a 'primeval force', expressed in human interaction by
instincts of self-preservation and sex. Social forms and strife were only
evolutionary modifications of such natural drives. Humans preferred to
live in peace, and early kinship groups based on sex and 'bloodbond'
discovered that survival was easier through association and co-operation.
However, population pressures caused war and forced peoples into 'a
condition of absolute hostility towards others'. War fragmented kin
groups, which came in time to differ in culture and race:

Contact between differentiated groups leads to flight or to battle. The conquest of
one such group by another leads to more complex social formations, held together
by common traditions and institutions of control, rather than by kinship.

Civilisation and the state arose out of society's need for coercion to curb
strife, and was based at first upon the slave labour of vanquished peoples.
Social controls became progressively more sophisticated, customary and
peaceable, while culture and commerce created social diversity and broke
down aggregations of power. The occasions for war and violence were
reduced as social structures became more complex. The 'culture' state
tended to displace the 'conquest' state. However, in his last work *Soziologie*
(1907) Ratzenhofer seemed to concede to the rising temper of *realpolitik*,
suggesting that races with innately superior mental capacity and aggressive
will were destined to rule the weaker. He postulated seven stages in history:
primal, primitive culture, barbaric (group conflict), warfare (living by
plunder and war), conflict of classes, spread of capitalism (cultural
expansion and class antagonism), and a new age to come enjoying
harmonious social life but achieved by domination of the stronger races.[20]

Positivism and Spencer: The bourgeois peace ideal

The history of peace biology, of 'scientific' pacifism, was to be interwoven
with that of positivist and Spencerean stage theories of social evolution.

These theories predated Darwin, and reflected the nineteenth century's optimism about progress, peace and science. (Whether war was in fact on the way out is disputable – the statisticians of war now tell us that the frequency and intensity of wars has not varied significantly since 1816.)[21] These theorists were confident about the possibility of constructing an all-revealing 'science of society' that would encompass all disciplines. Biology would be recognised as the vital science. Integrated into sociology, it would provide the basis for an instrumental and predictive social science. Stage theory had some disturbing, as well as utopian, implications. It gave a strong impetus to the use of comparative method and naturalistic analogy, for example between humans and animals, states and organisms, different races and cultures. Biological analogy was to be used, and misused, by a wide spectrum of social theorists, including racists and militarists. What gave abiding aid to the peace cause, however, was stage theory's dismissal of militarism as an outmoded phase of history, an evolutionary anachronism.

Positivism and Spencerism were congruent with bourgeois peace ideals and political rhetoric, used as polemical weapons in a series of struggles between established elites and emerging middling groups associated with the rise of industry and cities in Europe – the most conspicuous being the French Revolutions of 1789 and 1830, and the British reform agitations across the period 1790 to 1832. Middle-class rhetoric attacked the old aristocratic value system as militaristic and hierarchical, fated to be displaced by the more dynamic, cosmopolitan and peaceful ideology of the rising, industrious bourgeoisie. Ignoring the impulse given to militarism by the French revolutionary tradition of a democratic nation-in-arms, middle-class rhetoric depicted war as a barbaric legacy from a feudalistic and dynastic past, a pastime for lords and kings, glorified by knightly legends and tales of chivalry. The industrialised world of the future would cherish trade not force.

The French positivists put this thesis in naturalistic garb. In works such as *The Reorganisation of European Society* (1814) the Comte de Saint-Simon saw history as alternating between 'organic' periods, when social cohesion was great, and 'critical' periods of change and destruction, necessary because they carried the seeds of the next organic phase. (Thomas Carlyle and John Stuart Mill were among those influenced by this classification.) The world was only then, in the early nineteenth century, passing from the more primitive military and religious stage, into the 'positive' stage of industry based upon science. Although Saint-Simon cautioned against optimistic determinism, and visualised possible retrogression in human history caused by factors such as excessive class conflict, his lasting vision was of a liberal peaceful future. Mill praised the 'comprehensive liberality' of the Saint-Simonian spirit, which inspired progressive, secular radical movements throughout Europe.[22]

According to Saint-Simon, the future would see rising material standards, literacy, planning and active social sciences that would lay down naturalistic guidelines for human behaviour. The positivists talked about a 'law of association' (first sketched out by Saint-Simon's disciple Bazard). This law envisaged in history a widening association from family to tribe to city, nation state to universal human community. The last stage would see the rule of love, harmony and peace, and a rapid drive to human perfectibility. Saint-Simon forecast a semi-socialist future, dominated by a superior race of Europeans who would ultimately populate the globe, and run by an elite of technocrats, savants and social engineers. He even foreshadowed a Marxian-style utopia in which nation states and armies had naturally withered away with the triumph of positivist principles.

Auguste Comte's universalistic system was elaborated in *Cours de la philosophie positive* (6 vols, Paris, 1830–42). It was full of overtones of historical fatalism, even though Comte denied teleology, and insisted that the human will could at least adapt, curb or accelerate the invariant laws of history. It was the role of sociology (he coined the term) and the sociocratic order of the future to understand, and to facilitate, the laws of progress, to urge on desirable trends and oppose the undesirable (there was an anticipation of Marx's emphasis upon action rather than acquiescence in natural progress). Comte's 'law of the three states' postulated three historical stages in human intellectual development. This was a topic of vital importance to him, since his monumental ordering of the sciences assumed a close link between science and culture, and assumed causal connections between scientific methodology and changing historical patterns of intellectuality. These patterns progressed from a primitive theological stage, marked by crude animistic thought, through a transitional metaphysical stage, where natural phenomena were explained by recourse to abstract forces and entities, to an ultimate positive stage, dominated by empirical science. Militarism was the classical social structure correlated with the theological phase, while industrialism was that associated with the positive phase.

Comte was no believer in a mythical golden age at the dawn of history. Early humans lived in conditions of perennial and savage warfare, cannibalism, chaos and superstition. It was out of this devastation that the crudely authoritarian system of theology-militarism arose. War played a useful role in stimulating early technology (tools, weapons) and forcing social solidarity as a defence against enemy groups. Conquest resulted in ever-widening political groupings, culminating in the great empires of classical history. War and the division of labour were in fact the great agents of social evolution in this era. In ancient civilisations such as Rome, war created a large slave class, whose labour became the basis of industry. Industry progressively took over from war as the means of wealth creation.

The metaphysical stage was associated first with feudalism, where the supranational Catholic belief system constrained the military state; and then with the 'critical' era of Protestantism and natural rights radicalism. The self-interested individualism of that period, the basis of capitalism, was to be ultimately chastened and socialised in the positive stage. This era would see the hegemony of the scientific mind-set, the rule of harmony, altruism and progress, spiritualised by a Religion of Humanity.[23]

Comte's vision was, at one level, merely another variation of Enlightenment optimism. What was more prophetic was his effort to integrate the life sciences into his sociology. In his elaborate hierarchy of sciences, biology immediately preceded sociology, as simpler and more predictive. Biological models would need to be studied by sociologists. Social science was subordinate to biology, and social data must be viewed naturalistically (indeed could be reduced, as Comte said, 'to Positive theories' drawn from the sciences as a whole). Comtean positivism may be seen as materially aiding the 'naturalisation' of social science well before Darwinism did so.

However as Comte scholars always point out, there were differences between the Comtean and Darwinian modes. Herbert Spencer's shrill denunciation of Comtism as unscientific underlines the point; while deep divisions within republican, free-thinking French positivists in the 1860s over Darwinism permanently shaped French anthropology.[24] Comte rejected the whole idea of species change, even Lamarckian transformism (popular in France for political and cultural reasons). The geological age of the earth was too short (he argued, using the conventional wisdom of Cuvier) to permit transmutation of species. Environmental changes could induce modifications within organisms, but there were fixed limits to change, beyond which extinction would result.

Comte used biological analogy extensively in his social theory, borrowing from physiologists like Cabanis and the phrenologist F. J. Gall. From phrenology he took the concept that human faculties could be localised within the brain, a line of thought that led to instinct theory and images of man as fighting animal. Comte, however, believed that Gall had shown scientifically the innate sociability of man, and the dominance of the affective over the intellectual side of human nature. It was natural for humans to restrain their egotistic and violent impulses on behalf of the overall good of social orders.[25]

Comte's solidarist emphasis also owed much to biology, borrowing as it did from currently popular concepts of society as a living organism.

Organismic theories of the state, especially in Germany from Fichte to Bluntschli, spurned contract and individualistic explanations of the origin of political organisation. The organicists associated the idea of animate nature with the state, in the hope that this would enable them better to understand the state's juristic and political essence.[26] Comte saw a spontaneous harmony of structures and functions as the hallmark of human society. This paralleled the plant and animal world. A *consensus universal* emerged from the cooperative interaction of society's organic parts with each other, and with the environment. Within the social organism were 'naturally inherent' principles of sympathy and unity, but also of subordination, for example of the intellectually inferior – the mass of mankind – to the superior, the savants and leaders. This elitism was often ignored by Comte's republican followers.

Comte's stage theory was very compatible with the 'elevationist' strand of social evolutionism, with its optimism about a cooperative and warless future. However, his scepticism about human rationality emitted a jarring note. Despite his positivist epistemology, his faith that science would ultimately subsume all knowledge, and even obliterate the need for difference of opinion (this generated understandable alarm in liberal circles), Comte shared the Romantic movement's respect for the emotional, imaginative and transcendental dimension. John Stuart Mill, himself coming to realise the inadequacy of strictly material culture, in 1848 praised Comte's 'inculcation of the purely *subordinate* role of the intellect as the minister of the higher sentiments'.[27] Comte alleged that the 'affective impulses' played a more important part in most people's lives than intellect. However the selfish instincts created centrifugal tendencies in society, and threatened to undermine communal spirit based on humans' instinctive sociability. War was likely to spring from such egoism. Comte assumed that private advantage was the practical foundation for public good, but he also argued that social control and intellectual analysis were needed in the interest of the greatest good. Indeed his inclinations were almost Benthamite in this regard, although Bentham had more confidence in the potential rationality of the citizenry. Comte imagined an intelligent minority cultivating the mental progress needed for social advancement. This elite would monitor state intervention that would be primarily moral and cultural, working to enhance altruism and a sense of holism.[28] The trouble with this, from the liberal peace viewpoint, was that a warless world might only be accomplished at the risk of authoritarianism.

While optimistic rationalism continued to enjoy a lusty life in social evolutionary and peace circles, there were other discourses here sensitive to the connotations of noble emotionalism – Benjamin Kidd's 'emotion of the ideal' – as the agency of human reform. This raised the spectre of massive social conditioning, even a Pavlovian totalitarianism. Generally, however, the Victorians interpreted positivism as an optimistic doctrine: mindlessly optimistic, thought T. H. Huxley, who took a bleak view of the human condition. Comtism had a widespread influence in Victorian Britain.[29] The long-lived Frederick Harrison proselytised endlessly on behalf of the Religion of Humanity ('Catholicism *minus* Christianity' observed Huxley). In France Comtism had lasting appeal to republican activists, including in the later nineteenth century Jules Ferry, Leon Gambetta and Georges Clemenceau. Such republicans saw themselves as orchestrating a 'scientific politics' that would inevitably crush the institutions and religion of the *ancien régime*.[30]

The stage model was to reappear in many guises, and also the Comtean faith in experts, mandarins and scientists. Peace apostles were to invest much hope in a scientific sociocracy. It was to prove one of the great let-downs of history, for the experts turned out to be impotent to control war. The positivists would have found unthinkable the accusations made today that wars are manufactured by an unholy alliance of scientists, business and the military, the 'industrial-military complex'.

Despite Herbert Spencer's denigration of Comtism, he owed a considerable intellectual debt to positivism. However he owed an even greater debt to native English tradition and historical experience, most notably that evoked in the dissenting, radical, crusadingly middle-class world of the English midlands and north in which the young railway engineer-cum-intellectual grew up. This was also the nurturing-bed for the cosmopolitan bourgeois peace ideal that flourished in mid century, generally linked with Cobden and Bright and the Manchester School. Spencer came from a Wesleyan family in Derbyshire, although his spikily independent father seceded from Methodism to the Quakers, the purest of the English pacifists. There were family associations with both Enlightenment science – Spencer's father was at one time secretary of the Derby Philosophical Society – and political/religious dissent. There was a connection with Edward Miall, whose radical newspaper *The Nonconformist* campaigned for disestablishment of the Anglican Church. Spencer worked as managing editor of the liberal *Economist* from 1848, where he imbibed *laissez-faire* doctrine from one editor, James Wilson, and utopian ideals from another, the socialist Thomas Hodgskin. In his youth Spencer was exposed to clusters of ideas that were to persist in his mature philosophy: traditional suspicion of the state; resentment against a paternalistic old Poor Law; Lamarckian ideas of use-inheritance associated with Enlightenment optimism about the goodness of nature and a benevolent destination for humankind; phrenological concepts of innate faculties (from Franz Gall and George Combe he took up the idea of inherent moral and acquisitive senses); and engineering/physical principles that became the dynamic of his social theory.[31]

Spencer's grand project of creating a universal 'synthetic philosophy' does not appeal to the modern mind, and Spencer is no longer fashionable. He is dismissed as an arid system-spinner. It is with surprise that we read of his impact on an earlier age, not least in the United States. In his 1909 novel *Martin Eden*, Jack London has his autobiographical hero absolutely staggered by Spencer, 'organizing all knowledge for him, and presenting to his startled gaze a universe so concrete of realization that it was like a model of a ship such as sailors make and put into glass bottles'.[32]

There have been at least two competing historical images of Spencer. One, dear to the peace school, sees him as an enemy of militarism and imperialism, a stage theorist who saw human history marching inexorably towards an ideal end of freedom, individuality and international peace. The other, equally dear to socialist critics (but shared by many others), sees him as a bloody-minded Social Darwinist, a 'scientific' defender of a brutalising capitalism that endorsed violent struggle and had no compassion for the disadvantaged in society. The latter image has received the severer battering at the hands of historical revisionism, which has recuperated the complexity and context of his ideas – although recent studies recognise that an understandable backlash was generated by Spencer's harsher pronouncements: for example, against 'maudlin philosophy' for maliciously lowering the quality of modern society by artificially preserving 'imbeciles and idlers and criminals', an anticipation of degenerationist discourse, so influential in medical-psychological and political agendas in later nineteenth-century Europe.[33]

The more learned opinion now is that Spencer, far from being a deterministic Social Darwinist, arguing primarily from biology, rather exploited biology to legitimise an overarching metaphysical system.[34] His biology was subordinate to his ethical/social system, and served it. He was a transcendentalist who denied God, replacing Him by an abstract Unknowable, and who attempted to replace traditional sources of morality by hitching his ethical wagon to science (in Peel's apt phrase).[35]

It is contendable that Spencer's evolutionary system was not genuinely Darwinian, that it did not entail a real struggle theory (although his language often suggested otherwise), and that it was not strictly speaking the source of any normative system. Spencer, it appears, reluctantly squeezed Darwinian natural selection into his primarily Lamarckian theory, and Lamarckian theory was relatively uncommitted to concepts such as 'survival of the fittest' through struggle. (Spencer pushed it about as far as it would go in this direction.) Moreover, as suggested, it is possible to conceive of Spencer's ethics as deriving from an architectonic model and moral concepts that were essentially outside his evolutionary paradigm, even though there were dynamic interactions between the two worlds of discourse. This is probably enough theoretically to defend Spencer against the charge that he was an exponent of simple naturalistic ethics, committing the 'naturalistic fallacy' of deriving a normative 'ought' from Nature's 'is'.[36]

In *Social Statics* (1851) Spencer alleged that 'the course of history could not possibly have been other than it has been'. Its inexorable progress was from an unsubdued and chaotic early human state – a world filled with 'inferior creatures only' – to higher stages that led ultimately to civilisation ruled by the greatest happiness principle, a society ruled by peaceful, sympathetic beings, perfectly fitted to their environment, free and equal (indeed, as contemporaries like Kropotkin noticed, almost an anarchist or socialist utopia).[37] Of course such creatures would have been swiftly annihilated in the Hobbesian conditions of primal history. There the necessary task of 'clearing the earth' of inferior races of men was undertaken by 'aboriginal man', a killer, largely devoid of sympathy, but with dormant capability of evolving into 'the ultimate man' when conditions permitted (pp. 448–9). War, bloodshed, enmity and cruelty – these 'manifold evils' (p. 451) – were endemic and inevitable in early history, mandated by environment and predatory instincts. The forces that were working out the 'great scheme of perfect happiness' took no account of incidental suffering, and exterminated 'such sections of mankind as stand in their way, with the same sternness as they exterminate beasts of prey and herds of useless ruminants. Be he human being, or be he brute, the hindrance must be got rid of. Just as the savage has taken the place of lower creatures, so must he, if he have remained too long a savage, give place to his superior' (pp. 454–5). With a few exceptions, most primitives were unsociable and warlike. They were in the early 'egoistic' stage. However, the general direction of social evolution was from egoism to altruism. War and population pressure were the triggering mechanism that – despite their anti-social character – helped impel humanity forward into higher civilisation.[38]

Challenges like war and crowding fostered among conquering races qualities of social cohesion, mutual aid, inventiveness in artifacts and weapons, economic specialisation and human differentiation: 'From the very beginning the conquest of one people over another has been, in the main, the conquest of social man over anti-social man' (p. 455). As successful races carved out their own living space, and efficiently defended it, they were less subject to decimation by enemies. Peace descended for longer and longer periods of time, and commerce flowered. Slavery – the distasteful but necessary by-product of military expansionism – forced recalcitrant aboriginal man into productive labour. On these bases civilisation was founded.

Rather like Darwin, Spencer preferred not to linger upon the passing cruelties, the apparent purposelessness, of the evolutionary process, but to concentrate upon its regularities (and, infinitely more so in Spencer's case, upon its ultimate moral significance). Thus Spencer detected beneath appearances a subterranean tendency for man's 'latent capabilities' to flourish under the action of favourable circumstances. This happened according to the probabilistic laws of the organic world (laws that owed much to Spencer's engineering training): laws of division, differentiation, dissipation of motion, integration of matter, advance from simple to complex, incoherence to coherence, homogenous to heterogeneous. He used a botanical analogy. The 'seeds of civilization' inherent in aboriginal man, and distributed over the earth by his multiplication, were certain in the lapse of time to fall into fruitful environments, 'and in spite of all blightings and uprootings, were certain... ultimately to originate a civilization which should outlive all disasters and arrive at perfection' (p. 454).

Struggle, in a somewhat chastened Lamarckian form, played a pre-conditional role in the achievement of progress within Spencer's naturally-ordered, self-adjusting mode of social evolution. Race-improvement was dependent upon the constant exercise and struggle of faculties and instincts. The results were transmitted to progeny by use-inheritance. Spencer warned as early as 1842 that race-degeneracy could result from inactivity, from governments inhibiting people from exercising their natural faculties. He later supplemented this retrogression theory by reference to orthodox Darwinian natural selection.[39]

Going with this retrogression theory was Spencer's intriguing suggestion that human violence in the present was a survival of past socio-biological patterns, a reversion to primitive structures. In this Spencer anticipated theories prevalent at the time of World War I, and articulated more recently by thinkers like Arthur Koestler, Paul MacLean and Henri Laborit. Spencer explained modern 'murders, enslavings, and robberies – the tyrannies of rulers, the oppressions of class, the persecutions of sect and party', and other barbarous customs, as 'simply instances of the disastrous working of this original and once needful constitution, now that mankind have grown into conditions for which it is not fitted' (pp. 451–2). The persistence of man's 'destructive propensities' was not surprising, given the slow rate of change in the basic conditions of human life. Warfare had continued between man and the higher animals, between men in groups, between higher and lower races. Spencer targeted his *bête noire*, the state, whose interventionist activities resulted in national wars. The state thwarted the natural resolution of tensions, even the teleological thrust of evolution itself. However, revolutions and social convulsions were necessary to modify fixed and authoritarian structures. All of these historical forces caused man's belligerent faculties to be constantly exercised, and they were preserved (according to Lamarckism) by use-inheritance.

In Spencer's scenario, it was only with the coming of industrialisation that there arose genuine prospects of rapid progress towards global peace. Spencer's sociology paralleled the cosmopolitan pacifism of his intellectual forebears, the Manchester School. Like them he believed that global capitalism was basically peaceable. He predicted that the more settled conditions of international capitalism would generate a sort of 'take-off' into self-sustaining human growth, just as the Industrial Revolution had triggered a take-off into exponential economic growth. Now, at last, the Lamarckian reinforcements would be benign: the innately altruistic faculties of man would develop and be passed on to future generations through use-inheritance, while the more egoistic predatory instincts would dwindle through lack of exercise. However 'rebarbarisation' was still possible in the modern world, should the appropriate conditions call forth 'the old propensities'. Spencer cited the barbarising of colonists who lived under 'aboriginal conditions', and he pointed to the frontier settlers of America 'amongst whom unavenged murders, rifle duels, and Lynch law prevail' (p. 450).[40]

Sometimes Spencer wrote as if competition were a permanent necessity in human history, but sometimes as if it would fade away with the rise of a more moral industrial society, as social evolution led to social harmony and altruism. He attacked the 'might is right' school in *Social Statics* (pp. 477ff.), and kept up the assault in *The Study of Sociology* (1873) and *The Data of Ethics* (1879). Competition to the death, and violent elimination of unfit strains, were features of primal, not advanced, stages of evolution. Indeed they had a retrograde effect upon man's developing ethical sense as soon as human consciousness perceived violence to be at variance with the moral law; and 'to diminish men's moral sense is to diminish their fitness for acting together, and, therefore, to render the best producing and distributing organizations impracticable. Another illustration this of the perfect economy of nature' (*Social Statics*, p. 457).[41] Spencer's position, taken up by many peace biologists, was that the natural process itself generated in humans a self-regulating mechanism that virtually ensured emancipation from the brutal 'Darwinian' fight for survival. As their minds and consciences developed, humans would enter a higher 'cosmic' phase, marked by coexistence rather than confrontation. War would become an anachronism.[42]

It was Spencer's description of the historical stages of militant and industrial society that struck the public mind. In *Principles of Sociology* (1876–96, but especially Part V, 1882) he analysed these stages. He saw societies evolving rather like organisms, with internal competition (and co-operation) between organs, with survival of the fittest through individual variation and selective pressure. Societies, races, individuals all strove to reach a state of dynamic equilibrium with their environments. Conflict was endemic to the process, and had early on stimulated the growth of political organisation and complex social systems. Institutionalised conflict produced militarism. Spencer disliked militarism. Indeed he was one of its classic critics. Yet he recognised that the militant phase was a necessary, if unlovely, stage of social evolution. War had played a vital role in emancipating humans from an unruly, savage state. War had brought social cohesion, the basis for emerging nation states and empires. It had been the great consolidator of kingdoms.

Militant society was marked by strong cooperative traits (a useful corrective, this, to the glib leftist assumption that only socialist societies were truly cooperative – and Spencer was to remark some disturbing parallels between state-dominated military and socialist structures). War demanded joint action for survival, mobilisation of fighting forces for defence and offence, organisation of non-combatants, the restraint of self-interest: 'development of the militant type involves a close binding of the society into a whole' (*ibid.*, Part V).[43] With its hierarchy, discipline, strict group loyalty, ceremony and conservatism, the militant society placed severe curbs on individual liberty: 'the individual is owned by the State' (sect. 551). Early warring tribes had primitive chieftainship, out of which evolved more coercive and disciplined instrumentalities and despotic types of civil government: 'the citizen as well as the soldier lives under a system of compulsory co-operation' (sect. 561). It tended to become a rigid and unadaptive system, resistant to change and social mobility, marked by officialism and caste distinctions that often became hereditary, repressive of dissent and intellectual culture.

Economically, the militant society was closed and protectionist, concerned with self-sufficiency, suspicious of private combinations and enterprise, worshipful of state power. The system itself fostered a constipated, inward-turning national posture, and attitudes of fear and hostility towards neighbours. Militarism had endured for millennia, since it kept up the very climate of belligerence from which it drew strength. It was a self-sustaining system. The people brought up within such systems invariably acquired militaristic traits: physical vigour and courage, but allied with pugnacious, vengeful, destructive, obedient and patriotic, anti-artistic and anti-scientific, essentially intolerant and illiberal characteristics. In a milieu of recurrent struggle and warfare, selective pressures ensured the survival of people with such traits. Use-inheritance blue-printed aggressive characters into the tribal or national make-up.

Out of the travails of history would eventually emerge the higher stage of industrial society. The west was currently in a transitional phase of mixed structures. As more people became employed in peaceful pursuits, a less coercive, more individualistic society would appear. Spencer merely accepted the Victorian assumption that war was diminishing, and hardly explained the cause of such a critical change. His ideal type of industrial society was based on contract rather than status (terms borrowed from Sir Henry Maine).[44] It was to be democratic and decentralised, marked by plasticity and social mobility, economically open, a society of limited government, unlimited private initiative, enacting natural justice by allowing reward to be apportioned to merit.

The 'aggressiveness of nature fostered by militarism having died out' (sect. 564), there remained only the less brutal industrial struggle for existence. Societies would survive that preserved personal rights and produced the greatest number of the best people (sect. 567). The removal of the pressures of war would bring marvellous results: 'Nearly all public organizations save that for administering justice, necessarily disappear' (sect. 569). Despotism would wither away. With the spread of industrialism 'the tendency is towards the breaking down of the divisions between nationalities, and the running through them of a common organization: if not under a single government, then under a federation of governments' (sect. 572). The 'Religion of Amity', as Spencer put it, would slowly overhaul the 'Religion of Enmity'. Out of Spencer's early Quakerism and Manchester idealism came his mature vision – that of a pacific world order based on global free trade, with no militarism, no strong state or big bureaucracy, with citizens freely following their own ways, acting democratically through a myriad of voluntary associations.

The trouble was that the world did not move in this direction in the later Victorian age. Spencer was progressively disillusioned by growing threats to liberty in western history: by the Commune, corruption in Recon-structionist America under the presidency of Ulysses S. Grant, Gladstone's 'proto-welfare' measures.[45] But it was the rise of socialism – the ideology of state power – and the modern cult of jingoistic imperialism that most appalled him. They were, to his mind, related phenomena, survivals from the militant type of society. As early as 1875 (in volume I of *Principles of Sociology*, part II, sect. XI), he equated extensions of government regulation with a trend to authoritarian militarism: 'Along with the tacit assumption that State-authority over citizens has no assignable limits, which is an assumption proper to the militant state, there goes an unhesitating faith in State-judgment, also proper to the militant type' (p.

572). Spencer found alarming signs of 'rebarbarisation' in the expansion of Britain's army and volunteer forces; in 'a manifest extension of the militant-spirit and discipline among the police, who, wearing helmet-shaped hats, beginning to carry revolvers, and looking upon themselves as half soldiers, have come to speak of the people as "civilians"'. He was even alarmed by endowment of scientific research, registration of teachers and inspection of local libraries (*ibid.*, 1882, part V, sect. 559).

Spencer was never an out-and-out pacifist. He conceded that peace-loving nations might need to arm defensively against predatory rivals. However, he deemed British policy at the time of the Boer War as a naked struggle for mastery. His was a classic indictment of the threat to traditional freedoms posed by wartime controls and war psychology.[46] During war mania free discussion was muzzled, taxes raised, resources diverted to wasteful production of armaments. Irrationality reigned, and human traits were superseded by brute traits. Spencer attacked the militarism of the militia, the cadet corps, even the Salvation Army. He was one of the first to detect militaristic values in sport, and he lashed out at violence in literature and the popular press (such as Alfred Harmsworth's *Daily Mail*): 'In all places and in all ways there has been going on during the last fifty years a recrudescence of barbaric ambitions, ideas and sentiments and an unceasing culture of blood-thirst.'[47] He hoped that these bad signs were temporary. It was vital for higher evolution that peace should reign. However Spencer became an embittered old man. Towards the end of his life he wrote to a friend: 'Did I but think that men were likely to remain in the far future anything like what they are now, I should contemplate with equanimity the sweeping away of the whole race'.[48]

Walter Bagehot: a Whig view

A deft, cultured, and temperamentally undoctrinaire observer of humanity, Walter Bagehot surprised his cohorts in 1872 with the relatively abstract *Physics and Politics*, his one real effort – if a preliminary one – to devise a 'science of society', that elusive endeavour of the age. The Victorians were not overly impressed – partly no doubt because he was regarded as a brilliant journalist, not an academic. Modern commentary has often repeated the verdict. Even John Burrow, who has written a delightfully sympathetic essay on Bagehot, assesses the work as less a systematic treatise than an inspired extension of his perennial concerns with the social conditions of action, with the practice and possibilities of politics. The language of Darwinist selectionism does not (in Burrow's opinion) altogether hide the Bagehot who studied politics in its own terms, who set nothing beyond full political life, no supersession of politics by society, and no awesome extrapolations from historical laws to human predictions.[49]

Even so, Bagehot's speculations on war and civilisation, selection by conquest, racial mixture, the role of group norms, human progress and retrogression influenced Darwin's writing of the *Descent of Man*;[50] while historians of sociology and psychology have generously acknowledged Bagehot's pioneering work in their fields. According to C. H. Driver in 1933, Bagehot catalytically explored the implications for sociology of evolutionary theory, and marked the beginning of the psychological approach to political science. He applied the 'new knowledge' – the physiology of Huxley and Maudsley, the evolutionism of Darwin and Spencer, the history of Maine and Buckle, the anthropology of Lubbock, Tyler and McLennan – to human history and politics. In this way he wrote 'a sociological footnote to the doctrine of evolution prevailing in the sixties: a tentative peering not only outward into the remote darkness of pre-history, but also inward into the irrational and subrational forces of human nature inherited from the uncounted ages of the evolutionary process'.[51]

The first of Bagehot's five articles on 'Physics and Politics' appeared on 1 November 1867, in the *Fortnightly Review*. They were published in book form in 1872, with the subtitle 'Thoughts on the Application of the Principles of "Natural Selection" and "Inheritance" to Political Society'. It was symptomatic of the confused world of biological discourse at the time that a book making such a Darwinian promise should contain a high degree of Lamarckian theory.[52] Bagehot had little sympathy with the reputed materialism and determinism of Darwinian science, although he was careful to maintain that his own thesis was independent of any philosophy as to the nature of matter or mind. What he did object to was the historical materialism of works like T. H. Buckle's *History of Civilisation* (1857–61), which saw material forces as the mainsprings of human progress. Bagehot insisted on the primacy of mental and moral causes, an attitude suited to Lamarckian-style speculation. It was the action of the will (he said) that caused unconscious habits: 'it is the silent toil of the first generation that becomes the transmitted aptitude of the next':

Our mind in some strange way acts on our nerves, and our nerves in some equally strange way store up the consequences, and somehow the result, as a rule and commonly enough, goes down to our descendants ...[53]

Bagehot's theory that mental impulses became blueprinted into social heritage owed much to the work of T. H. Huxley and Henry Maudsley on the nervous system. Huxley's *Man's Place in Nature* (1863) and *Elementary*

Physiology (1866) stressed the complex physiology of reflex actions. Individuals seemed capable of converting what were originally the behavioural products of will, volition and brain into 'artificial reflex actions', or habituated responses. Bagehot translated Huxley's concept of physical drill, whose effects became embodied in man's 'nervous structure', into a concept of social drill, the basis of a heritable 'cake of custom'.

Maudsley, a controversial pioneer of criminal anthropology and psychiatric theories of degeneration, suggested inherited Lamarckian factors behind 'race' dynamics. His *Physiology and Pathology of the Mind* (1867) said that racial and social efficiency accelerated as increasingly complex interactions took place between reflex and voluntary faculties within humans. This had a powerhouse effect: 'stored up power' was acquired by one generation and transmitted as an 'inborn faculty' to the next; 'and the development takes place in accordance with that law of increasing speciality and complexity of adaptation to external nature which is traceable through the animal kingdom'.[54] Bagehot insisted that knowledge of the new theory of 'a transmitted nerve element' was crucial in understanding 'the connective tissue' of civilisation. Here we had 'the continuous force which binds age to age', which allowed improvement, 'which makes each civilisation not a set of detached dots, but a line of colour, surely enhancing shade by shade'.[55] Later 'social heritage' thinkers, such as Graham Wallas and Havelock Ellis, were to subtract the Lamarckian factor from this equation, and to consolidate Bagehot's accent on cultural evolution as the key to human progress. Peace philosophy found social heritage language appealing, for it bespoke the possibility of humans freeing themselves from a crippling dependence on violent selectionist processes embedded in nature.

Bagehot did not go quite so far. For a social heritage thinker he was unusually committed to the centrality of conflict, and specifically of military art, as an engine of change. It was a rough rule, especially in early times, 'that progress is promoted by the competitive examination of constant war' (p. 64). Evolutionary success, for most of history, had been a matter of the strong prevailing over the weak, 'and in certain marked peculiarities the strongest tend to be the best' (p. 42). (Huxley, and many others, objected that adaptive ability was not necessarily correlated with brute strength.) Bagehot saw human history as a bloody and uncertain affair. Progress was abnormal rather than inevitable: Darwin marked this passage when he read essay 2 in the *Fortnightly* in 1868. Bagehot observed that progress was a Eurocentric concept. Many societies – savage, Oriental – failed to improve: 'only a few nations, and those of European origin, advance; and yet these think ... such advance to be inevitable, natural, and eternal' (p. 41).

It was military progress that was 'the most *showy* fact' in human history. Fighting forces had invariably grown, and weaponry improved. There was, moreover, an indissoluble link between civilisation, intelligence and war. The great fighting powers were also the great civilised nations. If anything, that link had become stronger with time: 'In ancient times city people could not be got to fight ... But nowadays in all countries the great cities could pour out multitudes wanting nothing but practice to make good soldiers, and abounding in bravery and vigour' (p. 44). (The American Civil War had impressed upon the world the valour and impact of democratic levees.) Contact between modern nations and primitive peoples revealed vividly the superiority of the western races, both militarily and in terms of biological fitness (most notably resistance to disease). Bagehot explained the connection between military and mental growth thus:

Every intellectual gain, so to speak, that a nation possessed was in the earliest times made use of – was *invested* and taken out – in war; all else perished. Each nation tried constantly to be stronger, and so made and copied the best weapons; by conscious and unconscious imitation each nation formed a type of character suitable to war and conquest. Conquest improved mankind by the intermixture of strengths; the armed truce, which was then called peace, improved them by the competition of training and the constant creation of new power. Since the long-headed men first drove the short-headed men out of the best land in Europe, all European history has been the history of the superposition of the more military races over the less military (p. 45).

Sir Henry Maine, exploring the hinterlands between law, history and anthropology, had already in *Ancient Law* (1861) drawn attention to the primacy of custom in primitive society. Bagehot added another insight – one that almost certainly influenced Darwin. This was that primitive social discipline, a discipline stemming from customary sanctions, religious terrors, the power of chiefs, and an emerging law, conferred selective advantage on societies in warring situations. In passages that Darwin marked, Bagehot drew parallels between the process by which the wild and unruly members of herd animals were lost, or culled by their native keepers, and the process of man's own self-domestication. When humans were at the first stage in the struggle of life, the most obedient and 'tamest' tribes were the strongest, the conquerors:

All are very wild then ... But what makes one tribe – one incipient tribe, one bit of a tribe – to differ from another is their relative faculty [Darwin's underlining] of coherence. The slightest symptom of legal development, the least indication of a military bond, is then enough to turn the scale. The compact tribes win, and the compact tribes are the tamest. Civilisation begins, because the beginning of civilisation is a military advantage (p. 47).[56]

With a Spencerean touch, Bagehot described how the wild men, 'the absolutely incoherent men', were 'cleared away' during prehistory. The less coherent men lived on in protected, remote parts of the world, but in 'regions of rivalry' they died out. There whole families of civilisations took the essential first step of snapping the restrictive bonds to tradition. The most enduring civilisation began in the Mediterranean, from which it grew like a 'conquering *swarm*'. But most became 'arrested civilisations', primarily because they failed to generate 'beneficial variability' (a phrase Darwin liked). The primal compulsion towards customary discipline constantly recurred. Terrible sanctions imposed on early humans 'killed out of the whole society the propensities to variation which are the principle of progress' (pp. 147–50).

War usefully counteracted this. Wars were 'by their incessant fractures of old images, and by their constant infusion of new elements, the real regenerators of society' (p. 99). Wars encouraged innovation and variability. Darwin noted Bagehot's argument that warfare could result in racial mixtures that begat 'beneficial variability'. A genetically 'mixed and ameliorated' state, if its improvement 'even in part took the military line', would most likely gain 'a steady advantage in the battle of nations, and a greater chance of lasting in the world' (p. 58).

Bagehot discerned three main stages in the evolution of humanity: the preliminary (or race-making) age where custom reigned; the fighting (or nation-making) age where variability was needed; and the age of discussion. The first 'pre-economic' age of no-polity witnessed the critical emergence of race and kin groups from a Hobbesian condition only recently arisen from the brute level. The hardest step of all was the next step, to fixed polity and early civilisation. The problem was to nourish the 'little seed of adaptiveness' and originality, to gain variability without losing legality or the virtues of the savage age: valour, discipline, obedience, the warlike qualities that were 'the daily bread of human nature' (p. 52).

Bagehot recognised that social practices could be of evolutionary utility in one age, or context, but prove unadaptive in changed circumstances: 'The whole history of civilisation is strewn with creeds and institutions which were invaluable at first, and deadly afterwards' (p. 60). Thus, for example, despotism met the primary needs of early society, as it produced military efficiency ('so long as war is the main business of nations, temporary despotism – despotism during the campaign – is indispensable': p. 54). The trouble with despotism was that it discouraged the principle of variability. It kept people in the customary stage: 'its very fitness for that age unfits it for the next ... Some 'standing system' of semi-free discussion is as necessary to break the thick crust of custom and begin progress as it is in later ages to carry on progress when begun' (p. 55).

Slavery was another example. It was a useful spin-off (like race mixture) from early warfare. It conferred leisure upon conquerors, and thus created the opportunity for art, culture and intellectual advance. Slavery also made a nation more capable at war: 'slave-owning nations, having time to think, are likely to be more shrewd in policy, and more crafty in strategy' (p. 59). However, later, more moral ages deemed slavery, with its ruinous human costs, less apt, and ultimately rooted it out. Despotism, slavery, 'venerable oligarchy' and 'august monarchy' were only some of the 'preliminary forms' which at first brought 'many graces and many refinements, and often tend to secure them by the preservative military virtue' (p. 60).

Bagehot weighed war in the evolutionary balance. He accepted that war had placed a selective premium upon intellectual and moral vigour, even religious fervour: 'Mr Carlyle has taught the present generation ... that "God-fearing armies are the best armies"' (pp. 60–1). Against this, war had negative selective effects. While it nourished the preliminary, martial virtues, which gave nations military edge 'and make them more likely to *stay* in the race of nations' (p. 60), it did not foster humanity, charity, grace and 'a nice sense of the rights of others', apt qualities for the age of discussion:

Since war has ceased to be the moving force in the world, men have become more tender one to another ... and this is not so much because men are improved ... but because they have no longer the daily habit of war (p. 62).

The primitive contempt for physical weakness and women had also eroded, although the war spirit still coloured morality too much:

Metaphors from law and metaphors from war make most of our current moral phrases ... The military habit makes man think far too much of definite action, and far too little of brooding meditation ... Military morals can direct the axe to cut down the tree, but it knows nothing of the quiet force by which the forest grows (p. 63).

What was remarkable, indeed, was war's evolutionary persistence. Despite Bagehot's liberal optimism about a more humane future in a context of discussion, tolerant give and take, developing reason and conscience, there was a darker side to his thought that insisted upon man's retention of faculties and habits inherited from an ancient animal past. (Maudsley had only two years earlier claimed that there was a brute brain within man's modern brain, as revealed by morbid psychology and 'the degeneration of insanity'.)[57] An atavistic bio-psychological insight underpinned Bagehot's famous theory of gradualism, as expressed in *The English Constitution* (1867) and other works. The art of politics (he argued) was to avoid the pitfalls of ideological haste and human impetuosity. These flaws were inherited from a less reflective, action-oriented past. Over-activity was one of the great evils facing humankind. It was inherited from times when life was simple, when quick action generally led to desirable ends: 'If A kills B before B kills A, then A survives, and the human race is a race of A's.' But the issues of life were plain no longer. To act rightly in modern society required deep study, much passive consideration:

Even the art of killing one another, which at first particularly trained men to be quick, now requires them to be slow. A hasty general is the worst of generals nowadays; the best is a sort of von Moltke, who is passive if any man was passive; who is 'silent in seven languages'; who possesses more and better accumulated information as to the best way of killing people than any one who ever lived ... I wish the art of benefiting man had kept pace with the art of destroying them ...

Bagehot thought that while war 'had become slow', the mindless philanthropy of the age 'remained hasty', bringing 'great populations to suffer and be vicious'. All this because philanthropists and others had inherited 'from their barbarous forefathers a wild passion for instant action' (*Physics and Politics*, p. 124).

Bagehot's work certainly tapped some of the subterranean insecurities of the mid-Victorian age, and foreshadowed the cultural anxieties of the later century, with its fear of atavism and problematic sense of progress. At least one Bagehot scholar has linked 'the Victorian nightmare of evolution' to his fear of democracy, regard for difference and ordered progress, his growing conservatism:

More than any of his contemporaries, Bagehot stressed the time necessary for spirit to evolve from blood and brain. Evolution imbued Bagehot with an indomitable respect for gradualism and convinced him that natural growth is always slow ... Explosive changes in society were as dangerous as violent changes in biology ... Darwin's notation of the preserving as well as the creating factor in the development of new species profoundly impressed Bagehot and can be caught in his qualified concepts of 'verifiable progress' ... 'conservative innovation' ... and 'animated moderation'.[58]

One might contend that these evolutionary readings were substantially comforting, rather than disturbing, to Bagehot and the Victorians. They reinforced a Whiggish politics of middle-of-the-way restraint rather than Tory reaction or radical reconstruction. Bagehot's views on war fell well within such Whiggish parameters. He shared liberal hopes that the art of organised killing would wither away in a world dedicated to talk and trade, not war. Nevertheless he recognised with Whiggish caution that warfare was a biologically and culturally entrenched human institution – one that probably rested on an instinctive basis, and had been crucial in fostering innovation and variability. As such it would be long a-dying.

The opposition to imperial biology: Wallace and Huxley

If stage theory encouraged use of analogy from nature and comparison between man and animals, a quietly persistent alternative tradition emerged out of the anti-determinist elements within Darwinism. This tradition opposed explanatory systems that reduced humans to animals (violent, territorial), that foreshortened human complexity, flexibility and uniqueness, or denied human autonomy in the face of overarching bio-historical laws (such as 'survival of the fittest', or 'war is a biological necessity'). The anti-determinists affirmed human values and autonomy against an invading and 'imperial' biological science, that threatened everywhere to impose naturalistic models and ethics. As the 'new liberal' philosopher D. G. Ritchie complained, fatalism tended to result if man was approached only from the side of nature:

we see the individual only as a 'complex animal' whose actions are the result of inherited instincts and the influence of his environment... and in the nation [we see] only a social organism whose life is in the same way conditioned by phenomena (natural events) in the past and by the physical environment of the present.

However, the individual had a consciousness of self, of ends to be attained; and the nation (or people in it) had political consciousness of ends: 'History is the struggle for freedom from fate.'[59]

Although naturalism was the dominant mode in science, and the basis for Darwinism, some of the ablest critics of 'imperialist' biology were eminent biologists – such as A. R. Wallace, the co-founder of the theory of natural selection, T. H. Huxley, 'Darwin's bulldog', and the zoologist Peter Chalmers Mitchell (dealt with in chapter 7). It is perhaps not so strange that biology should have harboured free-wheeling humanistic as well as fatalistic trends. The general point has been made that elements of a philosophy of choice were injected into nineteenth-century biology from philosophy and the social sciences, which surreptitiously rendered biology into terms amenable to current social theory.[60] If this is so, a sort of two-way traffic in ideas was going on. Social theory was attempting to appropriate biology as a way of heightening its own explanatory power. At the same time, the mores of social theory were influencing biology in various directions: for instance, towards anthropomorphism, slanting biology into an obsession with the origins of human faculties and culture, which could lead to reductionism. However, Victorian mores also set biology towards the image of a humankind capable of directing its own bio-destiny.[61]

The legacy of the anti-reductionists and anti-determinists was potentially of great benefit to peace theory, suggesting the human capacity to escape from violent biological laws inherited from an animal past. However peace biology – like science itself – was divided by these philosophical issues (essentially matters of faith that could not be tested by observation). Within the discourse of peace biology were some strong addictions to naturalistic analogy of a non-violent kind. Even the opponents of determinism were capable of using evolutionary justifications for their own preferred social and political models, the very sin that they condemned in others.

As a committed social reformer, Alfred Russel Wallace was by temperament resistant to the view that naturalistic imperatives limited man's capacity consciously to ameliorate the human condition. As a young man he had imbibed Owenite socialism, with its Enlightenment confidence that reason had infinite potential to reconstruct social environment. He grew up also in 'Manchester culture' and was drawn to its cosmopolitan peace ideal. His new moral order of the future owed something to Owen and something to Spencer (also something to T. H. Buckle, Henry George and spiritualism). It is unlikely that his biology was quarantined from these values.

Although Wallace was in many ways a purer than pure Darwinist, he had by 1870 caused consternation in Darwinist circles by excepting the human brain from the usual processes of natural selection. Probably under the influence of spiritualism, but genuinely puzzled by the biological problem that early man had a larger brain size than was needed for the rudimentary struggle for survival, Wallace advanced 'my special heresy': he invoked teleological processes under the guidance of a higher intelligence to explain the qualitative gap between man and his fellow animals – in brainpower, consciousness, aesthetic and moral qualities.[62]

Wallace had started towards his 'heresy' in a paper of 1864, which described the human mind as a basically new cause in evolution, transforming all of the rules of the Darwinist game. Wallace showed how early man had begun to evade the action of natural selection by controlling environment, using intelligence, creating a new relationship with the circumambient world. Humans devised environmental answers to challenges, for example by inventing clothing and shelter, rather than evolving thicker fur or fat, in the face of climatic change. With hunting and fighting, man invented better weapons rather than evolving claws and fangs, and used intelligence and social capability to develop team hunting and warfare. Humans learnt how to develop higher social efficiency by cleverly exploiting their social and altruistic potential, rather than by enduring the culling of the 'unfit', the pain and waste of progress achieved by the brutish methods of the animal world. Wallace noted that selective premium was now placed upon groups and races that possessed higher mental and moral faculties. Human physical change thus stabilised, and major structural evolution came to a virtual end.

The paper ended on a note of utopianism that he would later amend. In some ways the utopia echoed Spencer's *Social Statics*, which he had read. The future would be peopled by humans with the same basic physical form, but with rapidly advancing mentalities, 'till the world is again inhabited by a single homogenous race, no individual of which will be inferior to the noblest specimens of existing humanity'. There would be perfect moral freedom and equality. Compulsory government would die away as unnecessary, to be replaced by beneficent voluntary associations:

the passions and animal propensities will be restrained within those limits which most conduce to happiness; and mankind will have at length discovered that it was only required of them to develop the capacities of their higher nature, in order to convert this earth, which has so long been the theatre of their unbridled passions, and the scene of unimaginable misery, into as bright a paradise as ever haunted the dreams of seer or poet.[63]

Wallace continued to admire Darwin, and to champion natural selection as the major agency in evolution in almost all cases except that of humanity. However, precisely because humans were unique, Wallace opposed the harsher kinds of Social Darwinism, especially the militarist and racist kinds that arose towards the end of the century out of a new genetics that seemed to undermine culturally-based agendas for human improvement. Unlike some other socialists, he wasted few regrets on the demise of Lamarckism, with its delusive hope that reformed culture could be directly inherited by the race.[64]

Instead, he hoped that a liberal-socialist reconstruction of society – 'when we have cleansed the Augean stables of our existing social organization' – would ensure the hereditary future of the race. With all reaping the full reward of their work, with men and women freely following their best impulses, when all were splendidly educated, then 'a system of selection will spontaneously come into action which will steadily tend to eliminate the lower and more degraded types of man, and thus continuously raise the average standard of the race'. Wallace borrowed openly from Edward Bellamy's utopian *Looking Backwards* (1888). Young males and females would be subjected to an intense education, including a three-year conscription in 'the industrial army', enabling them to make enlightened choices about jobs and life. Wallace was confident that 'a powerful selective agency would rest with the female sex', as women married later, and married 'fitter' males under conditions of social and economic security and independence. Cruel and violent males would be selected out. He also invoked Spencer's law that individuation and reproduction were antagonistic. Increased specialisation of the nervous system – as displayed in higher intellectuality – correlated with decreased fertility. This, said Wallace, was the ultimate answer to the global population problem. Clever societies would automatically control fertility. It was the reply to those sceptics who predicted a Malthusian disaster if the world found ways to curb the old 'positive checks' – war, pestilence and famine.[65]

Wallace became a spirited critic of modern war and imperialism. Tribal and race struggle had been essential (he said) in early history, leaving 'the stronger and higher, whether physically or mentally stronger' to survive. Not less potent was 'the greater vital energy and more rapid increase of the higher races, which crowds the lower out of existence'. This had happened in the case of the Tasmanians, the Maoris and the Red Indians: 'Here we see survival of the fittest among competing peoples necessarily leading to a continuous elevation of the human race as a whole, even though the higher portion of the higher races may remain stationary or may even deteriorate.'[66] At the same time Wallace considered that all peoples were roughly equal in innate brainpower. Brain size had not improved significantly since prehistoric times. As anthropologist he was most sympathetic towards the Polynesians and other fine races, whose customs and conduct compared favourably with those of rapacious western colonisers: 'in all essentials of true civilization these uncultivated people are fully the equals – perhaps even the superiors of ourselves'.[67]

In *The Wonderful Century* (1898) Wallace pleaded that a great scientific age like the present should be able to abolish the anachronisms of war and cruelty. In Cobdenite vein he urged that the natural influence of trade and science was towards peace. But he could not ignore the revival of the war-spirit in late nineteenth-century Europe, wracked by useless dynastic wars, a vast camp occupied by vast armies, equipped with new and deadly weapons. Technology was being immorally applied to war purposes rather than being used for the benefit of the people. He calculated that the cost of keeping three million men in arms in Europe came to at least £180 million. As the average working wage across Europe was about twelve shillings per week, this amounted to the constant labour of at least six million people, just to support 'this monstrous and utterly barbarous system of national armaments'. The so-called Christian powers of Europe 'do *not* exist for the good of the governed, but for the aggrandizement and greed and lust of power of the ruling classes – kings and kaisers, ministers and generals, nobles and millionaires – the true vampires of civilization'.

Wallace typified the leftist conspiracy theory of war. Conquest and war gave outdoor relief to the sons of the ruling and monied class. Great vested interests pressured governments into imperial and military adventures:

'anything to distract attention from the starvation and wretchedness and death-dealing trades at home, and the thinly-veiled slavery in many of our tropical or sub-tropical colonies'. Wallace anticipated the post-1918 disillusion about events:

It will be held by the historian of the future, to show, that we of the nineteenth century were morally and socially unfit to possess and use the enormous powers for good or evil which the rapid advance of scientific discovery had given us; that our boasted civilization was in many respects a mere surface veneer.[68]

Thomas Henry Huxley's credentials as an enemy of imperial biology, that was trespassing into the forbidden fields of ethics and politics, have been subject to debate. After all the youthful Huxley was a gladiatorial Darwinist, an exuberant 'bishop-basher' who exulted in using naturalistic weapons to demolish religious obscurantism. This was trespassing with a vengeance. To his death he shared Victorian racial and imperial stereotypes, the Victorian work ethic and respect for Victorian capitalism's central achievements, and was not unwilling (in his less guarded moments) to use evolutionary readings to serve his ideals. One vision of Huxley sees him converted in the late 1880s – in a cultural context of anxiety over Britain's degenerating role in the world economy and geo-politics – to criticism of evolutionary ethics out of essentially political opposition to the English extremes of *laissez-faire* individualism and land-taxing socialism. He identified the first extreme (perhaps uncritically) with Spencer, the second (more reasonably) with Henry George and A. R. Wallace. In this view, Huxley only denied the authority of evolutionary science to causes he disapproved of, while using it to justify his own middle-of-the-road social policy.[69] Instructively, in an essay of 1891 Huxley denounced Spencer's use of biology to justify 'Anarchic Individualism' ... mischievous system' that threatened Huxley's own programme of empowerment for science through educational reform. Almost in the same breath, however, he attacked 'despotic or Regimental Socialism' for abrogating biological laws: (a) by ignoring natural man's 'deep-seated organic impulses', which underlay the 'primary fact' of struggle between nations, empires and economies; and (b) by proposing a redistribution of wealth that would only aggravate the Malthusian population problem. Huxley less than modestly declared his own political perceptions to be scientifically objective, based on laws he had discovered 'as a naturalist'.[70]

Another approach finds greater continuity between the early and later Huxley, between the young naturalist who read Carlyle and was impressed by the poetic orderliness as well as the harsh justice of nature and the cosmic pessimist of the Romanes lecture of 1893. This view depicts Huxley gradually developing a humane repugnance to the pitiless amorality of nature, and becoming increasingly resistant to uncritical extrapolation from such a 'cosmic' process to human society and ethics.[71]

Even as a young man Huxley never capitulated to scientific tendencies to reduce humans to mechanisms, brutes or prisoners of some iron law of the universe. *Man's Place in Nature* (1863), the book that made him notorious as a spokesman of the 'monkey theory', that compared in detail human and ape anatomy and deduced an evolutionary connection, paradoxically celebrated the splendour of humanity. Huxley dismissed as puerile the claim that belief in 'the unity of origin of man and brutes' entailed 'brutalization and degradation' for humanity:

no one is more strongly convinced of the gulf between civilized man and the brutes; or is more certain that whether *from* them or not, he is assuredly not *of* them. No one is less disposed to think lightly of the present dignity, or despairingly of the future hopes, of the only consciously intelligent denizen of this world.[72]

During the 1870s, as a tall poppy in English science, a leader in the Endowment of Science and educational reform movements, Huxley became impatient with the 'administrative nihilism' of the Spencerean proponents of *laissez-faire*. He accused them of misusing biological analogy to legitimise minimal state theory, and to frustrate state-sponsored education. His own anatomical expertise suggested centralist rather than *laissez-faire* outcomes from analogy drawn between organisms and the state, most notably the idea of a coordinating authority being essential rather than anarchistic competition between organs, cells, muscles.[73] Perhaps partly as a political strategy, Huxley tended increasingly to dissociate natural and social discourse. However, he still maintained that 'the natural order was a vital factor in the state of art and that it must remain the focus of significant human activity'.[74] As late as 1886, in 'Science and Morals', he repeated his conviction that order pervaded the 'seeming disorder of the world', that 'the great drama of evolution, with its full share of pity and terror' had also 'abundant goodness and beauty'.[75]

The death of his daughter in 1887 changed things. He fell into melancholia and a sense of alienation from an uncaring and value-free nature. In a cathartic essay penned soon afterwards, 'The Struggle for Existence in Human Society', Huxley wrote bleakly of an animal world 'on about the same level as a gladiator's show', a sentient world dealing out malevolence as plentifully as benevolence, a natural world 'neither moral nor immoral, but non-moral'. Who could take comfort 'from the reflection that the terrible struggle for existence tends to final good, and that the suffering of the ancestor is paid for by the increased perfection of the progeny'? Evolutionary progress was itself uncertain: 'Retrogression is as practicable as progressive metamorphosis', while Kelvin's physics predicted the eventual heat-death of the universe.[76]

Huxley cautioned that his distinction between nature and human society was an analytical convenience, since, strictly speaking, society (like art) was a part of nature. This caution was to be widely forgotten in the debates that followed. And, indeed, Huxley's main emphasis was on man's elevation out of nature:

society differs from nature in having a definite moral object; whence it comes about that the course shaped by the ethical man – the members of society or citizen – necessarily runs counter to that which the non-ethical man – the primitive savage, or man as mere member of the animal kingdom – tends to adopt. The latter fights out the struggle for existence to the bitter end, like any other animal; the former devotes his best energies to the object of setting limits to the struggle (p. 203).

This was to become a major theme in peace thought. But Huxley stressed the primal pugnacity of man, and tended to equate primitive man with the brutes. This ran counter to a romantic faith in peaceful natural man that persisted in peace discourse and anthropology generally. Huxley thus provoked a counteraction from the apostles of a co-operationist and ethical nature, most immediately from the anarchist Peter Kropotkin, whose concern was to emancipate natural man from the violence and corruption of civilisation.[77]

Huxley rejected the noble savage myth. He saw early history as one of 'the Hobbesian war of each against all'. The 'weakest and stupidest went to the wall'. The toughest, shrewdest, and most adaptable survived. However, the history of civilisation was 'the record of the attempts which the human race has made to escape from this position. The first men who substituted the state of mutual peace for that of mutual war...created society' (p. 204). In doing so they limited the struggle for existence, and this became the basis of the higher civilisations. The ideal ethical man made peace both his ends and his means. He freed himself from his place in the animal kingdom, founded on the principle of non-moral evolution, and established 'a kingdom of Man, governed upon the principle of moral evolution' (p. 205). Aggressive primordial instincts persevered, however, particularly in the context of turmoil and war caused by overcrowding – the Malthusian spectre haunted Huxley to the end. Unlimited breeding (fostered by the socialist delusions of his friend Wallace, or by the charitable collectivism of General Booth and the Salvation Army) could end civilisation by reimposing the struggle for existence, 'the mitigation or abolition of which was the chief end of social organization' (p. 206).

In his dramatic Romanes lecture Huxley portrayed the natural (or cosmic) process as an almost dialectical antithesis to the ethical process. Buddhist and Stoic thought had solaced Huxley in his grief, and permeated the essay. Buddhism counselled 'total renunciation of that self-assertion which is the essence of the cosmic process'. Stoicism distinguished man's animal from his higher nature.[78] Huxley veered from the image of an indifferent to a malignant cosmos: 'cosmic nature is no school of virtue ... the cosmos works through the lower nature of man, not for righteousness, but against it' (pp. 75–6). Thus he denied naturalistic ethics that wanted the cosmic process to be an exemplar for human conduct, ethics to be 'applied Natural History' (p. 74).

Man had become 'the superb animal which he is', head of the sentient world, by virtue of the struggle for existence, through violence, cosmic strife, war, unscrupulous self-assertion, by exploiting those qualities that were shared with 'the ape and the tiger': ferocious destructiveness combined with cunning, sociability, imitativeness and organisation (pp. 51–2). Yet, in proportion as humans passed from savagery to social organisation, 'civilized man brands all these ape and tiger promptings with the name of sins ... there is a general consensus that the ape and tiger methods of the struggle for existence are not reconcilable with sound ethical principles' (pp. 52–3).

In almost an aside, Huxley conceded one axiom of evolutionary ethics, that moral sentiments had originated 'in the same way as other natural phenomena', by a process of evolution. But (like Hume) he refused to grant that 'is' logically entailed 'ought': 'Cosmic evolution may teach us how the good and evil tendencies of man may have come about; but, in itself, it is incompetent to furnish any better reason why what we call good is preferable to what we call evil than we had before.' It was a fallacious notion that 'because, on the whole, animals and plants have advanced in perfection or organization by means of the struggle for existence and the consequent "survival of the fittest"; therefore men in society, men as ethical beings, must look to the same process to help them towards perfection' (pp. 79–80). Survivalist ethics depended on identifying 'fittest' with morally best, an improper association since 'fittest', biologically, meant only those who successfully adapted to conditions. This criticism was to become a standard weapon in the kitbag of campaigners against militaristic Social Darwinism.

Swiping at Spencer once again, Huxley branded the fanatical doctrine of *laissez-faire* of the time as a theory of self-assertion masquerading as rights, and buttressed by cosmic analogy. The human future depended not on imitating the cosmic process but on combatting it, replacing it with the ethical process, a higher moral order. It was a matter of audaciously pitting 'the microcosm against the macrocosm'. In subduing nature, and acting ethically, humans would need 'in all respects' to reverse the behaviour that had led to success in the cosmic struggle: to replace self-assertion by self-restraint, to help fellows rather than tread them down, to fit as many as possible to survive rather than to aim at survival of the fittest (pp. 81–2).

Perhaps inconsistently, Huxley sought to strengthen this 'ought' by reference to the 'is' of the social evolutionary process, which he saw as steadily moving towards human control of violence and anarchic individualism. This seemed to cut across his stand that 'the cosmic process has no sort of relation to moral ends' (p. 83). Yet he could not resist a naturalistic sanction for his 'elevationist' beliefs. Huxley assured his Romanes audience that evolutionary theory did not entail the debasement of humanity, despite 'the cosmic nature born within us':

I see no limit to the extent to which intelligence and will...may modify the conditions of existence...And much may be done to change the nature of man himself. The intelligence which has converted the brother of the wolf into the faithful guardian of the flock ought to be able to do something towards curbing the instincts of savagery in civilized men (p. 85).

Refutations rained in upon Huxley, the dying old lion, and not only from offended Spencereans and Darwinians. The religious evolutionists Benjamin Kidd and Henry Drummond insisted upon the central significance of religious and ethical, 'ultra-rational' factors as agents of human evolution. Drummond's popular *Ascent of Man* (1894) argued a naturalistic ethic to counter the Huxleyan division of the cosmic and moral worlds. The natural condition was not, as Huxley said, one of selfish struggle and 'the unfathomable injustice of the nature of things'. The struggle for life, in Drummond's view, had always been matched – and was now being overmastered – by another evolutionary factor, 'the struggle for the life of others', based on natural forces of sympathy. Evolution was universal and, under God's aegis, evolution was good, embodying the Christian ideal of love.[79]

Stripped of its supernaturalism, this reading of altruistic evolutionism was also to become a feature of capacious peace biology. The internal tensions within Huxley's world-view were to be projected into peace theory at large, with naturalistic pacifism ranged against methodological disquiet about biological imperialism.[80]

3   Crisis in the west: the pre-war generation and the new biology

The context

In the generation that preceded the First World War, new elements intruded into the debate on the biology of war, stemming from such factors as the imperial rivalry of the great powers, a crisis of identity in western culture, and revolutionary advances in science, including biology. It was a time when strident declamations of western superiority and faith in inevitable progress were combined with widespread evidence of disenchantment and doubt. The optimistic human self-image associated with rationalism and liberal ideas came under attack from cruder, more reductionist, more violent and belittling views of humankind. The genetics revolution, and the hereditarian doctrines that came out of it, generated some extreme brands of biological determinism that had violent and authoritarian consequences. Yet, amidst the despair and alienation that marked western culture before 1914 – and despite the militarist assessment of war as a biological necessity – an anti-war tradition of biological thought became entrenched in the pre-war era. This peace paradigm was particularly strong in the Anglo-American world, feeding off the 'new biology' as well as more conventional respect for Darwin's ecological and co-operationist ideas.

The changing climate of world affairs affected all schools of thought. It was an age of rampant imperialism, a struggle for mastery among the European powers, arms races, cut-throat economic competition, a world recession (the so-called 'Great Depression' of the 1870s to the 1890s), bewildering social change and class unrest. There was industrial expansion, even a rising living standard, in much of Europe before 1914, but also a sharpened awareness of gross inequalities in wealth. The rise of revolutionary socialism, anarchism and syndicalism seemed to threaten the capitalist social order. Massive urbanisation and spreading technology ushered in a new world, a world of motor cars, telephones, electric light, the age of steel and oil, chemistry and electro-technics, a burgeoning state and bureaucracy.[1] It was an exciting age. Historians have looked back on it as the 'belle époch', an opulent, self-satisfied age, worshipping power and money rather than the older aristocratic values of style and duty. But beneath the surface there was much turmoil, resentment, anomie and potential for violence.

The internationalist peace ideal of the free traders and liberals began to wear thin with the growth of protectionism and the new nationalism. The rise of Germany signalled the end of the old complacency. Rather than countries being drawn together by commerce and better communications, as predicted by Spencer and the Manchester pacifists, nations seemed ready to fight each other for economic and geo-political leverage.[2] The new protectionists in Germany and elsewhere justified the use of force, since war promoted industrialisation, accelerated economic growth and planning, and helped bring about necessary changes to rigid class structures. Whereas free trade capitalism disapproved of war as a waste of resources, new protectionism tended to ally itself with militarism, seeing war as a legitimate and profitable instrument of state policy.

The classic theoretician of the new mercantilism was Friedrich List (1789–1846), the Tübingen professor of political economy, expelled from the Württemberg diet in 1821 for demanding liberal reform, but whose experience of Napoleonic warfare was to saturate his thinking on economic nationalism and permanently influence the German mind-set.[3] In his *National System of Political Economy* (1841) List treated war as part of a Providential design by which eternal strife, both moral and physical, took place between interest and interest, opinion and opinion, nation and nation. War enabled peoples to gain freedom and self-reliance. List agreed that war was an explosion of man's savage nature, and he shared the liberal belief that war was on the way out. Ultimately the world would be rationally organised on the basis of a world federation and a 'utopia of eternal peace'. Nationality was only a 'stage on the road to cosmopolitanism'. But while nations were still in this chauvinist stage, they could not afford to renounce the use of war, armed protection, or tariffs to foster industry.

Economic and biological thought illustrated some interesting parallels, hardly surprising given that human economic conduct is a special case of animal ecological behaviour. Within the German 'historical school' of protectionism there was general acceptance of biological struggle theory. War was endemic, at least in the imperfect present world, and it only made sense that one's country should ensure against losing in a war, and thus risking loss of its whole wealth, including its genetic capital. The Schleswig-born economist Lorenz von Stein (1815–90), a German nationalist who agitated against Danish rule in the Duchies, assumed that war was the externalisation of deeply rooted combative instincts and a propensity for domination within man. Hence armies, however high their cost, were a 'national premium of insurance'. Albert Schäffle (1831–1903), another Tübingen economist, derided pacifist plans for disarmament and world peace that did not grapple with the multiple causes of war: overpopulation, greed, thirst for power, religious fanaticism, etc. To prevent war there would have to be a vast human reform abolishing the destructive social struggle that endlessly went on within the race, or else iron rule by a dominant military power. Eternal peace also raised the problem: how would social evolution take place if peoples were kept in fixed positions based upon present economic and military strength? War often led to progress by breaking up undesirable social configurations. On this, Schäffle projected *laissez-faire* pacifism as having deeply conservative tendencies, opposing war because it might overturn the capitalist status quo. Schäffle was worried by the rising costs of militarism, and was not a proponent of brute force like some later German thinkers. But he considered that a balance of force was the most practical means to peace. Wilhelm Roscher (1817–94), professor of political economy at Göttingen and Leipzig, and actually trained as an historian, held that war preparations not only stimulated economies, but ensured peace through their deterrent effect. This was a variation on the theme, 'if you want peace, prepare for war', an old adage, but one with a very healthy future ahead of it.[4]

The American poet–philosopher George Santayana could write in 1913 that 'nationalism has become of late an omnivorous all-pervading passion'.[5] The rising tide of nationalism posed the most dreadful challenge to the peace cause. There was an historic tension in nineteenth-century liberalism between its cosmopolitan peace ideal and its traditional regard for the freedom of small nations and oppressed nationalities. This tension grew worse as the century wore on. Liberals had supported the cause of all sorts of subjugated minorities and nationalities: Greeks against Turks, Italians against the Habsburg Empire, Poles against Russians, etc. As the great revision of the European power balance took place after the 1860s, as submerged peoples struggled to free themselves from the rule of ramshackle empires and autocracies, many liberals favoured the use of force in the cause of freedom. As Michael Howard has argued, the power of nationalism ran counter to the growing ideas of arbitration, disarmament and non-intervention: 'To many continental liberals, these prescriptions seemed smug, insular and totally irrelevant to the historic movements of the century. For them the immediate object was not peace. It was freedom'.[6] The nationalist movements encouraged guerrilla 'wars of liberation' against imperialist rulers, wars that were to generate much of the world's tensions in the next hundred years (and still do).

Nationalism also fuelled the rivalry of the great powers. Like the insurgent nationalities, emerging powers such as Prussia asserted that nations had a right to expand to their 'natural frontiers' (whatever 'nation' or 'natural frontiers' meant, whether established by criteria of language, race, history or 'survival of the fittest'). Such doctrines also translated into economic chauvinism. The ideal of peaceful free trade was dismissed as a selfish dogma invented by top-dog nations such as Britain to perpetuate their privileged global position.

Even Marxism went down this road. Marxist theory – although regarding nationalism and war as ugly by-products of the capitalist system – also derided the free trade peace ideal as puerile, motivated by a desire to preserve capitalist hegemony and to forestall social revolution. Marx attacked Cobden as a capitalist stooge, whose ideal of universal peace and brotherhood was really 'cosmopolitan exploitation'. Engels in *Umrisse* (1848) accused capitalists of creating a brotherhood of thieves, of reducing the number of wars to make fatter profits in peacetime. The Marx–Engels analysis of war was flexible. If the economic factors of production within the capitalist system dictated war as an outcome, then war was inevitable. If the factors suggested a capitalist interest in peace (as alleged by pacifists like Bloch, Carnegie, Novicow and Angell), then peace was more likely.

As a historicist theory of struggle, Marxism saw history as a record of brutality, of bitter conflict between classes, rulers and ruled, exploiters and exploited, of dialectical clash of opposites. Only at the end, with the revolutionary triumph of the proletariat over the bourgeoisie, with the onset of the classless society, would conflict cease. In the meantime class struggle was essential to the historical process, and war could be useful to the cause of the working classes. If particular wars hastened the demise of the capitalist system, then they were to be welcomed. The tricky thing for Marx and Engels, and a host of later communist strategists, was to judge pragmatically just which wars and upheavals would aid revolutionary socialism, and which would not. Engels (who fancied himself as a military historian) foresaw a world war, and wavered over it. He feared it would inflame militarism and set back socialism. At the same time he convinced himself that, in the long run, such a war would lead to communist hegemony. Militarism would collapse under its own weight: it was horribly expensive, while conscripting the workers and training them in arms would make them better equipped to pull down the capitalist system. In *Einleitung* (1888) Engels presciently predicted a global war lasting four years, with ten million soldiers mutually massacring one another, and stripping Europe barer than any swarm of locusts had ever done. There would be famine, pestilence, general demoralisation, 'hopeless confusion of our artificial machinery in trade, industry and credit, ending in general bankruptcy; collapse of old states ... crowns will roll by dozens on the pavement ... only one result absolutely certain: general exhaustion and the establishment of the condition for the ultimate victory of the working-class'.[7]

Adding to the milieu of global strain provoked by imperialism and nationalism there was an identity crisis in western culture. It was closely affiliated with a revolt against reason and liberalism, and it encouraged the rise of philosophies glorifying power and will. 'The idea of violence was in the air', said Leonard Hobhouse of the pre-war years: 'There was a deliberate theory of force ... it was a philosophy most appropriate to a generation which was running headlong upon disaster.'[8] By the late nineteenth century, Hobhouse felt, there had been a loss of faith that human reason could triumph over a fatalistic, haphazard world. Other observers fulminated against cultural decay and the disappearance of intellectual and moral conviction. *Fin de siècle* pessimism, aestheticism and 'decadence' combined with 'modernism' in art and literature to convey a general sense of disorientation and revolt among the *avant garde*. Significant writers in almost every country – from France to Russia, Spain to the United States – openly rejected accepted literary forms, expressed alienation from the existing social system, flouted conventional moral standards, even repudiated any values or social engagement whatsoever. Many authors and artists retreated into 'an exquisitely private world of delicate perfumes and rich textures, of exotic experiences and perverse pleasures', or else favoured a Nietzschean 'brand of super-human assertiveness'.[9]

The novelists, poets and painters reflected a new awareness of human behaviour that was the product of the new biology and the new social sciences. Genetics reenacted the nature–nurture debate, while the new social sciences such as sociology, psychology and psychiatry revealed the importance not just of reason in human behaviour, but also of the will, the emotions, the unconscious and the irrational. Hereditarian themes were explored by Emile Zola, George Gissing and Henrik Ibsen. Zola's characters were (supposedly) trapped in a Darwinian web, their lives determined by inherited traits and conditioned by their everyday milieu (such as the mining community of *Germinal*, 1885). Gissing's *Demos* (1886) portrayed the working classes as lower evolutionary types. The careerist Mutimer – the proletarian anti-hero of the story – was destroyed because he could not adapt to new circumstances, because he still carried the inherited taints of his class. (The novel generated dramatic tension because of Gissing's ambivalence towards socialism, which he had once embraced; and was very topical, with its debt to Comtean positivism, Marxism, Spencerism, Schopenhaurian gloom and aestheticism.)[10] Ibsen's play *Ghosts* (1881) raised the spectre of congenital influence – the effect on a family of syphilis inherited from past generations. Heredity and environment, survival of the fittest, primal legacies, peace and war were topics that preoccupied later writers such as H. G. Wells and Bernard Shaw. Meanwhile a string of great writers interrogated the crisis in western life and values: Russians such as Turgenev, Tolstoy, Dostoyevsky, Chekhov; Germans such as Hauptmann and Mann (Aschenbach's mortal illness in *Death in Venice*, (1911) symbolised the sickness of art and society). French symbolists probed deeper levels of reality, while Proust and Joyce questioned the relationship of consciousness with time.

The idea of scientific certainty itself came under fire from the 'new physics', challenging the positivist aspiration to create an all-embracing system of knowledge. If science was fallible, if scientific laws expressed a relativist rather than an objective knowledge of reality – as argued by Mach, Poincaré and Bradley – then doubt was thrown over current attempts to model the social sciences on Newtonian or Baconian science. Doubt was also thrown over attempts to use Darwinian biology as a controlling paradigm in social theory. By 1915, the zoologist Peter Chalmers Mitchell was able to ask why any significant implications for humans could be drawn from Darwinian 'science', if scientific law had no absolute validity.[11] Philosophical movements such as German neo-Kantianism and Bergsonian intuitionism also attacked the primacy of naturalistic science and empiricism. Oxford idealism asserted the uniqueness of humanity, and its independence from deterministic laws based on scientific mechanism or evolution.[12]

Less liberal outcomes emerged from irrationalist philosophies, especially Nietzsche's, which penetrated biological speculation on war, fostering a cult of violence and an aggressive image of humankind motivated by unreasoning forces and untameable emotions, and led by ruthless superleaders. Nietzsche has an unsavoury reputation. He was the quarrelsome philosophy professor from Basle who became a recluse, went mad, and is said to have made much ammunition for the Nazi cause, besides accusing God of being dead. Much of this is sensationalism, and anachronistic (although even during his lifetime distorted versions of his work were spread by enemies). The Nietzsche who preached the 'will to power' and the doctrine of the *übermensch* was also the Nietzsche who admired the Jews as an intelligent race, and poured ridicule on the Prussians under the Kaiser. His thought in fact appealed to widely differing political camps. Instructively, the first serious appreciation of Nietzsche in Britain was made by the socialist-pacifist Havelock Ellis in *The Savoy* of 1896. Ellis did not champion Nietzschianism, but described Nietzsche as 'the greatest spiritual force which has appeared since Goethe... the nineteenth century has produced no more revolutionary and aboriginal force'.[13]

Indeed Nietzsche's destructive influence was the source of his magnetism for socialists and others of the 1890s and 1900s who were rebelling against the existing order. He attacked many idols: democracy, Christianity, humanitarianism, pacifism ('One has renounced the *great* life when one renounces war'), even Darwinism, although in some ways he took Darwinism further than its militant exponents did. His theories (if that is not too systematic a concept for his bursts of illumination) were anti-positivist and anti-progress, unlike Social Darwinisms that had a rational or teleological basis. Science (he said) was the handmaiden of decadent and materialistic bourgeois culture. History was a cyclical process of 'eternal return'. The Apollinian ideal of measure, restraint, reason and harmony needed to be subordinate to the Dionysian spirit, founded on the irrational passions, the gateway to truth.

Nietzsche was a quintessential individualist who was contemptuous of liberal individualism: 'the honourable term for *mediocre* is, of course, the word "liberal"'. Only the greatest individuals could lead the strenuous, passionate Dionysian life, could represent the evolution of the 'higher man', were entitled to transcend conventional bourgeois or herd morality. Nietzsche was a world apart from the chauvinistic militarists who lauded the 'Volk', who set whole peoples or races (usually skilled at war or trade) at the top of the ladder of natural selection. He believed in the exceptional man rather than the exceptional people.

However, there were parallels between his view that men were beyond good and evil, and the Treitschkean doctrine that great states were beyond the ordinary rules of international law. The militarists raided Nietzsche for what they wanted: approval of war and violence as cleansing, necessary, productive of change and courage, an antidote to timid and enervating democracy. They ignored his subtleties, and focused on his claim that 'this world is the will to power – and nothing else'. He was in fact sceptical about the outcome of the struggle for existence. He spoke of its result being the opposite of what Darwin's school desired: 'The species do *not* grow in perfection: the weak prevail over the strong again and again, for they are the great majority – and they are also more *intelligent*.' (Peace biology was to develop similar themes.) More appropriate to the militarist world-view was this comment:

Life itself is essentially appropriation, infringement, the over-powering of the alien and the weaker, oppression, hardness, imposition of one's own form, assimilation, and, at the least and mildest, exploitation.[14]

Philosophy offered some less violent responses to the corroding alienation of the age. Henri Bergson's *Creative Evolution* (1907) preached a mystic optimism based on the vitalist view that an animating life force was propelling humanity towards higher consciousness, and closer assimilation of humans into one cosmos. Social evolutionists like Benjamin Kidd also wanted a massive shift of human consciousness away from the dominating values of Mammon, ego, agnostic science, appealing to the 'emotion of the ideal', to man's capacity for self-transcendence and higher spirituality as the means of living a truly social life. One effect of such neo-religious reactions against materialism, it has been claimed, was to hasten the decline of 'a Darwinian naturalism which saw force as the law of life. Undoubtedly present, it was much less in evidence in 1914 than a generation earlier'.[15]

Empiricism received a new lease of life from William James's pragmatism, by which ethics were affiliated to human needs rather than to absolute values, a stance that was criticised as a new utilitarianism or philosophy of expediency, usable in authoritarian as well as liberal causes. James, it should be said, recognised 'the deeply penetrating appeal of some of the higher fidelities, like justice, truth, or freedom', opposed biological determinism, and advocated 'the strenuous life' of courage, concern for others and the vigorous exercise of free will.[16] Bertrand Russell made philosophy more logical and mathematical. Pinning his hopes for a peaceful and freer future on the use of reason, he was to become one of the more famous opponents of war. Meanwhile, in sociology Le Bon, Pareto, Michels and Sorel explored the significance of mass behaviour, violence and emotion in human behaviour. The new sociology suggested, disturbingly, that the collective might be more boisterous and destructive than the individual (an echo of Spencer and a blow to Kropotkin's mutualist ideal). Mosca, Pareto, Michels and Ostrogorski showed how leaders and elites controlled and manipulated the masses, now aspiring to power through advancing democracy.

The genetics revolution and militarism

Revolutionary changes in biological science itself were to condition the debate over the biology of war. Classic Darwinian theory came under siege as the rise of new specialisms in biology fragmented the tradition of natural history within which Darwin had worked, as study of heredity and variation produced results at odds with conventional selection theory, and as a revival occurred in older rival theories such as Lamarckism and orthogenesis.[17]

Biology in the 1880s and 1890s was deeply concerned with the phenomena of heredity, development, regeneration, cell structure and the nature of germ particles. There was a waning of the old theory of 'blending inheritance', which held that the characters of offspring struck an average between those of the parents. Experimentalists came to believe that heredity and sexual recombination preserved and promoted variability in populations. Out of all this arose germ plasm theory and (after 1900) genetics, exciting discoveries that seemed to herald a new understanding of human differences and prospects of biological control of the human future. These hopes rapidly influenced ideas about race, class and war.

The Freiburg zoologist, and free-thinking nationalist, August Weismann (1834–1914) proposed a germ plasm theory in the 1890s that rejected the Lamarckian idea of inheritance of acquired characters, which had survived the challenge of natural selection as an alternative explanation of trait development. Darwin himself had retained a significant Lamarckian element in his system, mainly in order to outflank the inconvenient implications of 'blending inheritance. Weismann denied any experimental evidence for inheritance of acquired characters. He claimed that natural selection was the sole cause of evolution, working through heritable variations resulting from changes in genetic particles (or germ plasms). He differentiated cells into body cells, which gave rise to the life-form, tissues, organs, etc., of the animal or plant, and germ cells, which remained generally unmodified and produced the next generation. Germ cells continued after reproduction as long as the species survived, each new individual being the direct descendant of the germ cells of its parent. Weismann thus seemed to postulate germinal continuity, even immortality. The offspring inherited not from the parent body but from the parent cell, which owed its characteristics, again not to the parent body, but to its descent from a pre-existing germ cell of the same kind. Germinal variations arose either by spontaneous change in the germ plasm, or by a combination of the different germ plasms of the two sexes. Natural selection worked its influence upon such variations. Without the pressure of natural selection, the germ plasm would degenerate.

Conservative eugenists were soon arguing that as germ cells were resistant to environmental modification, and were the sole source of inherited differences, humans could only make lasting improvement in their race by improving their genetic endowment. 'Positive' eugenics encouraged the breeding of the 'fit', 'negative' eugenics discouraged the breeding of the 'unfit'. Social reform was scorned as useless or an actual disincentive to healthy selection, by cushioning the inferior from competition and stimulating their feckless breeding. In Germany the shift from 'an individualistic theory of the cell as a creative person to a collectivist and authoritarian germplasm' was exploited for both socialist and elitist ends.[18] Weismannism did not necessitate violent and oppressive politics. Many liberals and social democrats, even Marxists, favoured eugenic reform. Benjamin Kidd, after an interview with Weismann in 1890, came away buoyed by optimism, because 'every new generation comes into the world pure and uncontaminated, so far, by the surroundings and life-history of its parents'.[19]

Although Weismann backed natural selection and mechanical explanations of evolution, Weismannism did not unequivocally dismiss factors of culture and nurture, or teleology. Weismann himself was much affected by the powerful tradition of German Idealism, and believed in a 'directive power' which did not interfere directly with the mechanism of the universe, but lay behind it as the 'final cause'. As he said in his *Theory of Descent*: 'The endless harmony revealed in every nook and corner by all the phenomena of organic and inorganic nature cannot possibly be regarded as the work of chance, but rather as the result of a "vast designed process of development"'. However he denied 'vitalism', and evolution through *per saltum* mutations or spontaneous creations. Evolution worked through natural selection of minute variations, gradually over eons of time. Change took place under natural laws. At the same time ideas of necessity or causality could be combined with those of purpose:

Mechanism and teleology do not exclude one another, they are rather in mutual agreement. Without teleology there would be no mechanism, but only a confusion of crude forces; and without mechanism there would be no teleology, for how could the latter otherwise effect its purpose?[20]

For Weismann science was, at the highest level, the revelation of the absolute. But science and reason alone could never make knowable the ultimate reality that embodied the world as spirit, that revealed the immanence of the divine in the actual. Weismann was not alone in such views. Despite Darwinian materialism, biology continued to be influenced by concepts of design, teleology, orthogenesis, vitalism, idealism, and other reactions against the image of a purposeless, chance-based, amoral universe. Scientific idealism was simplified and used as the staple of many popular varieties of biologically-oriented Christian apologetics.[21]

When in 1890 the Canadian-born science journalist Grant Allen surveyed the debate on heredity, he was struck by the impact of Weismannism: 'it has been enthusiastically accepted in England by the younger Darwinian school, and has become almost a test of orthodoxy with the Oxford and London biologists'. Yet the issues were still in hot dispute, and Allen, a sympathiser of Lamarckism (he was reformist, socialist and feminist) detected a reaction setting in against Weismann. Biology was split 'into an ultra-Darwinian or Weismannesque faction on one side, and a partly Lamarckian or Spencerian body on the other'.[22] Not a few old Darwinists, such as G. J. Romanes, sat on the fence.[23] Within the emerging eugenics movement in Britain and France, Weismannism and Lamarckism flourished side by side, with most eugenists believing that 'superior' and 'inferior' traits could be passed on directly to offspring.[24] Such ideas infiltrated the war debate.

The hoary figure of Spencer still stood ranged behind Lamarckism. To the end of his life (1903), he insisted that habit produced modifications of structure in organisms, and that these were inherited by progeny. Reformers, particularly in the Enlightenment tradition (very strong in France), found Lamarckism attractive – at least superficially – because it encouraged optimistic hopes of perfecting mankind genetically through institutional and educational reform. Towards the end of the century many who were dismayed by cultural decay, fatalistic philosophies and genetic determinism sought refuge in Lamarckism. This was primarily because Lamarckism allowed a key role for psychic factors in evolution – the purposeful non-violent striving of organisms to adapt to environment, a vital function for intelligence and consciousness – and it invested the matter of the evolutionary process with a 'life force' (borrowing from earlier associationist psychology and the writings of Bergson). A gamut of social theorists were drawn to such ideas, from mystics and believers to Fabians like Shaw and psychologists such as J. M. Baldwin and William McDougall.[25]

Looked at more closely, however, Lamarckism raised confusing and disturbing possibilities. The theory predicated long periods of evolutionary pressure before new characters could be acquired. This was more in accord with conservative thought than with reformist programs of thoroughgoing social change. Use-inheritance, although initially an adaptive process, was said to result in habits becoming fixed, and even directing further evolution as an internal force independent of environmental factors. The theory also allowed the possibility of the genetic fixation of non-adaptive characters.[26]

At the socio-political level, Lamarckism raised the spectre of ideological conditioning and directive rather than free politics. As Kidd feared, there was the gloomy prospect that intractable population problems, or social and economic change outside the control of planners, might lay down anything but a hopeful human inheritance. In Lamarckian terms, the misery that was observed to accompany massive industrialisation and urbanisation would have become genetically imprinted upon succeeding generations. Capitalism, with its alienating social effects, was seen to be inflicting widespread dysgenic modifications upon individuals and their children. Also, socially advantaged groups would be genetically privileged as a result of living for centuries in a benevolent environment. Socially generated diseases such as alcoholism and criminality would be passed on to the offspring of victims (on the other hand, some hereditarians claimed that these were inborn diseases). Warlike and pugnacious human habits would become congenital over centuries of violence. (One military man even suggested that particular strategies had become innate: the counter-attack in battle came 'as naturally to the British race as the crescent impi to the Zulu, the concealed stockade to the Burman, sniping and the ghazi charge to the wild Pathan, or the dense, thrusting advance by hordes to the modern German'.)[27] Even Spencer conceded that peaceful behaviour would not become congenital until all traces of the violent militant stage of history had been evolved out. Marx, who was also a Lamarckian, saw no real prospect of escape from the vicious legacy of the past until the proletarian revolution transformed the capitalist means of production. In any case, Lamarckist biology was vague about reversing habits already imprinted in a population. Nor were all Lamarckists liberals. Their ranks included racists and conservatives. Not surprisingly quite a few reformers in the 1900s welcomed the advance of 'hard heredity' theory that threatened the demise of Lamarckism.[28]

The drawback with Lamarckism, scientifically, lay in its imprecision and insusceptibility to experimental testing. This became obvious with the rapid advance of the competing theories of Mendelism and biometrics, theories that together encompassed the spectacular genetics revolution. Mendel's laws of inheritance were rediscovered by de Vries and Correns in 1900, and biometry was founded on the work of Francis Galton, Karl Pearson and W. F. R. Weldon.[29]

The biometricians, good Darwinians, focused almost exclusively on selection of small, continuous variations, which Darwin had thought to be the key factor in evolution. They used advanced statistical and math-ematical techniques in an effort to measure the way in which selective pressures, operating upon continuous variations, made themselves felt in large populations. The Mendelians, by contrast, concentrated upon discontinuous variations, usually large, transmissible to progeny and the probable origin of new species. Chalmers Mitchell wrote of this 'active and brilliant school' that they dismissed most small fluctuations as ephemeral, not transmissible to offspring, and playing no part in the origin of species: 'this Mendelian view does nothing to prove the existence of natural selection ... And it is to be noted that many of the most ardent Mendelians have such confidence in their own theory that they no longer think it necessary to invoke the operation of natural selection at all.' Mitchell believed that such opposing views could be synthesised under Darwinian principle, as happened in the 1920s with the work of the founders of population genetics: R. A. Fisher, J. B. S. Haldane and Sewall Wright. However, given the deep divisions over the selection issue, Mitchell regarded the Darwinian paradigm to be seriously eroded: 'It is merely ludicrous to assert that natural selection and the struggle for existence have any claims to be regarded as scientific law.'[30]

The biometricians and Mendelians in Britain became locked in a bitter feud. There was personal rivalry between the leading scientists – between the Mendelist William Bateson and the biometricians Weldon and Pearson – which reinforced the methodological differences between the schools. The use of statistics and a population approach was uncongenial to those like Bateson not trained in mathematics, and it ran counter to the typological thinking that still dominated traditional biology.[31] The biometricians promptly attacked Mendelism as a theory of discontinuity, and thus non-Darwinian. Clashes of this sort deepened the already existing anti-Darwinism of mutationists such as Bateson, while conceptual confusion on both sides lay at the heart of the controversy. Britain's elitist educational and institutional structure has been blamed for the depth of the dispute there.[32]

If the new biology was fragmented, its ideological implications were ambiguous. Hereditarianism (like Lamarckism) could be affiliated with a mix of doctrines, from free will to determinist, liberal to reactionary, pacifist to militarist. The free-will side of hereditarianism owed something to a broader moral discourse that was suspicious of biological determinism and uncritical use of analogy from nature, that recoiled from any system of ethics which derived right conduct by strict reference to natural criteria. Naturalistic ethics was widely opposed in Victorian and Edwardian Britain as repugnant to conventional morality, liberal values, rationalist regard for human autonomy, idealist philosophy and Romantic tradition. Like G. K. Chesterton, many declined to show any respect for those who 'close all the doors of the cosmic prison on us with a clang of eternal iron'.[33]

Some of the Mendelists shared current misgivings about an 'imperial' biology that was rampaging into the kingdoms of ethics and culture. The metaphor of aggression is apt. They were alienated by the violent component of Darwinist biology. Mendelism contributed to non-violent modes of thought in a number of ways. The scientific assault upon the Darwinist paradigm had the potential to discredit Social Darwinist doctrines based upon conflict. Then again, Mendelism downplayed struggle in favour of chance mutations as the key to selective evolution (although individual Mendelists varied in their attitude to competition as a filtering mechanism acting upon fluctuations).

One of the founding fathers of Mendelism, Hugo de Vries, put forward harmonious human ideals that starkly contrasted with the aggression of Karl Pearson, Britain's leading biometrician. (One would not wish to push such contrasts too far: Pearson was a highly idiosyncratic thinker, and there were many Mendelians who peddled harsh social doctrines in the eugenics movement.) De Vries, although respecting classic Darwinism, minimised the action of natural selection over long periods of history. He viewed *Homo sapiens* as one immutable race, and denied any analogy between an amoral, violent natural world and human progress. The American geneticist Thomas H. Morgan, an early enthusiast for de Vries's thesis, found the Darwinian vision of a violent world distasteful. This led him to put a genetic theory denying that nature was based on struggle.[34]

Genetics may not have been inexorably deterministic. However, the general thrust of genetics, of hereditarian social thought, was to foster images of humankind controlled by genes, human history dictated by ineradicable biological forces. Even peace biology – a complex phenomenon open to a variety of intellectual forces – came under the influence of 'hard heredity' theory. There arose a style of peace eugenics that put biology at the service of pacifism, that matched the biological determinism of the militarists with an opposite one. This was typified by the American peace eugenists David Starr Jordan and Vernon Kellogg. Jordan's best-seller *The Human Harvest* (1907) preached that 'the blood of a nation determines its history'.[35] His protégé Kellogg also veered towards genetic determinism, although this was qualified by his belief that 'we are a reasoning species' and that war was 'only an element of controllable tradition, not of ineradicable dominating heredity'.[36] There is a common impression that bogus science was the preserve of racists and militarists. In fact pseudo-biology featured on both sides of the propaganda war, both finding biologically predetermined patterns in human nature and history, both misusing metaphor and analogy to make sweeping generalisations about humanity from animal behaviour. (We shall return to peace eugenics in the next chapter.)

This is not to diminish the obvious connection between hereditarianism and the darker theorists, and alarmists, of reaction and war. Hereditarian discourses flourished in the late nineteenth century in British and continental intellectual and professional circles. The disciplines included medicine, psychiatry, anthropometry, criminal anthropology, eugenics and even the arts. There was evoked a fatalistic language of innate human criminality, bellicosity and atavism. This rhetoric crossed political lines, but seems to have been ultimately more congenial to the right as articulating deep social anxieties about the onset of socialism, mass democracy, urbanisation, the threats of immigration or a swarming population leading to racial decline. Hereditarianism generated political agendas that were diverse, but often directive, regulative and statist, aiming at goals of 'national efficiency' or racial unity and power. Even socialist reformers and right-wing zealots could share this instrumental agenda. As we shall see, instrumentalism became a general feature of the eugenics movement, although for its own social evolutionary reasons eugenics tended to dismiss the militarism that emerged from genetic theories of pugnacity.[37]

Coming under constant fire in all this were classic liberal values of individual autonomy, and the primacy of culture and milieu over nature. As the young Harold Laski, then a eugenist, put it, progress was 'a matter of genetics, not of training; of breeding rather than pedagogics'.[38] Kidd, after his early flirtation with Weismannism, came to believe that germ plasm theory promoted misanthropic and authoritarian values, with class, race and militarism seen to be irrevocable.[39] Under gene theory, man was projected as a 'fighting animal' dominated by aggressive territorial instincts. War was seen as a guarantee of biological health, the safeguard of nations.

Germ plasm theory gave a fillip to militarist and expansionist thought through Weismann's concept of *panmixia*, according to which struggle was necessary for the genetic health of a species. His 'law of retrogression' said that cessation of natural selection – for example, through general breeding unaccompanied by stern conditions of competition (*panmixia*) – would result in slow but steady degeneration of the species. Random mating would take place and a species would revert to an original 'species type'.[40]

Scientific speculation of this sort gelled with widespread *fin de siècle* alarm about 'degeneration' in western culture, both morally and physically. Recent research has amplified our understanding of the discourse of degeneration, exploring its roots in the early nineteenth century, showing how it varied according to the historical and discursive context in different countries, how it was a way of containing a sense of crisis and disorientation.[41] French psychiatric theory after the revolutions of 1848, from Morel and Taine to Zola and Le Bon, was saturated with awareness of disorder infiltrating the human system, while Cesare Lombroso's fatalistic image of 'criminal man' belonged to the political culture of post-unification Italy. Daniel Pick has suggested that in Victorian Britain degenerationist anthropology struggled against a national distaste for theory, the established liberal tradition and the free will principle of law. Yet beneath the surface of English isolationism were repressed visions of decline and pollution. By the Edwardian period Galtonian ideas had stimulated the rise of a new caste of eugenically-minded academics, journalists and doctors, intellectually centred at University College, London, the base for Karl Pearson, Henry Maudsley and Ray Lankester.[42]

Eugenists (Galton, Lankester, the young R. A. Fisher) blamed the advance of medicine and welfarism for causing a population explosion among the genetically inferior 'lumpenproletariat', while the better educated elites were voluntarily restricting their numbers. It was a recipe for genocide. The degeneration thesis was the biological analogue of Henry George's *Progress and Poverty* (1879): advancing 'civilisation' threatened a genetic impoverishment of the race. Biological pessimism reinforced the intellectual *schadenfreude* of the day. Harold Laski noted in 1910 that the work of Weismann, Pearson and Bateson had punctured the 'exuberant optimism' of the past fifty years:

In our enthusiasm for the theoretical advances resultant on Darwin's work, we did not realise that our social instincts militated against the force of natural selection ... We trusted to a biology that was often more reminiscent of Exeter Hall than of Darwin or Weismann ... We are beginning to realise that our life has not been based on a sound scientific foundation.[43]

Among the prophets of biological doom and retrogression was the Egyptologist W. M. Flinders Petrie, who saw 'no advance without strife' – civilisations only reached full expression by enduring centuries of military and mental struggle, after which they degenerated: 'Man must strive with Nature or with man, if he is not to fall back and degenerate.'[44] F. W. Headley's *Darwinism and Modern Socialism* (1909) was an anti-socialist tract that used biological reasonings to show that 'the continuance of competition and Natural Selection is essential to the well-being of a civilised community'.[45] In such works biology was conscripted in a rearguard action against the collectivist ethos of Fabianism, 'new liberalism' and Oxford Idealism, and against the more pragmatic threat of Lloyd George's plans for pensions and health insurance. In America Homer Lea – a truly bizarre figure, a self-made mercenary general who fought for the revolutionary cause in China against the moribund empire, and who feared Japan would invade California if the American empire weakened – declared that 'military vigor constitutes the strength of nations'. In *The Valor of Ignorance* (1909) he forecast 'gangrenous and fatal' results if humans thwarted the primal laws of struggle.[46] The Californian zoologist and eugenist Samuel Jackson Holmes included the 'civilizing' of war in a list of deleterious factors causing a 'vicious and defective' human heredity.[47]

Benjamin Kidd's best-selling *Social Evolution* (1894) was another work that took up Weismann's 'law of retrogression'. Although Kidd was in general orientation a reform Darwinist, his early writing insisted that human progress was the result of unrelenting natural selection. *Social Evolution* treated social systems as organic growths that possessed definite laws of health and development, controlled by biological laws. Struggle was central to his theory. He was suspicious of reason: by curbing competition along socialist lines, for instance, it threatened to bring about biological stagnation. However Kidd was no militarist, and he moved steadily away from pure conflict theory. Even from the beginning he pinned his faith upon non-rational factors, such as religion, and the operation of a civilising cultural evolution, to create a more humanitarian, unselfish and peaceful social environment, one that would raise competition from the level of primal violence to a higher phase of freer and fairer rivalry.

Arthur J. Balfour's *Decadence* (1908) flirted with, but refused to capitulate to, bio-medical doctrines of degeneration. Balfour was a rare breed, a British Prime Minister with serious claims as a philosopher. His writing, with its nuances and hesitations, helped explain in the eyes of his critics why his Conservative administration was ousted by the Liberals in 1906. There was, however, an aura of civilisation about Balfour. He recognised the primacy of social heritage, and rejected Weismannism and crude gene theory as a proper source for social thought. This contrasted with Pearson's eugenic creed: 'We have placed our money on Environment, when Heredity wins in a canter.'[48] Balfour questioned whether man's physiological inheritance would be significantly damaged (at least in the west) by racial mixture, immigration, conquest or differential class fertility rates. Culture could survive all such threats. Here Balfour saw hope in the alliance of science with industry, dismissing the doomster militarist view that scientific-industrial society had led to softness, materialism, ugliness. Such pessimism confounded 'accident with essence'.[49] Balfour's tone had changed somewhat since *Foundations of Belief* (1894), when he had been critical of the axis of rationalism, mechanism and technology, although agreeing that it was unlikely to lead to violent and authoritarian structures. The safeguard against a manipulative order of the future was man's evolving ethical and caring sense, emerging out of subterranean instincts and intuitions.

Typically Balfour hesitated over any doctrine of inevitable progress. This was, after all, Whig dogma. In *Foundations* Balfour vividly depicted the despairing Darwinian vision of a nihilistic universe. Man's story was 'a brief and transitory episode in the life of one of the meanest planets'. Famine, disease and mutual slaughter had gradually evolved 'after infinite travail, a race with conscience enough to feel that it is vile and intelligence enough to know that it is insignificant ... Man will go down into the pit, and all his thought will perish'.[50] In *Decadence* he recognised the process of 'social degeneration' in the history of great civilisations. Progress was perhaps the less usual condition of human history (Bagehot's insight). Progress was a typically western concept and type, and might be swamped if the west went under. The decline of the west was by no means unimaginable: 'by what right do we assume that no impassable limits bar the path of Western progress?'[51]

Kidd and Balfour were opponents of militarism. Others drew more extreme lessons from retrogression theory. Harold F. Wyatt held that, as the biological law of competition ruled the destiny of nations, war was 'God's test of a nation's soul'. Wyatt was a founder of the Imperial Maritime League, and an acrid critic of the Asquith government's 'anti-patriotic' naval policy in the pre-1914 years. He drew parallels with Rome, which had fallen because of the decay of the military spirit. Increasingly in history the 'higher and nobler' peoples secured victory in war, and superseded the lower races in the 'economy of God's providence'. If nations ceased to exploit one another's weaknesses, 'the processes of biological war, and therefore the evolution of man, would come to an end'.[52]

C. H. Melville, colonel in the Royal Army Medical Corps and eugenist, described war as the test of virility 'for most historical epochs in the life of active and dominant races'.[53] R. C. Hart defended great empires and racial supremacies in terms of biological necessity, arguing that war-struggle followed nature, while the peace-struggle thwarted natural selection. War was a check to over-population and an outlet for man's innate aggressive instincts. Hart endorsed the bleak view that man had brought needless suffering upon himself 'by his stumbling, half-hearted resistance to Nature's drastic method of purifying and strengthening the race, her remorseless slaughter of the unfit'.[54]

These discussions took place in a context of heightened militaristic sentiment in the west. Britain shared in this, despite its liberal individualism and historic dislike of standing armies. British militarism – although 'softer' than the Prussian variety – became perceptibly more strident in the generation before World War I. As the specialists have shown, it grew from deep historical roots: from the Victorian cults of muscular Christianity and public school Spartanism to the martial ingredients of nonconformity and working-class radicalism; from the racial and imperial insecurities evoked by the Crimean War and Indian Mutiny to the war scares of the later century and Britain's pathetic performance during the Boer War.[55] Liberal pacifists like Herbert Spencer saw 'rebarbarisation' everywhere – in the Boy Scouts, Lads' Drill Associations, the Volunteers (8 per cent of the male population had undergone military training by 1903), the patriotic leagues, the National Service League (which in 1901 launched a determined campaign for conscription, and by 1914 had 200,000 members), a Navy League agitating for more Dreadnoughts, and an expanding, newly popular regular army.[56]

The Boer War created a wave of despondency, especially when the Inspector-General of Recruiting reported that three out of four men applying to enlist at Manchester were rejected as physically unsound.

Benjamin Rowntree estimated that half the manpower in England was unfit for military duty.[57] This seemed to confirm the 'deteriorationist' prophecies of books such as C. F. G. Masterman's *The Heart of Empire* and Arnold White's *Efficiency and Empire* (both appearing in 1901). Masterman spoke of a 'new city type' that had evolved: narrow chested, excitable, weedy, degenerate, hardly a type for an imperial race.[58]

White was an outspoken radical of the right – far removed from Masterman's liberal reformism – a doomster journalist who spouted tirades against Jewish immigration, racial decay, socialist subversion, and the general inefficiency of the nation: witness its inept Establishment, flawed economy, administration, navy and army. (Kipling was to make similar complaints.) White's solution was a sort of Social Darwinist shake-up, the exposure of closed structures to a stringent struggle for existence. The talented and efficient individuals, races and societies would rise to the top in an ethos of fighting and competition. War was an instrument of God's iron law of evolution, a safeguard against moral decay. White's own bio-morality was exemplified by his call for a preventive war against the German navy.[59] The alarm about physical deterioration was taken to Weismannesque extremes in 1910 by Albert Wilson's *Unfinished Man: A Scientific Analysis of the Psychopath or Human Degenerate*, a work commended by White, which located the sources of anti-social behaviour in the human germ plasm, and explained it in almost exclusively biological terms.[60]

In France degenerationists, especially Morel, Taine, Zola and Le Bon, broadened their theory of degenerative traits – such as criminality and alcoholism, construed as 'throwbacks' to a primitive past – to political phenomena, such as riot, revolution and war. They saw such instabilities as taints infiltrating the race, taints tragically exposed by the German defeat of France in 1870 and the drama of the Commune.[61] In the pre-1914 years revanchists wanting to set France on a war footing against Germany used biological arguments in an effort to erode the ingrained anti-war sentiments that flourished in republican circles and social theory.[62] They used a mix of neo-mercantilist economics and Le Bonnian bio-sociology to show the need for a militarily strong nation. In 1905 Captain André Gavet depicted nations as organisms subject to a biological law of struggle for life. Wars were the inescapable result of a tussle between nations for territory, trade and means of subsistence, and nations that refused to fight abdicated their right to live.[63] Captain André Constantin used S. R. Steinmetz's ideas to justify war as 'an instrument of collective selection assuring superiority to the nations strongest in cohesion, will, intelligence, and number'. Generals Kessler and Bazaine-Hayter portrayed war as the test of a nation's fitness and social virtue. Lieutenant Peyronnet thought the lesson of biology to be that the feeble must disappear before the strong: 'extending these consequences from men to nations, one must admit that no sentiment of humanity or right would be powerful enough to prevent a strong state from taking possession of a weaker state'. The Nietzschean philosopher Jules de Gaultier, recoiling from Novicow's pacifist *Critique du darwinisme social* (1910), asserted that nations were an expression of Social Darwinism:

they are an expression of the difference which exists between men, of their ethnic and cultural differences and of the antagonism of their interests. It is because life is Darwinian that there are nations... culture, law, even kindness and the love of peace, all of which our civilization is proud, are the fruits of force, of force ready to prove itself by war.[64]

In Germany ideas of Darwinian militarism accompanied an expanding war culture that grew out of the nation's headlong leap into modernity after 1870. It was a leap into the world of big industry, big cities, a big army, new science, large geo-political ambitions, rapid and disorienting social and political change. The German cults of *Weltmacht*, naturalistic atavism, scientism and efficiency, futurism and idealised *Kultur* offered psychological resolutions to the problems created by flux, most notably a feeling of loss of identity and bearings, perceptions of disintegration and threat. There was a sense of threat to Germany, whether real or imagined, posed by a barbaric Russia or by an encircling Anglo-French coalition – bourgeois and determined to exclude Germans from the great power structure. This perception conditioned German thinking about power and the state, which repudiated orthodox liberal concepts. At least one historian has described a modernist Germany embracing the 'elemental' in diplomacy as well as the arts, rebelling against 'suffocating and stultifying norms, against meaningless conventions, against insincerity'.[65] War was glorified as a test of spirit and culture. Emblematic of this approach were men as diverse as Richard Wagner, Thomas Mann, Kaiser Wilhelm II and General Friedrich von Bernhardi.

Bernhardi insisted on judging war 'from the point of view of natural history'. A 'fundamental law of development', war exemplified the Darwinian struggle for existence, where nature was ruled 'by the right of the stronger', where the weak and 'unwholesome' were selected out.[66] Bernhardi's militarist writings were a compendium of German war philosophy 'declaimed not with the crass and naive brutality of the Pan-German pamphleteers, but with undeniable literary skill and the inflections of a man of culture'.[67] Yet they were too extreme, or too tactless, for the German General Staff, worried that Bernhardi was telegraphing their war programme to the rest of the world. Something of a loner and a political naive, Bernhardi headed the historical section of the General Staff from

1898 until transferred by Schlieffen, who disapproved of his 'radical' ideas. He retired from the army in 1909, and spent his time attacking Schlieffen's strategies, and mobilising German opinion against Britain and peace. He sneered at the strong world peace movement as 'supported by powerful private, and especially by large capitalistic, interests'.[68] His *Germany and the Next War* (1912) was a bestseller, and was translated into many languages, including Japanese. Bernhardi's name became synonomous with rampant Prussian militarism and the strategy of preventive war. He reworked the *Staatsräson* tradition, with generous additions of modish biological determinism. He rejected any higher law or power above the state, which was entitled to act according to the laws of self-interest and survival. Like organisms the state must dominate or degenerate.

Darwinism may not have figured centrally in Bernhardi's overall intellectual strategy – Goethe, Schiller, Treitschke, even Nietzsche contributed more powerfully to his thought. Even so, his use of biological analogy struck home, as a rash of refutations from western sources affirmed. War, in a long-remembered phrase, was 'a biological necessity'. It was not merely a necessary element in the life of nations, but 'an indispensable factor of culture, in which a true civilized nation finds the highest expression of strength and vitality'. The law of the stronger held good everywhere: 'Those forms survive which are able to procure themselves the most favourable conditions of life, and to assert themselves in the universal economy of nature. The weaker succumb.' International relations was governed by 'a persistent struggle for possessions, power and sovereignty', and those nations prevailed in war 'which can throw into the scale the greatest physical, mental, moral, material, and political power'. War furnished such nations 'with favourable vital conditions, enlarged possibilities of expansion and widened influence', and thus promoted the progress of mankind: 'Without war, inferior or decaying races would easily choke the growth of healthy budding elements, and a universal decadence would follow.' Strong and healthy nations increased in population and needed a continual expansion of living space:

New territory must, as a rule, be obtained at the cost of its possessors – that is to say, by conquest, which thus becomes a law of necessity ... Might gives the right to occupy or to conquer. Might is at once the supreme right, and the dispute as to what is right is decided by the arbitrament of war. War gives a biologically just decision, since its decision rests on the very nature of things.[69]

Eugenics and war

Oddly enough some relief from pro-war biology emanated from the much-maligned eugenics movement. Eugenics has been identified in the historical memory with ideas of Nordic racial purity and draconian programmes of 'social hygiene' that included controlled breeding, sterilisation of the congenitally 'unfit', constraint of anti-social types, anti-immigration laws and race segregation – much of this explicable in Foucault's terms of a quest for power by upper middle-class professionals and ruling groups wanting to replicate their own class. The historical reality, as usual, was much more diverse and multivalent than this stereotype suggests.

Eugenics assumed different forms in different cultures. For example, in France, largely because of Enlightenment and revolutionary ideals, the native tradition of reformist Lamarckism exerted a continuing influence upon eugenics. Luminaries of the French Eugenics Society, founded in 1912, included Adolphe Pinard, a neo-Lamarckian obstetrician at the Paris Medical School, and Charles Richet, a founder of the National Alliance against Depopulation. They strongly advocated 'natalist' programmes (improved baby care) and other reformist measures. Whereas in other countries a swarming population of lower-class degenerates was the great fear, in France the threat of degeneration was often perceived in connection with the country's falling birth rate. In this context, the French generally embraced 'positive' and reformist rather than 'negative' and reactionary eugenics.[70]

As we have seen, neo-Lamarckism continued to influence bio-social speculation in pre-1914 Britain, and remained an undercurrent in the eugenics movement there. There was a vigorous ameliorationist wing of that movement with leftist leanings – one thinks of A. R. Wallace, Grant Allen, Havelock Ellis, Ottoline Morrell, H. G. Wells, and the Webbs. Even Karl Pearson, usually thought of as a proto-fascist Galtonian, was a socialist eugenist, not such a rare breed a century ago. Socialists were fatally attracted to the Galtonian ideal of protoplasmic engineering. It might create superior human materials for the great socialist experiment, and also give socialism a modern and scientific image.[71]

However Galton also founded a rightist tradition, rooted in his directive and anti-democratic mores. One has only to read his authoritarian and eugenic utopian novel *Kantsaywhere* (written in 1910 near the end of his life). Here a master caste of Platonic-style Guardians was systematically bred (using ability tests actually devised in Galton's South Kensington laboratory), and labour camps were the punishment for unauthorised mating by the unfit.[72] The right in British eugenics gained little legislative or medical acceptance for its socially invasive therapies of population control and racial hygiene. Yet its language of pathology and national decline echoed the tone of politics and culture.[73]

In the United States eugenics achieved greater popularity, and legislative success (for example, state sterilisation schemes), and its racial discourse was more confrontationist than in Britain. This has been explained in terms of a greater perceived threat to the racial purity of the hegemonic white, Anglo-Saxon, Protestant, middle to upper class posed by the presence of a large black population, and by massive migration into America by European Jews and Catholics after 1900. The fact that peace eugenics was largely pioneered by Americans is no doubt related to the above factors: it too had deeply conservative and isolationist overtones, not least in the desire to preserve American capitalism from the disintegrating effects of external wars. In both Britain and America, the steam behind eugenics seems to have come from a taxpayer revolt against the burdens of pauperism, crime and insanity; while eugenic ideals attracted upwardly mobile professionals seeking to legitimise themselves – especially physicians, biologists and social scientists (business and the British aristocracy were notably absent).[74]

There was hope for peace idealists in the internal logic of eugenics. The new discipline promised a solution to the dilemma posed by the theory of retrogression: namely, that while struggle was a precondition for continuing human evolution, such struggle – and especially warfare – was often wasteful, inhumane, unpredictable and uncontrolled. The new biology stressed the genetic determinants of behaviour, and thus opened up the prospect of human self-control of biological processes. The Mendelian theory of single gene inheritance (later discredited) suggested that quite complex human characteristics – such as intelligence or aggression – could be traced to unit genes, and might ultimately be restructured by geneticists to accord with eugenic ideals.[75] If congenital diseases and malicious traits such as pugnacity could be eliminated by planned breeding and a variety of medical and legal policies, was there not an ultimate prospect of limiting war through genetic and political controls?

The more stringent eugenists branded a range of traits as genetically fixed, from alcoholism and criminality to imbecility and violent behaviour. The French Germanist Georges Vacher de Lapouge advocated capital punishment for degenerate criminals, and systematic breeding of an Aryan master race.[76] W. Duncan McKim in *Heredity and Human Progress* (1900) also wanted execution of 'weak and vicious strains', like epileptics, idiots, habitual criminals and drunkards. McKim's was a grim and obsessive book. He included war on the dark side of human existence. Racial development seemed to require an alternation of war and peace, 'although one tends to brutalize, the other to render vicious'. Each factor served to arrest the degenerative process induced by the other. He accepted Ruskin's view that war was the basis of high virtues and faculties in man. Peace had the greater merit of offering opportunity for the exercise of man's best attributes. However, the day of universal peace was far off. It must await the coming of the eugenic New Jerusalem, when the base instincts of human nature had been eliminated or subdued.

The trouble was, of course, that massive phenomena such as war, or poverty, were unlikely to yield to genetic tinkering. Indeed the whole late-century debate over the biology of war, heightened with Weismannism and Mendelism, was marked by the vast spectrum of issues that it evoked. The debate ranged from the specific – for example, was there an instinct of pugnacity in individuals? – to the cosmic, involving the role of war in human evolution, to the fate of peoples and empires. One of the most persistent questions raised was whether war had a positive (eugenic) or negative (dysgenic) effect upon human stock. This debate also broke out of any technical straitjacket into cosmic issues. No definitive answer emerged on the 'eugenics of war' problem before the close of the First World War (see chapter 6), although the inclination of most eugenists was to declare modern warfare, with its indiscriminate firepower and selective recruitment of armies, to be largely dysgenic in effect. Eugenists were perhaps predisposed to condemn the haphazard selection and waste occasioned by war, precisely because it offended their commitment to careful biological planning. However the whole matter bristled with difficulties.

There was, firstly, the continuing wrangle over 'nurture versus nature'. Just which physical or mental qualities of a people were genetically determined, and which moulded by culture or environment? What human traits were really desirable? Critics alleged that the eugenists simply wanted to replicate their own class or nation, that eugenics expressed the ethnocentrism of an upper-middle class. What limits should be imposed on eugenic policies in the interests of practicality or human freedom?

Francis Galton, who founded eugenics, conceived of it as a science, religion and social practice.[77] As science its purpose was to document the genetic effects of selective agencies upon human populations. As a social or 'religious' movement its purpose was to modify such selective effects in a eugenic direction. Neither purpose was easily fulfilled when it came to war (or other mass phenomena). When Galton coined the term 'eugenics' in 1883, he defined it as 'the study of agencies under social control that may improve or impair the racial qualities of future generations, either physically or mentally'. Was war an 'agency under social control'? Arguably war transcended, or defied, social control, or had done so historically. Many disputed the possibility, or desirability, of ever bringing war under control. Large social groups, vast historical forces, and perhaps ingrained instincts were involved in the causes, dynamics and effects of war. These were notoriously difficult to study scientifically, and yet understanding of such complex phenomena was necessary in order to appreciate, much less control, the 'racial' legacy of war.

Rather like Jeremy Bentham, Galton was intended for a legal career but escaped into social statistics. He developed new statistical techniques (such as chi square), and started a biometrics laboratory at University College, London (where Bentham still sits mummified in a glass case). Galton, however, took Bentham's social engineering to new levels, with his plans for a eugenic social order, based upon biometric analysis of the spread of human characteristics. The threat of degeneration would be met by a systematic eugenics (which he once defined as the study of the conditions under which men of a high type were produced).[78] Galtonism was a blend of old and new. His modern concern with the laws of heredity were integrated into a tradition of cerebral physiology associated with the Austrian phrenologist Franz Joseph Gall and the Belgian social statistician Adolphe Quetelet.[79]

Galton's most brilliant protégé was Karl Pearson, a founder of biometrics. He insisted upon the meticulous study of mass phenomena, in contrast to the pseudo-science employed by many Social Darwinists. Yet even Pearson was forced into spacious theorising and subjective speculation when it came to analysis of war and empire. Pearson's ideas were an idiosyncratic mix of current ideologies. He was a free thinker and sexual radical, a socialist and a pioneer of eugenics. At the same time he was out of step with a great deal of eugenic and socialist thought, not least because of his bellicose discourse on war and imperial expansion. On war he may be loosely placed among the group-selectionists, like the Dutch sociologist S. R. Steinmetz, who assessed war as the real test of group rather than individual supremacy in the struggle for survival.[80] As Pearson said in 1900: 'It is the herd, the tribe, or the nation which forms the fundamental unit in the evolution of man.'[81]

As a young Cambridge mathematics graduate, studying at the Universities of Heidelberg and Berlin, Pearson came into contact with the German tradition of statism, the Darwinist thought of Emil Du Bois Reymond, and the socialism of Marx and Lassalle. Pearson melded together Marxist economics, Gustav Smoller's democratic socialism, Fabian gradualism, and German Darwinist emphasis upon the survival values of group solidarity. He was one of the first eugenists fervently to combine hereditarianism with socialism. In *Natural Inheritance* (1889) he declared human abilities to be under genetic control. He later remarked that 'The sociology of the future – nay, the very science of history in the future – will be a biological science ... nature is more important than nurture'.[82] As socialist planning was the answer to the problem of inefficient capitalism, so genetic engineering would solve that of wasteful competition in nature. A rather jingoistic patriot, Pearson embraced an authoritarian 'national socialism'. *The Ethic of Free Thought* (1888) recommended that 'socialists have to inculcate that spirit which would give offenders against the State short shrift and the nearest lamp-post'.[83]

Pearson had no time for Weismann's theory of *panmixia*. It transgressed both his socialism and his biometrics.[84] The evidence suggested the opposite: that among gregarious animals, and especially civilised man, the intra-group struggle for existence had become progressively less important as an evolutionary factor, due to the growth of organisation and the suppression of anarchistic competition. According to Pearson the human future would inevitably be socialistic. Limitation of competition within the group would lead to increased social efficiency rather than to degeneration.[85]

Pearson however was warlike at the macro level. Socialists (he said) were acting in accordance with biological law by regulating internal conflict within their society, because by doing so they conferred advantage upon themselves in the wider struggle being constantly waged between societies for markets, living space, power and racial domination. There would be at least two types of selection under socialism. There would be 'physical selection', the struggle of the group against its physical environment, against disease and climate. Then there would be the selection caused by 'the struggle of superior with inferior races, especially of civilised with uncivilised man'. He frankly expected any nation under duress, short of food or resources, to attack its neighbours, 'especially if an obviously inferior neighbour is to be found', rather than 'gnaw its own vitals'.[86]

Pearson's bleak vision of a perennial racial struggle, a precondition for future human selection, was apt enough for a generation rushing headlong into the holocaust of 1914–18. One after another inferior races were being subjected to the white man, who excelled in science, material resources and endurance. Pearson rejoiced that Aryans had driven out lesser aboriginal races unable fully to work their lands, as in North America and Australia: 'This dependence of progress on the survival of the fittest race, terribly black as it may seem to some of you, gives the struggle for existence its redeeming features.' To turn swords into ploughshares would mean that mankind would no longer progress:

there will be nothing to check the fertility of inferior stock; the relentless law of heredity will not be controlled and guided by natural selection. Man will stagnate; and unless he ceases to multiply, the catastrophe will come again; famine and pestilence, as we see them in the East...

Hence Britain must take part in the imperial scramble, must compete for trade routes, markets, wastelands, food resources, for the day when Britain failed to hold her own among nations would be a day of catastrophe for British workers.[87]

The Boer War provoked his famous lecture on *National Life from the Standpoint of Science* (1900), a tirade against free-scrambling, free-market profiteering at the cost of class suffering and division. He urged eugenic and socialist efficiency at home – ensuring the rule of better brains and stock, reducing class oppression and inequalities – so that the nation might become 'an organized whole, kept up to a high pitch of efficiency by contest, chiefly by way of war with inferior races, and with equal races by the struggle for trade-routes and for the sources of raw materials and of food supply. This is the natural history view of mankind.'[88]

Pearson's sympathy for the workers was theoretical only. He had a fastidious distaste for the ill-bred proletariat, with its potential for anarchy or revolution. Like some of the Fabians, he wanted to reform or breed out of existence the country's lower stocks. He illustrated the elitist and authoritarian tendencies in positivist and socialist traditions of social engineering, as well as in hereditarian bio-politics. Pearson called for nations to be 'homogenous wholes' if they were to succeed in the global struggle for resources and power. That could mean social democratic reform, an emphasis on gregariousness, social instincts, and mutualism, all in the cause of 'national efficiency' (the 'buzz word' of the 1900s). But it could also mean human regimentation, social planning directed by a technocratic elite, controlled breeding and repression of alien or 'anti-social' groups not contributing to national homogeneity.[89] Pearson really preferred Bismarckian-style benevolent despotism to populist democracy. In the larger world where mixture of superior and inferior races was held to be biologically fatal, his policy of the 'homogenous whole' meant militarism and genocide.

Pearson's critics asked why he counselled suspension of crude struggle *within* modern societies, but commended brute force and genocide in international affairs. The 'new liberal' critic of empire J. A. Hobson approved of much of Pearson's socialism and eugenics, but asked:

If progress is served by substituting rational selection for the older physical struggle, first within small groups and then within the larger national groups, why may we not extend the same mode of progress to a federation of European states, and finally to a world federation? ... May not a ... biological and rational economy be subserved by substituting government for anarchy among nations?[90]

Hobson's bio-politics combined Hegelian dialectics with a pervasively evolutionary approach to social behaviour. In general this resulted in liberal optimism about the future. But there was a persistent sub-text of anxiety also in his writing. Hobson, like many reform Darwinists, opposed brute force and free-scrambling individualism, claiming that the best means to biological fitness was through a 'socialised' liberal capitalism.

This would maximise equality of opportunity. Less typical of the 'new liberal' agenda perhaps, Hobson favoured an 'organicist' analogy of society that would reconcile the claims of individualism with social order. He was an early critic of the 'military-industrial complex', seeing militarism as an outcome of capitalism's creation of surpluses.[91] He deplored the 'quantitative' view of human progress – one that promoted free breeding and imperial expansion, measuring success in terms of cotton bales and square miles of territory. He wanted 'qualitative' social progress. Human fitness should be measured not in terms of primal struggle, survival or possessions, but in terms of higher and more varied human character.[92]

Hobson believed that evolutionary processes were, in themselves, capable of generating more peaceful, rational and ethically 'fit' societies. However (like H. G. Wells) he warned that this was not automatic. Humans would need to exercise free will to achieve their ideals. Civilisation was fragile. There was a danger of reversion to a 'savage type of nature', and there were dark paths to be avoided: scientism unladen with humane values, biologism based upon reductionist images of humankind.

Impressed by Le Bon's crowd psychology, Hobson's *The Psychology of Jingoism* (1901) pointed to deep instinctive forces within national character that surfaced out of the subconscious during times of crisis, such as the Boer War, and were manifested in pugnacious patriotism. He was disgusted by the credulity and blood-lust of the British crowd-mind during the South African war. He speculated that 'the superstructure which centuries of civilization have imposed upon the ordinary mind and conduct of the individual gives way before some sudden wave of ancient savage nature roused from its sub-conscious depths'.[93]

Science itself was being used to reinforce savagery. Although he respected Darwinism and the new genetics, Hobson feared that they might provide a powerful new defence for the baser forms of war and imperialism. He was alarmed by the incursions of biological determinism into such disciplines as sociology. Theorists who tried to bring man under sweeping biological laws applying to the animal kingdom ran the danger of reducing human behaviour to simplistic patterns based upon primitive struggle. They underrated the fact that the laws of lower life were deflected or reversed 'by certain other laws, which attain importance only on the higher psychical levels of the *genus homo*'.[94]

That other great 'new liberal' Leonard Hobhouse took a similar line. His *Mind in Evolution* (1901) rejected a blind, struggle-based evolutionary reading of the human condition in favour of an orthogenic one. There was, Hobhouse insisted, a 'fundamental antithesis' between the organisation of, and the struggle for, life: 'Effort towards a higher development is made possible by a mitigation of the struggle for existence.' The telos of evolution was the expansion of Mind, the attainment of absolute self-consciousness through progressively cultural as opposed to physical inheritance: 'The generic function of Mind is to organise Life by correlating its parts. Its growth consists in the widening scope and increasing articulateness of correlation, with which it replaces that organisation of life which rests on heredity.'[95]

'Social efficiency' and 'Social Gospel'

Hobson singled out the doctrine of 'social efficiency' as a dangerous slogan of racist evolutionists. Through biological reasonings it seemed to give a moral sanction to race-struggle and imperialist wars. As Hobson paraphrased the doctrine, it held that progress required a selective struggle between races who embodied different powers, capacities and types of civilisation. Races of higher 'social efficiency' asserted their right 'by conquering, ousting, subjugating or extinguishing races of lower social efficiency'. But what was meant by 'social efficiency'? It was simply the antithesis of weak. Despite implications of moral and intellectual virtue, it signified nothing more nor less in a 'natural history' sense than capacity to beat other races. It was merely another form of 'survival of the fittest', where 'fittest' meant 'fittest to survive'. Those taking this view argued that the urge to enslave and kill other races was deeply rooted in human nature, and must continue:

So easily do we glide from natural history to ethics, and find in utility a moral sanction for the race struggle ... the doctrine soon takes on a large complexity of ethical and religious finery, and we are wafted into an elevated atmosphere of 'imperial Christianity', a 'mission of civilization', in which we are to teach the arts of good government and the dignity of labour ... This is the supreme principle of the imperialist statesmen, well expressed in Lord Rosebery's description of the British empire as 'the greatest secular agency for good the world has ever seen'.[96]

Hobson was brilliantly readable in deflating the pomposities of imperialist language. Whether he was entirely fair in categorising the logic of the social evolutionists on 'social efficiency' is another matter. His targets included a wide range of spokesmen, from Karl Pearson and the anglophile Edmond Demolins to Benjamin Kidd and American expansionists such as the sociologist Franklin H. Giddings. They took a variety of postures on the ethics of empire, and to reduce their moral theory indiscriminately to a biologically-based doctrine of conflict or racial superiority was risky, to say the least.

Kidd for one inclined to environmentalism, not hereditarianism. Although he accepted germ-plasm theory, and had no time for Lamarckism, his emphasis was upon cultural evolution as the pathway to a reformist future. Kidd's preferred model was, like Hobson's, a collectivised liberal capitalism. Indeed he had much in common with Hobson, as well as the positivists and Novicovians, except that he parted from them in his suspicion of reason.[97] Even Kidd's *Control of the Tropics* (1898), which influenced Joseph Chamberlain and President McKinley, combined a bio-political defence of empire with advocacy of social reform, and rested not upon racist genetics, but upon a decidedly cultural concept of 'social efficiency'.

Indeed Kidd detested Pearson's authoritarian eugenics, and spent many years fighting it. His eyes had been opened in 1904, at a meeting of the Sociological Society in London at which Galton first launched his eugenics programme. Kidd was appalled that, while Galton proposed to reconstruct the human race by scientific breeding, he could find no place in his plan for moral standards. It flashed home to Kidd that Darwinism was both the flower of western science and 'the organised form of the doctrine of the supremacy of material force'.[98]

Certainly Kidd was paternalist, advocating the spread of Anglo-Saxon imperialism which should administer the world's tropical resources as a trust for civilisation. But he was against military subjection of indigenous peoples as inconsistent with the high ideals of western culture. In his theory human evolution was governed by ethical rather than intellectual factors; and ethics was linked to non-rational – especially religious – forces. Hence Kidd denied that the world's presently dominant races had arrived there by dint of superior intellect. Rather they were 'socially efficient', and this was related to the presence in the culture of qualities of resolution, enterprise, energy, devotion to duty. The so-called 'inferior' races owed their humble position to social impoverishment, not to smaller brains or genetic defects. Anthropometric measurements had failed to show innate racial differences in terms of cranial capacity, and hence brainpower. Kidd noted that supposedly less intelligent groups such as Australian aborigines and American blacks learnt quite as readily as whites in elementary schools. Kidd opposed the theory of permanent racial types, as popularised by Robert Knox's *Races of Men* (1850). Taking his stance with Darwin, Kidd held that races were subject to evolution by adaptation and selection. He thus allowed the possibility that submerged races could achieve success by means of cultural improvement.

This also meant that no race could guarantee its continued survival at the top. Kidd was impressed by Japan's westernisation, enabling it to topple Russia in the war of 1904–5. 'Social efficiency' could obviously be acquired; it was not innate. Racial dominance was a matter of cultivating a society's life-sustaining forces, contained in its ethical systems, in order to outrun the destructive forces of self-assertive rationalism in the social system. However it was also true that bio-history had produced racial hierarchies over long periods of time. Hence racial dominances could not be abolished at a stroke. In his last book, *The Science of Power* (1918), Kidd renounced his belief in Darwinism and imperialism. Instead he placed his faith in a peaceful collectivist future, with women taking a higher role. He declared bitterly that racism based on genetic ideas of white superiority had led directly to the scramble for empire, 'one of the most pernicious and reactionary developments which has characterised the Western world for five centuries.[99]

Even Edmond Demolins' gushing works on Anglo-Saxon racial superiority with their simplistic stereotypes of Celtic, Norman, Gallic and German temperaments, amateurishly derived from the sociology of Le Play and Tourville, explained the predominance of the Anglo-Saxons in terms of commercial rather than bio-military supremacy. Demolins, a conservative Catholic, borrowed from Social Darwinism to pillory the 'solidarist ideology' of anticlerical republicans in France.[100] However his theories lacked biological determinism, explaining national character environmentally. The Anglo-Saxons had formed themselves historically into a 'particularist formation' (Tourville's term). This emphasised individualism rather than community. They had spread and prospered by dint of their 'superiority of private life' and greater capacity for work and colonisation. The Celts by contrast belonged to the 'Communistic Clan formation', which never attained social superiority, and dissipated its energies in political and professional activities. Peoples of a 'particularistic formation', such as the British and Americans, were better equipped institutionally and socially to succeed in the Darwinistic struggle for life. Community-oriented peoples, such as the French, were hamstrung by their paternalistic structures. Demolins allowed for military prowess in his law of human history. When one race showed itself superior to another 'in the various externals of domestic life, it *inevitably* in the long run gets the upper hand in public life and establishes its predominance'. Whether this hegemony was asserted peaceably or by feats of arms, 'it is none the less, when the proper time comes, officially established'. This law 'explains and justifies the appropriation by Europeans of territories in Asia, Africa and Oceania'. Yet Demolins clearly preferred the more peaceful methods of free trade imperialism to those of blood and iron. The new imperial Germany, he warned before 1900, was 'even already producing, and daily extending – Militarism, Officialism, and Socialism, which never yet brought in their wake social or economic prosperity'.[101]

In the United States the complex debates over the Cuban acquisition of 1898 indicated that there were few uniformities about race and war among social evolutionists. William Graham Sumner, the Yale sociologist and author of the classic *Folkways* (1906), combined anti-imperialism with a reputation for rugged 'Social Darwinism', and as a champion of brutish free market competition and survivalist ethics validated from nature. Revisionists have suggested that Sumner was more of a traditionalist than a Darwinist, harking back to Protestant cosmology and Malthusian economics in the face of Progressivist threats to the older American class structure in the late century. His thought was complex, his politics and his sociology frequently diverged, and we are reminded that he always insisted upon the distinction between nature's struggle for existence and 'the competition of life among men in society'.[102]

Sumner was a group selectionist like Pearson and the Steinmetz school, but, unlike them, disapproved of war and racial strife. However, he did see that the function of group solidarity within the *in-group*, as he called it, was to enable it to fight effectively against other groups, the *out-groups*. War was rooted in the human condition, arising out of the pressure of numbers, competition for resources, and from the drives of hunger, love, vanity and fear of superior powers:

While men were fighting for glory and greed, for revenge and superstition, they were building human society. They were acquiring discipline and cohesion; they were learning co-operation, perseverance, fortitude, and patience ... War forms larger social units and produces states.

War and revolution created new orders of society. However, as agencies they were also wasteful and irrational, never producing what was wanted 'but only some mixture of the old evils with new ones; what is wanted is a peaceful and rational solution of problems and situations'. Sumner fiercely opposed the Spanish war of 1898. He took the Spencerean line that peace went with industry: 'industrialism builds up; militancy wastes'. But peace would never be universal. It was evident that men loved war: 'There is only one limit possible to the war preparations of a modern European state; that is, the last man and the last dollar ... There is only one thing rationally to be expected, and that is a frightful effusion of blood in revolution and war during the century now opening'.[103] He and Engels were agreed on this at least.

Lester Frank Ward, the other big name in American sociology, and a reformist opponent of Sumnerian 'Social Darwinism', nevertheless regarded 'wars of men with their surroundings, with wild beasts, and with one another' as 'the strict analogues of those of the lower forms'.[104] He agreed with Daniel Brinton that 'war had probably been the highest stimulus to racial progress'. Brinton and Ward were Lamarckians, an indication that Lamarckism was not necessarily a peaceful or tolerant creed. American Lamarckists, such as E. D. Cope, tended to believe that long exposure to poor conditions had imposed a permanently inferior status on certain races and types, for example, blacks, criminals, women.[105]

It was essentially by war, Ward argued, that the Aryans had become the dominant race of the globe, 'the repository of the highest culture', the most socially efficient, displacing inferior races wherever encountered: 'From such transactions the element of justice is wholly excluded. It is only another form of conquest.' Although a professed peace lover, Ward's scientific judgment was that racial struggle and war were perfectly normal and healthy conditions, 'ethically colourless', the 'blind unconscious means' by which the cosmical laws of nature worked. Although he wanted a 'radical sociocracy' that would preserve human freedoms, Ward's views on war indicated a debt to the more authoritarian discourse of conflict theorists such as Ratzenhofer and Gumplowicz, whom he discovered at the turn of the century.[106] There were indeed huge ambivalences in Ward's attitude to international violence, because in general he favoured social planning and the supremacy of 'telic' forces – controlled by human intellect and purpose – over genetically-based natural forces. However he had only weak hope for a peaceful future: 'Under the operation of such a cosmical principle it seems a waste of breath to urge peace, justice, humanity.' Slow mitigation of the 'severity of the law of nature' was all that could be hoped for:

The movement must go on, and there seems no place for it to stop until, just as man has gained dominion over the animal world, so the highest type of man shall gain dominion over all the lower types of man. The greater part of the peace agitation is characterized by total blindness to all these broader cosmic facts and principles, and this explains its complete impotence. There is a certain kind of over-culture which instead of widening narrows the mental horizon.[107]

The Spanish war evoked a variety of responses from American social theorists. Many opted for war when the crunch came, but it was not without regret for the classical Spencerean stand against international strife as a reversion to the militant stage. Progressive industrial societies should compete through trade and not by main force. (Spain, however, might not be classified as 'progressive': it certainly did not in American war propaganda.) Again, the 'elevationist' tradition of Darwinism taught that evolution had raised humanity to new heights of rationality, co-operation and peace, traits that were hardly conspicuous in the unseemly war-fever of 1898. Apostles of racial purity warned, more cynically, that peaceful isolationism was more likely to improve the native American stock than an imperial conquest that would flood the United States with Cubans, Filipinos and other 'mezzotints'.

The Columbia sociologist Franklin H. Giddings, one of the founders of a 'scientific' and statistical American sociology, used Darwinian paradigms in his analysis of human behaviour. He justified American expansion into Cuba and the Philippines along the lines of Kidd's *Control of the Tropics* (1898). Kidd was lionised during a trip to the United States, still euphoric about its hundred days' victory over Spain but also torn by divisions over the acquisition of empire. His book was welcomed as supremely opportune, especially by the expansionists. Giddings solemnly cited Kidd's contentions in *Democracy and Empire* (1900). Tropical possessions were necessary for the 'northern nations' as vital sources of raw materials. However, imperialism should be as far as possible altruistic and irenic. Government should be firmly run by western administrators, the 'socially efficient', but as a trust on behalf of the world at large and the native inhabitants.[108] The anti-imperialists were cynical about such trusteeship concepts. They simply put a veneer, one critic said, 'on the old predatory instinct for land-grabbing and man hunting'.[109]

Hesitations about the war marked the 'Social Gospel' movement, made up of Protestant reformers who wanted to apply the 'social law of service' (Richard T. Ely's phrase) in the sphere of empire and world politics. The Social Gospellers included Ely (a Madison State University economist with Christian Socialist leanings, whose anti-trust sentiments influenced Kidd), Lyman Abbott (editor of the New York *Outlook*), Revd Washington Gladden (author of *Ruling Ideas of the Present Age*, 1895), Revd W. D. P. Bliss (editor of *Encyclopedia of Social Reform*) and Josiah Strong. Most of them were swept up in the general enthusiasm for the war. Gladden wrote a pro-war tract, *Our Nation and Her Neighbors* (1898). Strong's Anglo-Saxonist writings, especially his popular *Our Country* (1886), probably contributed to the intellectual climate favouring intervention in Cuba. Strong himself accepted annexation with misgivings, having earlier opposed expansion on Spencerean lines. He continued to hope that an era of peaceful industrialism would obliterate the need for atavistic wars between nations. Impressed by Kidd's *Control of the Tropics*, he accepted the need for continuing struggle as a condition of progress, while trusting that it would be waged at the intellectual and commercial level. In *Expansion Under New World-Conditions* (1900) Strong forecast that the Anglo-Saxons would use their biological advantages, acquired through long ages of strife, not to honour their own race but to exalt, enrich and free mankind generally: 'The movement is upward, and the greater altitudes will surely be gained.' He used the concept of 'social efficiency' to justify the ultimate displacement of competitive social systems by a 'New Solidarism', both at home and globally, struggle being replaced by the restraints of social control and higher evolutionary laws.[110]

Strong's uncertainty about annexation of Cuba reflected more widespread anxieties about Americans treading the European paths of power diplomacy and militarism. Recent scholarship has documented a continuing diversity and ambiguity in American 'Social Darwinist' writings on war, race and empire up to 1919, with doctrines of naked violence and *realpolitik* ethics more than outweighed in the serious literature by more sophisticated discourses based upon a preference for peaceful and rational modes of social evolution.[111]

Clearly, in the debate over the 'biology of war', as more generally, Darwinism bred a myriad of diverse doctrines, a plurality of connotations. Complex interactions took place between biological and social domains. Biological theories took on differing ideological shadings in differing historical climates. There were pro-war and anti-war biologies and pseudo-biologies. One is tempted to perceive such polarisations as perennial, like that between doctrines of original sin and human innocence, or nature versus nurture, reappearing in varied garb in varied historical seasons. The difficulty lies in distinguishing degrees of influence, emphasis and dominance across societies and time. To establish which paradigm was hegemonic at a particular time is rarely an easy task, requiring intensive counting of heads and scrutiny of a range of individual epistemologies. Moreover, individuals commonly wavered between discourses, were often inconsistent and often changed their minds. The prudent historian will generalise about such things in a suitably chastened frame of mind.

The evidence marshalled so far suggests a certain concurrence in the verdict that conflict Darwinism and the hereditarian theories of the 1890s and 1900s gave an impetus to biological militarism. But this tradition by no means dominated the debates on the biology of war before 1914. In the Social Darwinist world of discourse in the pre-war generation, the militarist assessment of war as a biological necessity was offset by a virile tradition of anti-war evolutionism. This tradition will now be explored in greater detail.

4 'The natural decline of warfare': anti-war evolutionism prior to 1914

The Future of War: Bloch, Wells, Angell

Ironically in the pre-1914 generation, as the world stood under the impending shadow of the First World War, thinkers were establishing beyond doubt the 'natural decline of warfare'. (The phrase was coined by Alexander Sutherland during the euphoria of Tsar Nicholas II's world peace proposals of 1898.)[1] While Jean de Bloch demonstrated that modern war was too costly and disruptive to be tolerated, and Norman Angell 'proved' that it was economically prohibitive, influential peace apostles such as Jacques Novicow, David Starr Jordan and Vernon Kellogg dismissed war as biologically destructive and outmoded. An age of fevered nationalisms and militaristic determinisms also brought forth 'peace eugenics', a discourse that brilliantly used the new genetics to reinforce mainstream peace Darwinism, and conducted a furious rhetorical offensive against the militarists. Ignoring their own inclinations towards determinism and use of analogies from nature, the peace eugenists blamed the enemy for breaching free will and the western moral tradition, for distorting nature and the nature of war. War was excoriated as dysgenic, an anachronism fated to disappear as human history moved into a higher phase of civilisation. Right up to August 1914 the optimists emphasised the basic peacefulness of the west's advanced civilisations.

This was based upon irrefutable fact. Europe had maintained a long, if fragile, peace since the Franco-Prussian war. This was despite the romantics who glorified war, the 'yellow press' who sensationalised war to make sales, and science fiction writers who prophesied war.[2] Lieutenant-Colonel G. T. Chesney's *Battle of Dorking* (1871) started a fashion for 'invasion scare' novels, while H. G. Wells added a new dimension with space invaders in his *War of the Worlds* (1898). The more perceptive experts foresaw utterly changed and terribly destructive new conditions on battlefields and behind the front as a result of new weaponry and firepower, better armour, submarine and air power. However, conservative military thought held that better weapons meant shorter wars with few disastrous consequences. There was still much complacency, based on the sheer unthinkability of western civilisation tearing itself apart in a great civil war. Some argued the case in distinctly modern terms of 'deterrence'. The horror of new weapons would surely deter nations from going to war. There was also the racist argument that, as the implements of war became more sophisticated and costly, only the wealthiest nations could afford them. As Robert Routledge put it in 1876, the 'poor and barbarous races' would be kept at bay this way, and the more certain would be the 'extension and permanence of civilization'.[3]

The most impressive case based upon deterrence came from Jean de Bloch. He was an extraordinary man. Born Ivan Bliokh in 1836 in Poland and originally a street pedlar, he became a confidant of Tsar Nicholas II, a railroad magnate and St Petersburg banker, a Zionist who fought for Jewish rights after the pogroms of the 1890s, and a pioneer of 'scientific' (as opposed to sentimental) peace studies, aiming to spread an exact knowledge of war in its sociological totality so that people would choose peace on the basis of enlightened self-interest. Bloch became a hero-figure in pacifist circles after the appearance of his six-volume *The Future of War*, published in Russian and Polish in 1898, and widely translated. W. T. Stead sponsored an English abridgment, and used all of his journalistic resources to push its message in Britain, while the American pacifist Edwin D. Mead and his friends arranged the American translation of volume VI and freely credited Bloch with masterminding the Tsar's peace rescript and the 1899 Hague peace conference.[4]

With uncanny accuracy Bloch predicted the shape of the holocaust of 1914–18; yet he was sufficiently a man of the nineteenth century, with its military concepts of limited war for limited ends, to call those who believed in war 'visionaries of the worst kind ... the great war cannot be made, and any attempt at it would result in suicide'.[5] Like most bankers Bloch preferred a world run on sound, peaceful business lines. War was a craziness that disrupted commerce, invited class disorder and revolution. Yet he perceived – unlike military staffs fettered to the past – that science was transforming war. Fourteen years of research convinced him that future war would be total war, with unbelievable butchery: rapid-firing rifles and machine-guns, powerful and accurate artillery, defensive entrenchments of great complexity, mass armies of conscripts, massive organisation and logistics. He forecast great armies bogged down in extended front lines. Wars would become prolonged sieges, the advantage resting with defenders behind barbed wire or in lines of fortresses. Millions would be slaughtered under conditions of unbearable terror, killed by shells launched miles away, or from sniper's bullets fired with devastating precision. The wounded would be left to rot in no man's land, a lethal fire zone between trenches. As death rates were highest among officers, soldiers would become a rabble, especially the city-bred conscripts unsuited to outdoor conditions. Defeatism and desertion would become endemic.

Bloch saw that total war thrust unbearable economic and civil burdens upon populations, first in escalating arms races, then to sustain a massive war effort. Civil resources were as vital as military capacity in this new type of war, which would be fought until the financial and moral exhaustion of the enemy. He estimated that in one year of world war the powers would spend £1,460 million merely feeding their soldiers, more than the total expenditure on all European wars waged from Waterloo to the Russo-Turkish war. A major war would disrupt the world system of supply and distribution of foodstuffs and materials, as well as the structure of international finance. Any attempt to finance war by the powers would cause a fall in securities, a tumbling market, sky-high inflation. A great war would cause famine as agricultural labourers were conscripted, would spark soaring food prices, astronomic taxes and disrupted industries, while the governing classes were being decimated at the front. It was a recipe for anarchy, and Bloch accused European governments (especially the French) of blocking inquiries into the economic and human madness of war.

Bloch, and economic rationalists like him, believed that the world's power and money elites would not allow such chaos to come to pass. They underestimated human ingenuity to tackle the huge logistical and economic problems posed by world war, or the capacity to persist in irrational behaviour. Ways were found to finance the First World War at the expense of economic orthodoxies. This gloomy possibility eluded Bloch: 'The soldier is going down and the economist is going up. There is no doubt about it.'[6] The romance of war had 'vanished into thin air with its gaudy uniforms, unfurled banners, and soul-stirring music'.[7]

However he became more pessimistic after his book was buffeted by European critics. He complained that few grasped 'the fell significance' of militarism: 'Military science has from time immemorial been a book with seven seals, which none but the duly initiated were deemed worthy to open.'[8] Bloch spent his last years campaigning for peace, arguing that war was a costly and destructive anachronism. What commercial or territorial gain was worth the price? Why waste money on arms races when it was incomparably better spent on education and social reform? Bloch travelled to Britain at the time of the Transvaal war to beard the admirals and generals in their den, winning the debate hands down if the press reports are to be believed.[9] His great vision was to set up War and Peace Institutions in the world's capitals, large museums that would portray the real significance of modern war by means of charts, panoramas and models. The Bloch Foundation funded the Lucerne Museum of War and Peace. He died on Christmas Day 1901, in Warsaw, in the midst of drawing up a vast propaganda campaign against continental militarism.[10]

One of those to read Bloch was H. G. Wells, who incorporated the Pole's ideas of futuristic war into his short story *The Land Ironclads*, fore-shadowing the use of tanks. Wells wrote even more imaginatively than Bloch about the way in which war was being mechanised, automated, and 'drawn into the field of the exact sciences'.[11] Wells agreed that the heavy firepower of new weapons gave great advantage to defence in the context of trench warfare. At the same time he saw more clearly than Bloch the potential power of offence, with the development of tanks, airforces, germ warfare and new bombs. He forecast the future horror, and futility, of atomic war in *The World Set Free*, written in 1913. In this story, and others including *The War in the Air* (1908), Wells pictured the destruction of the world's great cities and cultures, the death of millions, the end of industry, world credit and indeed government itself. There would be reversion to primeval tribalism and guerrilla violence. In *The Collapse of Civilisation* (1909) he warned that 'we have over-developed war'. It had become insane because of the expense of weaponry and the destructive potential of air power.[12]

Wells gave a terrifying new twist to Bloch's thesis. He had less faith in human rationality or the theory of deterrence. His stories were full of man's tragic failure to detect or act upon the fatal signs of impending disaster. The evolutionary legacy of the struggle for existence, the embedded aggression within the human constitution, the human capacity for senseless violence meant that there would be no easy end to national rivalries, race hostility, and the use of technology to wage war. At times he seemed to say that great wars, even human annihilation, had been biologically ordained. When had man ever refused to use a military invention? What could stop the inexorable industrialisation of war? Wells even expressed a theoretical preference for a holocaust that would cleanse the human race of its sins. A new order would be built upon the ashes, society stripped of the old evils of nationalism and class conflict. Some of his stories, however, suggest that social evolution would simply re-work itself in the same old patterns from a new primal start.

At times Wells was capable of equating the military state with the biologically efficient state.[13] In his unpleasantly illiberal eugenic writings – conditioned surely by his class insecurities and contemporary fear of biological swamping by the 'underworld' – he advocated rule by the 'Efficients', and ruthless elimination of the 'People of the Abyss' and 'those swarms of black and brown, and dirty-white, and yellow people' who were inefficient: 'the nation, in a word, that turns the greatest proportion of its irresponsible adiposity into social muscle, will certainly be the nation that will be the most powerful in warfare as in peace'.[14]

Wells was full of tormented ambivalence on the whole subject of the human future. His eugenics permitted some optimism that a technocratic elite, the Samurai of *A Modern Utopia* (1905), ruthlessly controlling selection, would maintain world peace by benevolent dictatorship. Balancing his apocalyptic nightmares of an end to history, either through human failure or external disaster (comet strike, Martian invasion, etc.),his social prophecy often took a more optimistic tone. Wells had studied Darwinism under Huxley at the South Kensington Normal School of Science. Many of his stories fictionalised Huxley's philosophy, including the idea that man must check nature at every point by means of the 'ethical process'. He looked forward to the next quantum leap in evolution when an almost godly human race would look back on this age as merely the crude and violent prelude of things to come, when reason, good order and peace would prevail.

With the onset of the new century, Wells briefly put aside his *fin de siècle* themes of dread, the themes that marked *The Time Machine* (1895), *The Island of Dr Moreau* (1896), *The Invisible Man* (1897) and *War of the Worlds* (1898), with their messages that evolution could end in a blind alley, that science was getting out of control, that civilisation itself was fragile. In *The Discovery of the Future* (1902) he declared himself a believer in the 'coherence and purpose' of the world, and the greatness of human destiny. *Anticipations* (1901), despite its gloom about militarism, proclaimed a hopeful gospel:

All that the human mind has accomplished is but the dream before the awakening. A day will come when beings now in our thoughts and hidden in our loins will stand upon this earth as one stands upon a footstool, and laugh, and reach out their hands amid the stars.

Such things, however, did not come about by automatic evolution. War, clashing imperialisms, population explosions, power and racial rivalries were symptoms of evolutionary maladjustment that threatened the end of the species. As one scholar has aptly put it, Wells may have been 'the indefatigable cheerleader for a human race liberated from its old, grim gods and breathing the clear air of reason'; but he was also the prophet who wailed that 'the human race was engaged in a life or death struggle with genetic entropy'.[15]

Economic rationalists like Molinari, Ferrero and Angell reinforced the brittle complacency about war being impossible. Although they conceded in theory that self-defeating behaviour could occur in economics, they were always in danger of falling into the trap of economic determinism, of believing that economic forces debarred war. But they did superbly document the exorbitant expense of military technology, and the ruinous costs of a great war. War didn't pay. That was their simple message, in the great liberal tradition of Ricardo, the Mills, Say and Bastiat.

In 1898 Gustave de Molinari, in *Grandeur et decadence de la guerre*, calculated that the profits of war no longer covered its cost. Territorial annexations, indemnities and the like would not in fact profit a victor nation, or would provide limited benefits at tragic price. War brutally disrupted trade between belligerents and affected neutrals, reducing revenue and purchasing power.

Guglielmo Ferrero's *Il Militarismo* (1898) praised global capitalism, and especially the rise of transnational corporations and a global consumer society, as forces for world peace. Militarism was an auxiliary of capitalism only when it did not entail 'such an immense expenditure on arms and war as to impede or arrest the accumulation of capital'. Despite Europe's 'mad fury for military inventions', war was unthinkable:

in those countries which possess a world-wide commerce, or where a vast national Caesarism exists, the State grows ever less bellicose ... war in Europe is today nothing but the ghost of dead injustices ... the civilized nations of Europe have renounced the exercise, to each other's hurt, of that systematic brigandage named warfare.[16]

However it was Norman Angell who was chiefly remembered – he thought very unfairly – as the man who declared war impossible on economic grounds, and was then proven wrong in 1914. It must be said that there were plenty of reverberations in his popular book *The Great Illusion* (1910) to justify the image, although he never actually prophesied the end of war. As he liked to point out in his mass lectures, why should he and other peace advocates bother to campaign if there was no danger of war? Angell's own concept of war as anachronism in fact threatened to geld the peace movement. He resorted to generalisations about man being naturally quarrelsome and irrational. War could only be restricted by perennial social controls, pending the eventual spread of a more enlightened culture. The pacifist literature of the pre-war era was racked by discursive tensions of this kind. Angell's materialistic pacifism irked the religious and 'moral force' pacifists. His conservative defence of finance capitalism as a force for peace ran counter to the militant left's image of war as a capitalist conspiracy. Peace activists freely proclaimed the obsolescence of war while bleakly warning about the arms race and the human propensity to fall back into atavistic savagery.

Angell had a large ego. He saw himself as a genius who would put peace studies on a new scientific basis, beyond mere moralism, a sure guide for statesmen. In fact his theories were flawed, his facts disputable, his scholarship sloppy. He was, rather, a great communicator, who updated the old free trade peace image for the early twentieth century. He was a moralist-rationalist in the Enlightenment tradition, who decked his dreams out in pseudo-scientific colours, whose writings were full of unsubstantiated value judgments about human nature. Nevertheless his work gave a tremendous fillip to a jaded peace movement at the right time.

A highly strung and lonely youth from a middle-class Lincolnshire background, Angell found solace in agnostic radicalism and a rather pretentious intellectualism. During a three-year stint at a French *lycée* from the age of twelve, he immersed himself in Mill, Voltaire, Paine, Kingsley, William Morris, Spencer, Huxley, Bradlaugh and Whitman. He led a cosmopolitan life as journalist, writer, peace apostle. As a young reporter he fraternised with exiled Russians at the university of Geneva. This inoculated him for life against the revolutionary virus. He had a fling at homesteading in California, worked on American and French newspapers, and moved into Lord Northcliffe's circle when he ran the French edition of the *Daily Mail*. He was dismayed by the popular hysteria generated by America's Cuban war of 1898, the Boer War and the Dreyfus affair, and wrote an unsuccessful pamphlet against militarism: *Patriotism Under Three Flags: A Plea for Rationalism in Politics* (1903). Echoing Le Bon's crowd theory, he argued that an uninformed populace was led into war by emotions that cut across their true interests.[17]

For seven years Angell worked as an editor for Northcliffe, whose *Daily Mail* supported the Boer War and an aggressive foreign policy against Germany. The two men had an odd relationship compounded of mutual respect and ideological difference. Angell did not leave until 1912, when he became a full-time peace worker on secret Carnegie money, helping to found the important Union of Democratic Control in late 1914. He was provoked to write his seminal pamphlet *Europe's Optical Illusion* (1909), the forerunner of *The Great Illusion*, in order to counter the bellicose attitudes and ignorance of Northcliffe's circle (especially Leo Maxse, J. L. Garvin and Lord Roberts). Typically Northcliffe backed his protégé while completely dismissing his message. However, financial interests, fearing the global consequences of an Anglo-German war, openly endorsed Angell. Bankers were prominent in conservative peace societies. Carnegie began the New York Peace Society in 1906, and recruited bankers such as J. P. Morgan and August Belmont. In 1910 Carnegie set up his own Endowment for International Peace, which quickly offered to finance Angell. He was also taken up by David Starr Jordan and the American pacifists. Jordan and Edwin Mead (the propagator of Bloch's ideas) were key figures in the newly formed, Boston-based World Peace Foundation.

Angell was a superb publicist, and the book became a splendid success, selling over two million copies in three years, and was translated into twenty-five languages. It was favourably received across a surprisingly broad spectrum of opinion, from establishment to peace movement. By 1912 over forty Angellite peace clubs had been formed in Britain, concentrated in the midlands, north and Scotland, and Angell's ideas were widely debated in working men's clubs across the land. Also by 1912 influential supporters such as Arthur Balfour and Lord Esher had founded the Tory-linked Garton foundation to promote Angellism.[18]

Angell blamed mercantilism for creating the 'illusion' that military and commercial power went together, that the wealth of defenceless nations was at the mercy of stronger ones. Such fear led to arms races, and war became a self-fulfilling prophecy. The truth was that war was impotent to alter the basic economic relations between states. Modern wealth was founded upon complex and interdependent financial and commercial networks. Any attempt at confiscation by a conqueror would cause the credit-dependent wealth of the defeated to vanish, 'so that if conquest is not to injure the conqueror, he must scrupulously respect the enemy's property, in which case conquest becomes economically futile'.[19] Angell liked to cite the case of Germany invading Britain and looting the vast wealth of the Bank of England. The effect would be a run on every bank in Britain, suspension of payments, global chaos in money markets, and the undermining of German banking as merchants the world over called in their German credits to offset London's collapse.

Territorial conquest in reality only added a new set of costs and benefits to a conqueror's budget, amounting to little more than an administrative reordering of the region's resources. Tributes or indemnities would likewise be self-defeating: indemnities paid in goods meant a flooding of cheap commodities into the victor country, while those paid in specie would send inflation sky high (an anticipation of the Versailles settlement). Confiscation of property was impossible as it would erode the financial credibility of the invader. Angell and the liberal economists had a touching faith in the sanctity of property and the unthinkability of genocide. Predators were assumed to act in the best traditions of the classical school of economics.

English patriots, from Frederick Harrison to the Oxford military historian Spenser Wilkinson, had advocated British naval expansion to counter Germany's threat to the empire and the British carrying trade. Angell scoffed at the whole idea. Trade was effectively cosmopolitan, he said (discounting protectionism). Success was a matter, not of battleships and armies, but of supply and demand, prices and entrepreneurship. If Germany conquered The Netherlands, Dutch merchants would still compete against German merchants, and on even keener terms as they would be within the German customs union. Solidarity and co-operation were in fact becoming more important than competition between nations (an economic analogue of peace biology). Unlike many socialist pacifists, Angell did not consider capitalism a warlike system, or finance capitalism a source of world tension. Like Bloch and Ferrero, he cast the financiers as the guardians of peace.[20] He spurned the thesis that imperialism and war were bred out of capitalistic greed for markets, raw materials and fields of investment. Rather capitalism favoured cosmopolitanism and peaceful trade. The free flow of goods and ideas could only aid international brotherhood.

In the tradition of Adam Smith, Bentham and Cobden, Angell declared great empires, armies and navies to be at best economically irrelevant, at worst millstones around a country's neck. He was himself a sentimental supporter of the British empire, but on grounds of kinship and social affection, not economics. His preferred models were the small, virtually unarmed states like Belgium and Norway that outdid the superpowers in economic performance. Empires and fleets were merely symbols of power, offspring of inglorious nationalism. Ultimately they threatened to spark a great conflict that would cause a collapse of world trade, economic dislocation on a massive scale, an end to civilised life and an opening for 'revolutionary and anti-national solutions' to the crisis.[21]

Peter Kropotkin and the mutual aid ideal

As already noted, there were strong analogies between the economic peace models built on the need for solidarity and interdependency in the world's trading and money systems, and biological peace models built on the fact of coexistence in the natural world. Peace biology of this kind was founded upon Darwin's holistic ecology, 'mutual aid' zoology, and anti-reductionist values that underlined man's biological uniqueness, and capacity to transcend genes and any warlike primal legacy. Humans, with their language, culture and ethics, had the potential to become 'imperial' animals in the best sense, mastering their environment, solving the age-old problems of poverty and war. This was the public image of peace biology. But within the discourse lay discordances, mainly over the issues of analogy and determinism, and these arose particularly in the fields of mutual aid zoology and peace eugenics. The Kropotkin image of a benevolent nature and humanity ruined by violent technologies and social structures prescribed a return to nature, and contrasted with Huxley's image of a violent nature and humanity needing control by a manmade, ethical culture. Peace eugenists flirted with an illiberal gene theory that denied culture, and sometimes simply substituted peace for war as a biological imperative.

Prince Peter Kropotkin's classic *Mutual Aid* (1902) in fact began as a refutation of Huxley, accused by Kropotkin of perverting the facts of nature and Darwinism.[22] Kropotkin endorsed and extended Darwin's ideas of natural coexistence; but he regretted that Darwin had inflated the factor of struggle, with widespread repercussions.

We have heard so much lately of the 'harsh, pitiless struggle for life', which was said to be carried on by every animal against all other animals, every 'savage' against all other 'savages', and every civilized man against all his co-citizens – and these assertions have ... become an article of faith.[23]

Kropotkin was to leave a twofold inheritance for the peace tradition: (1) his mutualist zoology provided a powerful tool for use against conflict and militarist schools of Social Darwinism; (2) his evolutionary ethics and positivist faith in biological science bolstered the analogical and determinist side of peace biology.

Kropotkin was, of course, with Bakunin, the great prophet of anarchism. Aptly enough, he universalised the anarchist's faith in human solidarity into an instinctive theory governing the whole animal world. He was seminally influenced by his naturalist studies of the rich animal life of East Siberia, which he observed during the 1860s in self-imposed exile as a young, reform-minded aristocratic Cossack officer. He read a flourishing literature on animal social life during the 1870s and 1880s, most notably the pioneering work of Alfred Espinas (*Les sociétés animales*, 1877) and George Romanes (*Animal Intelligence*, 1882).[24] As a political prisoner in France, Kropotkin read and embraced the mutual aid theory of the St Petersburg zoologist Karl Kessler.[25] But he steered clear of the sentimentalism of naturalists like Louis Büchner, whose 'hymn of love' on animal sympathy lacked evolutionary rigour. It was not love, but survival needs (argued Kropotkin) that induced a herd of ruminants or horses to form a ring to resist wolves, that induced wolves to hunt in packs, or even induced kittens or lambs to play. Social life and mutual aid depended upon 'an instinct that has been slowly developed among animals and men in the course of an extremely long evolution' (p. xiii).

Mutual Aid minimised overcrowding and species struggle as factors in evolution. This stance owed much to Kropotkin's political opposition to Malthusianism, a bourgeois ideology that threatened socialist meliorism, that shaped into 'a pseudo-scientific form the secret desires of the wealth-possessing classes'.[26] His observations in northern Asia led Kropotkin to emphasise struggle against environment, paucity of life and under-population to be the distinctive features of natural life. Nature's checks to population came from terrible snowstorms and frosts, torrential flooding and scarcity of food – factors so severe that, as with the semi-wild cattle and horses in Transbaika, wild ruminants and squirrels, whole portions of the species became so impoverished in vigour that 'no progressive evolution of the species can be based upon such periods of keen competition' (p. ix).

However where animal life was abundant – as with the teeming life on the lakes, the fallow-deer on the Amur, the heavy bird migrations along the Usuri – mutual support was the governing factor of life, not war and rivalry within and between species. In wonderfully evocative language Kropotkin illustrated his theme from microscopic pond-life, termites, ants, bees, locusts, beetles, land-crabs, eagles, pelicans, wagtails and parrots, to rodents, ruminants, wolves, monkeys and men. Evolutionary success went to the socially cohesive rather than to the merely strong and aggressive.

He described how bands of small lapwings or white wagtails, acting in concert, compelled powerful birds of prey, such as the sparrow-hawk, to retreat, even to relinquish its prey. The intelligent pelicans fished in bands: 'they form a wide half-circle in face of the shore, and narrow it by paddling towards the shore, catching all fish that happen to be enclosed in the circle' (p. 23). Kropotkin was fond of citing Darwin's example of the altruistic pelicans who kept alive a blind fellow by feeding it fish. Gregariousness and inter-dependence were the laws of animal life. Reciprocal caressing, grooming, defence and protection were common within species. Several displayed solicitude for their wounded, and, in higher species such as monkeys, even showed grief over death of comrades or mates. Kropotkin reversed the entrenched western view that selfish and pugnacious instincts were the real basis of animal and human biology. The real products of evolutionary history were altruistic and sociable instincts. Man's ethical foundations were therefore to be found in the evolutionary past. There was no need for a Huxleyan dissociation of biology and society, a dualism between natural and ethical humanity.

It followed that Kropotkin would have a highly sympathetic image of early and primitive humanity. He cited paleo-ethnology and zoology to show that the primitive form of organisation for mankind and its earliest ancestors (including the higher mammals) was not the family, but 'societies, bands, or tribes' (p. 79). The instinctive urge to live peaceably and cooperatively in groups was instilled early into humankind. This was indicated by the veritable workshops of stone implements found in the lake-shore traces of neolithic man in Europe, Asia and Africa; as also in the stone age settlements in Switzerland, at Lake Neuchâtel for instance, where life seemed to have been 'remarkably free of warfare' (p. 83). So too the life-style of primitive peoples contained laudable communal, other-

regarding values, often superior to the greedy individualism and materialism of western peoples. Kropotkin regarded the Eskimos, Australi-
ans, Fuegians and Bushmen as literal inheritors of early post-glacial
culture, since they lived within a girdle encircling the 'civilised' nations, at
the extremities of our continents. Far from living in Hobbesian disorder,
they had complex clan organisations and elaborate social codes.

Kropotkin was not, as he is sometimes represented, an uncritical devotee
of the 'noble savage' myth. He recognised the existence of primitive
practices such as infanticide, cannibalism, headhunting and vendetta. But
he explained them as adaptive responses to environmental pressure,
perpetuated through ritual and primitive religion. He blamed men of
science, anxious to prove man's animal origins, for going to the opposite
extreme to the Rousseauian idealisation of savages, charging them with
every imaginable bestial quality:

The savage is not an ideal of virtue, nor is he an ideal of 'savagery'. But the
primitive man has one quality, elaborated and maintained by the very necessities of
his hard struggle for life – he identifies his own existence with that of his tribe; and
without that quality mankind never would have attained the level it has attained
now (pp. 111–12).

Unhappily, as with other mammals, group solidarity was restricted to
those occupying allotted territories. This territoriality was the source of a
sort of split personality in humanity. Thus the life of savages was split
between two sets of actions and ethics, that applying within the group, and
that applying to outsiders:

Therefore, when it comes to a war the most revolting cruelties may be considered
as so many claims upon the admiration of the tribe. This double conception of
morality passes through the whole evolution of mankind, and maintains itself until
now (p. 113).[27]

This proposition was to be energetically maintained in twentieth-
century psychoanalysis, popular ethology and recent sociobiology.

For Kropotkin history was a great dialectical struggle and interaction
between self-assertion and mutual aid. War was an excellent example of
this. Military success depended upon social organisation and knowledge;
and it was mutual aid that created the conditions in which humans could
cultivate these capacities (p. 296). Yet a single war could produce more evil
than a hundred years of good that had come out of the mutual aid
principle.

However, Kropotkin saw mutual aid as eternally resilient in history.
This was despite the corruption of man's pristine collectivism through the
growth of property, accumulation of wealth, the influence of social

structures and political institutions. He highlighted the peaceful accomplishments of supposedly bloodthirsty barbarians, and lyrically praised the communalism and culture of Europe's medieval cities, which counterbalanced the militaristic forms of the feudal system. To his mind the most glorious ages in civilisation were those in which the mutual aid factor dominated, evoking a great flowering of arts, industry and science, as in the grand eras of the Greek city-state and the medieval guilds. He queried the current view that individualism and cut-throat competition explained the success of modern industrialism. Impressed by 'the astounding rapidity of industrial progress from the twelfth to fifteenth century', he asked whether the decay of medieval civilisation had not hindered, instead of hastening, the rise of industry (pp. 297–8).

Kropotkin invested his hopes for the future in those groups who had preserved the communalist ideals: the peasantry, the urban poor, artisans, guilds and trade unions, groups who would be emancipated from the thrall of capitalist artifice by revolutionary fiat. Humans would then be raised to the next stage of evolution, a peaceful, state-less, anarchist society based upon mutual sympathy, a morality in harmony with nature, and a truly existential and fulfilling individualism.

This was sound, and inspiring, anarchist doctrine. Less orthodox was Kropotkin's almost Comtean faith in science, especially biological science. Following Bakunin, anarchists almost ritualistically reviled rational systems and science as mental configurations that reinforced bourgeois hegemony and suppressed the natural impulses of the people. The *Pananarchist Manifesto* of 1918 denounced science as 'one of the stupidities of the European savage, just as religion is a stupidity of the Asiatic savage'.[28] Kropotkin, however, was a lifelong amateur naturalist, and he wanted to found a scientific anarchism, just as Marx wanted to found a scientific socialism. Anarchism was, to Kropotkin, 'a world-concept based upon a mechanised explanation of all phenomena, embracing the whole of nature ... Its method of investigation is that of the exact natural sciences.'[29]

A universalistic anarchist science would yield a system of ethics, grounded in biology and a true understanding of nature. During the 1880s and 1890s Kropotkin had tackled the massive task of creating a moral philosophy for anarchism, in the face of Nietzschean and Darwinian 'amoralism'. He returned to it in his last three years, after his return to Russia, when secluded in the village of Dmitrov from 1918. There he watched the Russian revolution hurtle off course (off the classical anarchist course), and he saw even greater need for an ethic that would provide a naturalistic ideology for the revolution. His unfinished *Ethics*, published posthumously in 1922, declaimed that man had been freed by science from 'supernatural hypotheses and the metaphysical 'mythology of ideas' ... He can derive his ideals from Nature and he can draw the necessary strength from the study of its life.'[30]

A lifelong student of the moralists, from Plato to Hume and Mill, Kropotkin was aware of the logical difficulties in naturalistic ethics. He riposted that it was less absurd to search for sanctions for right behaviour in nature and human nature, than it was to appeal to some external system of absolute values or metaphysical imperatives. These, on analysis, resolved anyway into formalisations of the mutual aid principle in nature. He believed that it was vital – but not sufficient – to give a naturalistic explanation of the origin of the moral instinct. This account would be couched in terms of the selective advantage of the mutual aid factor. However such an explanation did not translate logically into normative conclusions ('is' did not imply 'ought' as Hume and others had shown).

He tried a resolution in terms of evolutionary teleology. Humans acted morally when they acted in consonance with cosmic evolutionary forces – that is, in accord with the mutual aid principle, the ultimate agency of natural progress: 'It is the main factor in the progressive evolution of the animal kingdom in the development of longevity, intelligence, and of that which we call the higher type in the chain of living creatures' (p. 15). Science – because it was capable of unlocking the secrets of nature, capable of a 'deeper penetration into the *life of man and his destinies*' – could yield a 'realistic ethics' suitable for modern man (p. 5). If there were deterministic possibilities here, images of humanity swept along by great evolutionary-historical currents, Kropotkin held that humans retained the power of moral choice. They were steadily expanding their control over nature: 'science has taught man how powerful mankind is in its progressive march, if it skilfully utilizes the unlimited energies of Nature' (p. 4). In the anarchist utopia the distinction between determinism and free will would simply fade away, as the structures that had hindered the free expression of man's social instincts disappeared. People would have every incentive to act freely in accord with a cooperative natural law and their own sociable human nature.

Kropotkin spent many years in exile in Britain, where his ideas helped to generate a good deal of optimistic social evolutionism. Even Benjamin Kidd, increasingly prone to a doomsday economism that prophesied a global contest between the great powers for resources, wavered between angst and a millenarian faith that the world was becoming more ethical and peace-loving. In his *Two Principal Laws of Sociology* (1907–8), Kidd predicted a future of big states and empires, looking ultimately to one organic commonwealth governed by a futuristic and cooperative ethic. Although Darwinian science had combined with capitalist economics to make society materialistic and violent, the west still represented 'the enfranchisement of the future in the evolutionary process'. Despite the colossal arms race, and 'the taunt that force is everywhere omnipotent', Kidd believed that:

the social consciousness has been so deepened in our civilization that it is almost impossible that one nation should attempt to conquer and subdue another after the manner of the ancient world. It would be regarded as so great an outrage that it would undoubtedly prove to be one of the maddest and one of the most unprofitable adventures in which a civilized State could engage.[31]

Kidd's belief now seems a museum piece from an era predating total war. But many others were similarly sanguine, as John Haynes Holmes, the American pacifist, remembered in 1916, in the midst of the holocaust:

The mind of the world in the opening years of the twentieth century was most emphatically an optimistic mind. It beheld serious obstacles being overcome, knotty problems being solved, remote ideals being realised. It seems to see humanity, after centuries of wandering in the wilderness, now nearing the borders of the promised land. Long a barbarian, man had spoken as a barbarian; but now, if the signs were valid, man was becoming civilised, and lo, with his attainment to civilisation, he was resolutely putting away barbarous things...most forward-looking persons had come to believe that, so numerous and powerful were the forces making for peace, the old perpetual menace of international conflict had at last passed by forever.

Then came 1914: 'we awakened... to discover that we were still barbarians'.[32]

Jacques Novicow and 'scientific pacifism'

Novicow's was one of the most influential affirmations of anti-war evolutionism. We find his ideas rehashed constantly in popular science and peace propaganda, and reflected in serious speculation, right up to 1920 and beyond. Jacques Novicow (1849–1912) was a Russian-born, French-trained sociologist, a Kropotkinite and spirited critic of the conflict theories of Gumplowicz and Ratzenhofer. His distaste for force owed much to his early experiences under Tsarist despotism. As a young emigré to France he imbibed Enlightenment liberalism and an aversion to Bismarck's militarism.

He set out to study systematically the expressions of struggle and association – the universal laws of all things – at various levels, distinguishing between selective processes in animal as compared with human societies, and separating the biological from the social domain. He attacked the conflict Darwinists for uncritically applying biological criteria to social data. The narrow concept of the struggle for existence as a matter of bloody confrontation became less appropriate as the evolutionary ladder was scaled. If killing and predation were normal for animals, they were less adaptive in human societies. Humans had the possibility of rationally controlling and using resources, and wars were a 'disassociating' force that needed to be curbed. Novicow held that a genuine Darwinian interpretation of human evolution placed its emphasis upon a broadly conceived competitive process that included adaptation to environment, and factors such as social sympathy and co-operation. The movement was from lower levels of physiological, economic and political struggle to the elevated reaches of intellectual competition. This insight was to strike far and wide, indeed became a cliché in peace circles.

This is not to suggest that Novicow was a facile optimist. Each phase of struggle (he said) was affected by slow, irrational forces as well as by more progressive factors. Thus piratical, plundering modes of operation still occurred in the economic struggle alongside the more orderly methods of exchange. In world politics, conquering and warring modes contrasted with the peaceful building of ever-wider federations. The intellectual struggle was capable also of being waged at the authoritarian level: wars of ideas became wars of persecution and coercion of one school or civilisation by another, instead of the more elevating spread of ideas and ideals by free exchange. In this respect Novicow, despite his mutualist biology, was anti-socialist, since socialist ideology was coercive. In *Les luttes entre sociétés humaines* (*The Struggle Among Human Societies*, 1893), he hoped that the quicker-acting rational forces were predominating, as conflict became more intellectualised. There was a sort of snowball effect, since the most advanced civilisations were, almost by definition, those that welcomed the intense battle of ideas, where conflict was of the beneficial rational kind that led to greater human sympathy and justice.

In works such as *La guerre et ses preténdus bienfaits* (Paris, 1894), translated into English as *War and its Alleged Benefits* (1912), and *La critique du darwinisme social* (Paris, 1910), Novicow attacked supposedly Darwinian doctrines that considered 'collective homicide' as the mainspring of progress, and he exposed the economic, moral and biological waste of war. Like Kropotkin he rejected the 'anthropological romance' that early/primitive man was inherently warlike. He denied also that war had produced the state (rather than exchange of goods and services). War had always caused negative selection (Novicow ignored all contrary theories in this regard). It was the fit and brave who had always gone off to fight and die, the cowardly, sick and deformed who were left behind to propagate. The vanquished were commonly not killed, but made slaves who reproduced. The victors may have impregnated the enemy women, thus furthering their race domination, but this did not apply in modern warfare. He pointed to the decline in marriages between embittered French and Germans since the war of 1870 (ignoring rape and 'illicit' liaisons). Modern recruitment methods rejected the unfit, and ensured that 'the very flower of each generation are chosen for the butcheries'. Overall Novicow preferred a libertarian rather than a militarist social system, one where the free operation of sexual passion, combined with harsh economic competition, would advantage the strong and handsome, while killing off the inferior.[33]

Novicow favoured a European federation of states. This might contain warfare caused by rampant nationalism, and was in line with the trend of evolution towards the progressive expansion of association.[34] Like Comte and the Fabians, he put his faith in a cultivated elite that would persuade the people of the benefits of peace, that would hasten social evolution towards its goal of non-violent intellectual life. He justified this elitism from his organic theory: society was like a living organism and the elite – the experts and social scientists – were akin to the creature's nervous system, regulating and governing the living totality. Novicow himself became a fervent peace activist. He believed that the European masses were sound. In fact he wrote in 1912 that 'from the Ural Mountains to the Atlantic, the Europeans have the utmost horror of conscription and war'. However activism was essential. There were sinister minorities with a vested interest in aggression; and, anyway, according to his theory, relapse was always possible to lower and less desirable, irrational modes of competition.[35]

Novicow's 'scientific pacifism' became virtually the orthodoxy of French and German peace movements in the pre-1914 years. Charles Richet, leading French physiologist and eugenist, dismissed war as an outmoded evolutionary factor in his *Peace and War* (1906), in which he openly attacked the whole idea of 'war instincts' and anticipated Margaret Mead's celebrated dictum that war was a human invention rather than a biological necessity.[36] Novicow seems to have played an essential role in leading German pacifists to embrace the ideal of a federated Europe as the world's best hope for peace, in contrast to the French preference for a juridical solution along the lines of the Hague convention.[37] Alfred Fried, a one-time disciple of Bertha von Suttner and devotee of Bloch, was so impressed by Novicow's *Die Föderation Europas* (Berlin, 1901) that he became Novicow's German translator and publicist. However, despite Novicow's warnings, Novicovian peace ideas always ran the risk of generating a comfortable inertia, given that struggle was being 'inevitably' sublimated into peaceful competition, nations 'inevitably' evolving into the higher organic forms of continental federations or a world state. As

G. K. Chesterton observed: 'No political activity can be encouraged by saying that progress is natural and inevitable; that is not a reason for being active, but rather a reason for being lazy.'[38] It has been claimed that positivistic peace theories such as Novicow's threatened to undermine idealism and activism within the German peace movement, generating reactions such as the neo-Kantian revival within the German Peace Society.[39]

In Britain David Ritchie and Charles Harvey were also predicting world peace through imperial federations or a world state. D. G. Ritchie, a philosophy professor at St Andrews, and an innovative 'new liberal' theorist, combined Novicovian biology with a less liberal sympathy for British imperialism and 'realism' about war. Ritchie was a rationalist who had absorbed T. H. Green's Oxford idealism whilst at Balliol in the seventies, and he had debated evolutionary ethics in his widely read *Darwinism and Politics* (1889). He launched an onslaught upon *laissez-faire* politics, using biological arguments. The evolution of consciousness had enabled humans to attain to 'superorganic' evolution, to circumscribe the struggle for existence, to discover, control, and even to deny allegiance to the laws of nature, which were non-moral.[40] Customs such as war were 'natural' only in being primitive forms of the struggle for existence between races and nations, not in the sense of something that 'ought' to be. Primordial customs that survived after circumstances had changed could become hurtful, and far-sighted cultures discarded them.

Ritchie's book indicates how well entrenched had become the tenets of peace biology by the nineties. Ritchie paraded them deftly. Survival of the fittest (he said) meant not strongest, or ethically best, but merely best adapted to conditions. The largest and fiercest animals were not necessarily the most adaptive: 'The insignificant many more easily find food and escape enemies.' Struggle between races could result in backward evolution, degeneration, or the triumph of the cruel and despotic: 'The cruel polity of the bees, the slave-holding propensities of certain species of ants have their analogue in human societies.' At the same time, there were signs that selective premium had been placed upon man's developing social instincts and group morality, that human evolution was moving towards emancipation from heredity and mitigation of fierceness.[41] More avant garde was Ritchie's suggestion that cultural 'variations' – differences in mores, ideas, institutions – might be subject to selection in a climate of incessant debate and dissent, in much the same way that physical variations were subject to natural selection. Changes such as international arbitration, or economic co-operation, might prove to be the first of a set of variations that – if they proved their fitness – would bring about a new species of civilised society.[42]

Ritchie, however, sometimes sounded more militaristic, especially at the time of the Boer War, when he dubbed war as 'the great maker of nations ... a harsh form of dialectic, a rough measure of solving hard problems'. Races that triumphed in war, that gave security to subject peoples or spread civilisation over great portions of the globe, justified themselves at the bar of history as displaying superior discipline, moral and intellectual qualities. It was senseless to expect, as pacifists did, that the political map of 1900 should be frozen in time. Ritchie drew up hierarchies of war (rather in the style of the young Bertrand Russell). Wars of liberation and nationality were 'higher' than dynastic rivalries; wars fought by citizen-armies 'higher' than those waged by mercenaries. The next lofty stage might well be dominated by a few great empires, in which self-governing communities controlled the less advanced races, 'preparing the way for a federation of the world'.[43]

It is fascinating to trace configurations of militarism, and to map divergent logics, within the peace discourse. Charles Harvey's curious book *The Biology of British Politics* (1904) illustrates the point. Like Ritchie, Harvey switched disconcertingly between a positivist pacifism and a Pearsonite militarism; but unlike Ritchie he embraced 'biologism', treated nations as organisms, and believed that he had found the grand laws of history by subjecting it to applied biology and the law of 'association'. Human history began with hominid violence and chaotic individualism, and became 'a record of the continual substitution of combination for competition', culminating in an international state.[44] The break-up of the Roman empire was followed by ceaseless struggle between its fragments, absorption of weaker by stronger peoples, until the balance of power principle was arrived at: 'a kind of working theory established itself as the rule of European natural relations' (p. 146). It was creatively breached by Napoleon, whose ambitions caused a reactive combination of powers, the 'Concert of Europe': 'Napoleon rendered the life of Europe organic' (p. 127). The nineteenth century witnessed a dialectical dance between expansive nationality and steadily triumphant associationism. Humans were now in the final, most anguished stage, trying to emerge from state and imperial rivalry into world state. Harvey grew as lyrical as Cobden and Buckle about telegraphs and steamships, copyright con-ferences and peace congresses, Hague conventions and world courts, emblems of coming human unity. In fact Harvey felt that 'at the opening of the twentieth century we see in existence what is in reality an international state, practically identical with civilisation' (p. 143).

However, the dialectic demanded action from progressive, but also violent, nation-empires. Harvey rivalled Pearson in calling for coherence and social reform within nations, since these were the roads to 'external

efficiency'. His naturalistic defence of socialist reform turned the degenerationist thesis on its head. Social reform – rather than lessening fitness –
enabled society better to adapt to its milieu, and thus gave it power in the
global struggle. It was unruly individualism, allowing nature free play, that
led to deterioration: 'suspension of the individual struggle is necessary for
the more efficient struggle of the collective whole' (p. 155). Both social
reform and militarism were rooted in the instinct of self-preservation.
Armaments, however unpleasant, were 'a part of the same cosmic process
which developed a lion's claws' (p. 158). Harvey hoped that the great
powers would ultimately form a higher community, forsaking some
liberties for the common good, as did social units lower down the
evolutionary scale.

Norman Angell, whose antennae were sensitive, quickly took up
Novicow's ideas. Characteristically, he claimed to have arrived at the basic
insights independently; but he read *La critique du darwinisme social* hot
from the Paris press in 1910 and included large slabs of it in *The Great
Illusion*. He went on to 'puff' Novicow's writings in his pacifist lectures and
activities.[45] It is worthy of note that in their influential compendia of
pacifist polemics against war, publicists like Angell and Hiram M.
Chittenden regularly gave prominence, but rarely top billing, to biological
refutations of Bernhardi and militant Social Darwinists.[46] Angell attacked
Bernhardi, Steinmetz, von Stengel and Renan, as well as the Americans
Homer Lea and Theodore Roosevelt. He deeply believed that it was
essential to rebut the dangerous doctrines that war was a biological
necessity, or that man was an unchangeable 'fighting animal'. Yet overall
Angell is remembered for his economic, rather than his biological, thesis.
This is what struck a chord with his contemporaries too (although
reviewers duly recorded his assault on the Social Darwinist image of man).
All of this is fair comment about the limits to the biological debate on war.
There is an intriguing parallel with Bernhardi, whose war biology was
subsidiary to his *Weltmacht* philosophy – although ironically he was to be
remembered for his flamboyance on the lesser theme. In a practical
political sense, the British peace movement used texts from Novicow and
the peace eugenists as ammunition in the good fight, and no doubt most
genuinely subscribed to a nobler biological image of humankind than their
foes; but their everyday preoccupation was with tactics and strategy,
traditional moral-political notions, and more tangible propaganda issues
such as the economic. Nevertheless the flood of books and articles on war
biology in the generation before 1914 attests to an abiding general interest
in the question of man, nature and violence.

Angell proclaimed man's irresistible drift away from conflict, towards
greater intellectualism and completer adaptation to the environment:

The planet is man's prey. Man's struggle is the struggle of the organism, which is human society, in its adaptation to its environment, the world – not the struggle between different parts of the same organism.

War was both biological and economic disaster under modern conditions. Total war saw the carefully selected elite of two populations exterminated by battle and disease. There was a distinctly racist element in Angell's opposition to imperial war, as there was in much American peace eugenics. Foreshadowing 'yellow peril' doctrine, he blamed British conquest in India, Egypt and Asia for 'race conservation' that might eventually lead to an Asiatic takeover globally:

When we 'overcome' the servile races, far from eliminating them, we give them added chances of life by introducing order, etc., so that the lower human quality tends to be perpetuated by conquest by the higher.

Despite evidence that war was being revolutionised by science, Angell had difficulty in seeing any nexus between scientific-technological capacity and potential for militarism. He stuck to the Spencerean view that the scientific-industrial phase was a step above the militant society, and passionately defended commercial culture against Homer Lea and critics who saw only effeteness, materialism and spineless pacifism in the bourgeois state.[47] Angell viewed the leading industrial nations, even Germany, as essentially non-militarist. How could modern life 'with its overpowering proportion of industrial activities and its infinitesimal production of military, keep alive the instincts associated with war as against those developed by peace'?

Angell wavered on pugnacious instincts. He did not rule out the possibility that they were an inherent part of the human constitution. But he preferred to highlight the significance of cultural factors in modifying 'human nature', which was not fixed but malleable. The First World War and subsequent world history deepened his fear of biologically-rooted aggression in humans. However, instinct should be subject to cultural restraint and social intelligence, in international affairs just as in the ordinary world of police courts and parliaments. Behaviour was a mix of biological and environmental factors. One had only to look at the great variety in society and behaviours to realise how profoundly humans could be changed 'by the force of new ideas, new readings of experience, education, suggestion, institutions, conventions, disciplines'. Convinced that war was the ultimate waste of resources, Angell dedicated his life to education for peace and global control of war, receiving the Nobel peace prize in 1933.[48]

The birth of peace eugenics

If Novicovian biology pictured a comfortingly natural progression from brutish struggle to intellectual trial, and stressed the opportunity of moulding a plastic human nature by means of social controls, genetic theory fostered visions of history dictated by unchangeable biological forces, man dominated by genes, scenarios of primordial pugnacity and incessant warfare. As I have suggested above (chapter 3), peace eugenics drew sustenance from the new biology. In doing so it created both propaganda reinforcement and discursive tensions within the wider discourse of peace biology.

In one sense peace eugenics consolidated mainstream tradition by portraying war as dysgenic, and probably fated to pass away as humankind ascended the scale of civilisation. It was the streak of genetic determinism within peace eugenics that was worrisome to peace liberals. Even here, however, there was ambiguity. Peace eugenics also exploited that side of hereditarian discourse that favoured control over, rather than submission to, biological law; that favoured the use of human ingenuity to enable man to escape from a 'natural' situation of chance and *laissez-faire*, of waste and unknown consequences, into a more scientific world that recognised genetic realities and manipulated them in order to create an improved human stock and future. Peace eugenics envisaged the birth of a new moral order by short-circuiting nature through the use of reason and science, which were also part of the evolutionary inheritance. Humans were not bound by the law of the jungle, or any morality of nature. War would be solved by human policy and eugenic engineering. This was consistent generally with late-century enthusiasm for 'biological sociology', with its faith that social problems had biological solutions. Such faith was widespread among British and American geneticists, well to the fore in the eugenics movement.[49]

The peace eugenists resisted war because of its disastrous genetic effects, which they tried to demonstrate by daring sweeps through history as well as by more disciplined, if still controversial, empirical studies. Darwin's *Descent of Man* (1871) was the essential starting point, with its biological arguments against conscription and standing armies as inducing negative selection.[50] In the pre-war generation a whole school of pacifist eugenics was built upon this foundation, and raised great waves in the Anglo-American world. David Starr Jordan, Vernon L. Kellogg, Havelock Ellis and Norman Angell figured in the debate, and not only in peace circles. They penetrated into, if they did not necessarily capture, the eugenics movement. The English Eugenics Society constantly debated the eugenics of war. Jordan's works, for example, were quickly published in British eugenic journals, while Jordan himself lectured to British eugenic circles, including a salon at the Duchess of Marlborough's Sunderland House in 1913. Kellogg's work also gained wide currency in Britain. His address on 'Eugenics and Militarism', given to the First International Eugenics Congress held in London in 1912, roused a considerable storm.[51]

Roland Hugins remarked in 1914 that the pacifists had enlisted 'the youngest of the social sciences', eugenics, to show that war had led to 'cacogenic' or dysgenic selection. He deemed Jordan's *The Human Harvest* (1907) to be 'the text-book of this theory in English'.[52] David Starr Jordan (1851–1931) was arguably the highest profile scientific propagandist against war in the prelude to World War I. His ideas were spread in a torrent of popular works including *The Human Harvest, War's Aftermath* (1914), *War and Waste* (1914) and *War and the Breed* (1915). He lectured widely in the Anglo-American world, and published many articles on war in scientific and popular journals.[53] Jordan was a rare type: a pacifist university president. He combined political Progressivism with entrenched capitalist and racist values, and was a somewhat pompous figure whose fulsome prose and less than rigorous science led him to oddly radical conclusions. An eminent ichthyologist, a student of the famous Harvard zoologist Louis Agassiz, Jordan had clawed his way from humble beginnings in New York State to the presidency of the newly-formed Stanford University in California. A man of imposing figure and voice, much loved by his fellows, he crusaded endlessly in the United States and abroad for world peace.

Jordan preached a mixture of Galtonian eugenics, Cobdenite economics and Progressivist conspiracy theory. He portrayed war as a biological disaster, a threat to global economic interdependence, plotted by sinister interest groups. He shared the Progressivists' suspicion of politics – sordid, corrupt, self – interested – and applied his suspicions globally. Wars had no fundamental causes. They were sparked off by an 'Invisible Empire' of big corporations, arms merchants, military establishments, 'contractors, adventurers and ghouls', politicians and civil service moguls. Jordan was a fierce opponent of the theory of deterrence. Arms races only heightened jealousies between peoples. The more soldiers, guns, warships and missiles that neighbouring countries used to 'defend' themselves, the more likely a clash. Jordan's preferred model was the Canadian–American border: no soldiers, no scares, no war.

Jordan moaned endlessly about the iniquity of war debts. War had created the world's greatest problem, massive growth of government debt, a crippling burden on this and later generations, making a new class of paupers in Europe, everywhere inhibiting domestic reform and distorting economic growth. Mechanical invention had produced prodigiously expensive new war toys, dreadnoughts, torpedoes, giant guns, warplanes: 'No war can bring financial, social, or political gain to any nation, as the world goes today ... Wars of spoliation, imperial wars, must go the way of international wars, as too costly for the people of a modern industrial state.'[54]

Yet at bottom Jordan was a rock-solid optimist. The heart of western capitalism was sound. The 'Invisible Empire' would not prevail against the whole movement of civilisation 'from strife towards order'. Human history had passed from 'tribal wars, municipal wars, struggles of robber barons, and of rival dynasties, marauding expeditions, holy wars and wars unholy, to relative peace within the borders of the nation'. Disputes were increasingly resolved by arbitration and legal decision. Why not so in the international sphere, the only place where mass killing was still legal? With Manchester School rhetoric Jordan predicted a world in closer compass as world trade expanded, as missionaries, trade commissions and peace congresses brought peoples together in recognition of their common humanity.[55] Jordan homilised the world on this subject from the pulpit of the World Peace Foundation, to which he was appointed founding director in 1910.

Jordan's case reminds us that peace biology was by no means an exclusively leftist or necessarily liberal phenomenon. Jordan's mix of pacifism, elitism, Anglo-Saxonism and capitalism touched responsive chords in the heterogeneous Anglo-American eugenics movement. Peace theory gained an added edge when it was combined with eugenic discourse that appealed to (say) middle-class white professional Americans, a group that was inclined to favour attempts to organise the social order on the basis of 'biological worth', who were attracted to an authoritarian science of social medicine that empowered their own class and race.[56] American eugenics was saturated with the language of racial anxiety, and this tapped into a persistent national tradition of isolationism, with its image of a vibrant American capitalism concentrating peaceably upon its own destiny, avoiding the entanglements of a warring and corrupt Old World. It was not without symbolic import that Charles Davenport's Cold Spring Harbor eugenic research station at Long Island was set up in 1904 with funds provided by the pacifist Carnegie Institution of Washington.[57]

Jordan opposed war as a threat to good old American capitalism, an invitation to class war and revolution globally. It was not so strange, after all, that the president of Stanford safely preached his pacifism to the United States establishment. His eugenics also appealed to existing racial and class stereotypes. He feared racial and class degeneration following imperial wars and great power struggles. His anti-Semitism and anti-immigrant rhetoric struck an immediate response in America's age of the melting-pot, nativism, labour agitation and expansion of empire to include 'inferior' Caribbean and Pacific stock.

In *The Human Harvest*, which he rehashed unashamedly and which the peace movement peddled assiduously, Jordan spoke the idiom of genetic determinism: history was dictated by germ plasm, by 'the blood of a nation'. War was a genetic disaster because it destroyed 'the bravest and the best'.[58] War caused reverse selection and threatened racial decline through the annihilation of a virile, free-born Anglo-Saxon stock: 'like the seed was the harvest'. After wars nations bred from inferior stock, those left at home.[59] Jordan, however, gave little systematic analysis of the eugenics of war, such as we have later in the works of Kellogg, Gini, Johnson, Sorokin and Quincy Wright.

Jordan made cavalier use of classical history, on which he had been bred, picturing the Romans as a vital, free people decimated by incessant imperial warfare. *Vir*, the real man, went forth to battle, while *Homo*, the human being, remained in the farm and begat the new generation: 'The sons of the real man gave place to the sons of scullions, stable-boys, slaves, camp-followers, and the riff-raff'. Thus Rome fell before the vigour of the barbarians. Spain also fell from glory because of war, because (as one writer said of Castile) 'she makes men and wastes them'. Napoleon was one of Jordan's great villains. Not only had he snuffed out French democracy, he had lain waste the flower of Europe, crippling the French nation both culturally and physically.[60] In *War's Aftermath* (1914) Jordan attempted, with indifferent success, to show that the American Civil War had inflicted grave racial damage upon Southern society.[61]

Ultimately it was Jordan's humanitarian rhetoric rather than his science that was effective. His thesis was riddled with disputable assumptions: for example that societies had historically selected the best types, morally and physically, to go to war; that mortality was higher in these groups than in the population at large; that they were effectively prevented from breeding at the normal rate: Jordan used the phrase 'prevented from marrying', prudishly skirting the possibility of extra-marital conceptions, except to hint that war lowered standards by encouraging promiscuity and a semi-legalised system of polygamy.[62]

Critics had a field day exposing his errors and dubious methods. The British anti-pacifist G. G. Coulton alleged, with some justice, that 'Dr Jordan appeals impartially to whichever theory happens to suit his momentary necessities in argument'.[63] Coulton's *Main Illusions of Pacificism* (1916) made a devastating attack upon Jordan that seriously undermined his intellectual authority. Classical scholars disputed his reading of Roman history. Thorstein Veblen rejected his claim that war attracted idealists: rather it drew adventurers and bullies whose loss was of slight racial significance. Others appealed to Mendelian laws, claiming that within two or three generations the survivors of war would have regained the racial average. Jordan in fact was a biologist who fully understood Mendelian theory, even using it to dispute the militarist view that genetic virility could be improved by military drill. This did not stop him using loose Lamarckian reasonings to make debating points.[64]

Jordan ignored the critics and stuck to his guns. Who could deny (he asked) that the loss of millions of soldiers carrying superlative inheritances must have traumatic genetic effects? He liked to move his audiences with an account of his travels through English hamlets and parish churches. Everywhere were tablets in memory of the fallen, gentlemen's sons from Eton and Harrow, Oxford and Cambridge, who had died in some far-off petty war from Zululand to Cambodia:

In the parish churches these records are numbered by the score. In the cathedrals they are recorded by the thousand ... What would be the effect on England if all of these 'unreturning brave' and all that should have been their descendants could be numbered among her sons today?[65]

In an age of mass conscription and heavy firepower, war would annihilate the elite of western manhood, the sturdy Anglo-Saxon type, the natural leaders of society. When the First World War came, it lent terrible new point to his warning. How was it ever possible to replace the 'lost generation' of 1914–18?[66]

Havelock Ellis, the socialist sexologist, tailored Jordan's peace eugenics for the English left and feminism. He suggested that the inexorable progress of civilisation towards law, rather than war, would be reinforced by proletarian threats of a general strike if war became imminent. He also cast women as peacemakers, although noting that women had been delighted spectators of combat in more primitive times.[67] Ellis endorsed the call of another reform eugenist Montague Crackanthorpe for eugenic and demographic controls to curb causes of war such as overcrowding and poverty.[68] Ellis proposed that the warlike spirit was being selected out, as fighting stocks were naturally killed off in wars and the field left to the unwarlike. This was a variant on Veblen's approach. The idea that wars were waged by unpleasant martial types rather than by 'the bravest and best' appealed to part of the psyche of political dissenters. However, as some biologists pointed out, this hypothesis raised the problem that, as the modern period became more peaceful (Ellis subscribed to this), pugnacious martial types were more likely to survive and multiply.[69] Ellis also had a problem with armaments (as did other peace apostles). If social evolution was marching towards peace, why were arms proliferating? He speculated that the inherited timidity of modern peoples, plus their surplus wealth and luxury, had led them to seek the protection of overweening arms:

It is an alarming process because those huge and heavily armed monsters of primeval days who furnish the zoological types corresponding to our modern over-armed states, themselves died out from the world when their unwieldy armament had reached its final point of expansion.[70]

The age of dreadnoughts and Big Berthas encouraged the imagery of dinosaurs and extinction. Ellis's prophetic comment foreshadowed G. F. Nicolai's biological law of 'giganthanasia'. The carnage of World War I led Nicolai to propose that wars, like species, tended to grow larger until they exceeded the limits of primordial possibility and threatened the end of the world.[71]

Vernon L. Kellogg and military selection

The most disciplined and authoritative product of pre-war eugenics came from Jordan's protégé Vernon L. Kellogg, whose classic *Military Selection and Race Deterioration* was researched and publicised well before the war, although it was not published until 1916. It dominated the field until the 1920s and beyond.

Kellogg (1867–1937) was a zoologist, professor of entomology at Stanford 1894–1920. He collaborated with Jordan in a number of textbooks, most notably *Animal Studies* (1905) and *Evolution and Animal Life* (1907). Kellogg had studied at Leipzig and Paris, and was to become well known during the First World War as the Brussels director of the American Commission for Relief in Belgium. His autobiographical history of the commission, *Headquarters Nights*, attacked Germanic neo-Darwinist militarism, and was popular and influential in the United States. Kellogg had in fact been a long-standing pacifist. His polemical *Beyond War* (1912) had derided war as biologically stupid. As a biologist he declared that its like did not exist in nature 'outside the forays of the few degenerate fighting ant species'.[72]

Beyond War was in many ways more fascinating than the more famous *Military Selection*. In it Jordan displayed the ambivalence felt within peace eugenic discourse about determinism. *Beyond War* was in some aspects very deterministic:

Man is in the big brutal grasp of this world force we call Organic Evolution, and every one of his characteristics, physical, mental, and psychic, is subject to the dragging pull of his Evolution master; his maker and his modifier; his nearly absolute overlord.

But, more cheerfully, 'despite lines of degeneration and of sidewise specializations running into *cul-de-sac*', evolution was 'change plus-ward, or upward'. Its 'unescapable line' was towards intelligent altruism. Atavisms like war – 'ancestral vestiges, useless, even disadvantageous'– were still present, causing 'slipbacks in heredity'. But Kellogg hoped that: 'As a species Man may change ... to an animal to whom intraspecific War, at least War of blood and bullets, will be unknown and unthinkable.'[73]

Kellogg's determinism was qualified by his stress on human rationality and malleability. Today's human was both structurally and culturally different from yesterday's, even though substrata of 'primal instincts' were still necessary for life, 'reverberations of ... past struggles':

They are the accumulations of that extraordinary biological memory on which are based our heredity, our capacity to develop from embryo to man, and our instincts.

And almost all of these instincts had been modified ever more 'by that growing, crowning new capacity of ours, the intelligence, reason, self-consciousness, self-control'. Human nature had in fact been transformed, and was no longer (as the militarists would have it) a matter of fixed, pugnacious instincts. Human nature had become human mind: 'It is human tropisms and reflexes and instincts and habits and consciousness and reason and ethics and religion and philosophy', a function of structure impressed by age-long evolutionary control. Kellogg blended this liberal biology with racist eugenics, contending that the Blond or Caucasian races – 'the mode of the species' – exemplified human nature in its most rational and adaptive phase, the basal instincts being largely reduced to feeding and sex drives. In other races there was a balance between raw instincts and reason, while lowest on the scale of peoples human nature was dominated by inherited instincts.[74]

Kellogg's peace biology did not require a 'primal innocence' theory. Anthropologists had been eroding the peace myth of early man; while a new attack had recently come from J. J. Atkinson, who visualised primal law emerging from a homicidal communal situation where the patriarch lived in a state of constant threat from 'deadly rivals of his very own flesh and blood', out to wrench wife and life from the paternal tyrant.[75] The 'primal horde' parricide theory was taken up by William McDougall (1908), and of course by Sigmund Freud in *Totem and Taboo* (1912) offering a sexual theory of war and pugnacity. Kellogg described *Homo primigenius* as a fighting animal, battling cave lions and bears, hunting mammoth and bison, constantly warring with fellow humankind

for the privilege of place and food, and even for that of remaining himself uneaten: for the men of Krapina were cannibals ... Naked, hairy body straining to body, sinewy arm exchanging blow for blow ... a hacked and bleeding testimony to the great law of the Struggle to Live.[76]

Human history then became a dialectical contest between the evolution of altruism and war technology. Now, it seemed, 'The instinct for fighting is dying out of human nature.' Humankind was now characterised biologically by teachability, by adoption of a specialised 'communist' life comparable to that of the social insects, features that had been established by selection and reinforced by tradition. Kellogg passionately called for world peace through rational eugenics, a eugenics that would foster cooperative tendencies, and nurture 'clean-blooded, clear-minded, strong-bodied, disease-resistant, long-living individuals'. War headed his list of 'anti-progressive' tendencies that must be curbed at all costs, war with its 'wasteful, brutal atavistic slaughter of men, degradation of women, wrecking of children, and imperiling of race':

its evolutionary disadvantage to our species, especially in the present high and hence critical stage of our development, and our amazing hesitation to wipe it out – for it is only an element of controllable tradition, not of ineradicable dominating heredity – are matters that the biologist can hardly speak temperately about.[77]

Kellogg's big book *Military Selection and Race Deterioration* stemmed from a Carnegie conference held in Berne in 1912, which set up commissions to foster the scientific study of war. The first commission sponsored the eugenic investigations of Kellogg and his French counterpart Gaston Bodart. Bodart's painstaking research into historic loss of life caused by warfare in Austria-Hungary and France concluded that war deaths had contributed to population stagnation and race decline, especially in France, 'the most warlike nation of modern times'.[78]

Kellogg's study ranged more widely, and made a bigger impact. He gave a condensed account of his work to the First International Eugenics Congress, London 1912, and his findings were canvassed by eugenics societies in Britain and the United States before 1914.[79] When the book finally appeared in 1916, it gave detailed statistics on recruitment, war mortality, disease, physiological and demographic change in European populations in order to document the racial disadvantages of 'exaggerated militarism'. Modern recruitment methods ensured that a superior elite was removed from the population and exposed to death and disease. War also helped the spread of race-deteriorating diseases, notably venereal, among civil populations.

It is instructive to compare *Beyond War* with *Military Selection*, for the comparison indicates how scientific emphasis can be affected by a mediating social theory. In *Beyond War* Kellogg toned down heredity in favour of cultural factors in human evolution, presumably because he wanted to show that humankind was not inescapably burdened by primal aggressive instincts. With man, he said, factors such as 'conscious environing', teaching ('It is the conspicuous characteristic of Man to be teachable'), and control over tradition almost outweighed 'the more strictly evolutionary factors, the actual heritable controls'.[80]

However in *Military Selection* – where Kellogg wanted to show the evil genetic effects of warfare – the tone was markedly more hereditarian. Kellogg admitted that the issue was vexed, but he gauged that a preponderance of biologists and social scientists now favoured heredity over environment 'in the determination of racial characteristics and racial modifications'. It was the character of the stock from which the race reproduced that determined the future of the race. Thus he felt justified, in his study of the eugenic effects of militarism, in concentrating upon heredity, upon selective reproduction within a given population, rather than upon cultural milieu.[81]

Kellogg focused upon the better documented area of recruitment, agreeing that both voluntary systems and conscription ensured the selection of healthier and physically superior types. With Britain's volunteers, for example, half of those seeking to enlist were medically rejected for disease, infirmity or lack of stature, although in such a system the 'better classes' of young men may have avoided service. This hardly applied to the compulsory system of modern France and Germany, where from 30 per cent to 40 per cent of those examined were rejected as physically unfit.[82]

What were the race-effects of deliberately selecting an elite for armed service? Kellogg thought them vital. Firstly, the removal of an exclusively male elite from the population disturbed the sex equilibrium, preventing 'normal and advantageous' sexual selection. This claim was to generate controversy.[83] Next, the elite was of the age of greatest life expectancy, sexual vigour and fecundity. These men were banished, temporarily or permanently, from their needed function of race perpetuation, the task taken over by the less fit retained in the civil population. The negative hereditary effects could not be regarded as negligible, given that standing armies in Germany and France included more than 5 per cent of each country's men aged between eighteen and thirty-five, a proportion that would rise materially in a big war. Kellogg neglected the capacity of populations historically to make up losses after war, a criticism often made by demographers.

Kellogg showed that historically armies suffered higher death rates than civil populations, even during peacetime, mainly because of the higher incidence of disease within armies. This phenomenon was quite marked until the 1900s. Death-dealing diseases such as typhoid and dysentery were associated with barrack and camp life; for example, typhoid deaths averaged 30 per 10,000 annually in the French home army during the 1870s and 1880s, whereas the figure for the civil population was only 5 per 10,000. Since then medical advances and sanitary engineering had helped cause a marked improvement in army health. In 1909, for the first time, the death rate in the British army fell below that for males aged twenty in the civil population.[84]

Even before the carnage of World War I, Kellogg was able to document the heavy battle casualties occasioned by war. In a score of bloody battles in the last three centuries, losses of dead and wounded amounted to between 20 per cent and 35 per cent of the combatants. At Waterloo the French lost 36 per cent, the English and Prussians 31 per cent. Over five million men were lost in the twenty years of the wars of the French Revolution and Empire. Losses by disease far exceeded losses by gunfire. Napoleon several times lost up to half an army from disease. In the month of January 1855, during the Crimean War, the English army lost more men from disease than people who died in London from the Great Plague during the terrible month of September 1665. Unsanitary camps, crowding, exposure to infected food and water, the strain of prolonged fighting, long marches and sieges created conditions of high morbidity. Returning soldiers also spread race-deteriorating diseases such as typhus and smallpox among the civil population.

Kellogg was a pioneer in insisting upon close scrutiny of the categories of mortality caused by war. He was scornful of the muddled thinking on this subject by 'extreme' Darwinists such as Otto Ammon, the anti-socialist Karlsruhe engineer and Aryan racial theorist who introduced Galton's eugenics into Germany. Ammon argued in such works as *Zur Anthropologie der Badener* (1899), surveying 28,000 military recruits, that degeneration awaited any race that did not experience high mortality in the struggle for life.[85] Kellogg pointed out that war selection was complex. His study indicated that mortality by gunfire was probably non-selective (if anything, perhaps removing the braver and hardier). However, because such mortality worked upon an already selected group, its total influence tended to be dysgenic. As to mortality in armies by disease, this might perhaps be regarded as destroying the weaker and less immune. However, again, such mortality affected an already selected group, above average for vigour and health. Any reduction of these numbers was a eugenic loss to the population.[86]

During the nineteenth century medical and anthropological scholars (such as Villerme, Bodin, Broca, Livi, and Ammon) had accumulated much physiological data about European populations. Kellogg tested his hypothesis from this evidence. He focused upon what he thought to be an excellent sample, not racially homogenous, socially varied and all exposed to the selective effects of conscription and war. This was a series of data from 1816 on the stature and physical condition of twenty-year-old French recruits, contained in the official *Comptes rendus du recrutement*. These statistics indicated that average height began noticeably to decrease with the coming of age, from 1813 on, of males born in the years of the Revolutionary wars (1793–1802). Average height continued to decrease in the following years with the coming to age of youths born during the wars of the Empire. However, youths born after the end of these 'terrible man-draining wars' showed a genetic improvement. By their adulthood in the later 1830s and 1840s they averaged one inch higher than the war-born generation. Less conclusive, however, was a study of recruits' health, judged by exemptions for infirmities.[87] Kellogg concluded that the wars had had a more serious degenerative effect upon vigour than stature in the immediate post-war era. His claim that the French had been genetically crippled by extended warfare was to become almost eugenic folklore for decades.[88]

Military Selection also fostered alarm that militarism spread venereal diseases that had race-weakening effects. From 1865 to 1872 the hospital admissions of soldiers in the United Kingdom for VD averaged more than one case to every five men. The prevalence of VD was highest in the Russian, British and especially the American armies, lowest in the German army.[89] Generally rates of VD were markedly worse in military than civil populations. Moreover venereal diseases – especially syphilis and gonorrhoea – produced dreadful effects (ranging from paralysis, congenital blindness, idiocy, insanity, to chronic invalidism and barrenness in women) that were virtually heritable in their impact. Syphilis, for example, was transmitted from man to woman, from woman to her children, and from these children to their children. Gonorrhoea passed from man to woman, and could result in barrenness on the part of the woman or blindness in her children. Moreover as VD had a low death rate, it did not select out its victims by death. It did not kill but ruined its victims and contaminated others, including later generations. Soldiers not killed in service returned 'attainted and racially dangerous' to the general population: 'It is a very harmful influence on the species, and it is an influence strongly fostered by militarism.'[90]

5 The First World War: man the fighting animal

Instinct theory and *Homo pugnax*

The holocaust of 1914–18 did not transform the debate over the biology of war, but it lent terrible new meaning to the dry formulations of the ante-bellum years and gave theories of human violence a new lease of life. As the Oxford pragmatist F. C. S. Schiller later remarked, the war 'revealed all too clearly how ferociously unchanged beneath the thin veneer of civilization lurked the old *bête humaine*, and how illusory was the belief in moral progress'.[1] The bestiality of events lent new intensity to the mythology of the Beast Within, which was now encoded anew in biological terms.[2]

Wartime theories in a range of disciplines presented man as a 'fighting anima' whose primal instincts were tragically at odds with advanced culture, thus anticipating Freudian analysis and E. O. Wilson's present-day sociobiology. Instinct theory – which stemmed from animal psychology, physiology and the genetics revolution – encouraged the belief that pugnacity had been programmed into the ancient part of the human brain as a result of evolutionary pressures dating from prehistory. War was seen to be instinct-driven. Endemic violence and genocidal fighting were postulated as eugenic forces in early human evolution. 'Fighting animal' theory was closely associated with 'flawed humanity' theory that pointed the way to Arthur Koestler's concept of 'schizophysiology' and Paul McLean's 'triune brain'. War was explained in distinctly modern sociobiological terms as adaptive behaviour springing from territorial urges, crowding, competition for resources and reproductive advantage, ethnocentrism and pseudo-speciation.

Nineteenth-century talk of human instincts tended to be loose, using notions of compulsive feelings and elemental desires ('primitive volitions or cravings, or what the Germans call "Triebe"', commented William Morton Wheeler in 1910).[3] Of course there had always been analogies drawn between human and animal traits, and phrenology had anticipated the future by trying to locate instincts (such as pugnacity) on brain maps.

130

The later century saw more systematic – and more controversial – efforts to define terms, to establish comparisons with animals, and to detect physiological sources of 'instinctive' behaviour. The English zoologist Conwy Lloyd Morgan located the inherited basis for instincts in an organism's central nervous system. He refined and expanded Spencer's usage of instinct as 'compounded reflex'. Morgan defined instinct as 'an organised train or sequence of co-ordinated activities by the individual in common with all members of the same more or less restricted group'.[4] (Thus many people concluded from the events of 1914–18 that bellicosity was a species-specific instinct for humans.) Coordination involved in instinctive behaviour, and the transmission of physiological impulses to the viscera and vascular systems was 'the primary function of the lower brain centres'.[5] The American philosopher–psychologist H. Rutgers Marshall included an evolutionary dimension in his definition of instinct. He defined instinctive activities as the result of coordinations inherited with an animal's neural structure, and tending 'to subserve some biological end which has been of advantage to its ancestors'.[6]

The more stringent instinct theory of the *fin de siècle* owed much to animal psychology, which was being pioneered by the invertebrate physiologist and Darwinist George Romanes (*Animal Intelligence*, 1882; *Mental Evolution in Animals*, 1883; *Mental Evolution in Man*, 1887), and, with more sophistication, by Lloyd Morgan (*Animal Life and Intelligence*, 1890; *Habit and Instinct*, 1896). These works explored the continuities – and the differences – between animal and human instincts, intelligence and consciousness. The experiments of Douglas Spalding and Lloyd Morgan appeared to show that inherited nervous organisations underlay instinctive behaviour in animals (chicks, ducklings, etc.). Morgan's work also indicated the importance of the learning process in modifying instinct.[7]

Medical research seemed to confirm the claim, made by the psychiatrist Henry Maudsley in 1870, that there was 'truly a brute brain within the man's'.[8] Cambridge-trained Charles Sherrington's ground-breaking *Integrative Action of the Nervous System* (1906) claimed that reflex and instinctive responses in organisms (including humans) derived from the lower brain centres. Following the lead of Darwin and Spencer, Sherrington held that the bodily expressions of primary emotions such as anger – stemming from heart, blood vessels, respiratory muscles and secretory glands – were 'instinctive actions reminiscent of ancestral ways of life'.[9] They arose as behaviours useful to the animal for defence, escape, seizure, etc. It was not long before instincts associated functionally with the lower brain centres – including human aggression – were being described in the general literature as the evolutionary legacy of primal experience long ago in human and pre-human history. Atavistic readings of human nature were readily generated from such apparently 'hard science'.

In an important sense such readings did less than justice to these experimenters. They tried to avoid reductionism, or a downplaying of human consciousness. Romanes was in fact criticised (even by his friend Morgan) for the fault of anthropomorphism, attributing human qualities of consciousness to animals, the opposite sin to reductionism.[10] Echoing Darwin on man, Morgan judged that 'of definite instinctive performance he inherits perhaps a smaller share than any other organism'. Man, he said, was 'a reflective being who frames ideals of conduct', who could avoid the constraints of natural selection and 'organic thraldom'.[11] Sherrington's physiology placed the lower primal centres in humans under the regimentation of the brain. He held man to be 'the highest organism' in the sense that humans dominated the environment 'more variously and extensively' than other species.[12]

Along with animal psychology and medicine, the genetics revolution also contributed to the fashion for hard instinct theory, especially with its claim that human behaviour was governed by innate, unlearned faculties. As already narrated, Weismann's idea of 'an inviolate, eternal germ plasm, uninfluenced by the life history of the carrier organism' (surely foreshadowing Richard Dawkins' 'selfish gene') biologised the study of human behaviour, and focused attention on instinctive and heritable human traits that were supposedly embedded in the germ plasm.[13]

Germ plasm theory provided a devastating new tool for breaking down the walls between animal and human behaviour. No longer could human instincts be readily sequestered from the automatic patterned behaviour seen to be characteristic of animals. The germ plasm was believed to hold the secret of man's 'innate' instinct of pugnacity, to illuminate the origins of such traits in the primal and animal past of humanity. Animal studies before the war, such as R. M. Yerkes's experiments on cats and rats, concluded forcefully that 'savageness' or 'killing instinct' was instinctive, in Yerkes's phrase a 'heritable behavior complex'.[14]

Such evidence was readily extrapolated to humanity. Pugnacity (or its equivalent) was regularly included in the lists of human instincts that were compiled at the time. Some of these lists became inordinately long (Luther Bernard's *Instinct*, 1924, found hundreds of usages). J. R. Angell's *Psychology* (1904) located seventeen human instincts, including anger and hunting. He classed hunting among the 'disintegrating instincts', while William James associated the fighting and hunting instincts.[15] William McDougall's *Introduction to Social Psychology* (1908) listed eleven human instincts, including pugnacity, self-assertion and flight. The Columbia psychologist Edward Thorndike broke down McDougall's instinct of pugnacity into seven instincts, including combat in rivalry, fighting during courtship and counterattack.[16] Letourneau linked aggression with an instinct of property, one of 'the most primordial of needs', that led to territorial drives and constant warfare for space and resources.[17]

James Rowland Angell, a colleague of the behaviourist John B. Watson at the University of Chicago and exceptionally well versed in contemporary psychological theory, envisaged humans as sharing with animals instinct/emotions that emanated from an 'ancestral source' and were blueprinted into the brain. They were 'racial habits transmitted by heredity' but shaped by situational factors: 'reactions which express the pressure of untold ages of man, or his pre-human ancestors, engaged in the struggle for existence'. Human pugnacity stemmed from instincts of anger and fear (Ribot's 'egoistic feelings'),[18] and involved a series of elaborate organic activities of 'the unpremeditated hereditary type'. In anger, instinctive reactions were triggered by the appropriate stimuli: brows became wrinkled, the face crimson, veins gorged, nostrils dilated, lips drawn back, the teeth set and hands clenched – the individual was prepared for combat. Angell felt that such 'instinctive discharges', once of evolutionary use to the race, had now become disadvantageous to modern humanity. Warfare arose from the 'pugnacious element' within anger: 'The evolution of the race has been notoriously sanguinary, and we should feel no surprise... that under the excitement of actual combat the old brute should display the cloven hoof.'[19]

Henry Rutgers Marshall also believed that humans shared with animals inherited 'instinct feelings' that underpinned 'fight/flight' patterns of behaviour. But he added a prophetic insight when he explained the self-sacrificing behaviour of warriors in terms of biological sacrifice, a form of extreme altruism that paid off in 'tribal advantage', or what sociobiologists now call inclusive fitness of the group. Fighting instincts in man were an example of group 'instinct actions', common to the higher mammalia, that worked for the biological good of the tribe. In war men lay aside personal safety to join with their fellows to oppose a common tribal enemy. Soldiers helped their wounded comrades at the risk of their own lives, sparing no pain 'so long as they thereby aid one of their own kin'. Among 'tribal instincts of a higher type' Marshall included 'the patriotic instinct', which was aroused by aggressive threats from neighbouring nations, or by 'opportunity for tribal aggrandisement'.[20]

William James, like that other founding father of functional psychology William McDougall, subscribed to pugnacious instinct theory. He stated flatly: 'Man is once for all a fighting animal... A millennium of peace would not breed the fighting disposition out of our bone and marrow.'[21] James told a World Peace Congress in 1904: 'Our permanent enemy is the noted bellicosity of human nature.' Man, biologically considered, was 'simply the most formidable of all beasts of prey, and, indeed, the only one that preys systematically on its own species'.[22] Primal hunting men had found war both profitable (loot, females) and exciting, and these ingrained feelings persisted despite the irrationality and horror of modern war: 'The horrors make the fascination. War is the *strong* life; it is the life *in extremis*; war taxes are the only ones men never hesitate to pay.'[23]

This was not the judgment of a crude reductionist or militarist. James was a Harvard medical graduate who had studied physiology under Du Bois-Reymond and Helmholtz, but he had broken away from the mechanistic tradition that held sway in medicine and psychology at the time. Consciousness, he said, was a function of the whole psycho-physical context. James had survived a period of suicidal depression in his twenties by reading literature of free will, and his pragmatic philosophy denied determinism. His consequentialist view of values as rules for action was controversial, but its final referent was to the greatest social good, and his preferred human model was the free, rounded and other-regarding individual.

Nevertheless his method meant that he had to test war by its consequences on action. He felt forced to accept some of the militarists' claims that war had a biological function. In *Principles of Psychology* (1890), he surmised that in the early history of 'ruthlessly ferocious' man, it was of evolutionary value to kill off a few 'obnoxious' members of one's own tribe in order to better the chances of those who remained: 'And killing off a neighboring tribe from whom no good thing comes, but only competition, may materially better the lot of the whole tribe.' Combativeness became rooted in humanity, became 'a fatal reflex response'.[24] Here (as elsewhere in his psychology) James veered towards an automaton image of humanity, at odds with his free agent theory.

In his famous essay of 1910, 'The Moral Equivalent of War', James portrayed war and pugnacity as vestigial traits of a primal past, stamped upon humanity during a history that was a bath of blood: 'The *Iliad* is one long recital of how Diomedes and Ajax, Sarpedon and Hector, *killed*.'[25] War had been 'the gory nurse that trained societies to cohesiveness'. People realised this, even in civilised western societies, where military instincts were still strong beneath the surface, despite the apparent drift to a 'pleasure economy'. James saw some sense in the doctrine that war was 'human nature at its highest dynamic', a cheap price to pay 'for rescue from the only alternative supposed, of a world of clerks and teachers, of coeducation and zoophily, of consumer's leagues and associated charities, of industrialism unlimited, and feminism unabashed. No scorn, no valor anymore!' In the final resort though, James preferred 'the reign of peace'.

War had become 'impossible from its own monstrosity'. He dismissed the 'fatalistic view of the war function' as nonsense. War-making was due to definite motives 'and subject to prudential checks'. James suggested ingenious ways in which the martial virtues might be channelled into 'moral equivalents', for example, through youth conscription for peace, a programme later taken up by F. D. Roosevelt's Civilian Conservation Corps and John F. Kennedy's Peace Corps.

James's legacy for war theory was double-edged. His proposal about finding a moral equivalent for war rang around the world. But he also made a lasting impression with his talk of innate pugnacity, and with his suggestion that western man suffered a split personality about violence: reason taught that world disputes should be arbitrated, yet the vestigial traits of an irrational past underpinned national rivalries that made war likely. 'Split personality' theories were to flourish during the First World War.

There were parallels between James and McDougall, who was also trained in physiology (at Manchester, Cambridge and St Thomas's Hospital in London), and who also spurned mechanistic theory. His training was tempered by an anthropological approach, gained as a young member of the 1898 Cambridge anthropological expedition to the Torres Strait islands. A quirky and difficult figure, McDougall studied at Göttingen, and taught (often unhappily) at Oxford, Harvard and Duke.

McDougall's instinctivism, often misrepresented as a theory of fixed instincts instead of relatively open-ended responses, gave a high role to human pugnacity in the evolution of human organisation. He defined instincts as tendencies to respond to stimuli in a particular way, according to some goal, and accompanied by a specific emotion. Instinctive action implied 'some enduring nervous basis whose organization is inherited', an innate psycho-physical disposition which 'anatomically regarded, probably has the form of a compound system of sensori-motor arcs'.[26] Instincts could be modified by learning. McDougall's hereditarianism, tinged with Lamarckism, was to generate much derision in behaviourist America, which disdained his 'occult' psychic notions, his vitalism and teleology. Yet his 'hormic' psychology emphasised 'purposive' striving, anticipating modern goal-seeking psychology.[27]

McDougall developed Darwin's theme that social solidarity and altruism arose from the need to organise for war. As group combat superseded individual fighting in early human history, success came to depend more and more upon the capacity of individuals for 'united action, good comradeship, personal trustworthiness', and the capacity 'to subordinate their impulsive tendencies and egotistic promptings to the end of the group'. Moral codes originated out of this group conflict, but also out of sexual instincts and the archetypal struggle of young males for sexual access to the patriarch's women. Regulated at first by force, this struggle was later curbed by social sanctions and tradition. Self-control and law-abidingness became the essential conditions for social progress. McDougall was influenced in this area by J. J. Atkinson's 'primal murder' theory.[28]

Like James, McDougall judged pugnacity to be one of the strongest, most enduring instincts. He was not impressed by the material motivations for war, such as land and slaves. This loot was usually offset by the pain to the tribe of perpetual warfare. (This logic has been resurrected by present day critics of sociobiology.) Intelligence ruled against war. Therefore it must have been upheld by potent instincts. And it still was. Europe in 1910 was an armed camp of twelve million soldiers, even though war could not fail to be disastrous to all nations. McDougall even claimed that pugnacity was stronger in the European peoples now than in primitive man. Yet his theory of open-ended instincts allowed for pugnacity's modes of expression to change with the rise of civilisation. McDougall detected signs that warfare was being replaced by industrial and intellectual rivalry; that pugnacity was being modified by a more amenable instinct, that of emulation, the basis of game play and science, with a high component of 'social self-consciousness'. Natural selection was moving from the individual to the group, and might end altogether if nationalistic wars could be brought under global control.[29]

Right up to August 1914 the optimists were still affirming the 'natural decline of warfare', the basic peacefulness of western civilisation. (In the United States, when hostilities broke out, 'One heard everywhere the comment – "It is impossible. I thought we had got far beyond all that"'.)[30] The war dealt this facile optimism a fatal shock. Men flocked to the colours in all belligerent states, and even the intellectuals appeared to welcome the war with relief and joy. War was seen as an escape from bourgeois dullness and materialism, even a revolutionary act against capitalism, a means of recovering society's organic roots through martial unity, and a way of spiritual regeneration.[31] In England Hilaire Belloc celebrated 'the fruitful vision of a re-creative war', and many perceived an antidote to decadent civilisation in atavistic vitality, a condition of precariousness and ex-istential excitement.[32] Wartime literature was replete with metaphors about the fragility of civilisation and the 'wild beast' lurking within humanity. Freud merely systematised current opinion when he proposed in 1915 that culture was a fallible human construct whose function was to constrain violent and libidinal primal impulses.[33]

Observers of the period spoke, cynically or agonisingly, even voyeuristi-cally, of a new age of blood and iron and *Weltmacht*, of rule by the strong rather than the best, of human aggression rampant. 'War is still the supreme law of this imperfect world', wrote Seillière regretfully in 1914, as civilisation seemed to succumb to Pan-Germanism.[34] Five years later W. S. Lilley's *Invisible Kingdom* proclaimed war still 'the motive principle of the world', and 'the militant instinct' man's means of deliverance from egoism and 'the lust of lucre'.[35] The Scottish historian and Hegelian J. A. Cramb, whose *Germany and England* (1914) foretold an inevitable collision between these Teutonic powers, praised war as 'a phase in the life-effort of the State towards completer self-realization, a phase of the eternal *nisus*, the perpetual omnipresent strife of all beings towards self-fulfilment'. The wars of the future would be intoxicating conflicts of race and empires, and death would be glorious as the soldier was 'lifted to the heights of the highest, the prophet's rapt vision, the poet's moment of serenest inspiration'.[36] A more alienated vision was projected by John Burroughs, the New England nature writer, whose 'Arrival of the Fit' (1915) spoke of the war as 'a catastrophe on a scale with the cataclysms of geologic time when whole races disappeared', confirming life to be an amoral evolutionary drama based upon chance and prodigal waste. Aggregate humanity was unmasked as 'no more exempt from the operations of cosmic laws than are the sticks and stones'. Millions were locked in a life-and-death struggle that no one wanted, seized with 'a fury of destruction': 'Men become Christianised, but man is still a heathen – the victim of savage instincts.'[37]

The European war seemed indeed, in the phrase of the American evangelist Gerald Stanley Lee, 'the final, sublime and awful culmination' of a primal theory of human nature ('the Krupp theory of human nature – "Scratch a gentleman and you get a savage"').[38] Reductionist images of man as fighting ape or primal predator flourished during the war, especially in the fields of medicine and psychology. The more simplistic popular science drew crude analogies between human and animal kind. Humans were depicted as puppets jerked by biological strings, violence accepted as an evolutionary necessity. Thus the Massachusetts physician William Lee Howard – recoiling from a world in decline because of perverse sexuality, miscegenation and pacifism – insisted that human nature had not changed 'from the days of war clubs and war axes'. He warned that a nation 'produced from germ plasm whose determinants of pugnacity have been reduced to zero, would soon cease to exist as a source of power or progress'.[39] Even a more sophisticated thinker like William Ralph Inge, the 'gloomy Dean' of St Paul's, a liberal Anglican theologian and something of a pacifist, traced the 'perverted patriotism' that caused war back to 'the inborn pugnacity of the *bête humaine*'. The human species, he said, was 'the most cruel and destructive of all that inhabit this planet', and territorial aggrandisement was the chief occupation of the state. After the war, he doubted that much had been learnt: 'man remains what he has always been – a splendid fighting animal, a self-sacrificing hero, and a blood-thirsty savage. Human nature is at once sublime and horrible, holy and satanic.'[40]

The American zoologist Samuel Jackson Holmes (he became notorious later for suggesting that Christian or Hebraic moral codes be replaced by a Darwinian one) described early humanity as almost exclusively engaged in 'the destructive, but eugenically wholesome, occupation of fighting', which he saw to be a critical factor in the emergence of man from primate ancestors. Perennial combat had favoured the selection of brainpower, courage and communal efficiency: 'Gruesome as the struggle for existence may be to contemplate ... it is a process to which the race is largely indebted for its congenital improvement.'[41] L. T. Hobhouse denounced such eugenic doctrine as 'at bottom a part of a campaign waged against all progress in the peaceful arts by the active and plausible advocates of rebarbarisation'.[42]

At the outset of the war Sir Ronald Ross, the conqueror of malaria and professor of tropical medicine at the University of Liverpool, loudly defended warlike nations as the nations of splendid manhood. The combative instinct (he said) had led to the elimination of less efficient types, while the gap between man and the next highest creature had been caused by genocide stemming from this innate aggression. Social virtues, such as self-sacrifice and obedience, had emerged as part of tribal evolution under the moulding influence of war. The 'purely intellectual qualities of cunning, observation, accurate reasoning, the faculty of inventing tools, and of seizing opportunities' were clearly associated with the warlike spirit. However, like his spiritual descendant E. O. Wilson, Ross acknowledged that violent aggression and war – once selectively critical to human evolution – had become obsolete, making it necessary for new rules to be devised using culture and reason.[43]

The pre-war hypothesis that humans were physiologically programmed for fighting was massively reinforced by Walter B. Cannon's classic tract *Bodily Changes in Pain, Hunger, Fear and Rage* (1915). The son of a Wisconsin railroad engineer, Cannon became a brilliant young professor of physiology, pioneer of the principle of homeostasis. His experimental work at the Harvard Medical School from 1906 to 1914 led him to conclude that stresses like rage, fear and pain evoked reflex bodily changes associated with the autonomic division of the thoracico-lumbar region. Adrenalin was discharged into the blood, stored glycogen freed from the liver, etc., in order to mobilise organisms for fighting, fleeing or coping with emergencies. The rage-fighting reflex was neurally controlled by the phylogenetically ancient part of the brain and lower spinal cord.[44] Cannon's work was a major inspiration for Arthur Koestler's later theory about the tragic 'schizophysiology' of the human species, subject to paranoid and violent aberrations because of impaired coordination between the phylogenetically old areas of the brain (archicortex) and the neocortex or 'specifically human' areas.[45]

Cannon's book claimed that the fighting instinct was firmly fixed in human nature, and had served man well in the momentous struggle for life. 'Deeply ingrained instinctive reactions' invariably preceded combat. The world's war machines were animated by 'these surging elemental tendencies'. (The language echoed Wyndham Lewis's 'vorticist' school in Britain, or Marinetti's 'futurism', although the latter imagined war as the supreme expression of modernity and machine culture, rather than of primitivism.) Developing an idea put forward by the British Fabian Graham Wallas in *The Great Society* (1914), Cannon proposed that 'baulked disposition', due to the frustration of belligerent natural aptitudes, could lead to human maladjustment and aggression – an early 'frustration-aggression' theory of war. In a creative speculation Cannon alleged that war also thwarted intense human desires for beauty and social justice. War thus itself roused in people hostility against war. The pugnacious instinct itself became a source of energy in a war against war.[46]

The trench warfare on the western front provoked some memorable clinical studies of soldiers under psychic and physical shock. One such study was George W. Crile's *A Mechanistic View of War and Peace* (1915), which strikingly anticipated modern sociobiological attitudes. Crile, a pioneer in American surgery and authority on shock, was director of clinical research for the American expeditionary forces in France. He was a cultivated man who hated war. Yet as he reflected

upon the intense application of man to war in cold, rain and mud...hairy, begrimed, bedraggled, yet with unflagging zeal striving to kill his fellows...I realized that war is the normal state of man...the oceans would not hold the blood he has shed.[47]

The physiological evidence suggested to him that man was still programmed for primal combat. Under threat an individual's kinetic system was activated. There was increased output of adrenalin, thyreo-iodin, glycogen; increased chemical activity in brain cells; heightened heart beat, respiration, body temperature, sweating. The organs and tissues were mobilised for action or flight.[48] Aggression in humans and animals was essentially comparable. (Crile, dubiously, tried to clinch this by showing photographs of a giant gorilla and a soldier to show similarity in facial expressions when angry.)

Crile saw no break in evolutionary continuity between 'the savage grapple with wild beasts' and modern forms of struggle such as business competition or war. Human war sprang out of strong hunting and

territorial urges. Man was 'a hunting animal' (p. 13). Like wolves men
hunted in packs. In war they hunted each other. (This was unlike wolves
and most animals, he failed to add. Contemporary literature was weak in
distinguishing predatory behaviour between species and fighting within
species.) Hand-to-hand bayonet combat became 'an orgy of lustful
satisfying killing', a 'fling back in phylogeny' to a time before weapons,
when man tore his enemy's flesh with angry teeth. Modern defensive wars
were based upon the ancient instinct to preserve clan and cave, kith and
kin, against predators. Territorial behaviour was reflected in line fence and
boundary quarrels, and provided deep-rooted instinctive foundations for
national jealousies: 'The action patterns of ontogeny seem but shallow
tracings upon the deep grooves of phylogeny; in the cultivated man of
today is the beast of the phylogenetic yesterday' (pp. 21–2, 55, 64).[49]

Despite man's large brain and complex behaviour, Crile contended that
certain phylogenetic action patterns of killing had been established within
the brain as a result of eons of selective struggle. Ancient mammalian brain
mechanisms determined responses to stimuli. Certain adaptive responses
had become almost automatic as the result of repeated neural reinforcement. Unless this species-experience was counteracted by ontogeny,
humans would continue to be warlike. War had historically served the
survival of the fittest, and been birthmaid to civilisation. It was probably
impossible to eradicate from the web of life.

However, mass wars had become dysgenic, while the First World War
threatened civilisation itself. The war nations had lost 'the unit value of
millions of years of life' (p. 42). The west seemed trapped in a death-
struggle with the Frankenstein of its own creation. Man controlled a
'world of limitless force and endless machinery...yet fails to control that
all-important mechanism – himself' (p. 96). Taking a cue from John B.
Watson's *Behaviorism* (1914), Crile advised that humankind's only hope
for peace was to counter phylogeny with ontogeny, breeding by training.
There were echoes of H. G. Wells's *A Modern Utopia* (1905) in Crile's plan
for massive human conditioning against war: 'Backed by public money
and public opinion, a group of supermen may evolve a system of
mechanistic training which will mold the next generation into a higher
degree of adaptation to environment' (p. 103).[50] The First World War
evoked a number of potentially authoritarian solutions of this type,
signalling the serious breakdown of the liberal humanist tradition that had
once dominated western thought. Benjamin Kidd paralleled Crile in
calling for directive cultural conditioning. Within the life of a single
generation, Kidd said, the world could be made to undergo 'changes so
profound, so revolutionary, so permanent, that it would almost appear as
if human nature had been completely altered in the interval'.[51]

Another 'wild beast' theory of man came out of medicine, this time from the Scots physician Harry Campbell, who encountered cases of war shock at the West End Hospital for Nervous Diseases in London. Campbell wrote a series of articles for the *Lancet* from 1913, published as *The Biological Aspects of Warfare* (1918). Here he described man as an 'arch-slaughterer', a natural carnivore with combative instincts, exhibiting ferocious animal-like traits in anger and fighting: 'The untamed man, when enraged, assumes in very truth the aspect of the tiger: he puts himself in a threatening attitude, frowns, growls, or even roars.' However, humans had the more sinister capacity consciously to inflict pain and exult in cruelty. Campbell anticipated Robert Ardrey's hunting hypothesis by emphasising how critical to human evolution had been our ape ancestor's abandonment of the arboreal life for a hunting career in competition with the carnivores.[52] The severe new conditions of hunting (Campbell said) had intensified hominid combativeness, and probably precipitated the evolution of ape-man into *Homo sapiens*. The fighting instinct was further developed by constant inter-tribal warfare, waged for hunting grounds rich in resources. The aggressive and clever tribes wiped out their competitors. The ape-man's descendants not only killed and exploited other species, but – uniquely in the animal kingdom – sought genetic advantage by waging war against their own species. Fatalistically Campbell accepted that it was idle to seek to override 'the great biological law of struggle: throughout all living nature the battle is, and ever will be, to the strong'.[53]

A 'hunting hypothesis' about early man and war had been put as early as 1905 by the British philosopher turned psychologist, Carveth Read, and extended in his *Origin of Man* (1920).[54] He believed that humans had evolved from ape-like stock because of changes begun by the practice of hunting in packs for animal food. As packs of 'wolf-apes' multiplied and spread across the world, they came to regard each other as rivals on the same footing as the great cats and packs of dogs, 'and every attempt at expansion or migration provoked a battle'. From the outset the human pack came into competition with true carnivores, and discovered attack to be the safest defence, even without weapons. Pugnacity was bred into the pack, which 'has a disposition to aggression upon every sort of animal outside the pack, either as prey or as a competitor for prey'. The first wars were probably waged for hunting-grounds, and may have been reversions to the warlike behaviour of the carnivorous pack's primate ancestors. (Darwin had noted that baboons in Abyssinia, *C. gelada*, fought for feeding-grounds against troops of another species, *C. hamadryas*.)[55]

The physiology being pioneered by Walter Cannon and others ushered in a whole tradition of writing that branded modern man as a biological freak, handicapped by an archaic and pugnacious animal brain that impaired the working of the new 'human' cortex. (Morley Roberts, William Morton Wheeler, Arthur Koestler and Paul MacLean were to be the best known names in this tradition.)[56] One of the more notable exponents of such views during the First World War was the Iowa psychologist G. T. W. Patrick. In 1915 Patrick spoke of the 'asymmetrical development of the human personality', of an inbuilt imbalance caused by retention of 'the same old brain of our fathers and fore-fathers, deeply stamped with ancestral traits and primitive instincts', but no longer adaptive in an advanced social system. Under selectionist pressures favouring intelligence and co-operation, humankind had evolved into large-brained, toolmaking, versatile, environment-controlling beings, 'but working inevitably under high pressure and dangerous tension'. Something was bound to snap when the limitless development of intelligence was linked inseparably 'to a brain, a highly complex, delicate and unstable mechanism, which was originally intended as a motor center for hand, foot and somatic muscles'.[57]

According to Patrick 'man the fighting animal' had evolved out of conditions of incessant conflict between races, with extermination of the unfit. Survival had been the product of order and mutual aid *within* groups, but with fear, hatred and the rule of might prevailing *between* groups. Thus had arisen ethnocentrism and xenophobia, which now applied to modern states, the descendants of primitive tribes. The units of society – men with their ancient mammalian brains and instincts – had not changed, even though society itself had changed, making modern war 'insane' and dysgenic. War was a way in which over-stressed humans regained homeostatic balance, 'a temporary reversion to completely primitive instincts'. The First World War was a global 'fling' after the world 'has had a thinking spasm of unusual severity... Instantly when war was declared a great inward "peace" settled down upon the warring nations ... The brain centers were short-circuited.' Even though substitutes must be found for war, the underlying forces promoting human aggression would always re-emerge in social unrest. There were obvious parallels here with Freud's theory of war as id-releasing. Interestingly Patrick's essay appeared in the same year that Freud published his 'Thoughts for the Times on War and Death' in *Imago*.[58] After the war Patrick wrote *The Psychology of Social Reconstruction* (1920), which explored ways in which humans might regulate the violent and anti-social instincts that were deeply-seated in their brains.[59]

Henry Rutgers Marshall's *War and the Ideal of Peace* (1916) also developed a concept of man as 'fighting animal': 'deeply embedded in man's nature are instincts that lead him to fight: to fight as an individual, and to fight with others of his kind in groups'. Certain stimuli still triggered an inbred and immediate fighting reaction. Marshall – like other fighting animal theorists – denied the liberal pacifist view that war had become culturally autonomous, no longer biologically driven. Fighting instincts (he countered) still made up the basic sub-structure upon which depended the world's massive war machines and war politics. Anticipating Arthur Keith, he interpreted patriotism as an outcome of man's evolutionary skill in turning pugnacious instincts to the service of the clan or group.[60] Although he had been a long-standing pacifist, Marshall supported the Allied war against German militarism.[61]

He discerned hope for humankind in the extensive experimental evidence that instincts could be transformed in their functioning by appropriate conditioning. Marshall was influenced by the work of Pavlov and Thorndike in animal psychology, and by Watsonian behaviourism. Watson cited the work of Scott and Conradi, who found that bird songs could be changed in a controlled environment. Watson got from Mendelism the un-Darwinian insight that inherited characters and crude instincts (such as pugnacity) were commonly unadaptive. These defects might be recouped by behavioural plasticity and habit.[62] Graham Wallas had already suggested that restraint of war habits could be made habitual, as happened in the Icelandic sagas, where quarrels were by custom brought for resolution to the heads of families, despite the fierceness of the Icelanders.[63] With such ideas in the air, Marshall affirmed the feasibility of the peace ideal: 'the beginnings of effective control of instinctive tendencies may be found in intelligent effort to eliminate the stimuli which aroused the instinctive reaction ... man would no longer be describable as a fighting animal'.[64]

Ideas of entrenched racial fears, anger and destructiveness were vigorously circulated within psychological circles by one of the founding fathers of the American Psychological Association, G. Stanley Hall. His 'Synthetic Genetic Study of Fear' (1914) gave long evolutionary explanations of phenomena such as shock, fear and flight. He spoke of 'revivals of old, long-submerged, dendritic or even pelagic stages of evolution [that] may surge up and evict the judgment and master the will'.[65] Hall praised Patrick's innovative discourse on war, and agreed that 'it is more or less normal for men at times to plunge back down the evolutionary ladder ... to break away from the complex conventions and routine of civilized life and revert to that of the troglodytes in the trenches'.[66] Hall prefigured the sociobiological claim that teenage gangs represented a reversion to tribal organisation. He proposed that sport, play and fighting were a 'falling back to activities that are older than modern civilization and appeal to lower strata or neuro-muscular response':

Man has always been a fighter and his passion to kill animals ... and inferior races ... is the same thing which perhaps in the dark past so effectively destroyed the missing link between the great fossil apes of the tertiary and the lowest men of the

Neanderthal type. All these illustrate an instinct which we cannot eradicate or suppress, but can best only hope to sublimate.[67]

Even Raymond Pearl, who, as we have seen, blamed the perverted Darwinist mentality of German militarism for the war, accepted the current thesis that humans were programmed for fighting, that threats to territory from foreigners set off visceral mobilisation of the organism for conflict.[68] War, a fundamentally biological enterprise which transformed the whole environment of those engaged in it, was motivated by fighting instincts and entrenched racial differences, 'a deliberately planned struggle between biologically unlike groups of individuals for the purpose of maintaining or bettering their status in the general hierarchy of group domination or precedence'. Like E. O. Wilson today, Pearl interpreted human social heritage as highly dependent upon germ plasm, and thus greatly resistant to change. War in fact had been the one outstanding force that could break down the inertia of social institutions (an echo again of Bagehot). It had performed a biological function in the scheme of social inheritance 'analogous to that of mutation in physical inheritance'. This did not imply the deterministic selectionism of the German militarist school, which Pearl abhorred for ignoring man's mental and moral qualities: 'no war in this day and age is, in any proper sense of the word, literally a struggle for existence', while only genocide could destroy the imprinted group culture of a conquered nation or race.

We have seen that the basis for 'fighting animal' theory was laid down before the war in the discourses of instinct theory, physiology and comparative psychology. Morgan, Marshall, Sherrington and McDougall proffered evidence that instincts like pugnacity were associated function- ally with the lower brain centres, and were an evolutionary legacy from primal humanity. J. R. Angell, James and others argued that violence was endemic in human history, that war and aggression rested on substructures of pugnacious instinct in humans, who had been 'wired' for fighting during eons of evolution. The First World War gave new impetus to such bio- psychological ideas, with Patrick, Crile and Cannon among the more imaginative pioneers of a discourse that led ultimately to E. O. Wilson, with his claims that violent predispositions had been genetically encoded into humans. There were in the First World War era prefigurations of sociobiology's claims that similarities between animal and human traits – most notably aggression – were due to common genetic ancestry. It was a rule of biology that innate, genetically determined traits were usually ubiquitous within a species, and shared by its evolutionary relatives. The First World War enhanced the view that human bellicosity was under specific genetic control, because it seemed to show the ubiquity of war and pugnacity, and exposed the frailty of the peacemaking forces of reason and culture. Hence we have an abundant literature rich in metaphors about a lurking savagery masked by a flimsy curtain of civilisation, a literature that continued after the armistice, ranging from Aldous Huxley's novels of the twenties to Eric Ambler's thrillers of the thirties. This literary image was to have its biological analogue in Koestler's concept of human 'schizo-physiology'. Violence was anti-social behaviour triggered by phylo-genetically ancient areas of the brain and nervous system. In Crile's phrase, 'the cultivated man of today is the beast of the phylogenetic yesterday': war was a 'plunge into the primeval', an oedipal release from the tension of civilised life.[69]

In the pre-1919 years there were plentiful expressions of sociobiology's theme that evolution had conferred selective advantage upon groups who were naturally pugnacious, internally cohesive, and who practised genocide against competitors. Holmes, Ross, Campbell and Hall thought that factors such as genocidal warfare, or the abandonment of forest life for carnivorous hunting, had precipitated the evolution of ape-man into *Homo sapiens*. Out of early humanity's obsession with the 'destructive, but eugenically wholesome, occupation of fighting' (Holmes) had come fitter types, 'the nations of splendid manhood' (Ross), and ultimately, as McDougall contended, the whole rich phenomenon of civilisation and social morality. The evolutionary origins of war were sought in prehistory, in hunting and territorial urges, in ethnocentrism and the struggle for living space, resources and mates. This discourse was reinforced from Malthusian demography, which viewed war as a biological check over a swarming world population.[70] Man as fighting beast raised the vital issue, one that preoccupied the great minds of the age: was it ever possible for primal traits to be suppressed or regulated by culture? Freud warned of the difficulty – and psychological perils – of constraining man's deepest in-stinctual impulses, and told of the human propensity for reverting to primordial behaviour. Genetic theory of the pessimistic 'degenerationist' sort warned of racial decay should there be an end to the genocidal struggle that had (supposedly) shaped human heredity and history. The trap of biological determinism lay at hand. War could be seen as a biological, or psycho-biological necessity, to be fatalistically accepted, or even com-mended. As Eric Fromm later remarked, militarist determinism correlated well with conservative and quietist feelings:

What could be more welcome to people who are frightened and feel impotent to change the course leading to destruction than a theory that assures us that violence stems from our animal nature, from an ungovernable drive for aggression?[71]

However all was not lost. Even fighting animal discourse admitted that modern war was dysgenic. Paradoxically, the grisly nature of trench warfare served to preserve one element of pre-war optimism about the 'natural decline of warfare'. As we shall see in the next chapter, by seeming to decimate the racial and class elites of Europe, war still emerged as biologically obsolescent. The idea of war as biological necessity was also thoroughly hammered in Allied circles because it was identified with the Bernhardi–Treitschke school of Prussian militarism.

The instinct and 'fighting ape' theorists we have looked at in fact differed concerning the degree of biological determinism, or inevitability, that underlay human belligerence – ranging from the fatalistic pessimism of Holmes and Campbell to the relative optimism of Lloyd Morgan ('Man is a reflective being who frames ideals of conduct' and can avoid the 'organic thraldom' of his animal nature).[72] There was much residual faith that human morality and reason would prevail over destructive impulses, much that was assimilable into the scientific and mythic structures of the peace tradition. As Crile and Marshall argued during the darkest days of the war, man's hope for peace was to counter phylogeny with ontogeny, a lesson reinforced from the new discipline of Watsonian behaviourism. Psychology held out the prospect of a peaceful human future achieved through behaviour modification and the channelling of aggressive instincts into non-violent pursuits (new 'moral equivalents of war'). As Patrick warned: 'War is fast becoming irrational and a substitute for it must be found.'[73] That imperative was to become fixed in twentieth-century thought. However the felt need to counter gene theory by behaviourist conditioning raised new threats to human freedom. In a real sense the war of 1914–18 laid the foundation for the worlds of George Orwell's *Nineteen Eighty-Four* and Anthony Burgess's *A Clockwork Orange*.

The killing crowd

Crowd theory was very fashionable in the pre-1914 generation, and it was closely affiliated with fighting animal discourse, also insisting upon the primal pugnacity of the human 'herd' and anticipating Freudian notions of war as a return to an atavistic and instinctive kind of world. Crowd theorists such as Le Bon and W. H. R. Rivers were influenced by the earlier British neurologist John Hughlings Jackson. From eighteenth-century chain-of-being doctrine and recapitulation theory, Jackson represented neurological illness as a reverse recapitulation of the historical process of biological evolution. Injury or disease caused nervous functions to reverse back through earlier phases of evolution. Recapitulation theory has been shown to be replete with metaphors derived from the unstable politics of nineteenth-century Europe. It was hardly surprising that this anxiety was extrapolated into war theory. It was alleged that under pathological conditions, such as disease, social stress, or war, all that humanity had acquired under social evolution was suspended, and more ancient structures were exposed.[74]

Crowd theory, despite its location in psychology and sociology, was firmly rooted in biology, even though its biological usage was loose and ideologically loaded. Its pioneers were the Frenchmen Gustave Le Bon and Gabriel Tarde and the Italians Scipio Sighele and Pascal Rossi. Scholars have explained the new interest in collective sociology and elite theory as a conservative reaction to the protracted nineteenth-century crisis in European liberalism, a reaction to the erosion of customary society and the challenge to privileged classes posed by industry, urbanism, spreading democracy and socialism.[75] Crowd studies lent credence to militarist ideology by appearing to validate scientifically more authoritarian brands of politics. By contrast, in the United States collective psychology and sociology took a more democratic line in accord with the existing political consensus.[76]

From selectionist theory (as Nye has shown) elite-mass theory took the idea of the axiomatic inferiority of the masses, the losers in the struggle for survival; from organismic theory it derived the image of a collective mind; from hypnosis and clinical psychology the image of crowds as non-rational bodies, acting unconsciously under a process of 'mental contagion' at the suggestion of leaders. The image of crowd behaviour as atavistic owed much to instinct theory. Le Bon spoke of a return to the 'ferocious instincts' of man's savage evolutionary heritage.[77]

In wartime Britain Martin Conway and Wilfred Trotter popularised the concept of the primal pugnacity of the crowd. Cambridge-trained Conway, knighted in 1895 for mapping 2,000 square miles of the Himalayas, was the colourful Slade professor of fine art (1901–4), director-general of the Imperial War Museum from 1917, and a deeply conservative Unionist MP, sitting for the combined English universities from 1918. He had a penchant for biological fundamentalism unusual in an art critic. In Conway's schema, all crowds possessed the 'instinct of expansion' (thus stretching McDougall's instinct theory to cover collective behaviour, something McDougall himself did in *The Group Mind*, 1920). Nations, which were 'similar independent crowds', were thus mutually hostile, always seeking to absorb more people and land.[78] War was the natural condition of man – ancient, primitive and modern. Only restraining forces, such as the balance of power, kept modern nations in unstable equilibrium: 'It is not the cause of war that requires to be sought, but the cause of peace.' Conway tended to blame war upon the aggressive masses, placing less emphasis upon the formative role of leaders than did theorists like Tarde. War-passion was always latent in every national crowd, and was spread by 'contagion': 'Gusts of passion are the most frequent cause of actual war, and it is to these, coming on suddenly and with uncontrollable force, that democracies are especially liable.'[79]

Conway's 'war crowd' was irresistible, swallowing up 'all contained crowds of whatever sort', subduing any 'peace-crowd' (as was shown in the Crimean, Boer and First World Wars). He scorned as 'merest moonshine' the hope of socialists like Gustave Hervé that the world's workers would unite in a general strike against capitalist wars. (Hervé's notorious *My Country Right or Wrong* (1911), boasted that the masses would not give one centimetre of skin, or one drop of blood, for their mother country.) To the dismay of pacifists like Bernard Shaw, history seemed largely to vindicate Conway, with disconcertingly large sectors of the British left embracing the war effort in 1914.[80]

The only real force that could restrain the national-crowd (Conway said) was a superintending 'over-crowd', like the Roman empire, able to police unruly groups over great areas. This was unlikely to be set up, given the indifference of the mass of humanity to world peace, until some ultimate threat of annihilation (even planetary invasion) welded people together. In any case super-nationalism would not be viable unless it incorporated the strength of nationalism within itself – chastening national power, super-imposing a higher common ideal, but still cherishing the individuality of nation-crowds. Conway's hope for the future was for the triumph of a civilised ideal – like that of the Anglo-Americans – embodying the principle of national diversity, whereas the Germans fought for a militarist ideal of national discipline under the guidance of science. The historical function of wars was to set up and test such ideals. The one that survived won an epoch in which to realise itself.[81]

More influential, and egalitarian, than Conway was Wilfred Trotter (1872–1939), distinguished surgeon-physiologist and medical researcher at University College Hospital, London. Trotter was an instinctivist with 'fighting beast' ideas, one who wanted to explore the deeper biological and psychoanalytical dynamics of human psychology. Yet, unusually for a crowd theorist, Trotter's politics were left of centre, and he fiercely opposed the doctrine of war as biological necessity. He wavered between a deterministic pessimism about humankind, trapped by genetically-derived conventions that bred conformity and belligerent ethnocentrism, and a more hopeful belief that expanding altruism would prevail over the darker subconscious forces at work in the human 'herd'.

Trotter's *Instincts of the Herd in Peace and War* (1916), based upon two sociological papers he wrote in 1908–9, complained that anthropomorphic thinkers had exaggerated the role of reason in human psychology, and used a man-centred rather than a comparative method that would study humans as part of the animal world. Even Freud's great edifice of new theory was deficient in this respect: one could scarcely fail 'on coming into it from the bracing atmosphere of the biological sciences, to be oppressed by the odour of humanity with which it is pervaded'.[82] Humans had capacity for cerebration and for symbolising instinctive impulses, but instincts were 'enforced by the effects of millions of years of selection'. A few thousand years of civilisation, 'accompanied by no steady selection against any single instinct', could have had no effect in weakening them (pp. 95–6). Trotter advocated study of mass humanity, which was more homogenous and predictable than individual humans.[83] The gregarious or 'herd' instinct was fundamental to social life in humans, as with most organisms. It was the source of human anxieties and neuroses because the sanctions of the herd (social mores) often clashed with individual desires, ethics and rationality. Trotter anticipated Freud here, and there were reverberations from Emile Durkheim's pre-1900 discourse of 'social constraint', and from Boris Sidis, whose *Psychology of Suggestion* (1898) warned that individuality was imperilled by conformist crowd pressures.[84]

In Trotter's biology, gregariousness was advantageous because it shielded the individual organism – merged in the larger unit – from the immediate effects of selection, enabling it to vary with a freedom that would have been dangerous to an isolated being. Humans, like all gregarious animals, might develop towards increasing variety, more stringent integration, or extinction. There was in fact great probability that 'after all man will prove but one more of Nature's failures' (p. 65). Gregariousness had its restrictions: inability to live satisfactorily apart from the herd, dependence upon leaders and custom, credulity towards the dogmas of the herd, a weakness of personal initiative. But life in the herd conferred a sense of power and security. In times of war and emergency there was a capacity to respond to the call of the herd 'with the maximum output of energy and endurance, a deep-seated mental satisfaction in unity with the herd, and a solution in it of personal doubts and fears' (p. 110). Successful leaders were those who identified with the herd, not those with intellect or originality (in fact, Trotter suggested, these traits were disadvantages to a leader unless well camouflaged).

Trotter distinguished 'protective' from 'aggressive' gregariousness. Herd behaviour offered protective mechanisms, for example, grazing animals such as antelope were alerted against predators by a system of warning signals. Aggressive gregariousness gave the social group an immense accession of strength as a hunting and fighting organism. Man's primal past was unmasked both by mob violence – the aggressive passion of the pack – and by mob panic – the protective passion of the herd. However, man had raised the evolutionary stakes by prodigiously increasing the size of the unit in which the individual was merged. The nation was now the smallest unit on which natural selection acted unreservedly, and force was the ultimate regulator of competing nations. Trotter identified Germany and Britain as warring herds in the First World War, the Germans representing the aggressive 'wolf-like' herd, lower in the evolutionary scale than the socialised British type, which had affinities with social insects like bees (pp. 182ff.). He later came to regret this as wild wartime speculation. He too had been caught up in crowd hysteria.

Trotter blamed the 'restless pugnacity' of humans against their own species on man's complete triumph over natural enemies, allowing more leisure for intra-specific fighting. This was not such a handicap to the race when fighting units were small, although even then war encouraged insensitive and unoriginal types. War became more of a racial threat as the fighting units grew bigger, and herd unity became the biological defence mechanism of peoples under stress. Trotter vividly analysed the vague fears and xenophobia, rumours and irrational opinion that gripped populations in modern war. There was intolerance of independent thinking or maverick behaviour; an innate felt need for leadership ('It is touching to remember how often a people in pursuit of this ideal has obtained ... nothing but melodramatic bombast'); but also war provided a rare opportunity for breaking down archaic class distinctions as people huddled together within the greater 'war herd'. Trotter regretted that Britain had not seized the chance to reform its class system in 1914, when there was widespread readiness to sacrifice social privileges in the interest of national homogeneity.[85]

In Trotter's macro-biology total war threatened to arrest human progress by greatly reducing the variety and amount of human germ plasm available for selection. There was no other animal whose fighting involved one-fifth to one-quarter of the whole species:

It is plain that a mortal contest between two units of such a monstrous size introduces an altogether new mechanism into the hypothetical 'struggle for existence' on which the conception of the biological necessity of war is founded ... There is no parallel in biology for progress being accomplished as a result of a racial impoverishment so extreme, even if it were accompanied by a closely specific selection instead of a mere indiscriminate destruction.

Even where a supposedly 'superior' society destroyed a simpler one, Trotter thought that extermination of the 'inferior' race might deny to the species 'the perpetuation of lines of variation which might have been of great value' (pp. 128–9). To emphasise genetic variety rather than racial purity was a powerful analysis, rarely heard at the time.[86]

Trotter was dismayed by the war hysteria of 1914–18, which dismissed pacifism and internationalism as 'the vapourings of cranky windbags'. The dubious science of Social Darwinism, and the fashion for 'fighting animal' theory, forgot that man's instinctive pugnacity was balanced by an equally instinctive altruism, also growing out of the needs of the herd.[87] He declared pacifism to be perfectly natural, indeed 'ultimately inevitable in an animal having an unlimited appetite for experience and an indestructible inheritance of social instinct' (pp. 125–6). Although Trotter for a time promised an exciting contribution to an exact social psychology, his uni-causal bio-instinctivism came under damaging attack. Even the instinctivist McDougall complained that he reduced richly varied social phenomena to the 'herd instinct'.[88] Critics detected something distinctly occult in crowd psychology's use of sweeping collective instincts of 'imitation' or 'sugges-tion'.[89] Graham Wallas discerned an ideological content to crowd theory, historically the product of fear of democracy or socialism. For the Fabian it seemed not a case of the people being collectively ferocious or blind, but rather of them being culturally deprived.[90]

As the war ended some interesting efforts were made to synthesise crowd theory with psychoanalysis. In *The Psychology of War* (1918), the Cornell medical psychologist John T. MacCurdy attributed war to deep-seated, pathological human instincts. These combined Freud's unconscious and primitive anti-social instincts with Trotter's 'herd instinct'. MacCurdy accepted Trotter's portrayal of humans as herd animals owing blind allegiance to the group, and feeling rooted hostility to those outside the group. MacCurdy suggested that during times of war, humans still felt vestigial emotions of hostility to their enemies as species other than themselves. This foreshadowed the concept of 'pseudo-speciation' that was to figure in later sociobiology. According to MacCurdy, early tribal warfare for hunting grounds had fixed the idea that strangers were another species in the struggle for survival. Thus was overcome the natural taboo against killing con-specifics:

Advance of knowledge has taught that all the members of the species *Homo sapiens* are men, but it is doubtful whether that knowledge is a vital part of our automatic mental life.[91]

The New York psychoanalyst Everett Dean Martin branded the nation at war the 'classic example of the killing crowd'. Following Freud, Martin viewed war-making as a release from 'the deadening hand of social control'. The homicidal wish-fantasy could now become a reality. Repressed hostility within society was released in the respectable form of 'national honour'. However Martin rejected Freud's account of crowd behaviour as essentially sadistic, a simple impulse to cruelty caused by the temporary regression of the war-crowd to more primal conditions. Rather, Martin held, crowd behaviour during war was paranoid and compulsive.[92]

Crowd theory – as a sub-genre of instinct theory – made almost commonplace the image of the human herd moved by primal pugnacity and irrational unconscious forces, often conceived reductively to be genetically arrested at a primitive phase of evolution, still herd animals responding to innate dispositions that fostered xenophobia. Crowd behaviour in war and riot was read as regression back down the evolutionary scale to the race's ancestral mentality.[93] Even gregariousness, usually regarded as a civilising force, was now treated as a cause of violence. As MacCurdy said, humans by their herd nature were doomed to split into groups, and these behaved biologically like separate species struggling for existence: group norms prevailed, and an abnormal suspicion of strangers developed.[94]

Predominantly elitist in Europe, crowd theory tended to naturalise authoritarian politics and militarism. Yet not all the theorists believed that war was made inevitable by nature and history. There was multivalence in crowd discourse as in instinct theory generally. Gregarious instincts included the potentially peaceful instincts of sympathy and association. The war crowd might eventually translate into the global crowd, humanity itself. Elite theory allowed the possibility of control of the (supposedly) ferocious instincts of the masses by more intelligent and moral leaders, or by the 'better classes'. The politico-cultural context was critical, as illustrated by the democratic trend of collective social science in the United States, or by the appearance of Trotter's more radical herd theory in pluralistic Britain.

As with other 'fighting animal' discourse, there were limits to the threat that crowd theory posed to the liberal peace paradigm. Conway's insistence that war was the natural condition of 'similar independent crowds' was depressing. But he also suggested hopes of world peace being imposed by a global 'overcrowd' embodying the Anglo-American ideal of national diversity – something that many pacifists would have settled for. Trotter was ambivalent about instinctive pugnacity and the future of humankind, but he did perceive pacifism to be a 'perfectly natural' trait in an essentially social species. Indeed his scathing attack upon Bernhardian doctrine, and his conviction that great wars of extermination would disastrously limit the global variety of genetic material, put Trotter squarely in the peace biology camp. Overall crowd theory shared the eugenist belief that modern war was dysgenic.

6   The survival of peace biology

Reworking the mainstream tradition

Peace biology – always adaptive and resilient – responded inventively to the challenge and trauma of the war, reworking the mainstream tradition that had been founded on Darwin's holistic ecology. Its spokesmen regrouped, beat a strategic retreat on some fronts, launched an offensive on others, while managing to preserve the essentials of the liberal peace myth: faith in enlightened science and culture, human malleability and a better future. The massive destruction of life in the trenches seemed utterly to vindicate peace eugenics, while the 'unspeakability' of the Prussian foe helped greatly to discredit militaristic Social Darwinism. Nevertheless, there were submerged ambivalences and discursive tensions within the peace biology discourse. They arose during the debates over the eugenics of war and the legitimacy of analogies from nature. The logic of eugenics threatened to lead the peace movement into dangerous deterministic territory. Again, the critics of neo-Darwinist 'distortions' of selectionist theory were more than a little double-faced. They anticipated modern geneticists, such as Dobzhansky, in claiming 'fitness' to be a value-free concept, that must be cut away from undesirable (especially militaristic) social connotations. But they were less adept in dissociating 'fitness' from their own value system.[1]

Peace literature continued to endorse biologically the human capacity to escape the trammels of nature, despite man's apparent fall from grace during the First World War. As the Scots physician Robert Munro phrased it, humans had learnt 'the art of dodging many of the operations of the cosmic forces'.[2] The eugenist Theodore Chambers, who had the quintessential eugenist's contempt for naturalistic reliance on the blind forces of biology, declared flatly that humans now had the power to decide who and what was to survive. They might, if they chose, breed 'hideous, gruesome beasts', or cause degeneration of the race through mindless war or reproduction. But man could also choose to 'so influence environment as to give survival value to the highest and noblest characteristics'.[3]

Bernard Shaw had warned in his *Revolutionist's Handbook* that unless man did so shape his environment, 'war and competition, potent instruments of selection and evolution in one epoch, become ruinous instruments of degeneration in the next'.[4] The shadow of devolution constantly lurked behind the more optimistic discourses of the day.

The distinguished naturalist Sir Ray Lankester believed that man had been cut off from the dictates of natural selection by the evolution of consciousness: 'Man forms a new departure in the gradual unfolding of Nature's predestined scheme.' Through the power of will, humanity was able to modify its own history: 'Man is Nature's rebel. Where Nature says "Die!", Man says "I will live".'[5] Lankester – Director of the British Museum's Natural History department and Keeper of Zoology – was the dominating figure in British zoology. Darwin, Hooker, Tyndall and Huxley had been visitors to his family home when Lankester was a boy, and he maintained till the end of his long life (1847–1929) a grand and orderly Darwinian image of man and nature. His *Nature and Man* (1905) attacked reductionism, and celebrated man as an unparalleled 'piece of work', none the less significant for arising out of 'that system of orderly processes which we call Nature'.[6] Yet there was a persistent sub-text of anxiety in Lankester's work. His Sheffield lecture of 1879, *Degeneration*, became a source-book for discourses of atavism and eugenics. He forecast atrophy of powers, devolution and even extinction if humans succumbed to the 'prejudices and dogmatism of modern civilization'.[7] Although Lankester followed John Tyndall's famous Belfast Address (1874) in holding that the laws of nature were causally deterministic, his theory allowed a redemptive role for science. By giving humanity the power to assign the causes of its own evolution, science offered the prospect of ultimate control over human destiny and problems such as war. He continued to express this hope even during the dark days of the First World War.[8] As the Novicovian pacifist George Nasmyth put it, humanity needed an intellectual revolution: acceptance of modernity entailed faith in consciousness, and abandonment of counter-culture and fatalistic primitivism.[9]

Graham Wallas was also optimistic that man could bridge the gap between culture and an ancient inheritance of war instincts. Beatrice Webb was amazed by Wallas's cheery activism during the war, while she felt 'beaten by events ... The war is a world catastrophe beyond the control of my philosophy.'[10] Wallas is an interesting case: a Fabian who flirted with the fashionable instinctivism of the day in his widely read text *Human Nature in Politics* (1908), but who turned against the politics of impulse because of the war. In *The Great Society* (1914), a book that enjoyed a considerable vogue (especially in the United States), Wallas ultimately balanced nature and nurture, and found a naturalistic validation for rationalism. The 'intelligent dispositions' were not to be disregarded in favour of the 'instinctive dispositions', or treated as merely regulating primal impulses. Intelligence was a mature product of evolution, and should be used as a reliable guide to conduct. 'Non-intelligent dispositions', such as fear and pugnacity, were becoming less useful as guides to life.

Although Wallas explained war in terms of regression to primal instincts and a release from psychological frustrations, he had in fact never endorsed instinct-based racial stereotypes, and thought it 'the intellectual tragedy of the nineteenth century' that Darwinism had been used to justify capitalist and imperialist violence. In 1908 he prophesied that sterile concepts of nation and empire – underpinned by biological abstractions of struggle – would propel Germany and Britain into world war. This was tragically to twist Darwinism, which really stood for a new world ethic, not world conflict. During the war Wallas became a power-broker in English governmental and social science circles, and from this base he campaigned against the militant instinctivists of the right.[11] One strategy was to distinguish modern war, with its complexity and monotony, from primitive warfare. Rather in the later style of Arthur Koestler, Wallas denied that modern combat was the simple outcome of individual pugnacity (a point often ignored by today's sociobiologists).[12] By the war's end Wallas had virtually abandoned his instinct theory of social psychology for one based upon social transmission, writing in 1921: 'We have become ... biologically parasitic upon our social heritage.'[13]

Peace biology continued to put more sophisticated models of competitive and adaptive behaviour than the simplistically violent alternative proposed by the militarists. To this end Havelock Ellis went close to remaking Darwin into a pacifist:

That Darwin regarded war as an insignificant or even non-existent part of natural selection must be clear to all who have read his books. He was careful to state that he used the term 'struggle for existence' in a 'metaphorical sense', and the dominant factors in the struggle for existence, as Darwin understood it, were natural suitability to the organic and inorganic environment and the capacity for adaptation to circumstances.

Ellis contended that war – a formative (if comparatively innocuous) social force among early humans – was now inflicting a 'permanent loss in the material heirlooms of Mankind and a serious injury to the spiritual traditions of civilisation'.[14]

Leading naturalists such as Lankester and J. Arthur Thomson protested against the militaristic caricature of nature as a state of Hobbesian warfare. (That Hobbes had stirred the young Darwin's imagination was left unmentioned.) Selection, according to Lankester, was not so much a matter of direct struggle between con-specifics, but rather a more relentless struggle against environmental perils and overcrowding. It was essentially a desperate competition among a given species, in a given area, for food, to escape enemies, and for protection against climate. This natural struggle was to be sharply distinguished from human contests for wealth and advancement. In fact Lankester was much irritated by the fad for animal comparisons. He accused the 'literary politicians' of the west (and even novels, such as Paul Bourget's *Un Divorce*, 1904) of twisting Darwin: their 'inflexible law of the animal universe, the struggle between species, is one which is quite unknown to zoologists'. Fittest did not equate with strongest: 'Frequently in Nature the more obscure and feeble survive in the struggle because of their modesty and suitability to given conditions, whilst the rich are sent empty away and the mighty perish by hunger.'[15]

Lankester accused the *Homo pugnax* school of confusing predation with warfare. Predators preying upon their natural food, other species, were no more waging war than herbivores made war upon grass. If anything human warfare was 'unnatural' in that it departed from the rules of animal predation. These incorporated a natural limit to the destruction of victims (food species) by aggressors (predatory species). The supply of prey must not be seriously checked, or else the predator would starve. The true Darwinian struggle for existence was 'the unconscious competition between the super-abundant individuals of one and the same species' to survive nature's noxious agencies (predation, drought, storm) and 'to secure safety, nourishment and mating'.[16]

The zoologist J. Arthur Thomson also opposed the reductionism of the conflict school, which approved of war's 'rat versus rat mode of the struggle for existence'. Thomson was professor of natural history at Aberdeen (1899–1930), after training at Edinburgh, Jena and Berlin, and was well known as a popular writer on science and evolution, perhaps best remembered for his *Evolution of Sex* (1899), co-authored with Patrick Geddes. In Thomson's bio-view, responses to environment could be 'competitive or non-competitive, self-regarding or other-regarding, with teeth and claws, or with wits and kindness'. One creature sharpened its weapons, another thickened its armour, while yet another – man – experimented in state socialism. While competitive individualism paid, up to a point, in organic nature, 'survival and success are also to those types in which the individual has been more or less subordinated to the welfare of the species'. Especially among the finer forms of life, adaptive behaviour was more and more often 'something subtler, some parental sacrifice, some co-operative device, some experiment in sociality. The improbability of war being the saving grace of human history grows upon us.' Typical of reform eugenists, he regarded genetic inheritance as fundamental, but valued social heritage as supreme. Thomson's was one of the more eloquent pleas for a return to Darwin's holism: 'Darwin attached great importance to the web of life, to the manifold and subtle inter-relationships that bind creatures together in a vibrating *systema Naturae*.'[17]

This thesis was endorsed by George Nasmyth, who traced the pervasive philosophy of force to a 'profound misreading of the biological analogy'.[18] Nasmyth's 400-page compendium of anti-war biology, *Social Progress and the Darwinian Theory* (1916), was virtually commissioned by Norman Angell to popularise Novicow's peace ideas.[19] Nasmyth, a Quaker, had been active in the international student peace movement before 1914, when as a Cornell Ph.D. with interests in physics and sociology he studied at Berlin, Göttingen, Heidelberg and Zurich. He grieved that Darwinism – essentially a doctrine of moral law and social instincts – had been appropriated by brutal individualists, conservatives and militarists to legitimise the lower instincts of greed and brute force: 'Political theory in all Europe was based on the new "Social Darwinism", and it was proclaimed that might always makes right' (p. 40). The First World War demonstrated that biological error could mean death on a colossal scale (p. 113).

Within species (said Nasmyth) the biological rule was not unproductive struggle but 'relations of alliance and association' (p. 67). Militarists wrongly extrapolated from inter-species predation and hostility to intra-species human struggle; and they drew dubious analogies between collective combat in humans and mainly individual fighting in animals. Nasmyth anticipated Konrad Lorenz's celebrated theorem that humans lacked the instinctive inhibitory mechanisms that curbed excessive violence among animals.[20] Nasmyth suggested that early man had possessed such inhibitory instincts, but they had atrophied with the growth of human intelligence. Thus, tragically, humans had become able to attack their own kind, violating the law of mutual aid (pp. 73–4, 169). War was thus 'a rupture of equilibrium in biology' (p. 104). As civilisation advanced, war also advanced, becoming more dysgenic, diverting resources away from productive employment and social reform.

Nasmyth in fact wavered between a Kropotkinite faith in a placable human nature ruined by too much cerebration, and Novicow's model of humanity transcending a violent animal state, transforming physical into intellectual struggle (for example, p. 210). Ultimately he plumped for faith in human consciousness and freedom, fiercely opposing the 'fatalistic theory' that 'war is not, like law or constitutional government or any other human institution, the result of human effort and opinion, good and bad, but is imposed by outside forces which men cannot control' (p. 212).

Patriotic factors played a key role in the denigration of neo-Darwinist militarism, which was identified with enemy propaganda, and with the evil race 'science' of the Bernhardi–Treitschke school. That Anglo-Saxon xenophobia – all too evident in war propaganda – was based upon similar pseudo-science was conveniently forgotten.[21] The Scots clinical psychologist James Crichton-Browne, a pioneer in the treatment of mental illness, wrote a wartime tract against Bernhardi's evolutionism. He thought it appalling that Darwinism, one of science's 'most illuminative' theories, should have been appropriated 'in justification of German outrage'.[22] Popularisers such as W. C. D. Whetham and Robert Munro joined the fray. Whetham accused the enemy of eroding conduct based upon Christian ethics, of merging 'survival of the fittest' doctrine with Prussian power philosophy, stark and narrow. The Germans assumed 'with characteristic want of lucidity' that survival of the fittest for war, or for organised industry, 'would secure the survival of the fittest for the Art of Life as a whole'.[23]

In his tract *From Darwinism to Kaiserism* (1919) the Scots physician and lawyer Robert Munro accused Prussian *Weltpolitik* philosophy of using false readings of Darwin. The Prussian state tradition was naturally attuned to the militant side of Darwinism, and readily embraced the concept that 'war, strife and incessant contests are essential for success in life'. But analogies between natural selection and war were perilous. What possible parallel could there be between 'the almost unseen struggles and competitions' that took place between animals or human tribes 'and modern warfare, with its bombs, shells, projectiles, aeroplanes, submarines, torpedoes?' Only man was capable of genocide: 'Natural Selection does not deal with brutality of this kind.' Man also had built an edifice of ethics which was, at heart, the antithesis of the brute natural processes that the Prussians worshipped.[24]

At a meeting of American naturalists in December 1916, Jacques Loeb of the Rockefeller Institute for Medical Research decried Prussian bio-militarism as vitiated by false assumptions and antiquated methodology. The thesis that virility would disappear if not practised in the form of war rested on the assumption that functions and organs not used would vanish in an offspring. Yet sixty-nine generations of *Drosophila* had been raised in the dark, without any degeneracy in the eye or its function. Moreover, 'survival of the fittest' was not, like Ohm's law in physics or Mendel's law in biology, an exact law of nature; but rather a poor metaphor, not subject to quantitative verification. The fact that some animals, and some humans, were brutal did not make brutality a universal law. Racial justifications for war also rested upon dubious tradition and observation. Loeb reminded his audience that, although serious biologists would laugh at the war enthusiasts, 'the sad fact remains that this pseudobiology has had at least a share in the production of the tragedy which is being enacted in Europe'.[25]

American scientists were much struck by Vernon Kellogg's war reminiscences *Headquarters Nights* (1917), which gave a piercing insight into the violent mind-set of the German general staff and nationalistic biologists. Kellogg reported: 'The creed of the *Allmacht* of a natural selection based upon a violent and fatal competitive struggle is the gospel of the German intellectuals; all else is illusion and anathema.' Sickened by what he took to be the intellectual betrayal of German biology, Kellogg converted from pacifism to ardent support of a preventive war against the global rule of Prussian ideology.[26]

Raymond Pearl agreed with his friend Kellogg, condemning the Treitschke–Bernhardi school of war determinism as 'a proudly ruthless philosophy ... not only immorally cruel, but also immortally stupid'. Pearl blamed the Haeckel–Weismann tradition of mechanistic biology for woodenly rigorising selection theory into a closed philosophical system. Yet, as an experimentalist, Pearl knew that natural selection did not operate in nature with anything like 'that mechanistic precision which German political philosophy postulates'. The reality was messier, quirkier. Mechanistic Darwinism focused crudely upon physical selection, and was 'really most unbiological' since it ignored 'the most fundamental of human biological characteristics', mental and moral traits. Tragically, for thirty years German children had been brainwashed with this survivalist dogma, and modern Germany had been built upon these cornerstones of propaganda.[27]

War as genetic disaster? The vindication of peace eugenics

What helped keep peace biology alive when it was under almost unendurable wartime duress was the continuing strength of peace eugenics. The coming of Armageddon reinforced eugenics' historical opposition to war's waste and haphazard selection. It also seemed to confirm racist and conservative fears that a global war would annihilate virile Anglo-Saxon stocks, and create the potential for class war and revolution. The social, economic and 'racial' (read genetic) harm of the war seemed obvious to all but the wilfully blind. British war propaganda permitted this opinion, even encouraged it, by blaming the evil upon the Prussian enemy. It became conventional wisdom that war, perhaps once useful, was dysgenic in its modern forms. Darwin had said so, and it was quite consistent with Darwinian principle that practices once adaptive to a species could lose their utility when conditions changed. The debate over the war's genetic implications, however, embraced a diversity of readings of evolutionary history, while some critics in scientific and scholarly circles were dubious about the methodologies being employed in the argument.

The casualties on the western front provided sickening evidence against war. It became a cliché that the cream of the nation's manhood was being heroically sacrificed in the trenches. Everybody heard of the disproportionately high casualty rates among the officer elite, of whole classes of brilliant graduates from Oxford, Cambridge and the public schools laying down their lives for their country. These were the mythical 'lost generation', the nation's natural leaders cut down in their prime.[28] War, as Nietzsche said (in *Human, All Too Human*), squandered men of the highest civilisation, 'those who promise an abundant and excellent posterity'. Official and medical circles accepted the point. The National Birth-Rate Commission of 1916 flatly reported that war was 'generally admitted to exercise a selective power that is dysgenic'.[29]

British authorities kept the exact figures about casualties secret, and even after the war satisfactory statistics were never published. However it was obvious that war losses were heavy, by common consent the worst in modern times. The best recent estimate we have for British servicemen killed in the war is about 720,000.[30] The official judgment of the British Registrar-General, Sir Bernard Mallet, in 1918 was that the belligerent countries had experienced an unprecedented number of killed and disabled, and that population expansion was likely to be seriously impaired for some time.[31] Although discreetly silent on mortality in the field, Mallet estimated that war conditions in Britain had caused a loss of over half a million potential lives due to a fall in births from May 1915 to June 1918 (while enemy countries had suffered relatively heavier losses of future population, Germany of the order of 2.6 million and Austria–Hungary 1.5 million). There had been a jump in wartime marriages in the UK, but this was offset by deaths in the field and increased civil mortality due to the influenza pandemic, heart disease and bronchitis, possibly effects of wartime stress (and perhaps less important genetically as affecting mainly the old and feeble). Mallet and other social scientists were surprised that illegitimacy stayed constant, and that there was a drop in deaths from alcoholism, insanity and suicide, variously interpreted as due to wider employment (especially for women), greater social contact and a morale-boosting sense of engagement in the war effort.[32] The experts were in lively disagreement about the prospect of recouping wartime losses, the optimists contending that war losses were made good historically in relatively short time, while the louder pessimistic school focused on the tragic proportions of the bloodbath in Europe.[33]

Wartime casualties included the 'mind-wounded' as well as the body wounded. The horrific campaigns of 1915–16 caused a degree of wartime psychoses never before experienced in military history. 'Shell-shock' cases made up to 40 per cent of casualties from the major battlefields. Although the full reality was kept from public opinion, the scale of the phenomenon caused 'a managerial and conceptual crisis', with army statistics showing that officers were more than twice as likely to suffer from breakdown on the battlefield as men from the ranks.[34] Shell-shock not only revolutionised psychotherapy and brought Freudianism into medical acceptance, it also intensified anxieties that the war was incapacitating the ruling order as well as killing it off.

Alarmist fears spread about a possible genetic catastrophe in the west. In the Galton lecture for 1916, Professor E. B. Poulton, a leading neo-Darwinian, warned the Eugenics Education Society that the war threatened to carry the world backwards to lower and more brutal ideals and human types. He quoted a letter from an American scientist: 'We are unquestionably witnessing the most stupendously interesting step of human evolution that has occurred since that which differentiated man from the anthropoid.'[35] George Crile estimated in 1915 that the peoples of Europe had lost the equivalent of millions of years of life. He forecast a dramatic decline in physique, health and fertility in the belligerent nations after the war.[36] Anxiety about a 'lowering of the general biological level' permeated the discussion as the war revealed heavy losses of white European man-power, brain-power, capital and industrial resources.[37] This anxiety rarely translated into opposition to the war effort against 'Prussian barbarism'. Troubled humanists and realist eugenists shared a sense of patriotic duty to win a dirty, if necessary war, and hoped that a better planned world would emerge from the peace.

At the beginning of the war there was a lively debate on the question of which army system best served the country genetically. Military experts like C. H. Melville had argued before 1914 that regular volunteer systems as in Britain were mostly composed of working-class recruits, whereas conscription forced into the army a higher proportion of professional and middle-class recruits, normally regarded by eugenists as genetically superior.[38] The war changed the complexion of things. Those who rushed to volunteer in the first years of the war were deemed to be the fittest of the race, and these, especially the superior officer class, were being decimated. The alternative system of conscription had the genetic advantage of spreading human losses over a wider social spectrum. Its randomising effect – as Raymond Pearl observed – would reduce war's dysgenic effects.[39] However many feared that conscription would reduce the army's elitist efficiency: 'Although it might conceivably be beneficial to the race to place its least fit specimens in the front fighting ranks, one can scarcely imagine that such a course would commend itself from the military point of view.'[40] Attrition at the front finally resolved the practical issue in favour of conscription.

Many eugenists remained sympathetic to the view that military training, as distinct from battle, had racial benefits. It set high physical standards, increased national morale, and gave survival value to desirable human traits. C. H. Melville, Arnold White, Sir James Barr, Theodore Chambers and Rudyard Kipling were among those who lauded the eugenic effects of compulsory military training.[41] The issue was bedevilled by Lamarckian intrusions, even though Mendelism and biometrics had supposedly discredited Lamarckism. The genetic and environmental effects of training were often confused, and the assumption made that improved physical standards acquired in camp would be inherited by the next generation.

In an effort to minimise the genetic damage being caused by the war, eugenists supported the creation of the Professional Classes War Relief Council. This gave aid in education, training, maternity and employment matters to professionals and their dependents disadvantaged by enlistment.[42] Theodore Chambers and J. Arthur Thomson were leading publicists in this area. Chambers, an apostle of Jordan–Kellogg peace eugenics, thought that soldiers should be encouraged to marry in order to breed up better stocks, and reduce VD. Otherwise large armies equated with promiscuous sexuality, and the conception of 'less fit' babies by loose women, usually implied in the literature to be genetically inferior.[43] There was much subterranean anxiety, however, about the plethora of wartime marriages and liaisons. 'Breeding up' might get out of hand and shake the foundations of the family. An abiding fear in this discourse was that economic pressures arising from the war would crush professional, artistic and intellectual groups, as well as middle-class women. They would be inhibited from reproducing, a highly dysgenic effect. After the war authoritarian eugenists such as Lothrop Stoddard were to build their theories upon the perceived 'death of the middle classes', inflicted by a war that was 'unquestionably the most appalling catastrophe that ever befell mankind'.[44]

J. Arthur Thomson hoped that some sort of 'eugenic bulwark' would be provided by the nucleus of brave men who had to stay at home, but he worried that sexual selection would be adversely affected by a large pool of unmarried women caused by the war. He warned that the war was harming the whole of Europe, since 'prejudicial germinal variations of a heritable sort' would be induced as babies suffered arrested development through lowered physical vigour of mothers and poor nurture. He saw little chance of recouping war losses easily. Admittedly, the war had some social redemptions and 'the race does not live by the germ-plasm alone ... war with its terrible sifting may be worth all its costs. But who can predict of any war what *all* its costs may be?' Thomson feared a post-war ravaging of the middle classes and a resurgence of militarism.[45]

Charles Darwin's son Major Leonard Darwin, in a much quoted review of the issues in 1916, agreed that the First World War was causing racial harm by killing or sterilising a disproportionate number of those who were above the community's mean level of what Galton called 'civic worth'.[46] This category was correlated with intelligence, bodily fitness and socio-economic status. The high death rates among officers and university men was particularly alarming given the small size of Galton's select class. If Britain's fighting men were divided into seven classes 'differing equally from each other in average merit', there would only be about 2,000 men in the 'highest' class – and it was this class that was being massacred. At the same time shirkers and the physically and mentally handicapped were being protected from slaughter. The practice of invaliding out the weak within the ranks made negative selection more stringent. It was unlikely to be neutralised by opposing factors: the retention of a strong and competent workforce needed for the domestic war effort; or the winnowing of the weaker soldiers at the front by disease and wounds.

Darwin wanted an expert inquiry to collect data and suggest policy on the very complex issues at stake. The experts would need to know the average loss of progeny per head of those who had died in the war, taking into account such factors as the pre-war progeny of soldiers, the effect on the birth-rate of a higher wartime marriage rate (caused by 'war-excitement' and allowances), loss of fertility on the part of the wounded, the sterilising effect of VD, etc. His opinion that the greatest havoc was being wreaked upon the young, 'who would have been most valuable racially to the nation', has stood up well, given the exceptionally high death rates among eighteen to twenty year olds. Darwin gloomily looked to a future where the well-to-do declined, while the poor fecklessly multiplied, and eugenic reform was ignored by heedless politicians.[47]

The list of those endorsing the dysgenic nature of modern war was almost endless, crossed all political boundaries, and would be tedious to document.[48] One observer added a Mendelian dimension when he speculated that 'fluctuational variations' (for example, to height of population) would revert to normal over a few generations, although loss of a true mutation might permanently deprive the race of its benefits: 'Who can say that another and still more dreadful war may not be upon us before we have recovered from the racial injury of this?'[49] Wilfred Trotter, as we have seen, warned that the war threatened to arrest progress altogether by reducing greatly the variety and amount of raw material available for selection.[50]

Some interpretations showed an interesting tendency to expand into broader territory. The economist Harold Boag extended his analysis of genetic losses occasioned by war's mortality to include the concept of 'human capital'.[51] Giuseppe Sergi advocated study of the graver effects of prolonged war upon nations. This was not only because of the genetic battle losses, but because of a wider 'unbalancing of vital processes' by war and its economic repercussions.[52]

Also in this vein was William S. Rossiter's prophetic analysis of the revolutionary impact of the First World War.[53] Rossiter was a high official in the US Census Bureau, an authority on demographic trends 1815–1914. What proportion of a nation's human resources, he asked, could it spare for warfare without jeopardising economic life? With 30 million men drawn to belligerent colours by July 1916, the great European powers seemed to be fast nearing that limit (with the possible exception of Russia). By the end of 1915 the war powers had lost 12 million men, with about 15 per cent of males of virile age killed or incapacitated. These losses would be repaired with great difficulty (he calculated that Britain would need ten years, the Axis powers fifteen years, France an astronomic eighty-three years to recoup losses at normal fertility rates). A direct war loss of 12 million men in the war countries also meant that males would be 17.5 million fewer than females by the war's end. (Walter H. Page, the United States ambassador in London, described the Continent in 1916 as a 'bankrupt slaughter-house inhabited by unmated women'.)[54] Rossiter raised the spectre of a world economic system being shattered beyond repair:

The new activities of women, their numerical preponderance, and the new ideals and ambitions of war-aroused men, are likely to exert revolutionary influences upon reproduction, and upon the social and economic life of the nations concerned ... the ruthless hand of war may be fashioning a new age, to be far different from our own.[55]

The outbreak of the Russian Revolution in 1917, and the uprisings in post-war Germany, provoked much prophecy about an outburst of revolutionary change in Europe. This was often linked to the 'racial disaster' of the war, which had allegedly undermined traditional leadership in the west.[56]

From what has been said above, it appears that even within the ruling paradigm that war was dysgenic there were ambivalences, and varying evolutionary scenarios. The orthodoxy was often qualified. It was commonly recognised that there were some biological justifications for war; or that, for good or ill, bellicosity may have been ingrained in human nature. Eugenic thought also refracted discordances within anthropology and psychology over the issues of ancient war and the reputed pugnacity of early/primitive man. Authorities such as Sir Ronald Ross and William McDougall correlated the bellicosity of primitive peoples with physical and mental vigour. Ross saw the warlike virtues as the social virtues (self-sacrifice, constancy, courage, obedience, duty), and contended that warlike races – the Zulus, Masai, Sikhs, Pathans and Scottish clans – were 'the nations of splendid manhood'. Hand-to-hand conflict had been more discriminating genetically than later warfare by missiles.[57] McDougall's anthropological experience in Borneo led him to argue the racial benefit of war. He considered the Kenyahs, warlike highland peoples from central Borneo, superior to the peaceful Kayans from the coastal and lower river areas.[58] E. B. Copeland, a doctor living in the Philippines, claimed that the 'wild people' of the mountain regions of Luzon and Mindanao, a fighting race, were the best people in the archipelago.[59]

On the other hand, a persistent tradition in western thought held that man's natural life was Eden-like, the good and peaceful life, and that this had been corrupted by the serpents of vice and war, introduced by institutions and technology.[60] The British left, despite its flirtation with genetic theory, was historically amenable to structural explanations of disorder and injustice, whether Marxist/socialist (finding class, or economic-ideological reasons for war), anthropological (correlating the growth of organised warfare with degree of social complexity), or reformist psychoanalytical (such as Fromm's theory that anomie and violence were the fruits of disharmonious social order).

This socialist tradition was exemplified by Edward Carpenter's *Civilization: Its Cause and Cure* (1889). Carpenter's self-professed 'gospel of salvation by sandals and sunbaths' preached that civilisation had corrupted the unity of human nature, that the social life of the wilder races was 'more harmonious and compact', less criminal and violent, less class-ridden and sin-conscious than that of 'civilised' nations.[61] Kropotkin, Novicow, Wallace and Havelock Ellis projected an image of early/primitive man as basically peace-loving.[62]

Anthropological evidence could be assembled along similar lines. William Johnson Sollas, professor of geology and palaeontology at Oxford, pictured palaeolithic man as a peaceful hunter. In his *Ancient Hunters* (1911), he blamed farming and the domestication of animals for the beginning of systematic warfare. Sollas suggested that the Tasmanians, a race still living 'in the dawn of the Palaeolithic epoch', had lived essentially in peaceful equilibrium with their environment. Their extinction – the result of invasion by agricultural European settlers – replayed the archetypal drama by which war had originated in prehistory.[63] In *The Material Culture and Social Institutions of the Simpler Peoples* (1915),

L. T. Hobhouse, G. C. Wheeler and T. Ginsberg denied the prevalent view that early or primitive society was one of constant warfare. While concluding that only a few primitive peoples (for example, Eskimos and jungle folk) were highly peaceful, the authors suggested that 'organised war develops with the advance of industry and of social organisation in general'.[64] One of the more enthusiastic apostles of the idea of a 'golden age' of peace in early and primitive humankind was W. J. Perry, cultural anthropologist at the University of London, and a leading 'diffusionist' theorist. Perry held that war was not an essential feature of human society, but was a product of civilisation (originating in ancient Egypt) and the 'class state'.[65]

The sceptics

A number of critics braved orthodox opinion. They objected that the whole controversy over the dysgenics of war was clouded by methodological and empirical difficulties. Although some, like Sir Arthur Keith, perpetuated the militarist tradition, the sceptics in general eschewed ideological motives in favour of a dispassionate search for scientific truth. Chalmers Mitchell and A. G. Thacker, for example, were peace lovers, but neither was convinced that the prevailing 'laws of heredity' were rigorous enough to make judgments about war's selective effects. On closer inspection, however, evaluative factors lurked beneath the surface even of the more disciplined contributions to the debate.

Keith was one of those who took the grand approach, marked by sweeping claims for war's historical and racial benefits, tending to ignore or denigrate the micro-arguments about negative selection made by the peace eugenists. Keith moulded current instinctivist, degenerationist and group selectionist concepts into his own unusual race science. An immensely talented, if polemical, man of science, a polymath whose interests ranged from anatomy to human palaeontology, Keith was already in 1914 an FRS and president of the Royal Anthropological Society. His work as curator for the anatomy museum of the Royal College of Surgeons enabled him to explore Darwinian and Haeckelian explanations of man's antiquity and racial evolution – a matter of dead-ends, usurpations and slow change. However Keith was not in 1914 the bellicose Social Darwinist and self-advertising apostle of race and war that he later became, to the shrill disgust of H. G. Wells and Grafton Elliot Smith.[66] In fact before 1914 he seems to have been little interested in war as an agent of human evolution – indeed he largely accepted the thesis that war hindered modern nations by reducing fitness. He was preoccupied by the issue of racial isolation. Reading Darwin on the Tierra del Fuegons,

Baldwin Spencer on the Australian aborigines, McDougall on 'gregariousness' and Giddings on 'consciousness of kind', Keith found an
answer to the puzzle of how ancient tribes had protected themselves from
racial swamping. He postulated a deep human instinct of 'clannishness'
(Keith was a Scot), which kept tribes together in group solidarity, but
antagonistic to outsiders. Isolation, through group clannishness, seemed
the key to preserving race identity. He was to develop this into his
psychological concept of race.

It appears that Keith was converted to the idea of the 'evolutionary
naturalness and necessity of war' by the events of 1914–15.[67] He shifted his
focus from isolation to struggle, war now playing a key role in sustaining
mental apartheid between races. In a 1915 paper, he said that wars bound
a people together, isolated them racially from other 'tribes', and
discouraged them from breeding with lesser, or different, stock and thus
losing their special racial traits. Keith dismissed the war losses of the
Franco-Prussian war of 1870 as 'a detail', unimportant compared to the
Prussians' great achievement of racial unity. He said much the same about
the bloody American Civil War. Both the Germans in 1870 and the
Americans in the Civil War were 'race-builders in a true Darwinian sense'.
So also were the Russo-Japanese war and World War I essentially race
wars. By this Keith meant that the protagonists were impelled by ancient,
primal, race-preserving instincts of 'isolation' and pugnacity; and also
that war was a matter of territoriality and race-dominance. As an
anthropologist (only one of his personae) he accepted that the races
fighting the First World War were not ethnologically pure. The Germans
were in fact a mixed breed. Rather, what war was creating – by unifying
and isolating – was a 'psychologically' pure race. The bloodbath was
making an 'assemblage of allied peoples' into a 'true race of mankind'.[68]

With characteristic perversity, Keith rebutted Jordan's maxim that war
killed the 'bravest and best' with the quip that the bravest were not the
best, and that the brave man was relatively valueless in an industrial age.
His subsequent writings were to become increasingly militant and
outspoken. He spoke of them wryly as 'heresies'. *Nationality and Race
from the Anthropologist's Point of View* (1919) declaimed as biological
truth that war manifested nature's laws and registered deep human
structures inherited from an ancient past. To thwart racial struggle would
invite degeneration. However Keith did not use his celebrated phrase
about war being 'Nature's pruning hook' until 1931.[69]

If Keith sweepingly dismissed the doomster genetic theory about war,
others made more restrained criticism. The idea was often floated that war,
besides culling the brave, may also historically have selected out the
aggressive and anti-social elements. Roland Hugins suggested that the real

cause of decay in civilisations had not been war but hedonism, together with the refusal of elites to breed and pass on their genetic share to later generations. War may even have had a eugenic effect by eliminating the 'more ferocious and brutal elements in society'.[70] Chalmers Mitchell agreed that war culled the naturally martial:

If this consideration be pursued on theoretical lines, the inference might be drawn that forty years of unbroken peace have made Germany too ready to embark on war, as there has been no opportunity for her fire-eaters to be eliminated.[71]

Hugins considered that a military campaign had itself a selective effect upon an army, the survivors who returned home being sturdier than those who died. Variations on this theme were common in the early phase of the war, but faded away as the casualties mounted. As Rossiter remarked: 'Those who finally return from the war will be those who escaped shell, bomb and bullet by lucky accident, not those whose strength overcame adversaries.'[72]

The medical scientist Ronald Ross and the eugenist A. G. Thacker were sceptical that any causal link had been established between modern war and national degeneracy. Ross thought that the possibly dysgenic effects of modern missiles were offset by the way modern war raised the efficiency of the total social complex.[73] Thacker saw little evidence that Europe had suffered degeneracy because of the perpetual warfare that had plagued it until the nineteenth century. Nor was there proof of the militarist thesis that peace bred degeneracy – witness the healthy history of the Newfound-landers and Icelanders.[74]

Thacker and J. A. Lindsay were an energetic minority within the eugenics movement, urging a more rigorous methodology in dealing with the eugenics of war. How was it possible, Thacker asked, to apply 'the laws of heredity' to the known phenomena of war, and draw inferences about effects, when even biologists conceded that there were no generally accepted laws to apply? The field was still disputed between neo-Darwinists, Mendelo-mutationists and Lamarckians. Even the respected neo-Darwinian theory of 'reversed selection' could not be properly tested until a whole range of unknowns had been resolved, especially the quality and quantity of those killed at war, returned from war, and staying at home. As for Mendelian theory, it was necessary to discover how far military authorities selected soldiers on the basis of stable mutations rather than unstable fluctuations, for it was the selection of mutations that Mendelism claimed to be the key to permanent change in the character of populations. Much debate ignored the vital point that traits such as physical strength, stature and endurance were fluctuations, and extremes of fluctuations tended to revert rapidly to the racial mean. This reversionary process probably explained how nations had passed with little change through peace and war.[75]

J. A. Lindsay, professor of medicine at Queen's University, Belfast, warned that unproven theories were being paraded as dogmas in a debate over complex issues. It was simply being assumed that war wasted the best stock, that war (or peace) caused racial degeneracy, that any factor – including war – that lowered the birth-rate must be evil. In the latter instance, respectable demographers cautioned that over-crowding was a world peril. War's impact varied according to the economic and cultural level of the combatants, according to its duration and events, whether waged by conscripts or professional armies. The psychic effects were very different for victors and vanquished: 'The influence of war cannot be compressed into a single, simple or unambiguous formula.'[76]

The zoologist Chalmers Mitchell also condemned as vague and contradictory the evidence available on the eugenics of war. Mitchell (as we shall see later) was one of the more innovative peace biologists. However, his whole approach was conditioned by a healthy scepticism that any biological laws about human selection had yet been firmly established. He doubted that any real genetic modification of human stocks took place as a result of supposedly selective agencies, including war. In this case Mitchell was disturbed to find peace eugenics in the dubious company of the genetic determinists. He was very suspicious of the latter, since they were too ready to find hereditarian causes for social diseases, such as war, and too ready to propose authoritarian rather than liberal reformist solutions for them. Evaluative and political considerations thus coloured the 'objectivism' of even a disciplined and urbane thinker such as Mitchell. His critique highlighted some of the ambiguities in peace biology. While it was committed to the axiom that cultural rather than physical evolution was now the dominant mode for humans, peace biology was still obsessed by the need to show that war caused 'negative' physical selection.[77] Mitchell's misgivings were quickly taken up by the anti-pacifists, most notably by G. G. Coulton in his *Main Illusions of Pacificism* (1916), a searing polemic against Jordan and Angell.[78]

The Scottish doctor and science writer Ronald Campbell Macfie gave an iconoclastic critique of the whole debate, which he complained had been 'more often exploited by military or pacific partisans than elucidated by patient and impartial investigators'. The wary spirit of scientific inquiry was readily corrupted by 'the emotional psychology of war'.[79] Macfie (like Lindsay) insisted that each war was unique, involved a complex interplay of factors and had its own special consequences. A war of 'machine-guns and poison-gas, and serums' must be very different eugenically 'from a war waged with assegais and arrows'. Macfie had served on medical selection boards, and he doubted that the war was causing permanently dysgenic effects. Most men were rejected on account of acquired rather than hereditary defects, for example, flat feet caused by too much standing, heart disease caused by rheumatic fever: 'I doubt, indeed, whether ... the average enlisted man has three per cent more racial value than the average unenlisted person.' The epidemic of soldier weddings would probably nullify any procreative advantage enjoyed by the 'unfit' left at home.

Macfie saw armies as made up 'of all sorts and sizes, sons of Anakim and bantams', and it was an open question whether modern firepower selected the best or worst of them. Given the impartiality of machine-guns, 'the wholesale massacre of shrapnel, it seems very probable that death is indiscriminate in his harvest'. Better food and physical training in army life might have some eugenic effect, lowering vulnerability to TB and other diseases; but this was likely to be offset by greater wartime prevalence of 'drunkenness, nerve diseases, and vice diseases, and by the greater poverty and destitution that will follow the war'. However, overall, Macfie rated war quite low in the scale of factors causing negative selection in modern life, compared to the racial ravages of industrialism, drink and congenital disease: 'war is eugenic in so far as it takes men from the dysgenic industries of peace'. He noted that higher wages, less over-crowding and more food meant an improvement in the health of women and children of the lower classes in wartime. This point was rarely made at the time, but is now regarded as a major social consequence of the war. Macfie anticipated modern claims that wartime conditions were often an improvement for significant sectors of the British workforce.[80] He pointed out that only part of the male population was subject to war selection, many of these left children, many skilled workers were shielded in war factories, all females were unselected by war, while variations in physique 'even if selected, are often only nurtural' and all stocks remained well represented in the survivors.

Macfie's reference to the contentious issue of sexual selection raised a genuinely Darwinian concern, since sexual selection was a central feature of Darwin's theory. Macfie suggested that war's major historical impact had been upon sexual selection. In the modern era, war (he said) might even have a beneficial effect upon sexual selection, offsetting the destruction of male germ plasm at the front. If five million men were killed in the European war, some millions of women would be denied motherhood, while the surviving men would select as mates women with health, physique and beauty, 'for Nature has wisely arranged that men should be attracted by characters that imply capacity for motherhood'. Since such traits were heritable, and since civilised man was more and more inclined to choose types of female beauty that correlated with feminine virtues of sympathy, gentleness and unselfishness, 'every war, therefore, will do something to set up evolutionary tendencies opposite to its own brutal, truculent, anti-social spirit'.[81]

By the close of the war demographic studies were showing notable disturbances of the sex balance. According to one study, the ratio of females to males in the age class twenty to sixty had increased in Britain from 1,090 females to 1,000 males in 1910–11 to 1,150 to 1,000 in 1917.[82] Opinions varied about the likely genetic consequences of 'female pre-ponderance'. Hugins was sceptical about any major effect flowing from the war.[83] A number followed Macfie's line, hoping that womanly traits of gentleness and altruism might become fixed in the human character. Chalmers Mitchell suggested that, after a war, returned heroes were attractive to women and this was likely to result in 'high and selective reproductive activity'.[84] The continental demographers Gini and Savorg-nan argued that an over-supply of females would cause more hectic competition for mates, with the wealthier and 'fitter' females marrying and reproducing at the expense of the poorer and less 'fit'. Negative selection among males would be balanced by positive selection among women.[85] Such possibilities, plus the expansion of women's horizons triggered by the war, led one commentator to recall that 'one becomes a shade less impatient of the miserable waste and wreckage of war when one reflects how the exigencies of war have tapped unknown or forgotten reservoirs of national energy'.[86]

Raymond Pearl was another sceptic who discounted the thesis that war eliminated the best germ plasm.[87] Because females were not eliminated, half of the total racial germ cells of all qualities were preserved. Even if all the best males at the front were killed (an impossibility), within a few generations, on Mendel's principles, the remaining male genes at the home front could be bred up – given freely assortive mating – to make a 'preponderant stock of superior individuals'. In fact a considerable number of males killed in battle left progeny before their deaths, while a whole replacement generation of males and females under conscription age stood ready to perpetuate the race. Pearl observed that even in the most destructive of modern wars the killed were a surprisingly small proportion of the population. A death rate of 2 per cent for the American Civil War, or about 9 per cent of breeding males aged fifteen to fifty years, was not biologically decisive, in his opinion. Selective effects in the First World War became 'insignificantly slight', if account was taken of the randomi-sing effect of conscription and the mechanisation of war, with guns and shells destroying impersonally and non-selectively.[88]

Roswell H. Johnson, a eugenist trained in geology, systematised the manifold theories about war selection in an original multi-dimensional analysis.[89] Johnson had been appointed to one of the first chairs in eugenics in America, at Pittsburgh University in 1912. Like C. B. Davenport, D. S. Jordan, Frederick Adams Woods and Luther Burbank, Johnson was a member of the eugenics division of the American Breeders' Association, which has been described as a happy hunting ground for elitism and racism.[90] Racist values were to condition his theory of war's lethal selection.

Johnson urged that war's complex genetic effects should be studied under a number of modes. There were two major selective factors: (1) lethal selection operating through differential mortality; and (2) sexual selection working through differential mating. Also, selection occurred in two major contexts: (a) inter-group and (b) intra-group competition. One also needed to discriminate between selective effects *during* wartime – both upon armed forces and home population – and selective effects *after* the war.

Johnson hypothesised a crucial 'quality of race' factor affecting lethal selection. He rejected the 'sentimental equalitarianism' that denied important race differences. There were 'real average differences' between races: 'to think otherwise is to discard evolution and revert to the older standpoint of "special creation"'.[91] (This view, needless to say, itself depended upon deeply held racial assumptions that were impervious to scientific inquiry, and rested upon inconclusive data about race traits and their origins in heredity or culture.) Johnson said that the eugenic effect of war differed according to the race variation between the sides. There was significant variation when either the 'superior' or 'inferior' side lost notably fewer men: 'Where the difference has been considerable, as between a civilized and savage nation, it has been seldom that the superior does not triumph with fewer losses.' Johnson judged modern war, in general, to be less a test of racial efficiency than traditional war, because victory was increasingly a matter of alliance-making, with the weak uniting against a strong nation. However, he condemned the First World War as tragically dysgenic, a race war between 'members of the old Teutonic or Hebrew races, both stocks being preeminent for their contribution to science and art... The human species therefore on account of this is at present declining in inherent quality faster than in any previous similar length of time.'

As to selection *within* warring groups, this depended upon the method of raising armies. Permanent paid armies were probably little above the average of the nation, conscript armies probably superior physically. The quality of volunteer armies depended on the cause being fought for, whether one that appealed merely to adventurers only or to some moral principle. If the latter, heavy losses in a better quality army would be very dysgenic. The First World War was such a war, since through propaganda 'the soldiers of each country have been made to believe that *they* are the glorious defenders against unprincipled aggression'.

Lethal selection had worked historically within armies, because those killed were not 'a haphazard sample' of the whole army. A disproportionate number of the dauntlessly brave, reckless and stupid died. However with the modern increase of artillery, mines and bombs, those who fell were more and more chance victims. Again, the war selection once caused by disease was being nullified by advances in medicine and sanitation. Selection was also influenced by home-front conditions, often rendered severer than usual, with poverty rife, sanitation and medicine suffering. As the usual civilised restraints upon natural selection lessened, evolutionary pressures intensified.

Post-war selection also depended upon context. Inter-group selection could be changed by new agencies, as where a superior culture was forced by the victors upon the vanquished. However, victors could also introduce diseases and oppress conquered peoples. Conquerors themselves suffered when 'excessive spoliation' bred idleness, luxury and a diminishing birth-rate. Intra-group selection could be affected by such factors as reduced population pressure, making natural selection less severe. Alternatively, war could cause the loss of the economically creative part of a nation, or grinding taxation, leading to poverty and heavier selective pressures.

On sexual selection, Johnson agreed that the war's creation of an excess of women would intensify female selection. However the war also reduced male selection since relatively fewer men remained unmated. There was an over-supply of women in all classes, but some 'superior' women would not marry from 'the lack of sufficiently eligible suitors caused by the war'.[92] In the absence of hard data on this issue, Johnson and the other experts allowed conjecture and stereotypical thinking to condition their conclusions.

Johnson's multi-factorial model was a step towards the sophisticated paradigms used in later peace research on war. He was to expand his approach in *Applied Eugenics* (1918). However Johnson's model of 1915 was still rough-hewn, and lacked the empirical studies needed to challenge the authority of researchers such as Kellogg. Indeed, when dissected, Johnson's generalisations and hypotheses reflected his own eugenic leanings and current social and racial values.[93]

The 1914–19 debate over war's genetic and biological effects was revealing. One is struck by the authenticity of observations made in the midst of catastrophic events. The sense that Britain was witnessing a 'slaughter of social elites' has been largely confirmed by recent research.[94] At the same time, the debate yielded a diversity of readings of biology and history that illustrate yet again the perennial interaction between science and social theory. Eugenics was indeed still an infant study (and not yet discredited by its association with Nazi totalitarianism), while even the mind-boggling genetics revolution was only tentatively established. It was not surprising that 'unproven theories paraded as dogmas', as Lindsay complained; that scientific common sense came into conflict with pseudo-science and popular myth. The First World War, of course, raised massive issues of national and racial survival, so it was inevitable that scientific speculation should be stained with political and social colourings.

Overall the European crisis tended to confirm prevailing eugenic theory that modern warfare was a biological disaster for *Homo sapiens*. There was a pervasive anxiety that the First World War was decimating the racial and class elites of Europe. There was seen to be 'negative selection' caused by modern firepower and the mass recruitment of armies, nullifying any selective advantages conferred by warfare in earlier or primitive societies, or any eugenic effect of military training in modern nations. Under the screening methods of conscription, the medically 'fittest' were chosen for mass destruction in trench warfare, signalling a dramatic decline in the genetic quality of future generations.

People generally recognised that war's industrialisation and democratisation were among the most striking innovations in recent history, in humankind's rapidly changing environment. As with any dramatic ecological change, this necessitated adaptation and introduced new selective pressures. The contemporary judgment was that the human response to the challenge of the 'new militarism' was inadequate, and that the selective pressures were dysgenic. War had become an evolutionary anachronism. This verdict was to persist in biological circles. We find J. B. S. Haldane, the foremost evolutionist of our age, complaining in 1931 that 'eugenic organizations rarely include a demand for peace in their programmes, in spite of the fact that modern war leads to the destruction of the fittest members of both sides engaged in it'.[95]

Such a conclusion was satisfying to both traditional pacifism and to a eugenics movement committed to rational genetic planning. However, the alliance between mainstream peace biology and eugenics generated tensions and unmasked some of the ambiguities within the peace discourse. To some extent the tensions were camouflaged by the fact that both peace biology and eugenics were commodious movements, embracing a gamut of ideologies. Conservative racists like D. S. Jordan and liberal socialists like Havelock Ellis and Graham Wallas were accommodated within both traditions. Nevertheless there was a gulf between the free will, communitarian, optimistic school of peace biology and the starker brands of pessimistic, determinist eugenics. The rise of peace eugenics delivered a propaganda coup to the peace apostles, enabling them to deal a smashing new blow against the hated enemy, war, using the mailed fist of 'science'. But it also brought them into closer proximity to an alien and autocratic ideas system.

Galtonian eugenics focused upon genetic rather than cultural evolution, indeed tended to blame 'social evolution' – read reformist social change – for eliciting racial degeneration. In this dark scenario, war was only one of a series of characteristically modern social agencies causing dysgenic human effects. Precisely because war had become modern and 'techno-logised', it had ceased to be a healthy source of 'natural selection'. The logic of eugenics threatened to lead the peace movement into dangerous territory, for the eugenic 'utopia' was not only one of global peace, but one also of authoritarian genetic manipulation, eugenic population control and elimination of the 'unfit'. The criteria for 'unfitness' were essentially absolutes, or sociologically loaded rather than naturalistic.[96]

This discourse was fundamentally alien to the liberal peace vision. The main thrust of peace biology was to play down physical evolution through struggle, violence and natural selection, and to assert the primacy of cultural evolution in modern human history. Civilisation was assumed to have transcended genes and biological selection, to be motored by 'social heritage', and to be advancing almost automatically to a loftier plane of rationality, liberality and peace. If there was determinism here it was cultural rather than hereditarian. Far from human nature imposing ineluctable limits, it was seen to be limitlessly flexible and humans limitlessly adaptive, capable of solving the great problem of war through reason, co-operation and social reconstruction. The war dented, but did not destroy, this ideal. During this century of violence it has continued to show tough survival power.

Naturalistic fallacies and noble ends

Science and ethics

The war years elicited criticism of conflict-style Social Darwinism on grounds that it illicitly universalised data from the field of biological science, that it merged science and values, and tended to 'reduce' humankind to non-autonomous biological units. It is quite revealing that such methodological criticism was almost entirely directed at militaristic or aggressively capitalistic doctrines, rather than at the evolutionary models, or latent determinism, of peace biology. The privileged status of the latter model in this regard seems a telling sign of its entrenched intellectual position and respectability. Peace biologists were able to have their cake and eat it too. They commended cooperative models of animal behaviour as good examples for humans. At the same time they benefited from the epistemological difficulties of the enemy school when it used animal comparisons to legitimise war and human pugnacity. It has not been sufficiently noticed how peace biology 'cashed in' on major compatibilities between its value system and that of traditional mores, ethical and cultural. By contrast militarism – at least in the Anglo-American world – suffered by its association with unconventional standards, and found itself subject to more stringent analysis of its methods and philosophy.

The tendency to universalise from a discourse such as biology was rooted in pervasive nineteenth-century assumptions, especially the Comtean positivist assumption that all knowledge was reducible to science, that there existed an overarching system of natural laws that applied equally to science and society, that transactions and analogies made between the disciplines of biology, ethics and sociology were quite legitimate.[1] However these grand claims had generated methodological misgivings in the generation that preceded the First World War (see chapter 3). G. E. Moore tried to quarantine science from ethics in his *Principia Ethica* (1903), which developed a long-standing criticism of naturalistic ethics: namely, that it was logically objectionable to derive moral imperatives from factual descriptions, including scientific descriptions of nature or natural processes such as evolution.

The implications for 'Social Darwinism' were obvious. It was wrong to deduce unpalatable 'oughts' from the nasty and violent 'is' of nature; wrong to translate an observed natural law, for example, 'survival of the fittest', into a moral law or set of values. The implications for pacifist 'Social Darwinism' were less noticed. Of course, philosophy being what it is, endless discourse was possible on the subject. Evolutionary ethics had its defenders (such as Kropotkin); and some of them anticipated more modern discernments that Moore and his followers were heading towards a purely subjective theory of morals, one that replaced natural goods by 'self-evident' ideal goods that were in fact the 'comfortable intuitions' of Cambridge or Bloomsbury.[2]

T. H. Huxley's dissociation of evolution from ethics was taken up and expanded during the war by followers such as Peter Chalmers Mitchell, who, as we shall see, used Kantian idealism, the 'new physics' and schisms within biology itself to show the inadequacy of science as a source for rules of conduct. The historian James Bryce, following Mitchell, advised against the use of zoological analogies based upon the disputable hypothesis of natural selection. Human sequences (he said) were too complex and unpredictable, lacking the uniformity that marked things in external nature, to be subsumed under a set of natural laws. This did not, however, stop Bryce from commending adaptational, non-violent models from the animal world.[3] The Chicago sociologist I. W. Howerth declared that the whole case for war rested upon a profound misconception of natural law, which was not a service command but an observed sequence of events.[4] Theodore Chambers objected to the use made by militant Darwinists of evaluative and teleological concepts in discussions of evolution, which ought to be regarded as a natural, value-free law. Rather than attaching moral signs to whatever it was that survived, or accepting war's 'biologically just' decisions, humankind should 'so influence environment as to tend to give survival value to the highest and noblest characteristics'.[5]

Charles Waldstein, an Anglicised American who had studied at Heidelberg in the 1870s and became a leading Cambridge archaeologist, protested in his popular book *Aristodemocracy* (1916) that Darwinism was meant to be a scientific explanation of natural phenomena, not 'a practical or ethical guide for future conduct for man'. Pure Darwinism was not teleological but causal, while ethics dealt with ideal states, 'with things as man's best thought leads him to believe they ought to be'. Waldstein blamed the war on 'the defective moral consciousness' of the western world, the result of a crisis of faith in the face of scientised brute force.[6]

The English biologist F. A. E. Crew rejected the 'biological predestination' that marked the militarist–materialist concept of civilisation, 'the Darwinian standard of efficiency of the animal as the standard of fitness for survival of individuals and races in a civilised world'. Crew, believing that organic inheritance was always subordinate to social inheritance, grieved that biological–historical determinisms had threatened Britain almost as seriously as Germany: 'Haeckel, Nietzsche, Karl Marx and Treitschke were no more daringly dogmatic than were Herbert Spencer, Galton, Karl Pearson and Bateson.' Crew was fiercely opposed to the race, class and militarist extrapolations that had sprung from such grim biology. Yet he himself justified, as closer to the authentic historical design, nobler ideals 'more productive of benefit to humanity, and more in the direct line of the evolution of civilisation'. Peace apostles like Crew were willing to appeal to the verdict of arms when it suited them. He argued that Germany's defeat proved that materialist militarism was unable to survive in real battle against the more liberal values that lay closer to the heart of the biological process. This was hardly quarantining science from values.[7]

Chambers and Waldstein recognised that if Darwinism was to be safely sequestered into its own value-free realm, it needed to be distinguished from teleology. Since teleology usually envisaged a long march forward by evolution towards a final goal of ultimate absolutes, it was hardly ethically neutral. (Neither did it customarily locate its values in the natural process, in contrast to evolutionary ethics.) However, peace biology was by no means united on such theoretical issues. This study has already shown that ideas of purpose, progress, ethics and design kept intruding into peace biology, despite the existential bleakness of 'pure' evolutionism. 'Elevationist' biology tended to counter discourses of purposelessness and animal reductionism by restoring human dignity (or conceit), tended to put humanity back at the top of the ladder, to give biological reasonings for distancing man from the animals, almost to reformulate the idea of 'special creation'. Man, the favoured end-product of evolution, with distinctive talents, versatility, and ability to dominate a global habitat, 'man the imperial animal' was special. Humanity, by using its unique skills and reason to solve problems such as war and poverty, could become the ultimate master of the globe, the modern replacement for God, the fulfiller of evolutionary purpose. Meaning, even goodness, was restored to the universe. The reaction against determinism and reductive dogma had both liberal and illiberal potential. At its best it replenished concepts of human diversity and freedom. At its worst it threatened new forms of hubris and determinism.

Benjamin Kidd's *Science of Power* (1918) had a teleological view of humanity moving towards a higher destiny of benign competition. Ethical and mutualist modes of existence would eventuate (he predicted) under the influence of religion and feminism, with cultural evolution the key to a more humanitarian and irenic future. Despite his own tendency to see biologically determined patterns in history, Kidd had become disillusioned with Social Darwinism by 1916. He blamed it for generating exploitative capitalism, imperialism, and other forms of violent reductionism.[8]

Across the Atlantic the philosopher Ralph Barton Perry launched an angry wartime attack upon the 'new ethics' of Darwinian naturalism, which (he said) derived frightening criteria of right and wrong from an evolutionary process that in fact implied nothing as to value and offered no way of distinguishing between forms of survival. In his *Present Conflict of Ideals* (1918) Perry deplored the way in which a mechanistic Darwinism had been illegitimately extended to incorporate doctrines like Bergson's 'creative evolution' or Idealist teleology. The present age, understandably, found it hard to accept a Darwinian universe founded on chance, denying cosmic meaning or purpose, morally neutral: 'It has been widely supposed that since science has established the fact of evolution, the world is therefore growing better.' However, even if creation were moving towards some far-off event, why should it be good?: 'so far as the principle of evolution is concerned it might equally well be a *Götterdämmerung*'. Perry, a conventional moralist, tended to identify naturalistic ethics with philosophies of violence. This left out the Kropotkinite tradition of bio-ethics, and insufficiently allowed for benign ethics to emerge from Darwinian naturalism. Nevertheless his attack upon the Darwinian 'ideal of might' was well directed. The 'new ethics' had amputated moral criteria from the old standards of good. What one was morally obliged or permitted to do was now determined only by the measure of one's power: 'To the strongest all things are permissable; to the helpless, nothing.' The robust nation enjoyed a sort of universal right of way, and war became the test of nations.[9]

This approach, said Perry, was not only philosophically unsound, but biologically wrong-headed. Whereas the 'ideal of might' defined power simply in terms of survival, in the actual struggle for survival there were as many types of superiority as there were types of struggle:

The qualities required for success may be physical courage and chivalry, or they may be cunning and sanctimoniousness. Among nations, according as conditions change, success may be favoured by avarice or by martial vigor, or by scientific research, or by political submissiveness, or by revolutionary individualism ... [In the theory of might] Rome conquering the world by force of arms, is not less good than a Greece conquering it by force of ideas, or a Judea conquering it by the force of religious sentiment (pp. 144–5).

Perry might well have gone further, and shown that the common emphasis on might and violence within the discourse of militant evolutionary ethics bore a problematic relation to the pure theory that survival alone – whatever its form – was the criterion for superiority or value. Regardless of the latter, some people clearly preferred one sort of survival to another, possibly out of an absolutist preference for force. Perry himself preferred the conventional moral stance of those who wanted to differentiate higher from lower struggle, or even – like the socialists – to abolish human struggle altogether.[10]

Novicow revisited

Kidd and Perry exemplified a discernable late wartime reaction against hereditarianism, now encountering blame as a factor favouring militarism. That trend was accelerated by behaviourism in psychology and culture theory in anthropology. Social heredity became the thing, rather than instinct. Phrases abounded in the mould of H. G. Wells's 'tradition', James Mark Baldwin's 'social heredity', J. B. Watson's 'phylogenetic habit', Kidd's 'social inheritance' and A. L. Kroebner's 'superorganic'.[11] Cultural evolution promised salvation from the evils predicted by the degenerationists should natural selection be suspended. The optimists saw a hopeful human future caused by improvement to the social environment, progress that would be culturally transmitted to later generations.

In wartime America some intriguing contributions to the debate over the biology of war came from theorists preoccupied with the cardinal role of cultural, especially intellectual, evolution. Their work constituted a recuperation of Novicovian discourse. The prospect of United States intervention in the war seemed to stir greater interest in the evolutionary role of war in history. Americans, with their isolationist traditions, were wary about the effect upon their nation of immersion in the firestorm of Europe; although they were less wary, perhaps, about the benefits to civilisation if that event should be Americanised (one of the latest, the cynics said, in a series of cultural takeovers: the 'Americanisation of the world' had become a cant phrase of the period).

Thinkers like Teggart and Keller were fascinated by ideas-systems. They suggested that a more realistic version of Weismann's law of retrogression – which crudely emphasised physical competition – would focus upon the selective effects of rivalry between world-views and culture systems in explaining the rise of civilisations.

In his *Processes of History* (1918) the historian Frederick J. Teggart gave war the credit for two of man's major advances: the creation of the state, and the emergence of new ideas-systems. Prolonged and bitter wars, the result of group migrations, had finally broken up the early kinship systems, communities built upon blood-relationships, and paved the way for modern concepts of kingship and state, territorial structures and personal ownership, individual freedom from group dominance. The breakdown of customary fabrics was essential for human evolution, for progress depended upon the commingling of ideas through contact and friction between groups from dissimilar habitats. Without friction between peoples and cultures, and especially between ideas-systems, selection would have ended. Teggart, however, carefully delimited war's contribution to civilisation: it was mainly confined to 'the break-up of crystallized systems of organization and thought'. He distanced himself from the more extravagant claims of his fellow historian Crane Brinton that war had been 'the highest stimulus to racial progress', prompting an 'intellectual energy which nothing else can awake'.[12]

The sociologist Albert G. Keller, W. G. Sumner's follower and successor at Yale, author of the influential *Societal Evolution* (1915), anticipated modern sociobiology in his *Through War to Peace* (1918) by constructing a rudimentary gene-cultural mode of evolution. Keller speculated that social variations – like physical variations in nature – were tested by circumstance. The 'unfit' mores, ideas and social traits disappeared, while the 'fit' survived.[13] Reflecting Sumner's theory of mores, as expressed in *Folkways* (1907), Keller's concept of group selection was very deterministic. He saw evolution taking place 'Darwinistically' in an automatic and impersonal way, detached from the choices and intentions of most individuals. His theory allowed for various types of struggle, military, industrial, commercial and political. By insisting on the need for social traits to be tested by changing circumstance, it also entailed the conclusion that isolated peoples never developed an advanced culture (another echo of Bagehot). Keller was too realistic to claim that actual conflict took place between codes or mores. This was a figure of speech. The real conflict took place between groups or societies, with the victor extending and strengthening the code that it bore. A group's conviction that its code was superior was ethnocentrism.

Keller accepted the ancient and continuing importance of violence within human societies, but he argued, like Novicow, that as culture advanced, milder forms of struggle came to predominate.[14] They did so because they passed the evolutionary test. They were 'more expedient as adjustments to evolved life-conditions' than their parent-stock (p. 50). Cooperationist codes had a high survival value, since 'it is by peace and order within that a society is enabled to resist destruction or to concentrate its strength in pursuit of its interests against competitors'. Indeed the very definition of human society 'implies internal peace as an indispensable condition' (p. 51). However reversion to more primitive codes could easily occur if softened life conditions were replaced by harsher ones. Keller believed that war-selection was almost extinct in modern times, but could revive when milder modes of rivalry broke down. Unlike MacCurdy and others who saw war as pathological, Keller saw it as explicable behaviour under emergency conditions, as in the present world war:

Not for nothing has war been called the *ultimo ratio*. War has always been and is now the last expedient in bringing about selection in the mores (p. 57).

Keller rejoiced that the civilised mores of the Allied powers were triumphing over the primordial militarism of the enemy. This was in accord with the principles of societal evolution. The Prussian doctrine of war-selection by annihilation was the product of 'Teutonic half-knowledge' of Darwin's theory, and misuse of analogy: 'Germans have always been strong in applying theory from one field to matters of a quite different quality in another range.' It took the German mentality 'to work out in meticulous detail the analogy between society and an organism, and finally to identify the two' (p. 130). Darwin would never have countenanced the militarists' extrapolation from organic to social evolution: 'But a swift snatch at the analogy was satisfactory to the German mind, especially since the crude conclusions were in consonance with German mores' (p. 131).

The end of the war ushered in much celebration of the victory of the forces of reason and democracy over instinct and militarism. Patriotism and self-congratulation tended to prevail among scientists, but some, like the liberal Princeton biologist Edwin Grant Conklin, asked whether science itself was not partly to blame for the war: 'The sanction of science and especially of biology was claimed for the highly militarized state, for a hereditary aristocracy, for the beneficial effects of war.'[15] Conklin was an interesting case, a devout defender of democracy against racism and elitist theory, and willing to legitimise his values from biology. Yet he can be found issuing distinctly modern cautions against the use of analogy, warning that the application of biology to society was often of doubtful value. Biological sanctions could be found both for and against war:

Those who are searching for biological analogies to support almost any preconceived theory in philosophy, sociology, education, or government can usually find them, for the living world is large and extraordinarily varied and almost every possible human condition has its parallel somewhere among lower organisms (p. 404).

Nevertheless Conklin felt that the fundamental laws of biology applied to man no less than to other organisms: 'biology is a torch-bearer not merely into the dark backgrounds of human history but also into the still more obscure regions of the future development of the race' (p. 404). Conklin feared a resurgence of reactionary biology in the west, provoked by the democratic forces unleashed by the war, with thrones and autocracies crashing down everywhere. Strong enmity was arising in the United States against women's suffrage, popular education and the spread of world socialism, and hereditarian arguments were being exploited by the 'better classes' against the blacks and the disadvantaged. This pseudo-science needed to be exposed as politically motivated.

Conklin proposed using a biological insight to grapple with the classic dilemmas of democratic theory: how to reconcile individual freedom with the needs of social organisation, democratic equality with hereditary inequalities. Although man was never completely free from instinctive compulsions, the precondition for human freedom was man's evolutionary windfall: the growth of intelligence and memory, enabling a relative emancipation from organic inheritance. History could be read as a long evolutionary struggle for freedom and social emancipation, with individual liberty always balanced by the social good. As to which was the greater good, biology answered: 'Race preservation and evolution is the supreme good, and all considerations of the individual are subordinate to this end' (p. 406). If democracy maximised individualism and minimised social control, this would represent a return to the 'protozoan condition'. Hence Conklin provided himself with a biological case for the socialisation of democracy, in line with Progressivist and liberal welfarist tendencies. He used natural analogies. Humans could enjoy a freedom like that of normal cells of the body, each an individual unit preserving some independence, but fitting into an holistic system. Or else humans could aspire to freedom, not like that of the solitary wasp, but like that of the ants and bees in a colony, each best serving what Maeterlinck called 'the spirit of the hive'.

Conklin defended his holistic multi-racial ideal as 'the biological ideal of freedom', based upon the biological kinship of all humans. Humans were more alike than different, their instincts were fundamentally similar, and harmony was mainly a matter of education and milieu. He vigorously opposed the peace proposals to sub-divide Europe along lines of so-called race and nationality. Such differences were not inherent, but largely cultural and political. Biological progress lay in forming giant multi-cultural, democratic federations of peoples, like the United States, many cells making one splendid body. Human progress, as never before, depended upon 'the rational recognition of the great truth of universal brotherhood' (p. 410).

Peter Chalmers Mitchell: a 'modernist' objection to determinism

Peter Chalmers Mitchell's *Evolution and the War* (1915) constituted one of the more intelligent restatements of the 'optimist' tradition on the biology of war. It is the more interesting because it defied the tone of much bio-social speculation. Mitchell had epistemological misgivings about a universalist Darwinism, misgivings derived from twentieth-century physics and idealist metaphysics. This was quite unusual for biologists. He advanced the concept of scientific uncertainty to attack extrapolation from nature to man, to attack reductionist militarist doctrines as well as some brands of peace determinism.

Chalmers Mitchell (1864–1945) was an impressively cosmopolitan thinker, educated at the universities of Aberdeen, Oxford, Berlin and Leipzig. His pre-war publications included *Outlines of Biology* (1894), a biography of T. H. Huxley (1900), and a best-seller, *The Childhood of Animals* (1912).[16] Mitchell was examiner to the Royal College of Physicians (1892–6, 1901–3) and Secretary to the Zoological Society of London (1903–35). He wrote popular science for a range of journals and newspapers, most abundantly for the *Saturday Review* under the editorship of the flamboyant Max Harris. During the war Mitchell was recruited to the War Office as a captain in military intelligence (MI7), and worked for the Imperial General Staff and the War Mission. He was part of the Crewe House propaganda team assembled by Lord Northcliffe, and later had a hand in drafting the British peace terms. A Liberal in 1919, he became disillusioned by Lloyd George's vindictive peace policy and moved steadily to the left. He was living in Malaga at the outbreak of the Spanish Civil War and 'as a passionate "Red" fraternised with the anarcho-syndicalists'.[17]

Mitchell described himself as a 'hard-shell Darwinian evolutionist, a lover of the scalpel and microscope'. He disliked supernaturalism but admitted to a love–hate relationship with Hegelianism and was fascinated by issues such as vitalism in biology. As a raw twenty-year-old graduate from Aberdeen, he spent some months in Berlin at a time of militaristic fervour orchestrated by Bismarck, and found this deeply disagreeable. Yet he was drawn to Hegel: 'Schopenhauer had bored me, and Kant had beaten me, but the shining, fragile net thrown by Hegel over the universe had enchanted me.' Later as a brilliant Oxford zoologist Mitchell visited German universities and came to know many German scientists. But his heart and intellect turned steadily towards France, then Russia. He read Balzac, Flaubert, Zola, de l'Isle-Adam, Huysman – an 'amazing literature of beauty and insight' – then, after learning Russian for technical purposes, was led to the great Russian writers, Pushkin, Gogol, Dostoevsky and especially Tolstoy.[18]

Mitchell had a youthful fling with biological determinism. In an apocalyptic Wellsian-style essay for the *Saturday Review* in 1896, he spoke of nations as 'species in the making', and forecast an era of world wars fought between expanding giants, with feeble races wiped off the face of the earth. Armies and navies were like the teeth and claws of the tiger, the weapons of the 'species-corporate'. As conflict was most deadly in nature between species most similar, Germany was likely to be England's 'biological' rival. France and England were 'commensal mates'. The smaller nations were 'an assortment of incongruous breeds, imperfectly trained to live together in a harmony that requires the utmost vigilance of the keepers' (an interesting foretaste of Desmond Morris's metaphor of the 'human zoo'). Although the article drew little attention in Britain, it caused ripples in Germany where von Bülow saw it as a sign that the British were shaping up for an inevitable war against an emerging naval rival.[19]

Mitchell changed his ideas after reading Tolstoy, opposed the Boer War, rejected Bernhardian militarism, and played down struggle in natural selection. He soon forgot his morbid prophecies, visiting Germany in 1911, 1912 and 1913, feeling, like others, that 'war between great modern nations was a horror that no statesman would face'. Once a champion of evolutionary ethics, even against his hero Huxley,[20] he now denied that man as ethical creature was subject to biological laws governing the life of lower animals. He gave three lectures along these lines to the Royal Institution in February 1915. They provided the basis for *Evolution and the War*.[21]

Mitchell lived in the age of Ernst Mach, Henri Poincaré and Albert Einstein, F. H. Bradley and Alfred Whitehead, men whose scientific philosophies had demolished the old Newtonian certitudes and sown widespread doubt that scientific laws expressed an objective knowledge of reality. Scientific laws came to be seen as constructs, hypotheses about a world that was, in Bradley's phrase, a structure of emergent relationships. Mitchell absorbed the ideas arising from the 'new physics' and applied them to biology. He expressed scepticism that any significant implications for humans could be drawn from so-called Darwinian science, since a scientific law had no absolute validity, but was a generalisation from experience:

a scientific law is the result of the interplay of two factors, the extended world, at once the occasion and the subject of experience, and the human mind, ranging over the extended world, codifying, simplifying, schematizing. The resulting law is of the human mind and in the human mind, rather than of the extended world or in the extended world. It is an attempt at comprehension, subjective and not objective.

Rather like Mach, Mitchell melded physics with Kantian epistemology to deny that science was ever capable of understanding the 'ultimate, metaphysical reality which enfolds and permeates us'. He accepted Kant's view that science was theoretical and that one must look to a source other than science for the rules of conduct. This was the basic fallacy of the militant Social Darwinists, that they extrapolated from a biological 'law' such as the 'struggle for existence' to human rules of conduct (pp. 6–7).

In any case, given the war of paradigms within biology itself – with Mendelism, biometrics and Lamarckism vying for supremacy – had biological science in fact established satisfactory laws governing animal and human behaviour? Mitchell, as a good Darwinist, believed natural selection to be the best hypothesis of the cause of organic evolution. But he insisted that there was too much disagreement about its credibility among naturalists for it yet to be regarded as scientific law: 'many of the most ardent Mendelians have such confidence in their own theory that they no longer think it necessary to invoke the operation of natural selection at all'. Another school of zoology believed in directive rather than natural selection, which must be seen not as a law but a 'hypothesis much in debate' (pp. 14–16, 19–20).

Mitchell reinforced mainline peace biology by showing how people had misread Darwin's concept of struggle. Darwin's survivors, the 'favoured races' in the contest for life, were not meant to be the best armed necessarily, but rather the best suited to their whole environment 'including climate, food-supply, chances of mating and leaving offspring, general adaptation to their place in the composite web of life'. Whereas Darwin used the concept of struggle in a large metaphorical sense, including dependence of beings on one another, popularists gave it 'the special significance of fierceness and cruelty' (pp. 21–2). Mitchell accepted Kropotkin's emphasis upon mutual aid in evolution. Separate species had their niche in the ecological scheme, and there was rarely a direct struggle to take over an environment. Species tended to live side by side, the main competition being between members of the same species to survive in the face of severe Malthusian pressures. Often it was the more intelligent and hardier that displaced the more aggressive, as in the case of the disease-resistant dingo displacing the fierce Tasmanian wolf (thylacine).

Mitchell drew upon the infant study of ecology, publicising the researches undertaken by Victor Shelford, zoologist at the University of Chicago. Shelford's team had for years surveyed the life-systems of all animals, large and small, at field stations within one hundred miles of Chicago, concentrating on the Indiana sand dunes around Lake Michigan. Mitchell believed that Shelford's results were compatible with his own theory that evolutionary success depended less upon active violence done by dominant to weaker species, than upon general adaptive capacity. The team had found that animals in a region formed communities, consisting of a number of species that had selected a particular environmental complex. Different groups formed stream, pond, lake, prairie, thicket and forest communities. There was a finely balanced system of interdependence and unconscious co-operation, with no trace of the remotest resemblance to human warfare. Popularisers such as Havelock Ellis were soon passing on this version of Shelford's work to the British public.[22]

Mitchell objected to comparisons between animal predation and human warfare. Animals were ferocious, or used their weapons (beaks, claws, horns, teeth), to obtain food, or else in defence of themselves, their mates and young, or in the rivalries of sex. (He hardly considered that human warfare might involve extensions of such factors.) In any case could 'laws' derived from animal behaviour be applied to humans? Mitchell was sarcastic about the current obsession with animal analogies. As the augurs of imperial Rome inspected the entrails of animals before giving advice on grave matters of state, so 'modern philosophers explain and justify human conduct after a visit to the monkey-house at the Zoological Gardens'. Man's ferocity was explained by reference to the ape and the tiger: 'Human nature is interpreted in terms of protoplasm' (pp. 1, 93).

Unlike some present-day ethologists and sociobiologists, Mitchell advised extreme caution in making comparisons between different species, and especially between man and the lower animals:

It is merely futile to range up and down the animal kingdom, picking a resemblance here and a resemblance there; only the tracing back of human qualities down the exact line of ancestry of man, whatever that may be, could help us, and even were that done, no doctrine of origin, nor proved fact of origin could obliterate the distinctions between man and beast. However fruitful and interesting it may be to remember that we are rooted deep in the natal mud, our possession of consciousness and the sense of freedom is a vital and overmastering distinction (p. 94).

Another dilemma faced the lovers of analogy. What units were under discussion? The units of the animal kingdom – species, sub-species, varieties, races – were connected by blood relationship, linked by common descent. The units of human populations (or at least those favoured by militant Social Darwinists in their zoological analogies) were nations, and nations were now known not to be of the same order as units in the animal and vegetable world. They were not united by blood relationship. Anthropological studies had shown that the major racial types were intermingled in Europe, despite concentrations in certain areas. Employing the American William Z. Ripley's typology (*The Races of Europe*, 1899), Mitchell declared Britain to be Mediterranean and Nordic with an absorbed Alpine element. France had the three races in well-marked forms. Russia was typically Alpine, with Nordic strains in the north-west. Germany – despite the pan-Germanists – was diverse, predominantly Alpine in the south, centre and east, Nordic only along the north-west. Clearly Europe's political divisions did not correspond with the racial types of their inhabitants. Even if struggle were the biological law of life, it did not necessarily apply to political units that were the products, not of common descent or genetic links, but of 'bonds that are peculiar to the human race' (p. 64), i.e., cultural bonds.

Mitchell believed that cultural evolution, the characteristic means of human development, set human history apart from all other natural history. Of course nurture and nature were inextricably mixed in the shaping of individuals and peoples. But on the whole he was sceptical that wholesale genetic modification of human stocks took place as a result of supposedly selective agencies, even war (see chapter 6). Mitchell denied William Bateson's suggestion that mental and emotional aptitudes were genetically determined, saying flatly that 'nurture is inconceivably more important than nature' (p. 82).

In the long-standing biological debate between 'preformationists' and 'epigenesists', Mitchell thought of himself as an epigenesist.[23] Preformationists believed that organisms unfolded from a tiny pre-programmed precursor, epigenesists that the key influence was environment acting upon the germ to form the mature creature. Mitchell applied epigenesis to nations. The most important forces moulding difference in nationality (he said) were epigenetic, that is to say that they were cultural forces (education, social conditions, value systems) that were imposed upon the hereditary material, and had to be re-imposed in each generation.[24] While physical change caused by selection in humans was imperceptible, the role of the environment in shaping mental and emotional qualities of a people was critical. Attitudes were transmitted to the next generation, not directly by inheritance, but by cultural acquisition via tradition and literature, forming a 'permanent mental environment of the most powerful kind' (p. 90). This was part of *Kultur*, which gave a continuous life to national ideals, emotions, political and social systems, concepts of justice and religion. *Kultur* served to differentiate nations, however alike their initial racial composition, in a fashion that was new and peculiar to man.

Although humans were physiologically only slightly modified apes, they had during eons of evolution acquired a unique consciousness:

And it is consciousness that transforms all the qualities and faculties acquired by human beings from the animal world and that is the foundation of free and intelligent existence. It is not the existence of alternatives, not unforseeability or spontaneity but the consciousness of these that puts man and the nations he makes above the laws of the unconscious world. It is consciousness that gives man the power of being at once the actor, the spectator and the critic, that enables him to distinguish between self and not-self; and that brings him with it the sense of responsibility and of reality (p. 105).

Man was not therefore bound by supposedly deterministic laws derived from animal analogies. Mitchell opposed the extremes both of animal reductionism, and Bergsonian vitalism which suffused all life with a sense of consciousness, purpose and freedom. He wanted to show that humanity was unique, not according to traditional philosophy or religion, but according to Darwinian law. With Darwin he held that man's moral, intellectual and emotional qualities had evolved from the qualities of animals. Nevertheless animals were on the whole instinctive, man intelligent, animals irresponsible, man responsible, animals automata, man free. (There were strong echoes here of Lloyd Morgan.) Mitchell believed that there was no need to postulate an innate moral law within human nature, as did the Kantians. Writing as a 'hard-shell Darwinist', he concluded:

I assert as a biological fact that the moral law is as real and as external to man as the starry vault. It has no secure seat in any single man or in any single nation. It is the work of the blood and tears of long generations of men. It is not in man, inborn or innate, but is enshrined in his traditions, in his customs, in his literature, and his religion. Its creation and sustenance are the crowning glory of man, and his consciousness of it puts him in a high place above the animal world (p. 107).

It followed that humans could create peace, if they wanted. War was not fated.

Evolution and the War was respectfully received in Britain and abroad (it was translated into French and Portuguese), but it was symptomatic of the debate that Mitchell's ideas were seized upon to defend widely divergent viewpoints. Mitchell's friend James Crichton-Browne and Havelock Ellis used the book to show that adaptation to environment was more important than fighting in the evolutionary process, and most reviewers commended Mitchell for coolly and scientifically demolishing Bernhardi's war biology.[25] However G. G. Coulton's *Main Illusions of Pacificism* (1916) used Mitchell's scepticism about the methodology of peace eugenics to discredit pacifism and the Jordan–Angell thesis that war was dysgenic.[26] James Bryce used Mitchell to argue against the use of analogy to justify a theory of strife, as did the *Times Literary Supplement*:

German 'biological necessity' is seen to be based not on a law but on a very questionable hypothesis concerning Nature, and to be linked with that hypothesis not by relation but by analogy – and a false analogy.[27]

However, Ronald Ross was more confident than Mitchell about the reliability of Darwinian theory and inclined to think that laws derived from animal behaviour might legitimately be applied to humans.[28]

The last point created dispute when Mitchell's book appeared in French, with a preface by Emile Boutroux, Academician and philosopher of science. Naturalists in war-torn France tended to endorse Mitchell's peace evolutionism, and especially his critique of the German doctrine of omnipotent force. The Sorbonne biologist Etienne Rabaud hailed Mitchell for expressing 'the essential fact that absolute force is not dominant in biologic phenomena', but Rabaud refused to accept that man differed so radically from animals as to make analogies illegitimate: 'To endeavour to separate, from the metaphysical and sentimental point of view, organisms which one is obliged to assimilate from the biologic point of view, is a rather vain undertaking.' However the eminent biologist Joseph Grasset, of the medical faculty of the University of Montpellier, declared that man, as a fixed species for many centuries, presented characteristics so specific – notably from the 'psychical point of view' – that he should rationally be made the subject of a separate science, human biology: 'The human biologist must guard himself as carefully against the amibomorphic error as the general biologist guards himself against the anthropomorphic error.' Grasset approved of Mitchell's biology:

It is not the general biologic law of struggle, battle, the victory of the strong, which should be applied to man; it is the law of progress, mutual love and help, collaboration and emulation ... Human Biology enjoins international morality as well as individual morality, interindividual and social morality, for times of peace and times of war.[29]

As an enemy of biological militarism, Mitchell not only refracted current anxieties about the legitimacy of evolutionary ethics, he introduced an innovatory note – linked to the 'modernist' intellectual milieu of the time – when he put objections to the use of analogy on the grounds (1) that the Darwinist paradigm had not been properly established, and (2) that scientific laws themselves were uncertain and subjective. In respect of the first objection Mitchell encountered continuing Darwinist orthodoxy, not least from peace biology itself, while confusion was added by his personal devotion to Darwinism and his political suspicion of Mendelian hereditarianism. The later triumph of a new Darwinian synthesis under men like R. A. Fisher made Mitchell's criticisms seem outmoded. In the second respect, Mitchell's attack on the primacy of naturalistic science echoed the epistemology of the 'new physics' and German neo-Kantianism. However, positivism was still deeply embedded in Britain, indeed seeming to enjoy a resurgence from the 1890s.[30] Mitchell's critique of the Darwinist version of positivism seems to have been too novel and puzzling to influence a generation still convinced of the soundness of science.

He made more impact when he put his case against analogy on grounds of professional methodology. As a naturalist he could argue that it was impossible to make correct comparisons even between an insect and spider, 'two creatures so closely allied that only zoologists would separate them', unless one could trace the qualities of the insect and spider down to their

common ancestor, 'and in so doing we should almost certainly lose all that
made the comparison interesting and significant, and be left with little
more than the qualities common to all protoplasm':

It is quite true that the whole web of life is in physical and physiological
community, but considerations drawn from any part of it require so much
modification before they can be applied to any other part, that they become merely
verbal.[31]

This type of criticism was to have a more lasting heritage. Chalmers
Mitchell is worth remembering as an articulate early spokesman of a
persistent, if embattled, modern tradition that has resisted interpretations
of human nature and history that are based upon genetic determinants or
immutable biological laws, or that use animal analogies to generalise too
freely about human pugnacity and war.

8 Conclusion

It would be worthwhile to pursue the themes we have discussed to the present time. However I close with World War I. Another book (and another decade's work) would be required to do justice to the fascinating period after Versailles, and to energetic thinkers such as Raymond Pearl, Margaret Mead, Maurice Davey, Quincy Wright, Konrad Lorenz, Eric Fromm, E. A. Wilson and the sociobiologists. The lack of British names reflects their diminished contribution to a biological debate that British scientists largely pioneered. It would be interesting to gauge the extent to which the trauma of the First World War experience helped depopularise instinct theory, and accelerate the trend to behaviourism and 'culture theory' in bio-psychology and the social sciences generally. By comparing and contrasting national responses to the issue of war and human aggression (for example, Britain compared with the United States), one would hopefully glean deeper insights into the interaction between science and culture. That interaction would be dramatically illustrated also by analysis of the impact of Nazism and Stalinism upon biological discourse. For the moment, a few concluding reflections upon the present endeavour seem in order.

This study has attempted to trace the manifold implications of Darwin's theories for the debate over war and peace. It is suggested that, while Darwinism was translatable into almost every available idiom of political and social discourse, its usage in justifying war and generating a violent image of *Homo pugnax* has been exaggerated in the historical literature. That literature has undervalued Darwinism's peace implications, and especially Darwinism's capacity for assimilation into traditional value systems that spurned violence and stark survivor ethics. Such an interpretation is generally consistent with revisionist historiography on 'Social Darwinism', which argues for Darwinism's origins in, and absorption into, existent intellectual and moral paradigms. Our account of nineteenth-century conflict theory and biological militarism, of positivism and various stage theories of social evolution – including those of Spencer and Bagehot – hardly sustains an image of a 'revolutionary' Darwinism that broke down the existing framework of values on the questions of war and human pugnacity, although it would be foolish to deny elements of innovation and reorientation introduced by selectionist theory and language. The more radical brands of militaristic Social Darwinism were worsted in the Anglo-American world by a Darwinian-based 'peace biology' that accorded better than its rival with deeply held western moral values. Even in the more militaristic culture of Germany, biologically-based theories of state violence seem to have served largely as rhetorical appendices to more central justifications founded upon *realpolitik* and nationalism.

If my understanding of the evidence is correct, the scientifically versatile tradition of peace biology survived even the challenge of the 'new genetics' and the shock of the First World War. It is true that hereditarian and instinctivist ideas promoted a reductionist image of a belligerent and territorial humankind (chapter 5). However a revamped peace biology used new disciplines such as eugenics and ecology to consolidate and revivify a mainstream co-operationist tradition based upon Darwin, Kropotkin, and Novicow. Having said this, it is also true that the success of the peace paradigm obscured within it some long-standing tensions and ambivalences – dissonances that have continued to bedevil the movement.

A recurrent ambiguity was introduced into peace biology by influences derived from anti-determinist elements within Darwinism. Wallace and Huxley were emblematic figures in the creation of a tradition that affirmed human autonomy against the 'imperial' claims of biological science, a tradition that was sceptical about naturalistic analogy and ethics. This scepticism – carried on by innovative naturalists such as Chalmers Mitchell – ran counter to Kropotkin-style affection for mutualistic analogies taken from nature, and counter also to a Jordan-style determinist streak within peace eugenics. In the latter discourses, peace, rather than war, was seen as a biological necessity.

Both anti-war and pro-war camps used propaganda derived from bogus science, or dubious methodology and philosophy of science, when it suited their book. This was shown during the 1914–19 debate over the eugenics of war, when the sceptics who cogently posed some of the methodological difficulties at stake became an embattled minority. In general the peace school was able brilliantly to exploit the epistemological deficiencies of its enemies, whilst its own contradictions were rarely exposed to public criticism. As I have argued in chapter 7, the privileged status of the peace model in this respect reflects the way in which peace biology 'cashed in' on major compatibilities between its value system and that of traditional mores.

The First World War controversy over war's genetic ramifications was a particularly revealing one. It showed the strengths, but also unmasked the dissonances and dangers that imperilled peace biology. Peace eugenics had a splendid triumph, establishing as orthodoxy the proposition that modern war was dysgenic, that war had lost its tendency (if any) to maximise fitness. At the same time the peace alliance with eugenics exposed the movement to alien and autocratic influences (see the discussion at the close of chapter 6). The racial and class mythologies of conservative eugenics, its deterministic and reductionist world-view, threatened the liberal peace vision of an autonomous humanity making a peaceful human future – not by means of genetic manipulation and illiberal political controls – but by means of a voluntaristic process of cultural evolution. Fortunately for humanity the resilience of that liberal vision has enabled it to survive the challenges of twentieth-century totalitarianism and new forms of scientific absolutism.

Successfully concealed within the peace tradition were competing images of humanity and nature, each attracting strong allegiances. There was the 'Kropotkin paradigm' of a benevolent nature/humanity encountering violent technologies and state/class systems. This contrasted with the 'Huxley paradigm' of a violent nature/humanity curbed by an ethical, nature-transcending civilisation. The defence against the biological determinist's case on war used almost every conceivable variation on the above paradigms. The 'primitivist', or romantic, solution to war simply advocated the removal of structural factors that were distorting human nature. This was the mirror-image of the biological–militarist position, seeing peace – rather than war – as the natural outcome of man's placable – rather than vengeful – nature. However the concept of war as culturally specific, as function of society rather than biology, was not confined to the romantics with their image of an innocent humanity. It was also compatible with the 'realist' peace strategy that accepted the possible violence of humanity/nature, but denied that this explained war. War (in this view) was a question of politics rather than instincts, a matter of strategies, ambitions, plots and intentions rather than genes.

The modern dispute between sociobiology and sociology over war and the roots of social violence has replayed these themes. On the one hand, sociobiology sees war as the natural outcome of human pugnacity – in E. O. Wilson's phrase 'only the most organized technique of aggression ... endemic to every form of society'.[1] Sociology has questioned this linkage, and tended to explain war as a function of social organisation, of state, class, race and gender systems. (Race and gender, it might be objected, are not unrelated to biology but the sociologists reject utterly the logic of sociobiology on these subjects.) The sociologists Martin Shaw and Colin Creighton criticise the conceptual confusion, and 'the enormous amount of popular simplification', that mark discussion about war and pugnacity:

Aggression is not force, force is not violence, violence is not killing, killing is not war ... Not only must we deny that these terms are interchangeable; we must question any assumption of automatic connection between them. It really is quite absurd to suppose that it follows from the fact that individual people show aggression to each other in certain social situations, that superpower states must prepare to annihilate each other's populations with thermonuclear weapons. No such link makes any logical or scientific sense.[2]

On the other hand, there were predispositions within historic peace biology at least to consider that there might exist a biological basis to human aggression, and that this might entail causal linkages to the phenomenon of war. Even the most orthodox of peace biologists can be found accepting that human pugnacity derived from innate mechanisms (see the discussion of instinct theory in chapter 5); and can be found inclining to current assumptions that war had arisen historically out of 'fighting instincts', or else that war historically had conferred selective advantage upon victor groups in the struggle for survival. Nevertheless the main thrust of peace biology was to suggest that humans were progressively able to transcend their genes, to escape natural selection ('dodging many of the operations of the cosmic forces' as Robert Munro put it),[3] able to make culture ascendant over biology, will ascendant over instinct.

It was this confidence and emphasis that distinguished peace biology from modern ethology (in the Lorenz, Eibl-Eibesfeldt tradition) or modern sociobiology – and one says this without accusing these schools of welcoming biological militarism: it is rather that they are perennially sceptical that culture can control innate predispositions; indeed, more likely, as in E. O. Wilson's case, to see culture as sanctifying raw biological processes as encoded by genes. By contrast peace biology often spoke in Darwinian terms of war having changed from a once useful to a now hurtful structure, an evolutionary anachronism, a biological liability rather than necessity, no longer an adaptive option for humankind. Using the rhetorics and images of Darwin's holistic ecology, peace biology articulated possible solutions to war by means of normative social controls. Whether such controls were perceived to occur within, or outside, the 'natural' process was a matter of philosophical dispute (Huxley's waverings on the issue are instructive). However for many biologists higher ethics and a more humane culture had become part of the human evolutionary process.

The pre-1919 debate over the 'biology of war' may seem remote to us now. However the resonances of that debate still echo in modern controversies. This is particularly so, as I have already suggested, in the case of modern ethology and sociobiology. The founding fathers of these disciplines, most notably Konrad Lorenz and E. O. Wilson, put neo-

Darwinian interpretations of aggression based upon a speculative bio-history of humankind. So of course did a number of thinkers dealt with in these pages. However ethologists and sociobiologists seem to suffer from collective amnesia about their forebears. They have been remarkably reticent in acknowledging their intellectual ancestry, especially in the period before the great synthesising theories of Fisher, Sewall Wright and Haldane in the 1920s. When occasionally turning their hands to history, sociobiologists have given very garbled accounts of 'Social Darwinism', which they regard as an ideological taint to be avoided. Revisionist historians in their turn have defended 'Social Darwinism' as seeking to reconcile science with traditional religious and cultural values, and accuse sociobiology of abandoning such values in favour of a survivor ethic: 'Rather then being heirs of earlier social Darwinism, Wilson and his fellow sociobiologists are cultural radicals.'[4]

Such sanitisation of 'Social Darwinism' as essentially a quest for 'moral theodicy in nature' may take the revisionists too far. After all, the biological militarists were certainly seen to be one type of Social Darwinist, rightly or wrongly, and they suffered the same sort of embarrassment as the sociobiologists – precisely because their survivor ethic was viewed as anti-social and anti-traditional. They were seen as proposing a new, and unacceptable, morality, rather than reconciling science and tradition. They too were cultural radicals. Nevertheless, this study offers evidence that even 'fighting instinct' theorists recoiled from stark survivorism, denied the Bernhardi theorem about war's necessity, and in the last resort wanted their science to accord with the ethical and mythic structures of western tradition. 'Pure' militaristic Darwinists were more of an endangered species than has usually been acknowledged.

To return to antecedents. There were some remarkable anticipations of modern brain theory and sociobiology that occurred in the post-Darwinian debates over war and aggression. Of course, such anticipations lacked the syncretic power of today's models. But the basic insights were there. This can be illustrated, briefly, from E. O. Wilson's best-selling *On Human Nature* (1978). Almost every major theme in his chapter on aggression can be located in works written before 1919. Henry Rutgers Marshall, G. T. W. Patrick, George W. Crile and Walter Cannon prefigured Wilson's claim that pugnacious predispositions had been genetically encoded into the human brain (chapter 5). They said – in early sociobiological style – that modern man was still programmed for fighting, that the ancient bio-psychological roots of aggression persisted in humans. They thought that the institutionalisation of war rested on an instinctive foundation. In Wilson's phrase, war thus becomes 'a straightforward example of a hypertrophied biological predisposition'.[5] Many early biologists would have agreed with Wilson's view that war was endemic in human history (especially pre-modern history – the nineteenth century was more complacent than we are that modernity spelt peace). Samuel Jackson Holmes, for example, believed 'the destructive, but eugenically wholesome, occupation of fighting' to be ubiquitous, placing a selective premium on qualities of brain-power, courage, social solidarity and corporate efficiency. Genocidal warfare was thought to be a key factor in catalysing a critical species-change from hominid to *Homo sapiens*. Writers cited in this volume variously explained war in what have now become familiar sociobiological terms of territoriality, crowding, competition for resources, sexual and reproductive advantage, innate ethnocentrism and hostility to strangers, subspeciation, and enforcement of the rules of society.

Sir Ronald Ross strikingly foreshadowed Wilson's main propositions: for example, that humans had hereditary dispositions to aggressive behaviour; that combative instincts and war had been ecologically and selectively critical to human evolution; and even that the learning-rules of violent aggression had become obsolete, and that new rules must be devised using culture and reason. As Ross observed of war: 'Evolution has taken to itself a number of new and finer tools, wherewith to continue its great work, and the hatchet with which it formerly rough-hewed was no longer required.'[6]

Wilson's more liberal concluding reflections would not have been devoid of appeal to thinkers such as Havelock Ellis, Norman Angell and Graham Wallas. The eventual outcome of the evolution of organised aggression (Wilson says) will be determined 'by cultural processes brought increasingly under the control of rational thought'. He sees civilisations as propelled by 'the reciprocating thrusts of cultural and organized violence' – bringing the world at last even to the brink of nuclear annihilation – yet reason can be used as 'a last resort'. Wilson sees himself as bridging the nature–nurture controversy, conceiving of aggressive behaviour as 'a structured, predictable pattern of interaction between genes and environment'. Human pugnacity (he says)

cannot be explained as either a dark-angelic flaw or a bestial instinct. Nor is it the pathological symptom of upbringing in a cruel environment. Human beings are strongly predisposed to respond with unreasoning hatred to external threats and to escalate their hostility sufficiently to overwhelm the source of the threat by a respectably wide margin of safety.

However, aggressive learning rules that were once adaptive are now obsolete. They may be 'worked around', if hardly banished. Our only option is to undertake 'those difficult and rarely travelled pathways in psychological development that lead to mastery over and reduction of the profound human tendency to learn violence'.[7]

Today's critics of pop ethology and sociobiology – descendants of Chalmers Mitchell and his ilk of the pre-1919 era – continue to complain about theories that interpret human nature and history in terms of genetic programming or fixed biological laws, that misuse metaphor or analogy to make sweeping generalisations about humanity based upon animal comparisons. The old positivist ideal of constructing a unified science of behaviour that would synthesise the biological and social sciences may still be alive and well (as in sociobiology), but it is still met by liberal concern for human diversity and free will. This concern springs not only from the humanities and social sciences, but from within biology itself (again repeating history). The distinguished zoologist and science writer Tony Barnett warns: 'When the attempt is made to replace everyday knowledge, history or the social sciences by biology or physics, the most important missing concept is that of human beings as autonomous agents.'[8] Barnett dismisses as methodologically suspect attempts to apply concepts such as crowding, territoriality, dominance, stress and altruism directly from the animal world to human behaviour:

Detailed statements on the course or causes of the evolution of behaviour can be only surmise [a strong echo of Chalmers Mitchell]... General laws may be sought on the relationship of existing animal social systems with habitat or mode of life, but have still to be established. Man is uniquely versatile and has no single habitat or mode. Hence the human species must fall outside any analysis in which habitat and species-typical conduct are related. Human societies rest on verbal traditions maintained not only by imitation but also by teaching ['It is the conspicuous characteristic of Man to be teachable', said Vernon Kellogg in 1912: *Beyond War*, p. 165]... Current fashionable comparisons of man with other species reflect the prejudices of the writers, and have no scientific validity. The notion that men are ineradicably violent among themselves is a recent version of a pessimistic outlook which has been expressed repeatedly throughout history. Biological findings have been used, unjustifiably, to support both this view and its opposite... Man is a project of evolution, but he is not merely a puppet jerked by genetical or phylogenetic strings... Human diversity creates immense problems for man, but also provides means of solving them by conscious, voluntary action.[9]

The historian has a sense of *déjà vu* when scanning today's debates. The same old issues keep cropping up, although the language is now more sophisticated: heredity versus environment (despite the modern lip-service paid to epigenetic readings of human behaviour); instinct versus learning; the role of cultural evolution; the fixity or malleability – the pugnacity or placability – of human nature; the legitimacy of naturalistic ethics, etc. Protagonists on both sides of (say) the sociobiology debate still claim Darwin's authority, while denouncing their adversaries as 'pseudo-

Darwinists'. (There are strong parallels with the divisive Marxist world of discourse.)

Bio-social dissentions still have a distinctly ideological air, and still generate a mix of ideological derivatives. As Marvin Bressler has argued (echoing E. G. Conklin), the rich repertoire of animal societies can be linked to any number of preferred models of human behaviour, while any thesis can be supported 'by ignoring the logical and empirical requirements of establishing evolutionary continuities and by substituting poetic metaphor and analogy as principles of evidence'.[10] Barnett goes further and detects ideological agendas even within arguments favouring homologies of human and animal conduct. Homology (he says) is a special, biological type of analogy which is commonly misused to make unsubstantiated inferences about humankind. Common evolutionary origins are implied, although there is no way such implications can be scientifically confirmed or denied:

The existence of a superficial similarity gives no evidence concerning the genetics or the development of behaviour ... As for homologies of human and animal conduct, they may sometimes be thought of as descriptions, but often they emerge as rhetoric: they are an attempt to influence our opinions ...[11]

Biologists such as Tony Barnett and Stephen Gould are very suspicious about an alarming tendency in our modern world for hard science to be transposed into illiberal reductionist doctrines that can easily become part of pop culture. Barnett feels that reductionist dogmas have been repeatedly used to justify tendentious, usually pessimistic, portraits of humanity, political extremism and resistance to change. Gould agrees, and cautions us that biological determinism is not an abstract folly to be debated only within academic cloisters:

These ideas have important consequences, and they have already permeated our mass media. Ardrey's dubious theory is a prominent theme in Stanley Kubrick's film *2001*. The bone tool of our apelike ancestor first smashes a tapir's skull and then twirls about to transform into a space station of our next evolutionary stage ... Kubrick's next film, *Clockwork Orange*, continues the theme and explores the dilemma inspired by claims of innate human violence. (Shall we accept totalitarian controls for mass deprogramming or remain nasty and vicious within a democracy?)[12]

One can give a hearty amen to these warnings, while remembering that the historical record was complex, that Darwinian science was multivalent, that it inspired liberalism as well as reaction, and that misuse of science and methodological deceit were not the monopoly of the malevolent. Even those on the side of the angels – those wanting human peace, diversity and freedom – coveted nature and natural certitudes for their cause. What is surprising is how well they succeeded.

Appendix: Social Darwinism

The thesis of this book – namely, that Darwinism bred an influential tradition of non-violence – is hardly congruent with the familiar textbook scenario that Darwin's theory unleashed primarily harsh and divisive, conflict-based social doctrines. These were seen to apply both in the domestic arena of paupers, workhouses and *laissez-faire* politics, and in the global arena of clashing nation-states, empires and races

However, that orthodoxy has been under siege for some time. Recent scholarship has recognised that Darwinism generated social and political rhetorics and idioms that could readily be translated into a bewildering kaleidoscope of discourses; has accepted that Darwinism was multivalent, capable of generating a spectrum of ideological derivatives. Indeed there has been a lively (if sometimes sterile) semantic debate, whether the term 'Social Darwinism' should be applied to the gamut of these derivatives, or be delimited to social theory that used concepts supposedly central to Darwinian biology – such as natural selection, or differential reproduction. The generalists, for instance, are more inclined to accept (say) Lamarckism as a legitimate source of 'Social Darwinism', given that Darwin continued to use Lamarckian theory, while the restrictionists tend to exclude it. This obviously affects the status given to Lamarckians such as Herbert Spencer, who has traditionally been perceived to be a quintessential 'Social Darwinist'.

Revisionist historiography in this matter has emphasised continuity rather than discontinuity in intellectual history. It tries to absorb Darwinism into pre-existent intellectual and moral paradigms; while at the same time it questions the extent to which Darwin's theory penetrated and altered existing value-systems. The great nineteenth-century debates over the place of man in nature, and over the role of capitalism and the state, are said to have been less affected by Darwinian biology than by more traditional ethics, philosophy and economics. Let us pursue this issue, first with regard to the broader impact upon religion and philosophy, then in respect of secular Social Darwinism

The dimensions of Darwin's influence were most open to argument in the central issue of man's place in nature (not by accident the title of T. H. Huxley's famous essay). In a key respect Darwin seemed threatening, since his theory impinged upon the whole question of Nature, Man and God. We need hardly feel surprised that, in the fierce squabbling that followed the *Origin of Species*, the issue of scientific truth (always culturally relative) became highly emotive, or that perceptions of social consequence cut across the science–religion debate. It was not only fundamentalist Christians who feared the disintegrative effect of Darwinism upon values and social stability. Even non-Christian progressives such as John Stuart Mill, Leslie Stephen, George Eliot, Henry Sidgwick and Frederick Harrison were worried.[1] Even those who sided with science as a force for light and reason in its fight with religion and obscurantism found themselves harbouring liberal suspicions about Darwinism, not least because it could seem anti-democratic or militaristic in its implications. There were a number of possible responses to the cultural shock of Darwin. These included a sort of existential acceptance of a Godless universe or a harsh biological image of humanity, a prudent distancing from the new science, or ingenious reworking of Darwin to fashion a more acceptable episteme. Peace biology often followed the latter strategy

Darwinism seemed less threatening if it was seen to be containable within existing paradigms. Right from the appearance of the *Origin* efforts were made at *détente* between science and religion. Not all clerics were anti-science, nor all scientists anti-religious. Against the outspoken sceptics such as Huxley, Tyndall and Galton could be set devout scientists like Lyell, Faraday, Lister, Asa Gray and Clerk Maxwell. It is no longer fashionable to stress the 'warfare' between Darwinism and religion. The conventional wisdom now is that there were significant traffickings and continuities between science and religion, that the Darwinian paradigm had less than revolutionary religious and social repercussions. Robert M. Young and James R. Moore have contended, in the pioneering tradition of Walter Cannon, that any crisis of faith was resolved within the framework of established thought and belief. They see western science generally incorporating elements from canonical philosophy and theology. Darwinism itself is said to have owed much to William Paley's eighteenth-century school of natural theology, in which Darwin was raised, and especially to the Paleyite idea of universal natural laws embodying the concept of purposive adaptation of organisms to environment, supposedly part of beneficial Providential design. Since there is hot debate within 'the Darwin industry' over this claim, it may well be the Achilles heel of religious revisionism.[2]

The new orthodoxy downplays the 'dissonances' between Darwinism and religion, claiming that they were historically reduced in a number of ways. Darwinist science kept flirting with the heresy of teleology (the paradigm that it supposedly killed), while the various Social Darwinisms went well beyond flirtation. At the same time liberal theology seemed to be moving towards a vague rational Christianity that eliminated the mysterious and emotionally profound qualities of religious belief. This culminated in 'Modernism', a theological version of the Victorian doctrine of progress,[3] and in the ultimate counter-revolution of 'crisis theology' (Kierkegaard, Barth, Niebuhr and Tillich held that there were important dimensions of reality, such as the existential relations of humans to each other and God, that were inaccessible to science). James R. Moore has strained revisionism to full extent by viewing even orthodox Christian theology as basically congenial to the new biology, indeed more congenial to it than was liberal theology. Particularly attractive to orthodox Christianity was the doctrine of a contingent Creation 'ordered and superintended by a perpetual Providence'. As the young Anglo-Catholic Aubrey Moore saw it in the last century: 'Order, development, and law are the analogue of the Christian view of God.'[4]

The problem for the 'reconcilers', then and now, was that 'pure' Darwinist theory seemed quite simply to reject teleology unequivocally. It pictured evolutionary change as random-based, violent and purposeless, and regarded God as either unnecessary hypothesis or remote first cause. Influential studies like Edward Manier's *The Young Darwin and His Cultural Circle* (1978) have reinforced the Kuhnian view that Darwinism broke with natural theology and instituted a fundamental paradigm change.[5] John Halliday has insisted upon Darwin's philosophic materialism, his scientific contempt for Paleyite concepts of a single universal design:

While a degree of continuity between theology and science can be detected, hardheaded Darwinians and, more to the point, Darwin himself, saw that theological discourse was not cognitive in the scientific sense. The Darwinians' belief, indeed their whole ethos and commitment, was to the view that theological assertions could not be demonstrated in the way that scientific propositions could be. For them, the theory of natural selection had separated truth and belief, divorcing science and theology and forcing them apart

For Halliday 'the uniqueness and the severity of the Darwinian challenge to faith has to be accepted as fact'. More than this, Darwin threatened the deeply entrenched Victorian belief that man was truly unique and independent of the laws of organic evolution: a belief shared by reformed Protestant theology, rationalists, Marxists and Oxford Idealists.[6]

Some of the confusion on this subject may be sheeted home to Darwin himself. Studies of Darwin's language and rhetoric have suggested that it was Darwin's strategy to subsume earlier cultural forms and grammar –

especially those of natural theology and Scots common sense philosophy – in order to cushion his theory from criticism. He thus rendered the controversy over his work, as John Angus Campbell puts it, 'more a dispute *within* a common theological world picture than a debate *between* a radically naturalistic or "secular" world picture and a distinctively "religious" alternative'. In this way, according to Campbell, the real starkness of the Darwinian vision was slow to register in the nineteenth-century consciousness. Only in a violent twentieth century did there come full recognition of Darwin's anti-progressive implications, full understanding that 'the single most epochal and theologically subversive element in Darwinism' was not belief in animal ancestry, but 'its disbelief in any purpose for humanity in time other than biological reproduction'.[7]

Recent scholars of secular Social Darwinism have also put an 'assimilationist' thesis. They argue that the 'revolutionary' political edge of Darwinist thought was blunted so that naked doctrines of power, struggle, exploitation and domination were contained within a safer political and ethical tradition. Revisionists have challenged the received view, popularised by Richard Hofstadter and a host of textbooks, that assumed a hegemony within Social Darwinism of 'conservative' (Victorians would have said 'radical') social ideas emphasising free-scrambling survival

Hofstadter's reading is seen as a variant of the leftist indictment of Darwinism as an ideological support system for capitalism, along with classical economics and Benthamite utilitarianism. Darwinism was said to have originated in an aggressive capitalist economics and a despairing Malthusianism, and was in turn exploited by a buccaneering capitalism to justify its ethic of ruthless competition and its dislike of the state. As Gertrude Himmelfarb paraphrased this reading of Social Darwinism:

In society, as in nature, there was presumed to be a 'natural order' which, left alone, would insure the survival of the fittest. Any interference with that order, either to direct the organization of society or to protect special interests, would violate nature and enfeeble society ... Against this iron law of nature, there was no appeal to such fictions as equality, justice or natural rights. As there were no such principles in the jungle, so there were none in society. [In the words of William Graham Sumner] 'There can be no rights against Nature except to get out of her whatever we can, which is only the fact of the struggle for existence stated over again.'[8]

Detailed historical investigation, however, has undermined the claim that a naturalistic survivor ethic reigned supreme among business interests or supposedly quintessential Social Darwinists such as Herbert Spencer or W. G. Sumner. Irvin G. Wylie's 1959 study of nineteenth-century American businessmen,[9] and Robert C. Bannister's 1979 book on Anglo-American Social Darwinism pioneered the new interpretation.

According to Bannister, whose work is both analytically keen and thorough, Gilded Age defenders of *laissez-faire* and individualism 'rarely laced their prose with appeals to Darwinism, and virtually never in the way described in conventional accounts'. The real beneficiaries of Darwinism, in Bannister's narrative, were the 'reform Darwinists' – collectivists, New Liberals and other advocates of positive government – who used 'correct' readings of Darwin (theirs) to bolster their own positions, in contrast to the 'false' readings of their opponents, who were discredited by having pinned upon them the unwanted label 'Social Darwinist'. Bannister sees Social Darwinism as essentially propagandist stereotype. There were no schools of Social Darwinists: the unpleasant buccaneer types of the 1880s 'were, *as Social Darwinists*, the invention of their opponents of the left. Eventually the label was used, not merely to caricature the "let-alone-philosophy" (as it was termed), but to denigrate programs of other state activists one happened to oppose, whether New Liberals, fellow socialists, or eugenicists.'[10]

This kind of revisionism suggests that Darwinism was unattractive to the free marketeers, or of limited use to them as polemic – a contrast to the usual view that it conferred a much desired scientific prestige upon competitive doctrines. Why should this be so? The revisionists imply a conservative anxiety to preserve the status quo, to maintain conventional morality and established social relations. This dictated a 'hands off' policy towards biologically-based ideas of naked power or an expedient survivor ethic. Bannister's analysis assumes (in curious contrast to the religious revisionists) that Darwin envisaged an essentially savage and capricious nature, that the nineteenth-century mind largely accepted this as his message, but found ways to neuter it. Bannister portrays Darwin himself as recoiling from the social implications of his amoral and purposeless universe; Darwin found inspiration in Malthusianism, a more benevolent teleological paradigm, rendered it fiercer, then found a way out by distinguishing human from animal evolution: with the familiar story of human versatility, rationality, conscience and capacity for mutual aid. It is this reading of Darwin as an ultimate anti-reductionist that enables Bannister to present Darwinism as a foe of bio-social determinism, fostering the idea that 'men must transcend nature rather than following her dictates'.[11] Reform Darwinism thus becomes the logical heir of Darwin

This approach has invited attack from the 'Darwin industry', some of whom defend the overall coherence of Darwinian theory and deny that it 'opened a gap between society and nature'.[12] It has also been criticised for elevating a single brand of Social Darwinism – in this case 'reform Darwinism' – as 'the accurate reading of Darwin's theory'. John Durant claims:

Darwin's evolutionary writings were capable of any number of different interpretations, and they were pressed into service of a great variety of intellectual and social interests. It is these interests, rather than Darwin's original aims, or the internal logic of his writings, which give meaning to the debate on social Darwinism.[13]

The assimilationist position has some great strengths. Victorian culture was vital and commodious, and showed remarkable capacity to absorb dangerous new ideas. My own study of American democratic influence in the early nineteenth century convinced me of the British ability to accommodate potentially subversive doctrines into a safe and pragmatic national tradition.[14] In the Darwinist case, there is also the fact that major elements of order and continuity can be discerned in the Darwinian worldview: in its stress on history, on slow change over eons of time, in the uniformitarianism it inherited from Hutton and Lyell – all possible arguments for political gradualism as opposed to doctrinaire blueprinting.

At the same time Victorian culture was pliant and confident enough to tolerate and adapt ideas embodying change, revision and progress, provided they were not couched in 'unacceptable' ethical or political terms, i.e., terms breaching absolutely central civilised values. (Defining such values would of course be at the nub of the debate.) The culture shock induced in Britain by Nietzsche (for example) is explicable in these terms, since he frankly advocated a transvaluation of values. So too may we explain the stubborn resistance to ideas such as General von Bernhardi's of war as biological necessity. As Bannister has demonstrated, Darwinism might depend upon an essentially terrifying postulate of an anarchistic and violent universe, yet its main legacy (if he is right) was to 'reform Darwinism', a change-oriented and non-violent inheritance. Peace biology (which included conservatives and racists as well as quintessential liberals and socialists) benefited from the 'unthinkability' of any exclusively violent interpretation of Darwinism. (It also helped that its analytical tools and methodology seemed more sophisticated, more genuinely 'scientific', than its warlike rivals.)

One difficulty with revisionism, taken too far, is that it may underestimate the unsettling potential of scientific ideas – such as Darwinism – to disturb, to alter the rules of the game, to necessitate reorientations, to induce new intellectual inclinations and prejudices, for example, in areas such as race theory, or changing biological images of humankind and human history.[15]

Another difficulty, perhaps, is a disposition to exaggerate the acceptable face of traditional discourse. There is a tendency to dwell upon the social cohesiveness rather than the divisiveness of the Enlightenment and Protestant thinking upon which nineteenth-century capitalism was founded. Darwinism supposedly grew out of, and was accommodated into the more benevolent theodicies and teleologies of Malthusianism, classical economics and utilitarianism. This raises some enduring historical issues. To what extent did such socio-political doctrines really emphasise natural harmony and human collaboration rather than conflict, or a socially responsible 'moral theodicy' rather than a stark and irresponsible 'survivor ethic'? (Robert Richards would even argue the case that a responsible 'survivor ethics', or evolutionary morality, was possible.)[16] After all, whether justly or not, movements such as Malthusianism were deeply offensive to nineteenth-century humanitarian ethics. Have the revisionists maximised the elements of order, self-regulation and over-arching harmony in (say) the doctrines of classical economics, and undervalued the elements of class interest, the atomistic, anti-social, struggle-based elements? In any case, the insistence upon order and coherence within an intellectual or social system itself constituted an alarm signal, not only to traditional liberal-Whigs, who feared oppressive forms of autocracy emerging from such systems, but also to Chartists and socialists, who interpreted order as a prerequisite to an exploitative social structure.[17]

Notes

INTRODUCTION

1 Raymond Pearl, 'Biology and War', *Journal of Washington Academy of Science* 8 (1918), 341–60; reprinted in Pearl, *Studies in Human Biology* (Baltimore, 1924), pp. 534–49.

2 Even Trevor Wilson's magisterial history of World War I conforms to this mythology. He speaks of a 'Darwinian ethos of the age, expressed by the imperialist Lord Milner when he stated that "competition between nations" was "the law of human progress", "the Divine Order of the World"': *The Myriad Faces of War: Britain and the Great War, 1914–1918* (Cambridge, 1986), p. 11.

3 See, for example, Daniel Kevles, *In the Name of Eugenics: Genetics and the Uses of Human Heredity* (New York, 1985).

1 THE DARWINIAN LEGACY

1 Thomas Henry Huxley, *Evolution and Ethics* (New York, 1902; reprinted New York, 1969) p. 82. See ch. 2 for Huxley.

2 Lionel Tiger and Robin Fox, *The Imperial Animal* (New York, 1971). Fighting animal theory is dealt with in ch. 5.

3 Frederick Wertham, *A Sign for Cain* (New York, 1966), p. 9. See also Erich Fromm, *The Anatomy of Human Destructiveness* (New York, 1973) p. 2 and *passim*.

4 Arthur Koestler, *The Ghost in the Machine* (London, 1967), pp. 352–3. The Viennese-born Ludwig Von Bertalanffy helped to found general system theory. Among his numerous works was *Problems of Life* (New York, 1978).

5 For the above see Harriet Ritvo, *The Animal Estate: The English and Other Creatures in the Victorian Age* (Cambridge, Mass., London, 1987), pp. 1–5, *passim*.

6 For the above, see Mary Midgley, *Beast and Man* (New York, 1978), ch. 2. Plato's reference occurs in the *Republic* (quoted Midgley p. 571).

7 John Burrow, introduction to Charles Darwin, *The Origin of Species* ((Harmondsworth, 1969), p. 43.

8 John U. Nef, *War and Human Progress* (Cambridge, Mass., 1952), p. 410, and generally ch. 19. Nef does not directly link Darwinism with the cult of violence.

9 For Huxley on animal consciousness see T. H. Huxley, 'Mr. Darwin's Critics', *Contemporary Review*, 18 (1871), 443–76.

10 Keith Thomas, *Man and the Natural World: Changing Attitudes in England 1500–1800* (London, 1983), p. 141, and generally for this subject.

11 Norman Macdonald in R. D. Givens and M. A. Nettleship, *Discussions on War and Human Aggressiveness* (The Hague, 1976), p. 36. This comment makes a common confusion between predation and murder of one's own species.

12 Quoted Donald Worster, *Nature's Economy: A History of Ecological Ideas* (Cambridge, 1985; 1st edn, 1977), p. 185.

13 Benjamin Kidd, *Two Principal Laws of Sociology* (London, 1907–8).

14 Kenneth Bock, *Human Nature and History: A Response to Sociobiology* (New York, 1980), ch. 2, argues that the Darwinian contribution to social science was in fact disappointing.

15 Silvan S. Schweber, 'The Wider British Context in Darwin's Theorizing', in David Kohn, edn, *The Darwinian Heritage* (Princeton, 1985), pp. 36–7, generally 35–69.

16 John Dewey, 'The Influence of Darwin on Philosophy' (Columbia lecture, 1909) in P. Appleman, edn, *Darwin: A Norton Critical Edition* (New York, 1970), p. 393.

17 Robert M. Young, 'Darwinism *Is* Social', in Kohn, *Darwinian Heritage*, p. 611, also pp. 622, 638, generally 609–38. On scientific naturalism, see F. M. Turner, *Between Science and Religion* (New Haven, 1974).

18 Barry Gale, 'Darwin and the Concept of a Struggle for Existence', *Isis*, 63, (1972), 321–44, esp. 342–3.

19 Marx to Engels, 18 June 1862, in Marx–Engels, *Selected Correspondence 1846–1859* (Moscow, London, 1953), pp. 156–7; Engels to Lavrov, 1875, in Marx–Engels, *Correspondence* (2nd edn, Moscow, 1965), p. 302. It is also true that Marx and Engels welcomed Darwin's materialism, historicism and his erosion of teleology, thus liberating a whole new set of dialectics.

20 Oswald Spengler, *The Decline of the West*, I, (New York, 1947), pp. 369, 373; Benjamin Kidd, 'Darwinism', *Encyclopaedia of Religion and Ethics* (Edinburgh, New York, 1911), vol IV, pp. 402–5.

21 Silvan S. Schweber, 'Darwin and the Political Economists: Divergence of Character', *J. History of Biology*, 13 (1980), 95–289. Also Edward Manier, *The Young Darwin and His Cultural Circle* (Dordrecht, 1978).

22 Schweber, 'British Context', pp. 35–6; 'Political Economists', pp. 276–7. Darwin also used Bentham's optimalisation calculus, and visualised political and moral systems as biological problems. Schweber suggests that Darwin knew he was 'biologizing' explanations taken from political economy, but refrained from admitting it because 'Biology, like every other science, was not to be tainted with political ideology' ('Political Economists', p. 213).

23 C. C. Gillispie, *Current Anthropology*, 15, 3 (1974), 224. Gillispie denies that Darwin was an ideologist of early capitalism, but asserts that 'Darwin's theory did depend upon political economy for the possibility of its expression' (*ibid.*). See also Gillispie, *The Edge of Objectivity* (Princeton, 1960), p. 303: 'All the proverbs of profit and loss are there, from pulpit and from counting house.'

24 Gillian Beer, *Darwin's Plots: Evolutionary Narrative in Darwin, George Eliot and Nineteenth Century Fiction* (London, 1983), p. 9.

25 R. C. Stauffer, edn, *Charles Darwin's Natural Selection: Being the Second Part of his Big Species Book Written from 1856 to 1858* (Cambridge, 1975), pp. 172,

569 (hereafter Darwin, *Natural Selection*). Linnaeus's phrase, below, was used
by Erasmus Darwin in *The Temple of Nature* (London, 1803). See also Manier.

26 Gale, 'Darwin', p. 331 and generally pp. 321–44.

27 As Gale says, Darwin was working within 'a cosmographical framework of a
nondesigned, nonbeneficent, imbalanced nature. Within this context, the
rationalization of struggle was unnecessary. In fact, it was to Darwin's purpose
to show how unmitigated the struggle for existence in nature was and as a result
how important an effect it had upon the ecological balance of nature' *ibid.*, p.
332.

28 Darwin, *Natural Selection*, pp. 175–6.

29 Gale, 'Darwin', pp. 321, 323–4.

30 Worster, *Nature's Economy*, pp. 126, 167.

31 Darwin, *Natural Selection*, pp. 186–8. Also *Origin of Species* (London, 1859
reprinted Pelican, 1968), pp. 62ff.

32 Perceptively discussed in Manier, *The Young Darwin and his Cultural Circle*, pp.
13, 83, 177, and *passim*. Examining etymologies that may have influenced
Darwin, Manier concludes that the picture emerging has 'nothing to do with
competition, and less with combat' but much to do with '*vigorous* effort to
maintain life and vital activities' (p. 179). Darwin's usage also suggested a move
away from simple notions of direct contest towards more statistical concepts of
varying chances of survival and of leaving fertile descendants (p. 181).

33 Gillian Beer, 'Darwin's Reading and the Fictions of Development' in Kohn,
Darwinian Heritage, p. 570.

34 Beer, *Darwin's Plots*, pp. 167ff.; also *Origin of Species*, pp. 125, 415. Even this
interconnective vision of nature has been seen to stem from contemporary
social philosophy, especially from the Scottish Enlightenment school of socio-
economics, whose view of artificial economy paralleled Darwin's analysis of
interdependence, complexity and stability: Schweber, 'British Context', pp.
37–8.

35 Howard E. Gruber, *Darwin on Man* (London, 1974), pp. 117–18, 196–7.

36 Worster, p. 163.

37 Beer, *Darwin's Plots*, p. 170. Beer argues elsewhere that for Darwin evolution
was 'a lateral rather than simply an onward movement, whose power lies in
multiple relationships as much as in selecting out ... Neither the ladder nor the
pyramid are useful models for him': 'Darwin's Reading', pp. 564, 570–1.

38 Charles Darwin, *The Variations of Animals and Plants under Domestication*
(London, 1868), I, 10; also Darwin, *Autobiography*. Darwin had encountered
Malthus as early as 1833: Schweber, 'Political Economists', p. 195.

39 Darwin, *D Notebook* (September 29–October 3, 1838), quoted Dov Ospovat,
*The Development of Darwin's Theory: Natural History, Natural Theology, and
Natural Selection, 1838–1859* (Cambridge, 1981), pp. 61–2.

40 Sandra Herbert, 'Darwin, Malthus and Selection', *J. History of Biology*, 4
(1971), 209–17. In terms of biological theory, Malthus helped Darwin to see
that selection pressure was exerted by the exponential growth of population, an
insight that moved him from typological to a populational approach: M. T.
Ghiselin, *The Triumph of the Darwinian Method* (Berkeley, 1969), pp. 48ff.

41 In 1852 Spencer hypothesised that fertility decreased as the evolutionary ladder
was ascended, with the most intellectually and racially advanced humans (for

example, the British) producing more brain cells and fewer sperm cells: Herbert Spencer, 'A Theory of Population ...', *Westminster Review*, 57 (1852), 499.

42 On Malthus's 'rules of justice', see his *Principles of Political Economy* (London, 1820), p. 3; A. J. Field, 'Malthus's Methodological and Macroeconomic Thought', *History of European Ideas*, 4, 2 (1983), 135–49; S. M. Levin, 'Malthus and the Idea of Progress', *J. History of Ideas*, 27 (1966), 92–108. Cf. M. Ruse, 'Social Darwinism: The Two Sources', *Albion*, 12 (1980), 25.

43 Robert Young plays down Malthus's natural theology and sees a more direct link between a struggle-based Malthusian image of nature and society and later debates on the social meaning of evolutionary theory: 'The line from Malthus to Darwin and on to so-called "Social Darwinism" is unbroken ... The use of natural law as the basis for a given view of society became a commonplace in social, political and economic theory, and the theory of evolution was employed as a new, more powerful, justification for industrial capitalism.' For imperialism: 'The Historiographical and Ideological Contexts of the Nineteenth-Century Debate on Man's Place in Nature', in M. Teich and R. Young, eds., *Changing Perspectives in the History of Science* (London, 1973), pp. 372, 375. Donald Worster also argues that 'Darwin's reading of Malthus can make good claim to being the most important event in the history of Anglo-American ecological thought', because of its negative contribution to a dismal and violent image of nature through instrumental thinking, not least through Malthus's fixed concept of fertility: Worster, pp. 149, 154.

44 Peter J. Bowler, 'Malthus, Darwin, and the Concept of Struggle', *J.History of Ideas*, 37, 4 (1976), 631–50; also R. C. Bannister, *Social Darwinism* (Philadelphia, 1988). Bowler contends that Malthus emphasised struggle against environment, while Darwin emphasised intra-species competition. However Hodge and Kohn argue that Darwin saw Malthus 'as strikingly vindicating Lyell's appeal to inter-specific competition, by confirming that very small differences in conditions can make for large differences in the populational representation of species from one place to another'. Malthus showed Darwin 'how to construe intraspecific competition as analogous to interspecific': M. J. S. Hodge and D. Kohn, 'The Immediate Cause of Natural Selection', in Kohn, *Darwinian Heritage*, p. 194–5.

45 Bowler, p. 638; also Malthus, *An Essay on the Principle of Population*, 6th edn, 1826, I, 92–5. Hodge and Kohn point out that Darwin had already drawn similar analogies about primitive war before reading Malthus, and was aware of Lyell's 'extinction theorizing' that drew parallels with European conquests over American and Australian aborigines: 'Immediate Cause of Natural Selection', p. 195. Darwin had also written about the Spaniards' genocidal war on the Indians in *The Voyage of the Beagle*. See also Gruber, *Darwin on Man*, p. 118. Bowler's approach simplifies Darwin's concept of struggle (see above).

46 Darwin, *Autobiography 1809–1882*, quoted Ospovat, *Development of Darwin's Theory*, p. 72; also pp. 60–1, generally ch. 3. There is widespread dispute within 'the Darwin industry' on such questions.

47 Edward O. Wilson, *Sociobiology: The New Synthesis* (Cambridge, Mass., 1975), p. 573.

48 Darwin, *Beagle Diary*, 22 December 1835; *First Notebook on Transmutation of Species*, 89 (July 1837–February 1838); cited in Gruber, *Darwin on Man*, pp.

184–7, and see generally ch. 2. The first notebook denied that humans had an instinctive urge to conquer, or repugnance to breed together.

49 Gruber, ch. 2, esp. pp. 229–36. 'Darwin resisted the sharp distinction between instinct and reason. For him, an element of intelligent adaptation was an integral part of the lower instinct, even in the behaviour of worms and plants' (p. 230). In the *Descent* Darwin thought it possible that 'instinctive actions may lose their fixed and untaught character, and be replaced by others performed by the aid of free will' (1901 edn, p. 102).

50 Darwin, *The Descent of Man* (London, 1871; reprinted London, 1901), p. 166. Following page references in the text refer to this edition.

51 See, for example, Jim Moore, 'Socializing Darwinism', *Radical Science*, 20 (1986), 47–8. See also Greta Jones, *Social Darwinism and English Thought*, (Sussex, 1980) ch. 2.

52 Quoted J. W. Burrow, introduction to Darwin, *Origin of Species* (1859; reprinted Harmondsworth, 1972), p. 41; and *First Notebook on Transmutation of Species* (1837–8), quoted Gavin de Beer, *Charles Darwin* (London, 1963; reprinted Melbourne, 1968) pp. 209–10.

53 Darwin, *M Notebook*, 29 August 1838, line ref. 123, in Paul H. Barrett, edn, *Darwin's Early and Unpublished Notebooks*, in Gruber, p. 289. Darwin suggested that cultural imprinting could be akin to innate behaviour. He instanced numerous cases in primitive societies of the cultural fixing of 'many strange customs and superstitions ... It is worthy of remark that a belief constantly inculcated during the early years of life, whilst the brain is impressible, appears to acquire almost the nature of an instinct; and the very essence of an instinct is that it is followed independently of reason' (p. 187).

54 In a letter of 1860 he had given a more limited biological explanation: in a state of crisis, for example invasion by barbarians, force and ferocity would triumph. Quoted J. A. Rogers, 'Darwinism and Social Darwinism', *J. History of Ideas*, 33, 2 (1972), 272–3.

55 Darwin to W. Graham, 3 July 1881, quoted *ibid.*, p. 274.

56 According to recapitulation theory, the 'childlike' traits of uncivilised adults reappeared in the juveniles of the 'higher' white races: see Stephen Jay Gould, *Ever Since Darwin* (Penguin, 1987), pp. 214–21.

57 For background on theories of race see J. S. Haller, *Outcasts from Evolution: Scientific Attitudes of Racial Inferiority, 1859–1900* (New York, 1971); also Douglas Lorimer, 'Theoretical Racism in Late-Victorian Anthropology, 1870–1900', *Victorian Studies*, 31, 3 (1988), 405–30.

58 Lorimer suggests that racist thinking intensified, if anything, from the 1880s, fostered by 'the external reality of expanding European domination over the globe', and by the fact that 'the presumptions and values of the professional middle class gave focus to the scientists' inquiries'. Supposedly scientific racism became more entrenched as science itself became institutionalised and popularised, as what was in reality ambiguous theory went the rounds of the magazines and schools as accepted fact: Lorimer, 'Theoretical Racism', p. 428 and *passim*.

59 Gillian Beer, 'Darwin's Reading', especially pp. 564–9. For the *Beagle* quote, Darwin, *Journal of the Beagle* (New York, 1972), p. 235.

60 A. R. Wallace, 'The Origin of Human Races Deduced from the Theory of

Natural Selection' *Anthropological Review* 2 (1864), clviii–clxxxvii. Wallace argued that humans, through their social and sympathetic feelings, their power to superintend and guide the operations of nature, to make clothes, tools and weapons, had 'taken away from nature that power of changing the external form and structure which she exercises over all other animals'. As man ceased to be influenced by natural selection, 'mental and moral qualities will have an increasing influence on the well-being of the race'. Wallace spoke of the rise of 'better and higher specimens of our race', while 'the lower and more brutal would give way and successively die out'. Rapid mental advancement had raised 'the very lowest races of man so far above the brutes, (although differing so little from them in physical structure)' and had developed 'the wonderful intellect of the Germanic races'. (He was later to soften this stance on racial hierarchies.) Wallace spoke of the 'decreasing combative and destructive propensities' as an early factor in the development of man's social and sympathetic traits (clxii–clxiv).

61 See Beer's *Darwin's Plots* for Darwin on determinism. For a more pessimistic analysis, stressing the limited nature of Darwin's approach, and its inadequacies in explaining cultural or historical change, see Bock, *Human Nature and History*, esp. pp. 51–60. See also J. C. Greene, 'Darwin as a Social Evolutionist', in his *Science, Ideology and World View* (Berkeley, 1981).

2 THE AGE OF SPENCER AND HUXLEY

1 Woodruff D. Smith, *The Ideological Origins of Nazi Imperialism* (New York, Oxford, 1986), ch. 7. Smith sees German imperialism as an embattled ideology that tried to legitimate itself by an attachment to science and structures of ideas claiming transcendental and universal validity.

2 Ted Benton, 'Social Darwinism and Socialist Darwinism in Germany: 1860 to 1900', *Rivista Di Filosofia*, 23 (1982), pp. 93–7. Generally see Paul Weindling, *Health, Race and German Politics between National Unification and Nazism, 1870–1945* (Cambridge, 1989), esp. ch. 1.

3 For above see Paul J. Weindling, 'Darwinism in Germany', in Kohn, *Darwinian Heritage*, pp. 694–5, generally pp. 685–98. Haeckel even used the example of *Siphonophora*, who formed colonies, to show the existence of a 'state-forming' instinct (1896). Haeckel's more popular works included *The History of Creation* (trans. London, 1876; 1st edn 1868) and *Die Welträthsel* [The Riddle of the Universe] (Stuttgart, 1899). In 1869 the pathologist Carl Rokitansky sought the roots of aggression in 'protoplasmic hunger' but found this to be offset in higher organisms by integrating mechanisms (Weindling, 'Darwinism in Germany', p. 695).

4 Benton, 'Social Darwinism' p. 83, generally pp. 79–121.

5 Alfred Kelly, *The Descent of Darwin: The Popularization of Darwinism in Germany, 1860–1914* (Chapel Hill, 1981), p. 7, also pp. 4–8, 100–11. Weindling notes the earliest use of the term 'Social Darwinism' to be by Karl Steinmetz in 1901: 'Theories of the Cell State in Imperial Germany', in Charles Webster, edn, *Biology, Medicine and Society, 1840–1940* (Cambridge, 1981), p. 102 n. 5.

6 Weindling, *Health*, pp. 37, 48.

7 Kelly, *Descent of Darwin*, pp. 5, 106. Kelly comments: 'Neither racism nor Social Darwinism needed the other; they had arisen independently, and the fusion between the two was never complete' (p. 106).

8 *Ibid.*, p. 102. Kelly points out that it was almost impossible for high-status figures at this time to endorse Darwinism, given the anathema attached to it by advocates of the conservative power state. For Treitschke on the Kaiser assassination attempt, p. 103.

9 James Alfred Aho, *German Realpolitik and American Sociology: An Inquiry into the Sources and Political Significance of the Sociology of Conflict* (Lewisburg, London, 1975), pp. 33–9. Quote from Hegel is from G. W. F. Hegel, *Philosophy of Right* (Berlin, 1821; trans., New York, Oxford, 1952), pp. 209–10 (quoted Aho, p. 33). See also S. Avineri, 'The Problem of War in Hegel's Thought', *J. History of Ideas*, 22, 4 (1961), 463–74.

10 Aho, *German Realpolitik*, p. 14 and *passim*.

11 William Graham Sumner, *War and Other Essays*, ed, A. G. Keller (New Haven, 1911), p. 10, quoted Bannister, *Social Darwinism*, p. 109.

12 Bannister, *Social Darwinism*, p. 129; Aho, *German Realpolitik*, p. 14.

13 John F. McLennan's theory of wife-stealing was put in his *Primitive Marriage* (London, 1865), where he coined the terms exogamy and endogamy. For Herbert Spencer's criticisms of McLennan's views, see Spencer, 'Theories of Primitive Marriage', *Popular Science Monthly*, 10 (1876), 272–85. Johann Bachofen's *Das Mutterrecht* (Stuttgart, 1861) also argued the early significance of 'mother-rule'. There is a useful discussion in George W. Stocking, Jr, *Victorian Anthropology* (London, 1987), pp. 166–7, 200–4, *passim*.

14 Ludwig Gumplowicz, *Outlines of Sociology* (trans. of *Grundriss der Sociologie*, Vienna, 1877), edn, I. L. Horowitz (New York, 1963), pp. 194–5, 201, and generally Part 3, sections 1 and 2. *Outlines* was first translated into English in 1899. See also L. M. Bristol, *Social Adaptation* (London, 1915), pp. 162–70; Harry E. Barnes, 'The Struggle of Races and Social Groups as a Factor in the Development of Political and Social Institutions: An Exposition and Critique of the Sociological System of Ludwig Gumplowicz', *J. of Race Development*, 9 (1919), 394–419; D. Martindale, *The Nature and Types of Sociological Theory* (London, 1961), pp. 180–4. On modern debates see A. D. Smith, *The Ethnic Origins of Nations* (Oxford, 1986).

15 Horowitz, introduction to *Outlines* (1963), p. 23 and *passim*, arguing that Gumplowicz was an early critic of functionalism, with its equilibristic thinking, its tendency to draw inferences from strictly biological phenomena, and to make teleological substitutes for causal analysis.

16 Lester Ward's visit was, by the Austrian's own testimony, a key factor in qualifying his previous conviction that 'all humanity-tinkerers' were 'Utopians beyond the pale of science': Gumplowicz, 'An Austrian Appreciation of Lester F. Ward', *Am. J. Sociology*, 10 (1904–5), 643–53.

17 Kelly, *Descent of Darwin*, p. 105.

18 Gustav Ratzenhofer, 'The Problems of Sociology', *American J. of Sociology*, 10 (1904–5), 186, generally 177–88. He gave high priority to the world problem of population pressing upon resources, the primary cause of war, itself related to global economic processes being 'in the childhood of thoughtless robber

methods' (p. 182). For Ratzenhofer's impact on Lester Ward and Small, see R. C. Bannister, *Sociology and Scientism* (Chapel Hill, London, 1987).

19 Ratzenhofer, *Die Sociologische Erkenntnis* (Leipzig, 1898), cited Martindale, *Sociological Theory*, p. 185. Martindale has a useful eighteen-item summary freely rendered from Ratzenhofer's own outline of his theory of social process, pp. 185–6, which I draw upon below (also in Albion Small, *General Sociology*, Chicago, 1905, pp. 189–99).

20 Ratzenhofer in Martindale, *ibid.*, pp. 185–6; Ratzenhofer, *Soziologie* (Leipzig, 1907), summary in Bristol, *Social Adaptation*, pp. 175–6.

21 This revises the classical judgment of pioneer scholars like Quincy Wright, *A Study of War* (1942): see J. D. Singer and Melvin Small, *The Wages of War, 1816–1965: A Statistical Handbook* (New York, 1972), pp. 201ff. For the peace philosophy of the free trade Manchester School, see R. F. Spall, Jr, 'Free Trade, Foreign Relations, and the Anti-Corn-Law League', *International History Review*, 10, 3 (1988), 405–32.

22 John Stuart Mill to d'Eichthal, 7 November 1829, *The Earlier Letters of J. S. Mill, 1812–1848* (Toronto, 1963), *Collected Works of Mill*, XII, 41–2.

23 Auguste Comte, *The Positive Philosophy.* trans., Harriet Martineau (New York, 1853; reprinted 1979), pp. 556–600 (abridged version of *Cours de la philosophie positive*, Paris, 1830–42); A. R. Standley, *Auguste Comte* (Boston, 1981), pp. 80–90. I have also found useful: John C. Greene, *Science, Ideology and World View* (Berkeley, London, 1981), and Christopher G. A. Bryant, *Positivism in Social Theory and Research* (London, 1985).

24 Joy Harvey, 'Evolutionism Transformed: Positivists and Materialists in the *Société D'Anthropologie de Paris* from Second Empire to Third Republic', in D. Oldroyd and I. Langham, eds., *The Wider Domain of Evolutionary Thought* (Dordrecht, London, 1983), pp. 289–310. A key role in containing conflict within the *Société* was played by its founder, the neurologist Paul Broca, best known for his systematic skull measurements (positivism emphasised measurement). Broca, a polygenist on human origins, was ambivalent on evolution, and the debates suggest 'a response by French scientists to a fluctuating political, social and philosophical situation in which the scientific issues in turn shift both meaning and direction' (p. 304). See also Michael Hammond, 'Anthropology as a Weapon of Social Combat in Late Nineteenth Century France', *J. History Behavioral Sciences*, 16 (1980), 118–32.

25 Greene, *Science*, p. 67. For a revisionist approach, see Barbara Haines, 'The Inter-Relations Between Social, Biological, and Medical Thought, 1750–1850: Saint-Simon and Comte', *British J. History of Science*, 11 (1978), 19–35.

26 F. W. Coker, *Organismic Theories of the State* (New York, 1910), pp. 9–11; and on Comte, pp. 116–24.

27 J. S. Mill to Pringle Nichol, *Earlier Letters of J. S. Mill, 1812–1848* (Toronto, 1963), *Collected Works*, XIII, 738, quoted R. J. Halliday, *John Stuart Mill* (London, 1976), p. 48 and ch. 2 generally.

28 Standley, *Comte*, pp. 73–5.

29 Those influenced by Comtism included J. S. Mill, G. H. Lewes, Harriet Martineau, George Holyoake, Richard Congreve, John Morley, Leslie Stephen, Henry Sidgwick, Matthew Arnold, Mark Pattison, George Eliot, Thomas Hardy, George Gissing, H. G. Wells and Patrick Geddes: see T. R.

Wright, *The Religion of Humanity: The Impact of Comtean Positivism on Victorian Britain* (Cambridge, 1986); Martha S. Vogeler, *Frederick Harrison: The Vocations of a Positivist* (Oxford, 1984).

30 Robert A. Nye, *Crime, Madness and Politics in Modern France: The Medical Concept of National Decline* (Princeton, 1984), p. 68: 'In practice these politicians combined a radical conception of democratic sovereignty with a biological notion of society that employed organic metaphors and stressed social solidarity' (p. 68).

31 For the above see Robert J. Richards, *Darwin and the Emergence of Evolutionary Theories of Mind and Behavior* (Chicago, London, 1987), chs. 6, 7. Also J. D. Y. Peel, *Herbert Spencer: The Evolution of a Sociologist* (London, 1971).

32 According to the novel, London was most impressed by Spencer's *First Principles* (London, 1862), having failed with *Principles of Psychology* (London, 1855). Kant had 'given him the key to nothing', while Romanes had been 'hopelessly technical': 'the only idea he had gathered was that evolution was a dry-as-dust theory, of a lot of little men possessed of huge and unintelligible vocabularies'. Spencer made him 'drunken with comprehension ... There was no caprice, no chance. All was law': Jack London, *Martin Eden* (New York, 1909), pp. 107–8.

33 Herbert Spencer, *The Study of Sociology* (London, 1873), pp. 343–4. Earlier, in *Social Statics* (London, 1851), he claimed that it was part of the natural order of things for society to constantly excrete 'its unhealthy, imbecile, slow, vacillating, faithless members', and that this was thwarted by 'spurious philanthropists' (pp. 323–4).

34 Richards, *Darwin*, chs. 6, 7.

35 Peel, *Spencer*, p. 133.

36 Richards vigorously expounds this defence of Spencer, while making his own defence of some forms of evolutionary ethics. As he says, Spencer did not simply identify the evolutionary process with the moral process, but rather tried to construct three different arguments leading to the conclusion that certain trends in evolution were moral trends: 'The first argument ... tries to demonstrate that the general end of evolution is complete adaptation to the social state, which creates equal freedom. Spencer added that such adaptation requires as means benefits bestowed on self, progeny, and community. The second and logically independent argument is an ethical one: it proposes that the general moral end of man is greatest happiness, but specifies it as a matter of distributive justice. Spencer attempted to establish this conclusion by the sound strategy of contending that all ethical systems really do have happiness as their ultimate moral value and that all men logically assert it ... In essence, Spencer had constructed an abbreviated transcendental argument, which proposed that moral life and any conceivable moral system could make sense only under the assumption of the greatest happiness principle. The third argument attempts to demonstrate that the end of the evolutionary process also establishes, as a matter of natural rather than logical connection, the end of morality. If that identity may be made, then one can regard the laws determining the evolutionary process in man (i.e., principles of adaptation to advancing social relations) also as moral principles' (*Darwin*, p. 325).

37 Spencer, *Social Statics* (London, 1868; 1st edn, London, 1851), p. 447. Page references hereafter in text are to this 1868 edition. A Methodist critic declared: 'Never before was there a system so amazingly teleological': *Methodist Quarterly Review*, 40 (1880), 450.

38 For Spencer on population see his 'A Theory of Population, Deduced from the General Law of Animal Fertility', *Westminster Review*, 57 (1852), 468–501. In this article Spencer also argued that struggle preserved the ideal type of a species, by eliminating imperfect individuals. He missed Darwin's idea of struggle leading to species-change. (See also Greta Jones, *Social Darwinism and English Thought* (Sussex, 1980), pp. 6–7.) It is sometimes erroneously stated that Spencer coined the phrase 'survival of the fittest' in this 1852 article. In fact he coined the phrase in 1864: see Diane B. Paul, 'The Selection of the "Survival of the Fittest"', *J. History Biology*, 21, 3 (1988), 412–14.

39 Letter IX, *Nonconformist*, 23 November, 1842, quoted Richards, *Darwin*, p. 255; Spencer, *The Principles of Sociology* (London, 1893; 1st edn, 1882), Part V, sect. 438, pp. 240ff.

40 In *Principles of Sociology* (vol. I, 1876) Spencer claimed that elements of barbarism, characteristic of early phases of history, could recur in later historical stages, just as more 'civilised' elements of modern industrialised society could be detected in more primitive cultures. He listed a number of 'simple societies which have been habitually peaceful', including the Arafuras, Todas, Bodo, Mishmis, and Pueblos, societies that had failed to pass into the militant phase, and had thus not evolved the centralised authority and coercive institutions that were the usual response to habitual warfare. Hence these peaceful peoples foreshadowed the traits of the modern 'industrial type': (3rd edn, London, 1885), Part II, sect. X, pp. 552–3. For examples of retrogression from industrial to militant types, see Part II, sect. XI (he included Bismarckian Germany in his list).

41 As Peel paraphrases Spencer: 'The prime criterion of a high state of social evolution is that adaptation is not competitive but co-operative; and the end-product of history will be a society where the pursuit by individuals of their own goals will not be detrimental to others': Peel, *Spencer*, p. 147 and generally ch. 6: IV. Peel adds however that, by relativising the natural struggle, by conceding that war was appropriate for savage societies, Spencer undermined his absolutist ethical opposition to violence, and disjoined his sociology from his social philosophy (pp. 150–1).

42 For Spencer's discussion of animal and human altruism, see his 'On Justice', *Nineteenth Century*, 27 (1890), 435–48, 608–20. While seeing justification for defensive wars, he denied that offensive wars served human interests: 'It is only during the earlier stages of human progress that the development of strength, courage and cunning, are of chief importance. After societies of considerable size have been formed, other and higher faculties become those of chief importance; and the struggle for existence carried on by force, does not always further the survival of the fittest.' In proportion as capacity for 'a high social life' grew, 'offensive war tends more and more to hinder, rather than further, human welfare' (*Social Statics*, pp. 447–8). Also *Principles of Sociology*, Part V, sect. 438.

43 Spencer, *Principles of Sociology* (London, 1893; 1st edn, 1882), II, Part V, sect.

550, p. 571. References in text are to this edition. The whole of ch. 17, 'The Militant Type of Society', is relevant. Peel, *Spencer*, ch. 8, has a useful discussion.

44 Sir Henry Maine, *Ancient Law* (London, 1861), esp. ch. 5. Spencer categorised the militant society as one of *status*, 'the members of which stand one towards another in successive grades of subordination', whereas in the more commercial type of *contract* society voluntary association was supposed to govern relationships: *Principles of Sociology*, sects. 552, 562.

45 Bannister, *Social Darwinism*, p. 47, generally ch. 2, part 4.

46 See especially Spencer, *Facts and Comments* (London, 1902), and generally D. Wiltshire, *Social and Political Thought of Herbert Spencer* (Oxford, 1978), ch. 10.

47 Spencer, *Facts and Comments*, p. 133.

48 Spencer to W. S. Blunt, 10 October, 1898, quoted Wiltshire, *Spencer*, p. 244.

49 Bagehot's work generally 'is not what one thinks of as "science", and Bagehot's attempts at science or "physics" in *Physics and Politics*, the cribbings from Huxley on the nervous system to explain the acquisition of social habit and hence the formation of national character and public opinion, are jejune if portentous': John Burrow, 'Bagehot and the Nature of Political Understanding', ch. 5 in S. Collini, D. Winch, J. Burrow, eds., *That Noble Science of Politics: A Study in Nineteenth-Century Intellectual History* (Cambridge, 1983), p. 167.

50 See, for example, John C. Greene, 'Darwin as a Social Evolutionist', *J. History Biology*, 10, 1 (1977), 14–16.

51 C. H. Driver, 'Walter Bagehot and the Social Psychologists', in F. J. C. Hearnshaw, edn, *The Social and Political Ideas of Some Representative Thinkers of the Victorian Age* (London, 1933; reprinted 1967), p. 210.

52 It was Driver's shrewd judgment that 'one can hardly classify Bagehot as a Darwinian at all … There is a Darwinian gloss on the essay, it is true. But it might have been essentially the same without *The Origin of Species*': Driver, 'Bagehot', pp. 215–16.

53 Walter Bagehot, *Physics and Politics: Or Thoughts on the Application of the Principles of 'Natural Selection' and 'Inheritance' to Political Society* (London, 1872); reprinted in *The Collected Works of Walter Bagehot*, ed. N. St John-Stevas (London, 1974), VII, 22. Subsequent references in text are to this reprint.

54 Henry Maudsley, *Physiology and Pathology of the Mind* (London, 1867), quoted Bagehot, *Physics and Politics*, p. 20. On Maudsley as degenerationist see Pick, *Faces of Degeneration: A European Disorder, c. 1848–c. 1918* (Cambridge, 1989), pp. 203–16.

55 He added: 'Unless you appreciate that cause in its subtle materialism, unless you see it, as it were, playing upon the nerves of men, and, age after age, making nicer music from finer chords, you cannot comprehend the principle of inheritance either in its mystery or its power': *Physics and Politics*, p. 21.

56 See Greene, 'Darwin as a Social Evolutionist', pp. 14–16 for possible influence on Darwin. Francis Galton, in an article in *Ethnological Society's Transactions* (III, 137), was the source for Bagehot's remarks on wild flocks, and Darwin also marked this quotation. Greene notes that Darwin may also have been reminded of Galton's emphasis on the selective importance of affections making for social

solidarity. Bagehot's opinion on the supremacy of customary norms and morality in early society influenced Nietzsche, contributing to his concept of 'herd' conformity: see D. S. Thatcher, 'Nietzsche, Bagehot and the Morality of Custom', *Victorian Newsletter*, 62 (1982), 7–13.

57 In *Body and Mind* (London, 1870), Henry Maudsley put an atavistic theory that was to re-emerge later in the century. There was, he said, 'truly a brute brain within man's', as shown by morbid psychology and degenerate types: 'We may, without much difficulty, trace savagery in civilisation, as we can trace animalism in savagery; and in the degeneration of insanity, in the *unkinding*, so to say, of the human kind, there are exhibited marks denoting the elementary instincts of its composition' (pp. 52–3, quoted Pick, *Faces of Degeneration*, p. 208).

58 Martha Westwater, 'The Victorian Nightmare of Evolution: Charles Darwin and Walter Bagehot', *Victorian Newsletter*, 64 (1983), 9–10. Also S. A. M. Westwater, 'Walter Bagehot: A Reassessment', *Antioch Review*, 35 (1977), 39–49; D. Spring, 'Walter Bagehot and Deference', *Am. Hist. Review*, 81, 3 (1976), 524–31.

59 David G. Ritchie, *Philosophical Studies*, with memoir by R. Latta, ed. (London, 1905), pp. 252–3. Ritchie added: 'The worst kind of dogmatism may be that of the scientific specialist who applies some one conception with which he has worked successfully in his own space, to unlock all mysteries' (pp. 111–12). Also, Ritchie, *Darwinism and Politics* (London, 1889), and *Studies in Political and Social Ethics* (London, 1902), esp. 'War and Peace', pp. 134–76.

60 Jones, *Social Darwinism* pp. ix–x. Jones speaks of a 'tension between the precepts of social theory and the actual structure of biology', which is at the heart of the history of Social Darwinism from the mid nineteenth century to the present day (p. x).

61 See *ibid.*, ch. 1.

62 A. R. Wallace, *Contributions to the Theory of Natural Selection* (London, 1870), essay 10, 'The Limits of Natural Selection as Applied to Man'. Wallace argued that man's origins were inexplicable purely in terms of natural selection. He extended his argument to other facets of man's physical and mental nature; for example, hairlessness was seen as harmful, mathematical and ethical traits not useful to pre-civilised man. This breached Darwin's maxim that natural selection acted for the present, not future, utility of the species, and required a teleological view of human evolution. For an illuminating discussion see M. J. Kottler, 'A. R. Wallace, the Origin of Man, and Spiritualism', *Isis*, 65 (1974), 145–92. For Wallace's later views, see his *Darwinism* (London, 1889), ch. 15. T. H. Huxley dismissed Wallace's reservations, arguing that savage man needed all his brainpower to survive: 'Mr. Darwin's Critics', *Contemporary Review*, 18 (1871), 443–76.

63 Wallace, 'The Origin of Human Races and the Antiquity of Man Deduced from the Theory of "Natural Selection"', *J. Anthropological Society of London*, 2 (1864), clviii–clxx; reprinted (with changes) in Wallace, *Contributions*, essay 9 (quote, pp. clix–clxx). See also Kottler, p. 153. As Kottler points out, by 1870 Wallace began to worry that unrestricted reproduction of mediocre types was hindering progress in advanced civilisations, a worry shared by Darwin, Huxley and later degenerationists.

64 Wallace found solace (as did Benjamin Kidd) in the reflection that 'non-inheritance of the results of education and training...also prevents the continuous degradation of humanity by the inheritance of those vicious practices and degrading habits which the deplorable conditions of our modern social system undoubtedly foster in the bulk of mankind'. He also rejoiced that the legacy of idleness and debauchery created by the life-style of the rich 'as soul-deadening...in its effects as the sordid struggle for existence to which the bulk of workers are condemned' would leave no permanent inheritance: Wallace, 'Human Progress, Past and Future', *Arena* (January, 1892); reprinted Wallace, *Studies: Scientific and Social* (London, 1900), II, 505–6. Also Benjamin Kidd, 'Darwin's Successor at Home', *Review of Reviews*, 2, 12 (1890), 647–50.

65 Wallace, 'Human Selection', *Fortnightly Review*, 48 (1890), 331, 333ff. (also reprinted *Studies*, I, 509–26). He still had niggling worries about the disappearance of natural selection in humans. By saving the lives of the weak and maimed, there was a threat to race-improvement, 'but it has improved us morally by the continuous development of the characteristic and crowning grace of our human, as distinguished from our animal, nature' (p. 337). It was ironic that Wallace should give female sexual selection a key role in his socialist future, given that he had opposed Darwin on female choice as an evolutionary agent. Generally see M. Fichman, *Alfred Russel Wallace* (Boston, 1981), ch. 5; also Roger Smith, 'A. R. Wallace: Philosophy of Nature and Man', *British J. Science*, 6, 2 (1972), 177–99.

66 Wallace, 'Human Progress' p. 495.

67 Wallace, 'Polynesians and Their Migrations', *Quarterly J. of Science* (April, 1867); reprinted *Studies*, I, 412. In *The Malay Archipelago* (London, 1869) he commented on the 'remarkable fact' that among 'people in a very low stage of civilization we find some approach to...a perfect social state', lacking those 'wide distinctions, of education and ignorance, wealth and poverty, master and servant, which are the product of our civilization' (II, 460).

68 Wallace, *The Wonderful Century: Its Successes and Failures* (London, 1898), pp. 335, 337, 340 and ch. 19 generally. In 1899 Wallace responded to a questionnaire from the editor of *L'Humanité Nouvelle* on the causes, effects and solutions of war, sent to more than 130 writers including Tolstoy. Wallace claimed that the majority of people in civilised nations opposed war, and suggested a programme of civil conscription to cultivate the fine qualities called into existence by war and military training: 'Oh! that some great ruler of men would arise to benefit humanity by organising industrial armies, leading to the elevation and happiness of a whole people, and thus proving that peace may have its victories far greater and more glorious than those of war!': Wallace, 'The Causes of War and the Remedies', *L'Humanité Nouvelle* (May, 1899); reprinted in *Studies*, II, 384–93 (quote, 389–90).

69 Michael S. Helfand, 'T. H. Huxley's "Evolution and Ethics": The Politics of Evolution and the Evolution of Politics', *Victorian Studies*, 20, 2 (1977), 159–78.

70 T. H. Huxley, *Social Diseases and Worse Remedies* (London, 1891), pp. 23–33, quoted Pick, *Faces of Degeneration*, pp. 220–1. Pick shows how Huxley's

obsessive fear of overcrowding (dismissed by reformers such as George and Wallace) led him into using current degenerationist language.

71 James G. Paradis, *T. H. Huxley: Man's Place in Nature* (Lincoln and London: University of Nebraska Press, 1979).

72 T. H. Huxley, *Man's Place in Nature* (London, 1863); in *Collected Essays*, VII, 153 (London, 1896; reprinted New York, 1968), p. 153, also pp. 155–6. He described man as 'that great Alps and Andes of the living world', but based (like mountains) on 'the hardened mud of primeval seas' (p. 155).

73 Huxley, 'Administrative Nihilism' (1871) in *Collected Essays*, I, 251–90. For discussion see Richards, *Darwin*, p. 313, Helfand, p. 162. (Helfand claims that by adapting Spencerism, Huxley justified the practice of states modifying ethics and policy according to changing circumstances, making him 'a philosophical relativist in the tradition of naturalist ethics.)'

74 Paradis, *Huxley*, pp. 173–4.

75 Huxley, 'Science and Morals' (1886), *Collected Essays*, IX, 146. Nature, he said, dealt justly: 'the safety of morality lies neither in the adoption of this or that philosophical speculation, or this or that theological creed, but in a real and living belief in that fixed order of nature which sends social disorganisation upon the track of immorality, as surely as it sends physical disease after physical trespasses' (*ibid.*).

76 Huxley, 'The Struggle for Existence in Human Society' (1888), in *Collected Essays*, IX, 197–200. While his tone was gloomy, Huxley denied that either pessimism or optimism was a logical response to nature whose governing principle was 'intellectual and not moral … it is a materialized logical process' (p. 202). Following references in text are to this edition.

77 As Paradis says: 'Unlike Kropotkin, who formulated his ethical vision on Darwin's concept of "social instinct", arguing that morality and instinct were one, Huxley declared that the two were profoundly at war, that human aggression, rather than human co-operation, was the great factor behind man's early success in nature … Huxley began to think in psychic dimension, to conceive of man as a divided entity, one foot in a primordial past and the other in his civilized present, unable to possess completely either his primitive or his civilized self': Paradis, *Huxley*, pp. 150–2. Kropotkin will be dealt with in ch. 4, anthropological images of peaceful man in ch. 6.

78 Huxley, 'Evolution and Ethics' (1893) in *Collected Essays*, IX, pp. 68, 74. Text references are to this edition.

79 Henry Drummond, *The Ascent of Man* (London, 1894), pp. 3, 10–11, 53, 69–70. Kidd criticised Huxley's bifurcation of ethical/social and cosmic processes, 'the lesson of evolution, like the lesson of religion, being, of course, that they are one and the same': B. Kidd, 'Darwinism', *Encyclopaedia of Religion and Ethics* (Edinburgh, New York, 1911), IV, 405. Ironically the liberal Leslie Stephen's *The Science of Ethics* (London, 1882) based ethics upon natural selection 'to show how morality is independent of theology': see Jones, *Social Darwinism*, pp. 39–40. Stephen, an opponent of collectivism, was sceptical of Huxley's theorem that higher ethics went with a curbing of the struggle for existence: 'the more moral the race, the more harmonious and the better organised, the better it is fitted for holding its own … It holds its own, not merely by brute force, but by justice, humanity and intelligence, while … the

possession of such qualities does not weaken the brute force, where such a quality is still required. The most civilised races are, of course, also the most formidable in war': 'Ethics and the Struggle for Existence', *Contemporary Review*, 64 (1893), 168 (discussed Jones, pp. 49–50).

80 The young Peter Chalmers Mitchell, not yet a critic of evolutionary ethics, was unimpressed by the Romanes lecture, although he admired Huxley and was to become his biographer: 'The mere fact that we do prefer, and call good, the rules of social life which make for peace ... is a result of the cosmic evolution. This moral sentiment has in nature a higher cogency than the immoral sentiment of the thief and the murderer. Both sentiments are natural; but the cosmic evolution has given to one a superior claim on the allegiance of civilized mankind, which they freely recognize. If we know how good tendencies and evil tendencies come about, is there much more to be known of them?' Huxley himself had admitted that natural selection was in abeyance in human society: 'he is hardly fair to some of his scientific colleagues in silently identifying natural selection with the "cosmic process". There are other agencies at work': 'A Word with Mr. Huxley', *National Review*, 21 (1893), 713–15 (attributed to Mitchell by *Poole's Index*, IV, 190). The Catholic naturalist St George Mivart analysed the tension in Huxley's thought, but approved his 'approximation' towards Christian philosophy in distinguishing the human from the natural. Mivart thought that the term 'nature' was best used in its narrow sense of excluding humanity, 'since man, by his intelligence and will, is able to change the whole course of physical causation': 'Evolution in Professor Huxley', *Nineteenth Century*, 34 (1893), 198–211 (quote, p. 208). Huxley tried to resolve some of his inconsistencies in a *Prolegomena* to the Romanes lecture prefaced to it on publication in 1894. In this he placed greater emphasis upon the evolutionary context in which ethics had developed, essentially in terms of the selective advantage conferred upon groups by social bonding. In a rare reference to military selection, he conceded that 'the effect of military and industrial warfare upon those who wage it is very complicated': *Collected Essays*, IX, 36. Manuscript notes written shortly before his death show him still wrestling with the problem: 'In respect of external relations the Natural History process and the dawning of the ethical process work in harmony.' But, from the truce arising from mutual help 'the "Natural History" struggle for existence is at an end. If social progress takes place it can owe nothing to the struggle for existence. And the whole foundation of modern individualism is cut from under its feet ... Unlimited self-assertion is the foundation of the struggle for existence (and the cause of progress) in Natural History ... Civil History begins with self-renunciation ...': *Huxley Papers*, XLV, ff. 42–50, 1–4, cited in Richards, *Darwin*, pp. 318–19, n. 72 (also Paradis, *Huxley*, p. 183).

3 THE CRISIS IN THE WEST: THE PRE-WAR GENERATION AND THE NEW BIOLOGY

1 See, for example, Geoffrey Barraclough, *An Introduction to Contemporary History* (Harmondsworth, 1964), ch. 2; Modris Eksteins, *Rites of Spring: The Great War and the Birth of the Modern Age* (Boston, 1989).
2 Geoffrey Blainey, *The Causes of War* (London, 1973), p. 22 and *passim*.

3 List was one of the architects of the German *Zollverein*, but he committed suicide in 1846, feeling that he was a failure. See E. Silberner, *The Problem of War in Nineteenth Century Economic Thought* (trans., Princeton University Press, 1946), pp. 134–71, and Silberner, Book 2 generally for 'new protectionism', on which I have drawn below.

4 For above, *ibid.*, pp. 172–92. Gustave Schmoller (1838–1917), professor of political economy at Halle, Strasbourg and Berlin, and member of the Prussian *Staatsrat* from 1884, attacked liberal pacifism. He regarded war as a necessary element of international life, and accused Spencer of glorifying the peaceful type of society, which decayed into egoism. For an American version of deterrent theory see General John McAuley Palmer, 'The Insurance of Peace', *Scribner's Magazine*, 51 (1912), 186–91: 'The assumption that the cause of war can be reduced to an adjudicable dispute will rarely bear the test of historical examination... Nature unerringly decides these conflicts in favor of the strongest, and it is questionable whether a human contrivance for insuring the survival or supremacy of the weakest... would be a good thing for the world' (p. 186).

5 George Santayana, 'The Intellectual Temper of the Age' (1913) in N. Henfrey, edn, *Selected Critical Writings of George Santayana* (Cambridge, 1968), p. 6.

6 Michael Howard, *War and the Liberal Conscience* (London, 1978), pp. 46–7, and generally for background.

7 Those wishing to pursue this topic should consult Martin Berger, *Engels, Armies and Revolution: The Revolutionary Tactics of Classical Marxism* (Hamden, Conn., 1977). Also Karel Kara, 'On the Marxist Theory of War and Peace', *J. Peace Research*, 5 (1968), 1–27; and L. S. Feuer, 'Marx and Engels as Sociobiologists', *Survey*, 23, 4 (1977), 109–36.

8 L. T. Hobhouse, *The World in Conflict* (London, 1915), pp. 50–1. Another liberal, C. F. G. Masterman, warned in 1909 that only a thin crust separated European society from 'the central elemental fires... how slight an effort of stupidity or violence could strike a death blow to twentieth century civilization': *The Condition of England* (London, 1909), pp. 302–3. The Bishop of Winchester in 1914 described the recent past, 'in spite of all its peace and beauty, as a nightmare time, with an appalling climax': Edward Talbot, *The War and Conscience* (London, 1914), p. 7.

9 Michael D. Biddiss, *The Age of the Masses* (Penguin, 1977), pp. 156–7, and generally ch. 5. I have drawn on Biddiss for a good deal of material that follows. See also Barraclough, *Contemporary History*, ch. 8; Samuel Hynes, *The Edwardian Turn of Mind* (Princeton, 1968) and *A War Imagined: The First World War and English Culture* (London, 1990); Jonathon Rose, *The Edwardian Temper* (Athens, Ohio, London, 1986).

10 See, for example, John Goode, 'Gissing, Morris and English Socialism', *Victorian Studies*, 12, 2 (1968), 200–26.

11 Peter Chalmers Mitchell, *Evolution and the War* (London, 1915), pp. 6–7, and ch. 7 below. Also Biddiss, *Age of Masses*, chs 2, 5.

12 See A. Vincent and R. Plant, *Philosophy, Politics and Citizenship: The Life and Thought of the British Idealists* (New York, 1985); also R. J. Halliday on above, *Victorian Studies*, 30, 3 (1987), 412.

13 *The Savoy*, Nos. 2, 3, 4 (April/July/August 1896), quoted Patrick Bridgwater, *Nietzsche in Anglosaxony* (Leicester, 1972) p. 12.

14 Quotes from Friedrich Nietzsche, *The Twilight of the Idols* (London, 1896), Books 3, 14; *The Will to Power*, edn W. Kaufmann (New York, 1967, London, 1968), p. 462; *Thus Spake Zarathustra*, edn, Roy Pascal (Heron, 1957), p. xiii. Also Biddis, pp. 84–8, Barraclough, pp. 236–7. The Scots poet John Davidson, much influenced by Nietzsche but no uncritical disciple, lauded English imperialism: 'the word "overman" is supposed to be an index of evolution in humanity. This seems to me very foolish. Nietzsche has nothing to tell the Englishman of the "overman"; the Englishman is the "overman" in Europe, in Asia, Africa, America, he holds the world in the hollow of his hand': letter to *Daily Chronicle*, 22.5.1902, quoted Bridgwater, *Nietzsche*, p. 54.

15 R. N. Stromberg, 'The Intellectuals and the Coming of War in 1914', *J. European Studies*, 3 (1973), 112, n. 14.

16 William James, *The Will to Believe* (New York, 1897), p. 211; L. R. Rambo, 'Ethics, Evolution and the Psychology of William James', *J. Hist. Behavioral Sciences*, 116 (1980), 50–7.

17 Peter J. Bowler, *The Eclipse of Darwinism: Anti-Darwinian Evolution Theories in the Decades around* 1900 (Baltimore, London, 1983), ch. 1 and *passim*. Bowler suggests that the crisis in Darwinism was partly due to the professionalisation and vocational changes within the biological community, to the desire of groups such as experimental Mendelians to establish credibility, and possibly to an increase in dogmatism on the part of late-century Darwinists (pp. 13–15). See also Bowler, *Theories of Human Evolution: A Century of Debate*, 1844–1944 (Baltimore, London, 1986).

18 Weindling, *Health*, p. 92.

19 B. Kidd, 'Darwin's Successor at Home', *Review of Reviews*, 2, 12 (1890), 650. Also R. J. Halliday, 'Social Darwinism: A Definition', *Victorian Studies*, 14, 4 (1971), 389–405; F. B. Churchill, 'August Weismann and a Break from Tradition', *J. History of Biology*, 1, 1 (1968), 91–2; Ernst Mayr, 'Weismann and Evolution', *ibid.*, 18, 3 (1985), 295–329. For a contemporary socialist critique see Herman Whittaker, 'Weismannism and its Relation to Socialism', *International Socialist Review*, 1, 9 (1901), 513–23.

20 August Weismann, *Studies in the Theory of Descent* (trans., London, 1882), II, 695, 708–12.

21 For example, J. B. Crozier, *Religion of the Future* (London, 1880), *Civilization and Progress* (London, 1885); Henry Drummond, *Natural Law in the Spiritual World* (London, 1883), *The Ascent of Man* (London, 1894).

22 Grant Allen, 'The New Theory of Heredity', *Review of Reviews*, 1 (1890), 537–8.

23 Jones, *Social Darwinism*, p. 88.

24 Pick, *Faces of Degeneration*, p. 101.

25 Jones, *Social Darwinism*, ch. 5. As Bowler puts it: 'The great advantage of Lamarckism was that, although apparently naturalistic, it came very close to satisfying the requirements of a morally acceptable alternative to selection. Lamarckism did not require struggle, since all individuals adapted themselves to new conditions and passed on their acquired characters to their offspring. Instead of living things being reduced to mechanical puppets, they could be seen as active, purposeful entities choosing their own response to the environment and thus directing their own evolution. Many American neo-

Lamarckians saw use-inheritance quite explicitly as the means chosen by a benevolent God to allow life the power of designing itself': *Eclipse of Darwinism*, pp. 15–6, and ch. 4.

26 Bowler, *Eclipse of Darwinism*, pp. 61–4: 'Far from opening up the prospect of life being in charge of its own destiny, nonadaptive physiogenesis reduced living things to the status of automata passively reacting to the environment in a totally purposeless manner' (p. 64). Bowler suggests that there was a strong historical link between Lamarckism and orthogenesis, 'the latter being based on an extremely pessimistic concept of an evolutionary process driven by inbuilt forces that may push a species blindly into extinction' (p. 17).

27 Major W. H. F. Basevi, 'The Great Transition', *J. Royal United Service Institution*, 59, 438 (1914), 419–20.

28 According to Haller and Bowler, American neo-Lamarckians were 'fervently committed to the biological justification of a hierarchy of human races': Bowler, *Eclipse of Darwinism*, p. 19; John S. Haller, *Outcasts from Evolution* (New York, 1971), ch. 6. 'One could make a strong case for treating nineteenth-century neo-Lamarckism as the last bastion of the hierarchical interpretation of nature that Darwinism in principle set out to destroy' (Bowler, p. 19).

29 De Vries's claim to have independently revived Mendel's laws has been subject to controversy: for example, M. J. Kottler, 'Hugo de Vries and the Rediscovery of Mendel's Laws', *Annals of Science*, 36 (1979), 517–38.

30 Mitchell, *Evolution and the War*, pp. 18–19.

31 L. A. Farrall, 'Controversy and Conflict in Science: A Case Study. The English Biometric School and Mendel's Laws', *Social Studies of Science*, 5 (1975), 283.

32 Ernst Mayr, 'The Recent Historiography of Genetics', *J. History of Biology*, 6, 1 (1973), 147, generally 125–54. The importance of cultural factors was shown by the more civilised disputation between biometrics and Mendelism in the United States. Leading geneticists like Thomas H. Morgan, E. G. Conklin and Raymond Pearl (a biometrician) found difficulties at first in Mendelism, but most were willing to consider Mendelian experimental work seriously. Morgan converted to Mendelism in 1909, as eventually did biometricians such as Charles B. Davenport. D. J. Kevles blames English elitism in 'Genetics in the U. S. and Great Britain', *Isis*, 71 (1980), 447–8.

33 G. K. Chesterton, *The Thing* (London, 1929), pp. 280–1.

34 P. J. Bowler, 'Hugo de Vries and T. H. Morgan: The Mutation Theory and the Spirit of Darwinism', *Annals of Science*, 35 (1978), 64–5, citing de Vries, *Die Mutationstheorie* (2 vols., Leipzig, 1901–3), trans. as *The Mutation Theory* (London, 1910), I, 155–6. Bowler argues that de Vries specifically excluded the possibility that human races were sub-species produced by mutation. By choosing to proclaim the unity of humankind, he denied evolutionary justifications of both racial and individual struggle. In Morgan's case: 'It was thus not enough merely to separate man from the natural process of development... nature itself must be purged of its Darwinian associations' (p. 73). Mendelism has been seen as more 'individualist' in temperament than (say) Pearson's collectivist and pro-eugenics stance: for example, Donald A. MacKenzie, 'Sociobiologies in Competition: The Biometrician-Mendelian Debate', in *The Roots of Sociobiology* (London, 1978); B. Norton, 'The Biometric Defense of Darwinism', *J. History of Biology*, 6 (1973), 283–316.

Against this, as Kevles points out, many eugenists in Britain and America were Mendelians, and some biometricians were anti-eugenics: Kevles, 'Genetics', p. 445.

35 David Starr Jordan, *The Human Harvest: A Study of the Decay of Races Through the Survival of the Unfit* (Boston, 1907), p. 39.

36 Vernon L. Kellogg, *Beyond War: A Chapter in the Natural History of Man* (New York, 1912), p. 170. For his hereditarianism see his *Military Selection and Race Deterioration* (Oxford, 1916) p. 169. Jordan and Kellogg are treated in the next chapter.

37 See references on degeneration below.

38 Harold J. Laski, 'The Scope of Eugenics', *Westminster Review*, 174 (1910), p. 29.

39 B. Kidd, *The Science of Power* (London, New York, 1918).

40 August Weismann, *Essays on Heredity* (Oxford, 1888), *The Germ-Plasm* (New York, 1893). Karl Pearson denied that retrogression would take place to a racial mean.

41 Pick, *Faces of Degeneration*.

42 *Ibid.* See also Robert A. Nye, *Crime, Madness and Politics in Modern France: The Medical Concept of National Decline* (Princeton, 1984); R. Gilman, *Decadence* (London, 1979); S. and C. Gilman and J. Edwards, eds., *Degeneration* (New York, 1985).

43 Laski, 'Scope of Eugenics', pp. 26, 56.

44 W. M. Flinders Petrie, *The Revolutions of Civilisation* (London, New York, 1911), pp. 125–6. (Petrie was professor of Egyptology at the University of London, 1892–1933.) Also predicting biological decline were John Berry Haycraft, *Darwinism and Race Progress* (London, 1895) and G. Chatterton-Hill, *Heredity and Selection in Sociology* (London, 1907).

45 F. W. Headley, *Darwinism and Modern Socialism* (London, 1909), p. v.

46 Homer Lea, *The Valor of Ignorance* (New York, 1909), p.11 and *passim*; discussed in Bannister, *Social Darwinism*, pp. 238–9. See also the debate between Professor D. Collin Wells of Dartmouth College and Lester Ward. Wells put degenerationist views to the American Sociological Society in 1907: 'The human species and its foremost races developed under a rigorous weeding-out of the weak. Is it a priori likely that it can be maintained in physical efficiency upon the cessation of that rigorous selection?': Wells, 'Social Darwinism', *Am. J. Sociology*, 12 (1907), p. 702, generally pp. 695–716. Ward replied by criticising 'the oligocentric world-view which is coming to prevail in the higher classes of society, and would center the entire attention of the world upon an almost infinitesimal fraction of the human race and ignore all the rest': *ibid.*, p. 710.

47 Samuel Jackson Holmes, 'The Decadence of Human Heredity', *Atlantic Monthly*, 114 (1914), 302–8.

48 Karl Pearson, *The Problem of Practical Eugenics* (London, 1909), p. 34.

49 Arthur J. Balfour, *Decadence* (Cambridge, 1908), p. 49, generally pp. 44–57 (Henry Sidgwick memorial lecture, Newnham College, 25 January 1908).

50 Quoted D. P. Crook, *Benjamin Kidd: Portrait of a Social Darwinist* (Cambridge, 1984) p. 93, generally pp. 92–5.

51 Balfour, *Decadence*, p. 39. The zoologist E. Ray Lankester also thought that

assumptions about human progress rested upon 'an unreasoning optimism ... We are subject to the general laws of evolution, and are as likely to degenerate as to progress.' Lankester speculated that science might enable some control over human destiny through the power to know the evolutionary causes of change: 'we and our successors on the globe may expect to be able duly to estimate that which makes for, and that which makes against, the progress of the race': 'Degeneration' in Lankester, *The Advancement of Science: Occasional Essays and Addresses* (London, 1890), pp. 48–50.

52 Harold Frazer Wyatt, 'War as the Supreme Test of National Value', *Nineteenth Century*, 45 (1899), 216–25; and 'God's Test by War', *ibid.*, 76 (September 1914), pp. 489–510 (originally published *ibid.*, April 1911, but reprinted after the outbreak of war as 'appropriate to the present moment'). See also Wyatt and L. G. H. Horton-Smith, *The Passing of the Great Fleet* (London, 1909, 678pp.), and *Britain's Imminent Danger* (London, 1912, 200pp.), part I, by Wyatt, pp. 1–64. These books put dire forecasts that within a few years the German fleet would be greatly superior to the British. The Imperial Maritime League (est. January 1908) was prominent in the successful campaign to defeat the Declaration of London and the Naval Prize Bill. Wyatt, formerly a leader of the Navy League, contrasted an ambitious, over-populated Germany, imbued with military spirit, with 'the unmilitary spirit' of a free-trade Britain, whose birth-rate was dwindling. He hysterically attacked the 'anti-patriotic and degenerate part of the nation, especially the dominant Radical and Socialist party' (*Great Fleet*, p. xiii).

53 C. H. Melville, 'Eugenics and Military Service', *Eugenics Review*, 2 (1910–11), 53–60.

54 R. C. Hart, 'A Vindication of War', *Nineteenth Century*, 70 (1911), 226–39. (Hart was quoting Ray Lankester, who is dealt with in ch. 6.) One colonel wrote to *The Times*, complaining about Andrew Carnegie calling war a degrading evil: 'Does Mr. Carnegie really understand human nature and the immutable laws which govern and guide it? Is the grand law of "selection of the fittest" to give way to the miserable mediocrity of compromise fostered by charity?': Colonel A. C. Yate, *The Times*, 27 December 1910.

55 Anne Summers, 'Militarism in Britain before the Great War', *History Workshop*, 2 (1976), 104–23; Ian F. W. Beckett, 'The Nation in Arms, 1914–18', in Beckett and K. Simpson, eds., *A Nation in Arms: A Social Study of the British Army in the First World War* (Manchester, 1985), pp. 1–7; Geoffrey Best, 'Militarism and the Victorian Public School', in B. Simon and I. Bradley, eds., *The Victorian Public School* (London, 1975), pp. 129–46; O. Anderson, 'The Growth of Christian Militarism in mid-Victorian Britain', *English Historical Review*, 86 (1971), 46–72.

56 H. Spencer, *Facts and Comments* (London, 1902), p. 133; Summers, 'Militarism', p. 106, *passim*. Also [Anon], 'The Intellectual Charm of War' *Spectator*, 58 (25 April 1885), 542–3.

57 For full discussion, R. Soloway, 'Counting the Degenerates: The Statistics of Race Deterioration in Edwardian England', *J. of Contemporary History*, 17, 1 (1982), 137–64.

58 C. F. G. Masterman, edn, *The Heart of the Empire: Discussions of Problems of Modern City Life in England* (London, 1901), esp. pp. 1–52. The book was a

young liberal tract against the Boer War, seen to be exacerbating home problems. It included essays by A. C. Pigou, F. W. Head, G. P. Gooch and G. M. Trevelyan. Gooch wrote: 'the doctrine of evolution that recognises [war's] value in the early stages of the long ascent [of man] demands other instruments for other times. General Sheridan's dictum, "War is hell", becomes increasingly true as the civilisation of the combatants rises' (p. 337). B. B. Gilbert has a useful discussion, introduction to the Harvester edition of Masterman (1973), pp. xxiv–xxvi. The controversy resulted in a government enquiry into physical decline: Cd. 2175, 'Report of Interdepartmental Committee on Physical Deterioration' and Cd. 2210, 'Minutes of Evidence, *ibid.*' (1904).

59 See G. R. Searle, introduction to Arnold White, *Efficiency and Empire* (London, 1901; reprinted Harvester, 1973). A eugenist, White wanted medical certificates of fitness before marriage, and lamented that 'our species is being propagated ... from undersized, street-bred people' (p. 100).

60 Albert Wilson, *Unfinished Man: A Scientific Analysis of the Psychopath or Human Degenerate* (London, 1910), esp. chs. 1, 10, 11. Wilson devoted most attention to criminal types. See also J. J. Stevenson, 'Is This a Degenerate Age?' *Popular Science Monthly*, 60 (1902), 481–94; Alfred A. Mumford, 'Physical Degeneration of the British Race', *Fortnightly Review*, 76 (1904), 324–38; E. S. Talbot, *Degeneracy* (London, 1898); T. S. Clouston, *The Hygiene of Mind* (London, 1906). For a wartime account, see A. F. Tredgold, 'The Problem of Degeneracy', *Quarterly Review*, 228 (1917), 31–50.

61 Daniel Pick, 'The Faces of Anarchy', *History Workshop*, 21 (1986), 70–3. I am indebted to Dr Claire Addison of the University of Queensland for advice on French literary and historical themes. Her early death, on 30 April 1993, has meant a tragic loss to scholarship.

62 Linda L. Clark, *Social Darwinism in France* (Alabama, 1984), pp. 165–71, on which this section relies. Clark shows that military men were to the fore in using Darwinian justifications of war, partly out of desire to restore the glory of the army after the scandals of the Dreyfus affair.

63 André Gavet, 'L'Idée de patrie', *Revue politique et parlementaire*, 45 (1905), 434–50, quoted Clark, *Social Darwinism in France*, p. 166. Gavet distinguished 'la guerre fatal', war for national survival, from 'just and useful wars' that served humanity (for example, 'civilising' colonial wars). All humanitarian and pacifist teachings were treason.

64 André Constantin, *Le rôle sociologique de la guerre et le sentiment national* (Paris, 1907), pp. 142, 168–70, quoted Clark, *Social Darwinism in France*, p. 167. Constantin used anthropometric studies by Colligen and Ammon to support his thesis that wars caused individual selection advantageous to the species. Also Charles Kessler, 'Le Pacifisme', *Le Correspondant*, 221 (1905), 855–64; Georges-Albert Bazaine-Hayter, 'Société de sociologie de Paris...' *Revue internationale de sociologie*, 19 (1910), 196, 265, quoted Clark, pp. 167–8; Jules de Gaultier, 'Le présomption sociologique', *Mercure de France*, 96 (1912), 254, 276, quoted Clark, pp. 169–70.

65 Modris Eksteins, *Rites of Spring: The Great War and the Birth of the Modern Age* (Boston, 1989), p. 86, generally Part II for above themes.

66 General Friedrich von Bernhardi, *Britain as Germany's Vassal*, trans. J. Ellis

Barker (London, 1914), pp. 106–7, ch. 4 generally. Barker translated the book in order to warn the British of German war plans: 'decadent England is described as Germany's principal enemy, and she is to be made subservient to that country either by war or by an "alliance", under which England would have to give up her naval supremacy, leave the triple Entente, abandon her allies, disarm … and would have to allow Germany to smash France and to dominate the Continent of Europe, North Africa and Asia Minor' (translator's introduction, p. 5).

67 Gerhard Ritter, *The Sword and the Scepter: The Problem of Militarism in Germany*, trans. Coral Gables (Florida, 1970), II, 116; generally pp. 112–17.

68 Bernhardi, *Germany's Vassal*, p. 118.

69 Bernhardi, *Germany and the Next War* (trans. London, 1912), pp. 6, 10ff. Bernhardi added that the social order that would prove strongest was the one pursuing the highest moral aims (*Germany's Vassal*, p. 108). W. H. Mallock conceded that Bernhardi 'attempts to temper the extreme doctrine of war as a process which is justified by physical force only, and bring it into harmony with those ideals of moral and intellectual civilisation of which … men like Kant, Fichte, and Goethe are amongst the most shining examples'. He agreed with much of Bernhardi, although finding some of his overstatements 'morally monstrous': 'General Bernhardi on the Moral Logic of War', *Nineteenth Century*, 76 (1914), 1360–76. For an American attack on 'the evil genius whose hand is felt everywhere', see Norman Hapgood, 'Bernhardi and the United States', *Harpers Weekly*, 59 (1914), 367–8.

70 For the above see William Schneider, 'Toward the Improvement of the Human Race: The History of Eugenics in France', *J. Modern History*, 54, 2 (1982), 268–91; also Pick, *Faces of Degeneration*, Part 1.

71 For the attraction of eugenics to socialists in Germany see Paul Weindling, *Health*.

72 Peter Morton, *The Vital Science: Biology and the Literary Imagination, 1860–1900* (London, 1984), pp. 127–33, 142, generally ch. 5. Morton has an interesting account of eugenic 'utopias', including Ellis Davis's *Pyrna* (1875), which employed Spartan techniques of selective infanticide. No one grew up 'with a shattered frame, with a feeble pulse, with an aching head, or with that worst of all evils that is bred in a decaying civilisation, a nervously diseased constitution' (quoted p. 142).

73 Pick, *Faces of Degeneration*, ch. 7.

74 Daniel J. Kevles, *In the Name of Eugenics: Genetics and the Uses of Human Heredity* (New York, 1985), chs. 4, 5. Large numbers of women interested in issues of marriage, sexual mores and reproduction were involved in Anglo-American eugenics; as were geneticists, for example, Charles Davenport, Herbert Jennings, Raymond Pearl in the US, R. A. Fisher (statistician), J. B. S. Haldane (population genetics) and Julian Huxley in the UK. Kevles suggests that such groups were often looking for new political creeds and a secular substitute for religion. He sees in American eugenics a blend of conservatives (for example, Davenport), Progressives (for example, Gifford Pinchot, Charles W. Eliot, D. S. Jordan), and radicals (for example, Emma Goldman, Hermann J. Muller – a Marxist: p. 64). See also Mark Haller, *Eugenics: Hereditarian Attitudes in American Thought* (Rutgers, 1963);

Kenneth Ludmerer, *Genetics and American Society* (Baltimore, 1972); Mark B. Adams, *The Wellborn Science: Eugenics in Germany, France, Brazil and Russia* (New York, Oxford, 1990); Pauline M. H. Mazumdar, *Eugenics, Human Genetics and Human Failings: The Eugenics Society; its Sources and its Critics in Britain* (London, New York, 1992).

75 Ludmerer, 'American Geneticists and the Eugenics Movement, 1905–1935', *Journal of the History of Biology*, 2, 2 (1969) pp. 342–3 and generally 337–63. William Bateson looked to a future when it would be definitely known 'that liability to a disease ... addiction to a particular vice ... is due to the presence or absence of a specific ingredient, and finally that these characteristics are transmitted to offspring according to definite, predictable rules, then man's view of his own nature, his conception of justice, in short his whole outlook of the world, must be profoundly changed': *The Method and Scope of Genetics* (Cambridge, 1908), pp. 34–5, quoted Ludmerer, 'American Geneticists', p. 344.

76 Georges Vacher de Lapouge, *Social Selections* (London, 1896; trans. of *Les sélections sociales*, Paris, 1896); *The Aryan and His Social Role* (London, 1899; trans *L'Aryen, son role social*, Paris, 1899); also *Race et milieu social* (Paris, 1909). Also E. Seillière, *The German Doctrine of Conquest: A French View* (London, 1914), pp. 79ff.; and Gunter Nagel, *Georges Vacher de Lapouge* (Freiburg, 1975); Victoria C. Woodhull Martin, *The Rapid Multiplication of the Unfit* (London, 1891).

77 C. P. Blacker, *Eugenics: Galton and After* (London, 1952), p. 104.

78 Kevles, *Eugenics*, esp. ch. 1. It is psychologically interesting that some of the most enthusiastic apostles of 'race regeneration', such as Galton, Havelock Ellis, even Bernard Shaw, had barren marriages (p. 9).

79 Jones, *Social Darwinism*, ch. 5.

80 S. R. Steinmetz, *Der Krieg als Soziologisches Problem* (1899) and *Die Philosophie des Krieges* (Leipzig, 1907) praised 'collective selection' as promoting the national efficiency of a people, in contrast to the atomistic effects of individualistic selection. Steinmetz argued a retrogressivist line that humanity regressed morally without war, which unified peoples and encouraged a sense of mutual responsibility. André Constantin, who translated *Der Krieg als Soziologisches Problem* into French, included an essay by Steinmetz in his *Rôle sociologique de la guerre* (Paris, 1907): see Clark, *Social Darwinism in France*, pp. 166–7.

81 Karl Pearson, *National Life from the Standpoint of Science* (2nd edn, London, 1901; 1st edn, London, 1900), p. 55.

82 Karl Pearson, *Social Problems: Their Treatment, Past, Present and Future* (London, 1912; reprinted Garland, New York, London, 1984), pp. 4–5.

83 On Pearson see B. Semmel, 'Karl Pearson: Socialist and Darwinist', *British J. Sociology*, 9, 2 (1958), 111–25; and D. Mackenzie, 'Karl Pearson and the Professional Middle Class', *Annals of Science*, 36 (1979), 125–43.

84 A. R. Wallace and C. Lloyd Morgan, zoologist and comparative psychologist, also denied that *panmixia* entailed biological degeneration: for example, Wallace, 'The Future of Civilisation', *Nature*, 49 (12 April 1894), 550.

85 Pearson, 'Socialism and Natural Selection', *Fortnightly Review* (1894);

reprinted as *The Chances of Death and Other Studies in Evolution* (London, New York, 1897), I, 103–39.

86 'No thoughtful socialist, as far as I am aware, would object to cultivate Uganda *at the expense of its present* occupiers if Lancashire were starving': *ibid.*, p. 111; also p. 122.

87 Pearson, *National Life* (2nd edn, London, 1901), pp. 26–7: 'Being as we are, we cannot give up the struggle, and the moment dearth of ability, the want of brains and physique in the right place, leads to serious defeat, our catastrophe will come.'

88 *National Life*, pp. 46–8; also *The Grammar of Science* (1st edn, London, 1892; 2nd edn, London, 1900), ch. 9, part 16. For similar views on race war see T. B. C., *A War Policy for Greater Britain* (London, 1910); Chatterton-Hill, *Heredity and Selection in Sociology*, part 2, ch. 5; and S. J. Holmes, *Human Genetics and its Social Import* (New York, London, 1936), ch. 20.

89 Pearson wanted the barring of undesirable aliens (he was alarmed by the number of foreign names, especially Jews, in the commercial directories of London and Manchester), expatriation of criminals, exclusion from welfare of congenital paupers and the insane. By 1912 he was denouncing the factory acts and medical science as opposed to Darwinism: see *The Problem of Practical Eugenics* (London, 1909); *Darwinism, Medical Progress and Eugenics* (London, 1912); *Social Problems* (1912); also Semmel, 'Pearson', pp. 120–1.

90 John A. Hobson,'The Scientific Basis of Imperialism', *Political Science Quarterly*, 17 (1902), 468–9.

91 See, for example, Hobson, *Forced Labour* (London, 1917), *Democracy After the War* (London, 1917), and *The New Protectionism* (New York, 1916).

92 See Michael Freeden, *The New Liberalism: An Ideology of Social Reform* (Oxford, 1978), pp. 82–5, and Freeden, edn, *J. A. Hobson: A Reader* (London, 1988).

93 Hobson, *The Psychology of Jingoism* (London, 1901), pp. 19–20. He spoke of the 'animal hate, vindictiveness, and bloodthirstiness' that lurked in the mildest-mannered patriot, 'a convincing testimony to the descent of man' (p. 31). See also Jones, *Social Darwinism*, pp. 123, 128; John Allett, *New Liberalism: The Political Economy of J. A. Hobson* (Toronto, London, 1981), pp. 38–9, 228–9, and *passim*.

94 Hobson, 'Scientific Basis', pp. 462–5.

95 L. T. Hobhouse, *Mind in Evolution* (London, 1901), pp. ix–xiv. For Henry Sidgwick's criticism of Hobhouse's social evolutionism and 'naturalistic fallacy', see John A. Hall, *History of European Ideas*, 9, 4 (1988), 520.

96 Hobson, 'Scientific Basis', pp. 462–5. Hobson's eugenic ideas sometimes severely qualified his liberalism; for example, he considered that a 'rational stirpiculture in the wider social interests might require a repression of the spread of degenerate or unprogressive races' (p. 485). The First World War, however, evoked all of his liberal sympathies. He defended civil liberties against government intrusion and censorship, and fulminated against war profiteering, erosion of the democratic party system, conscription and growing militarism in Britain. See, for example, Hobson, *Forced Labour* (1917), *Democracy After the War* (1917) and *The New Protectionism* (1916).

97 Even here Hobson conceded that the dawn of a rational stage in human history

from the beginning of 'instinctive organic economy' meant the dawn of selfishness. Freeden attributes this to Idealist influence. Hobson wanted a society transcending individualism, similar to Hegel's civil society: M. Freeden, 'J. A. Hobson as a New Liberal Theorist', *J. History of Ideas*, 34 (1973), 424.

98 Kidd, *Science of Power* (1918; 8th edn, 1919), pp. 77–82.

99 *Science of Power*, p. 272; also Kidd, *Social Evolution* (London, New York, 1894), *The Control of the Tropics* (London, New York, 1898); D. P. Crook, 'Was Benjamin Kidd a Racist?', *Ethnic and Racial Studies*, 2, 2 (1979), 213–221; and Crook, *Kidd*, pp. 24–5.

100 Clark, *Social Darwinism in France*, p. 131, generally pp. 129–33.

101 Edmond Demolins, *Anglo-Saxon Superiority: To What it is Due* (trans. from 10th French edn, London, 1898), p. xxxix and *passim*; *Boers or English: Who are in the Right?* (trans. London, 1900), pp. 24–5. Ideas that national characters were racially ingrained were commonplace. One imperial writer, citing with approval Lord Rosebery's dictum 'What is empire but the predominance of race?', perceived British superiority to lie in an inherited blend of Anglo-Saxon pluck and common sense, Norse enterprise and Celtic vivacity: See T. B. C., *War Policy*, pp. 8, 57.

102 Bannister, *Social Darwinism*, pp. 98–9, and generally ch. 5.

103 W. G. Sumner, *War and Other Essays* (New Haven, 1911); reprinted L. Bramson and G. W. Goethals, eds., *War* (New York, London, 1964), pp. 205–27.

104 L. F. Ward, 'Cosmic and Organic Evolution' (1877), 'The Scientific Basis of Positive Political Economy' (1882), quoted Bannister, *Social Darwinism*, p. 127, generally ch. 6. See also on Sumner and Ward, Richard Hofstadter, *Social Darwinism in American Thought* (Philadelphia, 1944).

105 Peter Bowler, *Theories of Human Evolution: A Century of Debate, 1844–1944* (Baltimore, London, 1986), pp. 19, 127. Also Irish embryologist E. W. MacBride, *An Introduction to the Study of Heredity* (London, 1924), ch. 9.

106 Bannister, *Sociology and Scientism: The American Quest for Objectivity, 1800–1940* (Chapel Hill, London, 1987), p. 25, generally ch. 1. Also ch. 2 above.

107 L. F. Ward, *Pure Sociology* (New York, 2nd edn, 1909; 1st edn, 1903), pp. 238–40, 215–16; and 'Social and Biological Struggles', *American J. Sociology*, 13 (1907), 289–99.

108 Franklin H. Giddings, *Democracy and Empire* (New York, 1900), pp. 284–5. On Giddings, see Bannister, *Sociology and Scientism*, esp. ch. 5.

109 *Rochester Post Express*, 1 October 1898 (by a socialist observer): 'We are asked to accept as a philosophical political system the vague proposition that certain nations shall take charge of a great part of the earth and its inhabitants "in trust for civilization", leaving the nature of the trust, the character of civilization and the means to the end all to the discretion of the so-called trustees.'

110 Josiah Strong, *Expansion Under New World-Conditions* (New York, 1900), pp. 10, 213, *passim*; also D. R. Muller, 'Josiah Strong and American Nationalism: A Re-evaluation', *J. American History*, 53 (1966–7), 487–503.

111 Bannister, *Social Darwinism*, pp. 228–31, generally ch. 12.

4 THE NATURAL DECLINE OF WARFARE: ANTI-WAR EVOLUTIONISM PRIOR TO 1914

1 Alexander Sutherland, 'The Natural Decline of Warfare', *Nineteenth Century*, 45 (1899), 570–78.
2 I. F. Clarke, *Voices Prophesying War, 1863–1984* (London, 1966), esp. ch. 3. Alfred Harmsworth (Lord Northcliffe) a founder of tabloids, worked on the principle that 'a paper has only to be able to put on its placard "A Great Battle" for its sales to mount up' (quoted p. 66). The French military expert Demetrius Boulger declared war sooner or later inevitable: 'great issues have arisen which can only be settled by the sword ... War is nearest at hand when there is most talk of peace and when the Pacificists are most confident in the arrival of the Millennium': 'The Peace of Europe', *United Services Magazine*, 44, 995 (1911), 1.
3 Robert Routledge, *Discoveries and Inventions of the Nineteenth Century* (London, 1876), quoted Clarke, *ibid.*, p. 78.
4 Jean de Bloch, *The Future of War in its Technical, Economic, and Political Relations*, trans., R. C. Long (Boston, 1902, reprinted Garland, New York, London, 1972), hereafter *The Future of War*. This one-volume translation is from volume VI, a summary and conclusion of the six volume series, published in French as *La guerre: traduction de l'ouvrage russe – la guerre future aux points de vue technique, économique et politique* (Paris, 1898–1900, 6 vols.); and in German as *Der Krieg: ... Der zukunftig Krieg in seiner technischen, volkswirthsschaftlichen und politischen Bedeutung* (Berlin, 1899, 6 vols.). Abridgments of vol. VI appeared in English as *Is War Now Impossible?* (London, 1899), and *Modern Weapons and Modern War* (London, 1900). Mead described Bloch as 'a sort of Polish Rothschild': introd. to *The Future of War*, p. iv. Bloch supported Zionism although he was a convert to Calvinism. W. T. Stead, although a champion of Cecil Rhodes and a strong navy, opposed the Boer War, and until his death in 1912 (on the *Titanic*) campaigned for peace through arbitration.
5 *Future of War*, pp. ix, xi.
6 *Future of War*, p. lxii.
7 Bloch, 'Wars of the Future', *Contemporary Review*, 80 (1901), 311.
8 Bloch, 'Wars of the Future', pp. 307–8, 321: 'The warrior-caste has alone succeeded in shutting out the light of day and carrying over the prejudices, abuses and cruel usages of a barbarous epoch into the refined atmosphere of the twentieth century'. For British analyses see Colonel F. Maurice, *War* (London, 1891); Spencer Wilkinson, *War and Policy* (London, 1910).
9 *The Times*, 25 June, 2 July, 10 July 1901; also 14 July 1899. He lectured to the military experts at the Royal United Services Institution.
10 R. E. C. Long, 'Jean de Bloch', *Fortnightly Review*, 321 (1902), 228–36. For description of the Lucerne Museum, *Review of Reviews*, 26 (15 July 1902), 37–40. Generally see introductions by Edwin. D. Mead and W. T. Stead to *Future of War*; Mead, 'Jean de Bloch and the "Future of War"', *New England Magazine*, 28 (1903), 298–309; Stead, 'A Russian Cobden', ch. 5 of his *United States of Europe* (London, 1899), and Stead, 'Character Sketch: The Late M. Jean Bloch', *Review of Reviews*, 25 (15 February 1902), 136–42; P. Van Den

Dungen, introductory note to *A Bibliography of the Pacifist Writings of Jean de Bloch* (London, 1977); *Jewish Encyclopedia*, vol. III (1902); *Encyclopaedia Judaica*, vol. IV (1971).

11 H. G. Wells, *Anticipations of the Reaction of Mechanical and Scientific Progress upon Human Life and Thought* (London, 1901), p. 204. He refers to Bloch, p. 181.

12 Wells, 'The Collapse of Civilisation', *Works of H. G. Wells* (New York, 1924–7), vol. XX, pp. 472–3, cited T. H. E. Travers, 'Future Warfare: H. G. Wells and British Military Theory, 1895–1916', in *War and Society: A Yearbook of Military History*, ed. Brian Bond and Ian Roy (Croom Helm, London, n.d.), p. 85.

13 Wells 'drew upon his training in biology to conceive of the State as one organic whole, which achieved wartime efficiency in so far as the highest percentage of its members became organised and prepared for war, in fact, so far as the whole nation was transformed into one fighting unit': Travers, 'Future Warfare', p. 71.

14 *Anticipations*, pp. 212, 317.

15 Frank McConnell, *Victorian Studies*, 27,1 (1983), 116–17. Quotes from *Discovery and Anticipations* in Lovat Dickson, *H. G. Wells* (Harmondsworth, 1972), p. 116. Generally see N. and J. Mackenzie, *The Time Traveller* (London, 1973); Peter Kemp, *H. G. Wells and the Culminating Age* (London, 1982); J. R. Reed, *The Natural History of H. G. Wells* (London, 1982). Also on Wells and war, see Clarke, *Voices Prophesying War*, pp. 91–103.

16 Guglielmo Ferrero, *Militarism* (London, 1902; trans. and revised from *Il Militarismo*, Italy, 1898; reprinted Garland, London, 1972), pp. 306–7, 317. The Italian liberal Boccardo, a follower of Molinari, declaimed: 'For the ancient proverb *war feeds war* we today substitute the maxim *war will kill war*, which signifies that when the means of killing, mining, bombarding, and ruining will have attained the apogee of perfection (and we are rapidly nearing this goal), war will become almost impossible': quoted Silberner, *The Problem of War in Nineteenth Century Economic Thought* (trans. Princeton, 1946), pp. 116–17.

17 Howard Weinroth, 'Norman Angell and *The Great Illusion*: An Episode in Pre-1914 Pacifism', *Historical J.*, 17, 3 (1974), 553, generally 551–74. Also A. Marrin, *Sir Norman Angell* (Boston, 1979), and J. B. D. Miller, *Norman Angell and the Futility of War* (London, 1986).

18 Marrin, *Angell*, p. 79; Weinroth, 'Angell', pp. 551ff.; P. D. Supina, 'The Norman Angell Peace Campaign in Germany', *J. Peace Research*, 9 (1974), 161–4. Jordan even recommended the first edition to Homer Lea, a former student of his at Stanford, after Lea had sent him a complimentary copy of *The Valor of Ignorance*. Jordan was to harass Lea ruthlessly in later years; and typically advised Angell to cut references to Lea's work from *The Great Illusion* as folly 'hardly worth remembering': quoted T. C. Kennedy, 'Homer Lea and the Peace Makers', *The Historian*, 45 (1983), 489. Angell and Jordan formed a mutual admiration society, each energetically publicising the other's ideas.

19 Norman Angell, *The Great Illusion* (London, 1912; 1st edn, 1910), pp. vi–vii.

20 'Disturbance in New York involves financial and commercial disturbance in London, and, if sufficiently grave, compels financiers of London to cooperate

with those of New York to put an end to the crisis, not as a matter of altruism, but as a matter of commercial self-protection': *Great Illusion*, p. 46. Also on this topic, see R. S. Hamilton-Grace, *Finance and War* (London, 1910).

21 In a letter of 1912 to Maurice Brett, Angell warned: 'If military expenditure ... is not attacked scientifically, revolutionary and anti-national solutions like that of Hervé in France and the extreme socialists in Germany will gain more and more favour': quoted Weinroth, 'Angell', p. 565.

22 *Mutual Aid* was written originally as eight articles in James Knowle's periodical *Nineteenth Century* (November 1890–June 1896), to refute Huxley's 1888 paper on 'The Struggle for Existence'.

23 Peter Kropotkin, *Mutual Aid: A Factor of Evolution* (London, 1902; reprinted 1903), pp. xiv, xvi. Following references in text are to this edition.

24 Kropotkin referred also to the writings of Jean Charles Houzeau, Maximilian Perty, Louis Büchner and J. Lanessan. From Büchner's *Liebe und Liebes-Leben in der Thierwelt* (1883), he detected a line of influence to works such as Henry Drummond's *Ascent of Man* (London, 1894), Alexander Sutherland's *Origin and Growth of the Moral Instinct* (London, 1898) and F. H. Giddings' *Principles of Sociology* (London and New York, 1896). Sir John Lubbock's *Ants, Bees and Wasps* (London, 1872) was a major English source for the social insects. The subject of animal behaviour will be taken up in ch. 5.

25 He read Kessler's lecture 'The Law of Mutual Aid', *Proceedings St Petersburg Society of Naturalists* (1880), quoted *Mutual Aid*, p. 8. Kessler concluded that 'the progressive development of the animal kingdom, and especially of mankind, is favoured much more by mutual support than by mutual struggle' (*Proc.*, p. xi).

26 Kropotkin, *Fields, Factories, and Workshops* (London, 1899; reprinted London, 1901), pp. 84–5.

27 Kropotkin's authorities on early/primitive man included Sir John Lubbock, *Prehistoric Times* (London, 1865), J. F. McLennan, *Studies in Ancient History* (London, 1886), Lewis H. Morgan, *Ancient Society* (New York, 1877), J. Bachofen, *Das Mutterrecht* (Stuttgart, 1861), E. B. Tylor, *Primitive Culture* (London, 1871) and Elie Reclus, *Primitive Folk* (1891).

28 A. L. and V. L. Gordin, *Pan-anarchist Manifesto* (Moscow, 1918), pp. 3–6, in Paul Avrich, *The Anarchists in the Russian Revolution* (London, 1973), pp. 49–52. Also: 'Pan-anarchism declares that religion and science were invented as a means of distracting attention from oppression and the real tangible world, substituting for it an intangible world, either supernatural (religion) or abstract (science)': (quotes p. 50).

29 Kropotkin, *Modern Science and Anarchism* (Paris, 1913), in R. N. Baldwin, edn, *Kropotkin's Revolutionary Pamphlets* (New York, 1927; reprinted New York, 1970), p. 150. Anarchism's aim 'is to construct a synthetic philosophy comprehending in one generalization all the phenomena of nature – and therefore also the life of societies' (p. 150; also p. 192).

30 Kropotkin, *Ethics: Origin and Development* (trans., London, 1924; 1st edn, Moscow, 1922), p. 3. Following references in text are to this edition.

31 B. Kidd, *Two Principal Laws of Sociology* (London, 1907–8), II, 13–14. He added that militarism was mainly defensive among advanced nations, a means of resistance against the use of force by others 'under the influence of less evolved standards of conduct'.

32 John Haynes Holmes, *New Wars for Old* (New York, 1916), p. 8. See also W. L. Grane, *The Passing of War* (London, 1912), L. C. Jane, *Nations at War* (London, 1914), F. A. Woods and A. Baltzly, *Is War Diminishing?* (Boston, 1915). The historian G. P. Gooch wrote in 1911: 'We can now look forward with something like confidence to the time when war between civilised nations will be considered as antiquated as the duel': *History of Our Time* (London, 1911), p. 249. Also the National Peace Council *Yearbook* for 1914: 'peace, the babe of the 19th century, is the strong youth of the 20th century; for War, the product of anarchy and fear, is passing away under … that social sense and newer aspect of worldwide life which is the insistent note, the *Zeitgeist* of the age': quoted A. Marrin, *The Last Crusade: the Church of England in the First World War* (Durham, N. C., 1974), p. 66. Also J. J. Stevenson, 'Is This a Degenerate Age?' *Popular Science Monthly*, 60 (1902), 490–1.

33 Jacques Novicow, *War and Its Alleged Benefits* (London, 1912), pp. 26–8, and *passim*. Novicow's earlier works were more sympathetic to Spencer's theory that a militant stage was necessary in human evolution. Norman Angell was sceptical of 'peaceful savage' anthropology: *Peace and the Plain Man* (London, 1935), p. 257.

34 Novicow, *La fédération de l'Europe* (Paris, 1901), *Méchanisme et limites de l'association humaine* (Paris, 1912).

35 *War and its Alleged Benefits*, p. 111. See also Sandi Cooper, introduction to *La fédération de l'Europe* (Paris, 1901; reprinted, Garland, 1971); and H. E. Barnes, 'A Sociological Criticism of War and Militarism: An Analysis of the Doctrines of Jacques Novicow', *J. International Relations*, 12, 2 (1921), 238–65.

36 'If the law of nature was to be the rule, no society would be possible: the human race would be given up to pure anarchy … The belief that war is inevitable owing to the nature of man has no scientific support; war between nations is a social invention, not a natural phenomenon': Charles Richet, *Peace and War* (trans. from French, London, 1906), pp. 62–4. Cf. Margaret Mead, 'Warfare is only an Invention – Not a Biological Necessity', *Asia*, 40 (1940), 402–5. Richet combined his peace ideas with degenerationist fears about the cessation of natural selection in a semi-socialist world.

37 Roger Chickering, *Imperial Germany and World Without War: The Peace Movement and German Society, 1892–1914* (Princeton, 1975), pp. 96–105, 347–8, and ch. 3 generally, on which I have drawn for this discussion.

38 G. K. Chesterton, *Orthodoxy* (London, 1909), p. 49.

39 Chickering, *Imperial Germany*, pp. 105ff. Also endorsing the federationist ideal were major figures in German medical science, such as Oscar Hertwig (1849–1922) and Wilhelm Waldeyer (1837–1921), organicist cell state theorists who opposed pan-Germanist Social Darwinism 'which proclaimed the inevitability of war as a racial struggle'. Hertwig hoped that, as cells cooperated in an organism, so states should cooperate in the federation of *Mitteleuropa*. Although Waldeyer signed the scholars' 'Address to the Civilised World' in 1914, defending German policy, Hertwig continued to attack Social Darwinism and eugenics: see Paul Weindling, 'Theories of the Cell State in Imperial Germany', in Charles Webster, edn, *Biology, Medicine and Society, 1840–1940* (Cambridge, 1981), pp. 136–7.

40 'Those who really wish to trust to Natural Selection in its original form, which

operates by the extinction of the unfit, must be ready to strip the human race of all the painfully won results of civilisation and to return, first to barbarism, and then to a general scramble for nuts in the primeval forest': D. G. Ritchie, *Darwinism and Politics* (London, 3rd edn, 1895; 1st edn, 1889), p. vi. Social inheritance was 'the great advantage that mankind possesses over the brutes' (p. 132).

41 *Darwinism and Politics*, pp. 13, 15, 96–7. Mutuality is discussed in his additional essay 2 for the 2nd edition: 'Natural Selection and the Spiritual World', pp. 87–118, where reaction is expressed to Leslie Stephen's *The Science of Ethics* (London, 1882) and Samuel Alexander's *Moral Order and Progress* (London, 1889).

42 *Darwinism and Politics*, pp. 36, 126–32. The latter is from an essay 'Natural Selection and the History of Institutions', added to the original edition in reply to Emil Reich, *Graeco-Roman Institutions from an Anti-evolutionist Point of View* (Oxford, 1890). In it Ritchie warned that 'uncritical use of biological formulae only leads to bad results in sociology and in practical politics' (p. 141). For Keller's similar ideas on selection of mores, see ch. 7.

43 Ritchie, 'War and Peace', in his *Studies in Political and Social Ethics* (London, 1902), pp. 136, 156, 158 (first published in *International J. Ethics*, January 1901). However he still warned against 'crude applications of biological conceptions to social evolution. The nation is not an organism in the biological sense ... human evolution does not take place only by death and war' (pp. 164–5). He said he got his biological premises from his friend E. B. Poulton (see ch. 6). Also Ritchie, 'Social Evolution', *International J. Ethics* 6 (1895–6), 165–81; *Philosophical Studies* (London, 1905); 'Darwinism and Politics', *Fortnightly Review*, 86 (1909), 519–32. Bertrand Russell divided wars into types (colonisation, principle, self-defence, prestige) in 'Ethics of War', *International J. Ethics*, 25 (1915), 127–42.

44 Charles H. Harvey, *The Biology of British Politics* (London, New York, 1904), p. 115. Following references in text are to this source. Harvey acknowledged his debt to Spencer, Bagehot, J. R. Seeley, James Bryce and Karl Pearson.

45 Angell claimed that by the time he wrote *Europe's Optical Illusion* (London, 1909), Novicow was 'unknown territory' to him, although he had arrived at similar views 'by very different roads but by pretty much the same method of travel': see Angell, introduction to Novicow, *War and its Alleged Benefits* (London, 1912), xiii–xv; and Marrin, *Angell*, pp. 88–9.

46 Hiram M. Chittenden's *War or Peace: A Present Duty and a Future Hope* (London, n.d., c. 1911) was endorsed by Carnegie, and popularised peace biology in the mould of Angell and D. S. Jordan.

47 Anti-commercial sentiments were common in the military and service journals. For example, Estelle Blyth: 'Who, today, perpetrates the blackest deeds of shame, and violence, and cruelty? Not the soldier, whose trade is war; but the peaceful trader, the speculator who ruins thousands, the financier, who battens on "corners" in food, while children starve': 'On the Use of War', *United Services Magazine*, NS 44, 997 (1911), 247–51. Demetrius Boulger denounced nations that lacked patriotism; they 'only cumber the earth, and deserve to disappear'. Boulger preferred war to socialist unrest, strikes and sabotage: 'The Peace of Europe' (1911). Also Homer Lea, *The Valor of Ignorance* (New

York, 1909), *The Day of the Saxon* (New York and London, 1912). Lea blamed materialistic industrial society for eroding Anglo-Saxon civilisation in its race struggle against the 'yellow peril' and 'the swarming of the Slav'.

48 Angell, *The Great Illusion*, pp. 144–5, 149 n. 171; and his *Peace and the Plain Man* (London, 1935), p. 262 and *passim*.

49 Kenneth Ludmerer, 'American Geneticists and the Eugenics Movement, 1905–1935', *J. History of Biology*, 2, 2 (1969), 340. As the Nobel Laureate H. J. Muller wrote to Charles Davenport in 1918: 'I have never been interested in genetic problems as an abstraction, but always because of its fundamental relation to man – his characteristics and means of self-betterment' (quoted p. 340). Prominent in the American eugenics movement were the geneticists Davenport, Harry H. Laughlin, and Paul Popenoe, while other geneticists participated in the movement in its early years, for example, T. H. Morgan, William E. Castle, Edwin G. Conklin, Edward M. East, Herbert S. Jennings and Raymond Pearl.

50 Darwin, *Descent of Man* (reprinted 1901), p. 207, discussed in ch. 1.

51 D. S. Jordan's Boston address 'War and Manhood' (4 July 1910) was immediately published in the British *Eugenics Review*, 2 (July 1910), 95–109; his Sunderland House speech to the Eugenics Education Society on 'The Eugenics of War' was promptly published in *Eugenics Review*, 5 (1913), 197–213. Also V. L. Kellogg, 'Eugenics and Militarism', in *Problems in Eugenics: Papers to the First International Eugenics Congress* (London, 1912). For full documentation see D. P. Crook, 'Nature's Pruning Hook? War and Evolution, 1890–1918: A Response to Nancy Stepan', *Aust. J. Politics and History*, 33, 3 (1987), 237–52; also G. R. Searle, *Eugenics and Politics in Britain, 1900–14* (Leyden, 1976), pp. 36–8. Nancy Stepan has suggested that most British eugenists were either indifferent to the eugenics-of-war issue before the war, or else favoured military service: see J. M. W. Bean, edn, *The Political Culture of Modern Britain* (London, 1987), 138ff. I have argued against this view in 'Nature's Pruning Hook' above.

52 Roland Hugins, 'The Eugenic Judgment of War', *South Atlantic Quarterly*, 13, 4 (1914), 303. Although Hugins testified to the strength of peace eugenics before the war, he felt that peace advocates 'in their crusading zeal' had pushed the eugenic argument against war 'so far that it stands in need of qualifications'.

53 Full details in Alice N. Hays, comp., *David Starr Jordan: A Bibliography of His Writings, 1871–1931* (Stanford, London, 1952).

54 D. S. Jordan, *War and Waste* (New York, 1914; reprinted Garland, 1972), pp. 8–9, 19, also 53. He noted that even the US spent two-thirds of its annual income on the military. There was a secretary for war and navy, but none for economy, sanitation or internal peace.

55 'The steady extension of unification in international life is a guarantee that international war among civilized nations has already come to an end. The old impulses for international war have passed away': *War and Waste*, pp. 6–9; also p. 46: 'War is dying. It dies because it cannot pay its way.' Like Angell he believed that the great financiers, especially the Jewish interests such as the Rothschilds, who once skimmed the cream off war loans, would now never give the signal for a great war (p. 44).

56 See D. Kevles, *In the Name of Eugenics* (New York, 1985), and ch. 3 above.

57 Kevles, *Eugenics*, p. 45. As Kevles shows, the $10 million endowment of Cold Spring Harbor exceeded the total endowment for research in American universities at the time.

58 Jordan, *The Human Harvest: A Study of the Decay of Races Through the Survival of the Unfit* (Boston, 1907), p. 39 and *passim*.

59 'The delusion that war in one generation sharpens the edge of warriorhood in the next generation, has no biological foundation. It is the man who is left who always determines the future': Jordan, 'War and Manhood', p. 96. Jordan's race ideas owed something to Edmond Demolins's *Anglo-Saxon Superiority* (1898): *Human Harvest*, p. 47.

60 *Human Harvest*, pp. 24, 116 and *passim*.

61 D. S. Jordan and Harvey Ernest Jordan, *War's Aftermath: A Preliminary Study of the Eugenics of War as Illustrated by the Civil War of the United States...* (Boston, New York, 1914). This anticipated modern social science techniques in using public opinion polls, questionnaires sent to surviving Confederate officers and citizens. Their opinions were collected on thirty propositions, most formulating Jordan's 'reverse selection' theory as applied to the Civil War. The results, despite some interesting comments, were basically inconclusive, the hypotheses inexactly phrased and open to various interpretations. The authors concluded that there had been grave racial hurt, but conceded that the results could be read as 'more or less matters of environment as well as of differences in germ-plasm, of euthenics as well as of eugenics' (77–8).

62 Jordan, 'War and Genetic Values', *J. of Heredity*, 10 (1919), 225.

63 G. G. Coulton, review of *War and the Breed* (1915) in *Eugenics Review*, 7 (1915–16), 288. Coulton accused Jordan of assuming inheritance of acquired characters when it suited him, and of wilfully misrepresenting classical historians such as Otto Seeck. Coulton was also polemical against Angell. Coulton publicly corrected Jordan's errors at a joint meeting of the Eugenics Society and the War and Peace Society of Cambridge University, and repeated his exposure in *The Nineteenth Century and After* (October, 1914). He complained that Jordan chose to ignore such criticisms except for silently deleting the more obvious blunders: Coulton, *Eugenics Review*, 7 (1915–16), 287–92. For Jordan's personal campaign against Homer Lea, see T. C. Kennedy, 'Homer Lea and the Peace Makers', *The Historian*, 45 (1983), 489ff.

64 C. Roland Marshall charges that Jordan often used ideas of genetic inheritance of moral qualities, even acquired physical characters. He implied that qualities such as cowardice, viciousness, etc., would be passed on genetically by the unfit to their sons, and even that the maimed and crippled would pass on genetic effects: introduction to *Human Harvest* (Garland, 1972), p. 9. Jordan certainly knew better, saying on drill for instance: 'No training, mental or physical, can raise a man above his possibilities and it is the possibilities only that his children inherit. The events in a man's life leave no trace in actual heredity and none in transmission unless the events have consequences which impair the vigor of the germ cells': *War's Aftermath*, pp. 79–80.

65 *Human Harvest*, pp. 87–8.

66 Jordan, 'War and Genetic Values', 223–5; 'War Selection in Western Europe', *Popular Science Monthly*, 87 (1915), 143–54; 'The Repair of Human Wastage', *Independent*, 89 (1917), 179–80. Chittenden's *War or Peace* (1911) digested

Jordan's work for general readers, blaming war for absorbing 'the flower of nations', denying the 'strenuous life' thesis that military life was more exacting and elevating than civil life.

67 Havelock Ellis, *The Task of Social Hygiene* (London, 1912; 2nd edn, 1927), ch. 10. Ellis was best known for his controversial seven-volume *Studies in the Psychology of Sex* (1897–1928).

68 Montague Hughes Crackanthorpe (M. H. Cookson), *Population and Progress* (London, 1907). Ellis believed that spreading civilisation would in itself curb population growth: 'The only nations nowadays that can afford to make war on a grand scale are the wealthy and civilized nations. But civilization excludes a high birth rate: there has never been any exception to this law, nor can we conceive any exceptions, for it is more than a social law; it is a biological law': *Task of Social Hygiene*, p. 323.

69 For example, P. C. Mitchell, *Evolution and the War* (London, 1915), p. 78, and ch. 5 below.

70 Ellis, *Task of Social Hygiene*, p. 335. Also Ellis, *Philosophy of Conflict* (London, 1919), and ch. 5 below.

71 G. F. Nicolai, *The Biology of War* (trans. from German, New York, 1919), p. 176.

72 Vernon L. Kellogg, *Beyond War: A Chapter in the Natural History of Man* (New York, 1912), pp. 167–70.

73 *Beyond War*, pp. 6–8, 18, 112. On determinism Kellogg distinguished between three factors: (1) 'automatic determinism by the cosmic causal agents of evolution'; (2) the factor of 'the self-controlling determinism of Man's own acquired consciousness and understanding working through conscious selection, control of heredity, direct influence of the acquirements or losses of the parents on their young, etc.'; (3) the imposition upon these biologic conditions of 'the stores of accumulated knowledge and qualities of soul that may be handed on in ever increasing mass and importance through the life of the species, by tradition, oral and written, of customs, of social consciousness and ethical realization' (p. 153).

74 *Beyond War*, pp. 108–10, 112–13, 118–19. Also Kellogg, 'Race and Americanization', *Yale Review*, NS 10 (1921), 729–40. Kellogg's race theory had parallels with that of Ernst Haeckel, for whom see R. J. Richards, 'A Defense of Evolutionary Ethics', *Biology and Philosophy*, 1 (1986), 266: Haeckel judged that 'natural men', for example, Australian aborigines, were closer in psychology to higher vertebrates (for example, apes and dogs) than to civilised Europeans (*Die Lebenswunder*, Stuttgart, 1904).

75 J. J. Atkinson, *Primal Law* (London, New York, 1903), pp. 220–1 and *passim*. See ch. 6 for debate over the warlikeness of early/primitive humans.

76 *Beyond War*, pp. 121–2.

77 *Beyond War*, pp. 124–5, 166–7, 169–70.

78 Gaston Bodart, *Losses of Life in Modern Wars: Austria–Hungary*; *France* (Oxford, 1916), pp. 155–6 and *passim* (bound with Kellogg, *Military Selection*, cited below). Bodart found that large numbers of the youth and best blood of nations were exterminated in battle or by disease, or else suffered enfeebled health in post-war life.

79 Kellogg, 'Eugenics and Militarism', pp. 220–31. For heated debate at the

Congress on Kellogg's paper see *Report of Proceedings: Problems in Eugenics*; *Papers to the First International Eugenics Congress* (London, 1912), pp. 47–50; also Kellogg, 'Eugenics and Militarism', *Atlantic Monthly*, 112 (1913), 99–108; 'The Bionomics of War: Race Modification by Military Selection', *J. Social Hygiene*, 1 (December 1914), 44–52.

80 *Beyond War*, pp. 152, 165.

81 V. L. Kellogg, *Military Selection and Race Deterioration*, edn H. Westergaard (Oxford, 1916: published under the auspices of Carnegie Endowment for International Peace), pp. 164, 169. In fairness, Kellogg offered his study as a partial pioneering work, and admitted the difficulty of distinguishing military selection from other factors, for example, industrial change, in causing race-modification.

82 *Military Selection*, pp. 173–4. Colonel C. H. Melville and others disputed some of Kellogg's figures at the 1912 Congress. Melville argued that the bad figures for army health in Britain stemmed from the fact that 'the Army was recruited chiefly from the unemployed'. The young R. A. Fisher (and others) complained that Kellogg did not distinguish between the effects of war and those of 'militarism', i.e. 'the racial effects of training for war', regarded by many as 'race-hygienic': *Proceedings*, pp. 47–50; and R. A. Fisher, *Eugenics Review*, 8 (1916–17), 264–5.

83 *Military Selection*, pp. 177–8. Scholars such as Gini and Savorgnan were to put an alternative interpretation, that negative selection among males was balanced by positive selection among females: see P. Sorokin, *Contemporary Sociological Theories* (New York, London, 1928), p. 333; discussed in ch. 6 below.

84 Thus Melville was able to be more optimistic about army health using more up-to-date data than Kellogg. While the death rate in the British army was 1 per 1,000 in 1907, the civil death rate for males aged 15–20 was 3.47 per 1,000: C. H. Melville, 'Eugenics and Military Service', *Eugenics Review*, 2 (1910–11), 53–60.

85 On Ammon see Weindling, *Health*, pp. 96–103.

86 *Military Selection*, pp. 185–96. Kellogg was very cautious about civil mortality caused by war-induced diseases, admitting that if such diseases fell evenly upon the whole population they could select out the less immune people.

87 Fluctuations in the number of exemptions for undersize roughly paralleled those of exemptions for infirmity during the twenty years of war. But exemptions for infirmity declined more slowly than exemptions for undersize after the wars.

88 R. A. Fisher agreed about the dysgenic effects of soldier deaths in battle, but regarded deaths by sickness as a more dubious issue, while on civilian mortality he wanted more data on age distribution (since it was unknown whether the higher mortality induced by war mainly affected those unlikely to reproduce). As to French army figures, Fisher complained that it was impossible to compare them with the corresponding rise in height observed in other countries during the last century: *Eugenics Review*, 8 (1916–17), 264–5. Ch. 6 below deals with the First World War debate over the eugenics of war.

89 In 1905 the Russian rate was 62.7 per 1,000; in 1907 the British rate was 68.4 and the American rate 167.8; Germany had brought VD under closer control with a rate of 19.8 in 1905–6, a fact that led German generals to claim that really

effective 'militarism' was the answer to VD, for example, General von Bardeleben at the 1912 International Eugenics Congress. Also C. H. Melville who agreed that VD infected American and British soldiers, who were less hard worked, better paid and had more leisure than German soldiers: 'Militarism was a eugenic influence with regard to those diseases if carried out thoroughly, as in Germany'. He also disputed Kellogg's figures for syphilis in the British army: *Proceedings* (1912), 47–8. For an earlier discussion of VD see Robert Reid Rentoul, *Race Culture; or Race Suicide?* (London, New York, 1906), ch. 17. Rentoul was a physician and eugenist who favoured sterilisation of 'mental and physical degenerates'.

90 *Military Selection*, p. 202.

5 THE FIRST WORLD WAR: MAN THE FIGHTING ANIMAL

1 F. C. S. Schiller, *Social Decay and Eugenical Reform* (London, 1932), p. 2. I borrow the evocative classification *Homo pugnax* from Tony Barnett: see S. A. Barnett, *Biology and Freedom* (Cambridge, 1988), and other writings.

2 Fred T. Lane had expressed *fin de siècle* despair in *The Violet Flame* (1899; reprinted New York, 1975): 'the Beast of the Revelation is with us and the mark of the Beast is on the foreheads of men' (p. 66). See also Rudyard Kipling, 'The Mark of the Beast', in *Life's Handicap* (London, 1908), pp. 240–59.

3 William Morton Wheeler, *Ants: Their Structure, Development and Behavior* (New York, 1910), p. 529.

4 Conwy Lloyd Morgan, *Introduction to Comparative Psychology* (London, 1894), p. 336.

5 Morgan, *Instinct and Experience* (London, 1912), p. 7.

6 Henry Rutgers Marshall, *Instinct and Reason* (New York, London, 1898), p. 88.

7 For the instinct theory of Romanes and Morgan see Robert J. Richards, *Darwin and the Emergence of Evolutionary Theories of Mind and Behavior* (Chicago, London, 1987), ch. 8.

8 Henry Maudsley, *Body and Mind* (London, 1870), p. 52. Maudsley later wrote that every person could be sure 'that he is living his forefathers essentially over again ... and furthermore suspect that the vicious or virtuous ancestral quality, imbued as silent memory in his nature may leap out to light on the occasion of its fit stimulus': *Organic to Human: Psychological and Sociological* (London, 1916), p. 267, quoted D. Pick, *Faces of Degeneration* (Cambridge, 1989), p. 207.

9 Charles S. Sherrington, *The Integrative Action of the Nervous System* (New Haven, 1906; reprinted London, 1911), p. 257. Sherrington's experiments with decerebrate and spinal animals, plus those of Goltz in Germany, seemed to indicate that anger was associated with a lower nervous organisation than were fear, joy or affection. Pioneering work on the physiology of the brain had been done in the 1900s by G. Elliot Smith: 'Notes Upon the Natural Subdivision of the Cerebral Hemisphere', *J. Anatomy and Physiology* (London), 35 (1901), 431–54; 'The Morphology of the Occipital Region of the Cerebral Hemisphere in Man and the Apes', *Anatomischer Anzeiger*, 24 (1904), 436–51; 'The Term "Archipallium" – a Disclaimer', *ibid.*, 35 (1910), 429–30. Sir Thomas Smith

Clouston, physician-superintendant of the Royal Edinburgh Asylum, described the bodily changes associated with fear and anger in *The Hygiene of Mind* (London, 1906; 6th edn, London, 1912), p. 90.

10 Echoing Darwin on man, Morgan judged that 'of definite instinctive performance he inherits perhaps a smaller share than any other organism'.

11 Morgan, *Habit and Instinct* (London, New York, 1896), p. 327; *Comparative Psychology*, pp. 376, 359, 334, 340–2. Richards shows that Morgan, while an impeccable evolutionist, always insisted on the difference in kind between animal and human consciousness: 'our species enjoyed bright reason, perceived abstract relationships, and pursued moral and aesthetic ideals; animals lived on a darkling plane of sensory associations, chased after fleshy objects, and had no knowledge of the goals of their instinctive behavior': *Darwin*, p. 387. Morgan agreed with D. G. Ritchie, who in *Darwinism and Politics* (1891), asked: 'Might we not define civilization in general as the sum of the contrivances which enable human beings to advance independently of heredity?': *Comparative Psychology*, p. 342.

12 Sherrington, *Integrative Action*, pp. 237, 388–90, 391, 393.

13 John C. Burnham, 'Instinct Theory and the German Reaction to Weismannism', *J. History of Biology*, 5, 2 (1972), 321. Burnham claims that Anglo-American scholars (for example, Lloyd Morgan, James Mark Baldwin) were preoccupied with the social implications of germ plasm theory, whereas German thinkers were more interested in the philosophical implications, such as vitalism versus reductionism.

14 Robert M. Yerkes and Daniel Bloomfield, 'Do Kittens Instinctively Kill Mice?', *Psychological Bulletin*, 7, 8 (1910), 253–63; Yerkes, 'The Heredity of Savageness and Wildness in Rats', *J. Animal Behavior*, 3 (1913), 286–96. Yerkes influenced John B. Watson's *Behavior* (New York, 1914). Yerkes also wrote *The Dancing Mouse* (New York, 1907), *Introduction to Psychology* (New York, 1911), *The Mental Life of Monkeys and Apes* (New York, 1916) and *Almost Human* (New York, London, 1925).

15 James Rowland Angell, *Psychology: An Introductory Study of the Structure and Function of Human Consciousness* (New York, 1904; 4th edn, New York, 1908), p. 349; William James, *Principles of Psychology* (London, 1890), II, 411–15. Commentators found trouble fitting the hunting instinct into their systems. James Drever claimed that the fear/flight impulse aroused the hunting instinct. He suggested that the ferocity of World War I might be explained in William James's terms as due to the co-operation of the fighting and hunting instincts, raised to high pitch by 'contagion' of emotions associated with these instincts. Drever also saw sport and play as expressions of hunting instinct: James Drever, *Instinct in Man* (Cambridge, 1917; reprinted 1921), pp. 180, 183, generally ch. 8. See also Edward Thorndike, *Educational Psychology: Briefer Course* (New York, 1914; reprinted New York, 1927), pp. 18–19.

16 Angell, *Psychology*, ch. 16; Thorndike, *Educational Psychology*, pp. 23–4; Drever, *Instinct in Man*, p. 166; Knight Dunlap, 'Are There Any Instincts?', *J. Abnormal Psychology*, 14 (1919), 307–11; Luther L. Bernard, *Instinct: A Study in Social Psychology* (London, 1924); David L. Krantz and David Allen, 'The Rise and Fall of McDougall's Instinct Theory', *J. History Behavioral Sciences*, 3 (1967), 326–38.

17 C. Letourneau, *Property: Its Origins and Development* (London, 1892), pp. 2, 5; quoted Jones, *Social Darwinism*, p. 126. Thorstein Veblen even found it possible to write a book on *The Instinct of Workmanship* (New York, 1924). One wartime writer attributed an 'ovine instinct' to people holding back the advance of civilisation: F. H. Skrine, 'War and German Universities', *J. Royal United Service Institution*, 60, 439 (1915), 469.

18 Théodule Ribot, *The Psychology of the Emotions* (London, 1897).

19 Angell, *Psychology*, pp. 339–51. J. R. Angell was a student of John Dewey and William James, and wrote about the theories of Wilhelm Wundt, Lloyd Morgan, E. L. Thorndike and J. M. Baldwin.

20 Marshall, *Instinct and Reason* (1898), pp. 120–1, 138–46. Marshall anticipated, however vaguely, William Hamilton's seminal proposition of 1964 that altruistic, even self-sacrificing behaviour, could be biologically justified if it increased inclusive fitness by aiding the survival of kin: W. D. Hamilton, 'The Genetical Evolution of Social Behavior', *J. Theoretical Biology*, 7 (1964), 1–51.

21 William James, 'Robert Gould Shaw Oration', Boston 1897; reprinted James, *Essays in Religion and Morality* (Cambridge, Mass., 1982), pp. 64–74; 'Speech to World Peace Congress', Boston, 7 October 1904, *ibid.*, pp. 120–3.

22 'Speech to World Peace Congress', p. 38. Later writers were to forget James's distinction between humans and animals as hunters, and to assert inconsistently that man as hunter was consequently violent towards his own kind.

23 James, 'The Moral Equivalent of War', *McClure's Magazine*, 35 (1910); reprinted, *Memories and Studies* (Cambridge, Mass., 1911), pp. 267–96.

24 James, *Principles of Psychology*, II, 409–14: 'If evolution and the survival of the fittest be true at all, the destruction of prey and of human rivals *must* have been among the most important of man's primitive functions, the fighting and chasing instincts *must* have become ingrained. Certain perceptions *must* immediately, and without the intervention of inferences and ideas, have prompted emotions and motor discharges; and both the latter must, from the nature of the case, have been very violent, and therefore, when unchecked, of an intensely pleasurable kind. It is just because human bloodthirstiness is such a primitive part of us that it is so hard to eradicate ... Our ferocity is blind, and can only be explained from *below*.'

25 James, 'Moral Equivalent', pp. 267–96. Following quotes from this source. John Dewey was critical of James's 1910 essay. Dewey thought it more important to rectify social inequalities than to siphon off 'martial energies': James, *Essays*, p. xxvi.

26 William McDougall, *Introduction to Social Psychology* (London, 1908), pp. 26–9.

27 Edna Heidbreder, 'William McDougall and Social Psychology', in Mary Henle, *et al.*, *Historical Conceptions of Psychology* (New York, 1973), pp. 267–75.

28 James Jasper Atkinson, *Primal Law* (London, 1903), ch. 2.

29 *Social Psychology*, ch. 11. For his later views, see *The Group Mind* (New York, 1920), and *Janus: The Conquest of War* (New York, 1927).

30 G. T. W. Patrick, 'The Psychology of War', *Popular Science Monthly*, 87 (1915), 162–4.

31 Roland Stromberg, *Redemption by War: The Intellectuals and 1914* (Lawrence,

Kansas, 1982); Modris Eksteins, *Rites of Spring: The Great War and the Birth of the Modern Age* (Boston, 1989); Trevor Wilson, *The Myriad Faces of War: Britain and the Great War, 1914–1918* (Oxford, 1986), ch. 1. Graham Wallas noted that in the ante-bellum years many Europeans 'honestly felt from time to time that they would be improved by war, and are only restrained by the fear of "the infinite" – by the strong probability that they may get more war than is necessary to improve their digestions': *The Great Society* (London, 1914), p. 182.

32 Hilaire Belloc, *A General Sketch of the European War: The Second Phase* (London, 1916), p. 17, quoted Samuel Hynes, *A War Imagined: The First World War and English Culture* (London, 1990), p. 19, and generally Part 1.

33 Sigmund Freud, 'Thoughts for the Times on War and Death', in *Imago* (1915); reprinted John Strachey, edn, *Standard Edition of Complete Works of Freud*, vol. XIV (London, 1957), pp. 275–88.

34 E. Seillière, *The German Doctrine of Conquest: A French View* (London, 1914), p. 17. John St Loe Strachey, editor of the Conservative *Spectator*, had predicted in 1909 that a world of blood and iron would come about, dominated by the perception that 'man is still a wild beast, that the race is to the strong and not to the well-intentioned'. The 'Sunday-school view of the world' would be irretrievably smashed: *A New Way of Life* (London, 1909), pp. 12, 47–8.

35 W. S. Lilley, *An Invisible Kingdom: Being Some Chapters in Ethics* (London, 1919), pp. 85, 96, 99. Also Henry Maudsley: 'throughout the whole system of nature conflict, destruction of life is the inexorable law': *Organic to Human* (1916), p. 158. An English eugenist reflected: 'War tears off the decent garments of custom and leaves the soul naked. There is no greater revealer of the hearts of man': T. G. Chambers, 'Eugenics and the War', *Eugenics Review*, 6 (1914–15), p. 273.

36 J. A. Cramb, *The Origins and Destiny of Imperial Britain* (London, 1915), pp. 114, 121, 147, 150. Cramb (1862–1913) studied philosophy as Glasgow, under Edward Caird, and at Bonn, before being appointed professor of modern history in 1892 at Queens College, London. The above, published after his death, was a series of lectures inspired by the Boer War, commending an age of empires and bigness, in the style of Joseph Chamberlain, and warring competition, in the style of Weismann. Sir Charles Waldstein criticised Cramb's glorification of war in *Aristodemocracy: from the Great War back to Moses, Christ and Plato* (London, 1916), pp. 44ff.

37 John Burroughs, 'The Arrival of the Fit', *North American Review*, 201 (1915), 197–201. Burroughs (1837–1921) had long laboured to reconcile evolutionary science with monist transcendentalism, and he blamed the Huns for turning Darwin's reasonable theory of struggle into a militarist abomination. See his *The Light of Day* (Boston and New York, 1900), *Time and Change* (London and Cambridge, Mass., 1912), *The Breath of Life* (Boston and New York, 1915); also Perry D. Westbrook, *John Burroughs* (New York, 1974); and Anon., 'The Evolution of John Burroughs', *Current Opinion*, 70 (1921), 646. George Santayana also wrote in alienated vein in 1922: 'there is eternal war in nature, a war in which every cause is ultimately lost and every nation destroyed': *Soliloquies* (New York, 1922), pp. 104–5.

38 Gerald Stanley Lee, *We: A Confession of Faith for the American People During*

and After the War (London, New York, 1916), p. 66. Lee himself blamed 'hate-technology' for the war, not human nature. Lee's *The Voice of the Machine* (New York, 1906) influenced Graham Wallas.

39 William Lee Howard, 'The Psychology of War', *New York Medical Journal*, 101 (1915), 15–18. A character in H. G. Wells's novel *The Croquet Player* (London, 1936) says: 'man is still what he was. Invincibly bestial, envious, malicious, greedy. Man, sir, unmasked and disillusioned, is the same feeling, snarling, fighting beast he was a hundred thousand years ago' (p. 73).

40 Willian Ralph Inge, 'Patriotism', *Quarterly Review*, 224 (July 1915), pp. 73–5, 83; *Outspoken Essays* (London, 1919), p. 2. Inge also lashed out at survivalist Darwinism that had encouraged militarism. Like Burroughs he saw aimlessness in nature, not progress: 'It is not certain that there has been much change in our intellectual and moral endowments since pithecanthropus dropped the first half of his name. I should be sorry to have to maintain that the Germans of today are morally superior to the army which defeated Quintilius Varus': *Outspoken Essays*, p. 25.

41 Samuel Jackson Holmes, 'The Decadence of Human Heredity', *Atlantic Monthly*, 114 (1914), 302–8. Among primitive peoples (he argued) the weak and congenitally ill were put to death; sexual selection was improved under exogamy when wives were won by fitter men after a trial of strength or skill; while war multiplied the best stock. Civilisation had put an end to these eugenic practices. He later described education as more devastating to the race than war.

42 L. T. Hobhouse, *The World in Conflict* (London, 1915), pp. 24–6, 41 (originally articles in the *Manchester Guardian*, March–May, 1915).

43 Sir Ronald Ross, 'Evolution and War', *Science Progress*, 9 (1914), 514–16 (paraphrased by G. Taylor-Loban). The parallels between E. O. Wilson and thinkers discussed in this chapter, including Ross, are further treated in ch. 8.

44 Walter Bradford Cannon, 'The Interrelationships of Emotions as Suggested by Recent Physiological Researches', *American J. Psychology*, 25 (1914), 256–82. Also Cannon, 'Neural Organization for Emotional Expression', in Martin L. Reymert, edn, *Feelings and Emotions: The Wittenberg Symposium* (Worcester, Mass., 1928), ch. 22, pp. 257–69.

45 Arthur Koestler, *The Ghost in the Machine* (London, 1967). The older 'animalistic' brain, part of the limbic system, was said to be primarily responsible for aggressive-defensive, fearful behaviour and self-assertive tendencies, the emotional expression of which depended upon the sympathetic division of the autonomic system and the action of adrenal hormones. The built-in 'schizophysiology' of the human species was said to provide a physiological basis 'for the paranoid streak running through human history' (p. 336). Koestler included Cannon among the pioneers of his theory, which also owed much to the medical psychologist Paul MacLean.

46 W. B. Cannon, *Bodily Changes in Pain, Hunger, Fear and Rage: An Account of Researches into the Function of Emotional Excitement* (New York, London, 2nd edn, 1919; 1st edn, 1915), pp. 377–92. For biography see Jean Mayer, 'Walter Bradford Cannon', *J. of Nutrition*, 87 (1965), 3–8. Cannon did medical work at the front, with the Harvard Hospital unit at Bethune in 1917, resulting in distinguished work on the physiology of shock. In some respects Cannon's

theory of anger and fear had been anticipated by the French psychologist Théodule Ribot: *La psychologie des sentiments* (Paris, 1896), pp. 207–29.

47 George Washington Crile, *A Mechanistic View of War and Peace*, ed. Amy F. Rowland (New York, 1915; reprinted London, n.d. *c.* 1916), pp. 4, 64. Following page references in text are to London edition. Crile was the first to make a direct blood transfusion, pioneered the 'nerve block' system of anaesthesia (anoci-association), and invented the 'pressure suit' (adapted for use by fighter pilots in World War II). He was at the front with the American ambulance unit at Neuilly-sur-Seine. See Peter C. English, *Shock, Physiological Surgery, and George Washington Crile: Medical Innovation in the Progressive Era* (Westport, London, 1980).

48 Darwin had initiated analysis of this kind in *Expression of the Emotions in Man and Animals* (London, 1872).

49 Crile detected evidence for 'savage recall', signs of genotypical behaviour patterns, in modern man's liking for fishing, hunting, camping, sporting contests (boxing reenacted the savage grapple of primitive men), even in children's play. Play was a neural training for adult behaviour. Thus infant hunting animals played at fight, herbivora at escape, while 'strategists – monkeys and men – initiate in their games the activities of hunting, fighting, lovemaking, and rearing of offspring ... The play of children shows their line of descent' (p. 54). The English comparative psychologist Carveth Read speculated that hominids and early humans formed hunting packs that were predisposed to be aggressive towards every animal outside the pack. The hunting pack always claimed territory: 'this is the first ground of the sense of property': *The Origin of Man and of His Superstitions* (Cambridge, 1920), p. 43.

50 Crile's tone of genetic determinism turned here into environmentalism: for example, 'Man's action patterns reflect as in a mirror his environment', 'The child of man is most plastic. If a child remain in a Christian portion of the web of life, Christian action patterns are formed ... if in a peaceful web, peaceful action patterns result' (pp. 99–100). Crile compared Germans raised under their militaristic *Kultur*, and those who emigrated to America's melting-pot and adopted less militant ways. For more details on his kinetic theory of shock, see Crile, *The Origin and Nature of the Emotions: Miscellaneous Papers* (Philadelphia, London, 1915; reprinted College Park, Maryland, 1970).

51 Benjamin Kidd, *The Science of Power* (London, 1918), p. 106. There is no evidence that Kidd read Crile. Kidd's idea was taken up by the British biologist F. A. E. Crew: 'We know that the mind can be swayed to a new and permanent endeavour by an appeal to the emotion of the ideal. We know that, properly led, we can build a new Britain, and that all that is needed is a new social inheritance': 'A Biologist in a New Environment', *Eugenics Review*, 11 (1919–20), 119–23.

52 Cf. C. Robert Ardrey, *The Hunting Hypothesis* (New York, 1976). The Yale palaeontologist Richard Swann Lull also suggested an evolutionary narrative that covered man's descent from the trees, the assumption of an erect posture, liberation of the hands, and the transition to hunting from tropical fruit-gathering. By inventing clothing and going to an omnivorous diet, humans were no longer limited to one definite habitat; they dispersed, devised communal life and the division of labour, and, by means of intelligence and

mutual aid, found themselves no longer subject to the laws which governed animal adaptation. Lull believed that physical evolution in man had virtually ceased (may even have become retrogressive, for example, loss of keen sight and sense of smell). Future evolution would be primarily mental and spiritual: *Organic Evolution: A Text-Book* (New York, 1917), pp. 672–85. See also F. Wood Jones, *Arboreal Man* (London, 1926).

53 Harry Campbell, *The Biological Aspects of Warfare* (London, 1918), esp. pp. 5–32; reprinted from *Lancet* vol. 1 (1913), 1260–2, 1333–5, 1408–10, 1473–6; and vol. 2 (1917), 433–5, 469–71, 505–8. Campbell hypothesised that, since man's precursors lacked 'the stereotyped equipment for slaughter, instinctive and anatomical' of the carnivora, they were forced to live by their wits in hunting prey, to devise hand weapons, and to take full advantage of their agility, intelligence and prehensile hands, a situation that aided the natural selection of *Homo sapiens*.

54 Carveth Read, *The Origin of Man and of his Superstitions* (Cambridge, 1920). Read, formerly Grote professor of philosophy, was a lecturer in comparative psychology at University College, London. He first adumbrated his hunting-pack theory in his *The Metaphysics of Nature* (London, 1905), ch. 13, *Natural and Social Morals* (London, 1909), a paper to the British Association in 1913 and his 'On the Differentiation of Man from the Anthropoids', *Man* (November 1914), 181–6.

55 Read, *Origin of Man*, pp. 43, 58–9. Read rated war as one of the most influential factors in the development of society: 'Wars strengthened the internal sympathies and loyalties of the pack or tribe and its external antipathies, and extended the range and influence of the more virile and capable tribes' (p. 59). Gregariousness had also been ingrained, but 'man is still imperfectly sociable' (p. 35). 'The pack was a means of increasing the supply of food per unit; and gregariousness increased by natural selection up to the limit set by utility. Hence ... Man is in character more like a dog or a wolf than he is like any other animal' (p. 8).

56 Morley Roberts, *Bio-Politics* (London, 1938), esp. ch. 9; William Morton Wheeler, *Emergent Evolution and the Social* (London, 1927); Koestler, *Ghost in the Machine* (1967); Paul D. MacLean, 'Man and His Animal Brains', *Modern Medicine* (Chicago), 32 (1964), 95–106, and *The Triune Brain in Evolution* (New York, 1990).

57 George Thomas White Patrick, 'The Psychology of War', *Popular Science Monthly*, 87 (1915), 155–68. Subsequent quotes from this source.

58 Freud, 'Thoughts for the Times' (1915).

59 G. T. W. Patrick, *The Psychology of Social Reconstruction* (Boston, New York, 1920), for example, pp. 58–9, 246. Patrick depicted modern citizens as restless, aggressive, city-based, addicted to excitement (gambling, cars, trains, planes, 'crazes' like dancing and movies), to technology for war and destruction, and to drugs (tobacco, alcohol), subject to chronic fatigue, suicide and small families. At times he seemed to be universalising the traits of modern America. However it was also classic degenerationist doctrine, going back to Morel and Baudelaire, to blame human decay upon the frantic conditions of modern life, which produced 'nervous exhaustion and fatigue, together with a craving for stimulants': Stephen G. Bush, *The Temperature of History: Phases of Science*

and Culture in the Nineteenth Century (New York, 1978), p. 104. Writings in this genre included G. M. Beard, *American Nervousness: Its Causes and Consequences* (New York, 1881) and G. F. Lydstrom, *The Diseases of Society* (Philadelphia, 1904).

60 H. R. Marshall, *War and the Ideal of Peace* (London, 1916), ch. 4; and Sir Arthur Keith, *Darwin Revalued* (London, 1955), ch. 21.

61 Marshall, 'The Pacifist at War', *Atlantic Monthly*, 121 (1918), 665–7.

62 John B. Watson, *Behavior*, pp. 141–6, 169.

63 Graham Wallas, *Human Nature in Politics* (London, 1908), pp. 292–4.

64 *War and Ideal of Peace*, pp. 107, 130.

65 G. Stanley Hall, 'A Synthetic Genetic Study of Fear', *American J. of Psychology*, 25, 2 (1914), 163, also 189, 197; and *ibid.*, 25, 3 (1914), 368. See also Hall, 'A Study of Anger', *ibid.*, 10 (1899), 516–91.

66 Hall, 'Psychology and War', *J. of Heredity*, 8 (1917), 444.

67 Hall, 'Recreation and Reversion', *Pedagogical Seminary*, 22 (1915), 510–20. This paper also explored the concept of sport as canalisation of the fighting instinct, as did Pierre Bovet, *The Fighting Instinct*, trans. J. Y. T. Greig (London, 1923; from French edn, 1917), p. 91. Also R. A. Acher, 'Spontaneous Constructions and Primitive Activities of Children Analogous to Those of Primitive Man', *American J. Psychology*, 21 (1910), 114–50.

68 Raymond Pearl, 'Biology and War', *J. Washington Academy of Science*, 8 (1918), 341–60; reprinted, Pearl, *Studies in Human Biology* (Baltimore, 1924), 534–49. See opening paragraph in Preface, above.

69 Crile, *Mechanistic View*, p. 22. The parallels between 'fighting animal' discourse and modern sociobiology are further debated in the Conclusion, ch. 8 below. For modern criticism of sociobiology on war see Stephen J. Gould, *Ever Since Darwin* (Penguin, 1980), ch. 8, part B; and S. A. Barnett, *Biology and Freedom* (1988).

70 G. H. Perris popularised the phrase 'the human swarm', and explained war in terms of population pressure, the migration of tribes and peoples in *A Short History of War and Peace* (London, 1911). The American demographer Edwin D. James concluded that, while the west had brought under basic control Malthus's checks of famine and pestilence, it had tragically intensified the destructiveness of that other great check, war, by means of technology. War was not simply a possibility when economic crisis arose through over-population, 'but is of the nature of an economic certainty'. He pinned his hopes for world peace upon programmes of global contraception, agricultural science, free trade and the spread of republican government: 'The Malthusian Doctrine and War', *Scientific Monthly*, 2 (1916), 260–71. See also Adelyne More, *Uncontrolled Breeding or Fecundity Versus Civilization* (New York, 1917), and John E. Grant, *The Problem of War and its Solution* (London, 1922), pp. 53–72. Grant criticised biology for cultivating a belief in 'Nature angular and spare-framed' that went with the theology that 'was naturally vicious, greedy and faithless' (p. 86).

71 Eric Fromm, *The Anatomy of Human Destructiveness* (London, 1974; reprinted, Penguin, 1982), p. 22.

72 Morgan, *Comparative Psychology* (1894), p. 359; *Habit and Instinct* (1896), p. 334.

73 Patrick, 'Psychology of War', p. 168.
74 On Jackson's influence see Jonathan Miller, 'Crowds and Power', *International Review of Psycho-Analysis*, 10 (1983), 262–3. In the jargon of the day, 'pathogeny repeated phylogeny', an application of the embryological theory of recapitulation, with its slogan 'ontogeny repeats phylogeny', i.e., the embryological development of individuals recapitulated transitions from lower to higher rungs of nature's ladder of progress.
75 Robert A. Nye, *The Anti-Democratic Sources of Elite Theory: Pareto, Mosca, Michels* (London, 1977), pp. 9ff.; Leon Bramson, *The Political Context of Sociology* (Princeton, 1961), p. 53. Scipio Sighele wrote *Psychologie des sectes* (Paris, 1898) and *La Foule criminelle* (Paris, 1910). Pascal Rossi wrote *Les suggesteurs et la foule* (Paris, 1904) and *Sociologia e psicologia collectiva* (Rome, 1904).
76 Bramson, *Political Context*, p. 53 and *passim*. E. A. Ross and Robert E. Park were the main pioneers; for example, Park's doctoral dissertation *Masse und Publikum* (*The Crowd and the Public*) (Bern, 1904; trans., Chicago, 1972, and not available in English until the latter date). Also Gerald Stanley Lee, *Crowds* (London, 1913).
77 Nye, *Elite Theory*, pp. 11–12, generally ch. 1. As he says: 'Wild animal metaphors, and descriptions emphasising emotionality, or low intelligence and morality were the ones most frequently employed.' Also Nye, *The Origins of Crowd Psychology: Gustave Le Bon and the Crisis of Mass Democracy in the Third Republic* (London, 1975), esp. ch. 4. Le Bon's *La Psychologie des foules* (Paris, 1895) was translated into English as *The Crowd* (London, 1896). Gustave Flaubert wrote to Georges Sand in 1870: 'the natural state of man is savagery ... war contains within itself a mystic element which enraptures the mob ... We shall see, before another century, several millions of men killing each other': *Lettres de Gustave Flaubert à Georges Sand* (Paris, 1884), pp. 115, 118.
78 Conway's axiom was that 'all similar independent crowds are mutually hostile'. He defined 'similar crowds' as those in which membership of one excluded from membership of the rest, for example, nations were similar crowds; clubs and political parties were dissimilar crowds. 'Independent crowds' were those not united by any common 'overcrowd'. Nations constantly struggled for resources: 'Existing nations are like so many bladders, large and small filled with gas, and all squeezed together within a box which they are united to fill. If one of these bladders is to expand another must contract': Sir Martin Conway, *The Crowd in Peace and War* (London, 1915), pp. 265–8.
79 Conway, *The Crowd*, pp. 269–70. He thought Cobdenite belief in democracy as a force for peace 'a pure superstition without an atom of fact to rest on'. A number of observers blamed the First World War upon 'herd spirit', including the Dutch socialist Henriette Roland-Holst: 'This war has not only shown that international ideas were infinitely less deeply planted in the proletariat than we believed', but also that such ideas 'remained powerless in the face of feelings, instincts, emotions which break forth from the sub-conscious with irresistible force, even if rational interest stands on the side of the ideas': quoted R. N.

Stromberg, 'The Intellectuals and the Coming of War in 1914', *J. European Studies*, 3 (1973), 111–12.

80 Most of the Fabians supported the war, and the society ejected Shaw and other pacifists from the *New Statesman*. However a minority on the left kept alive a spirit of opposition to the war, including some socialists, ILP activists, labour journalists and members of peace organisations like the Union of Democratic Control and the No-Conscription Fellowship: Samuel Hynes, *A War Imagined* (1990), pp. 81, 86–7. Also Stromberg, 'Intellectuals', p. 118, arguing that many leftists and reformers hoped for social change from the great nationalist war: 'In the trenches, Herbert Read tells us, men dreamed of a better social order that would emerge from the comradeship of the war – one more equalitarian, less selfish.' The British suffragettes were aggressively pro-war, especially Emmeline and Christobel Pankhurst.

81 This did not sit too well with his original hypothesis that wars happened simply because crowds were habitually combative, and not really because of ideological issues: 'Wars happen first and the ideals are discovered, or at least formulated, afterwards.' In almost the same breath he declared the First World War a test of ideals, yet said that Britain fought Germany, not out of righteousness, 'but because Germany has been a strongly growing crowd which upset the equilibrium of Europe and aimed at the hegemony of the world.' There was also paradox in his solution of a peace imposed by an Allied supernational over-crowd embodying the ideal of national diversity and freedom, since this ideal proclaimed: 'all nations would be elements of supernational over-crowds to which they would belong side by side, not one above another': *The Crowd*, pp. 288, 293–94.

82 Wilfred Trotter, *Instincts of the Herd in Peace and War* (London, 1916; 2nd edn, London, 1919), p. 78. Page references hereafter to the 2nd edition. The book includes an early section essentially the same as his papers in *Sociological Review* for 1908 (pp. 11–41) and 1909 (pp. 42–65), plus a long section (pp. 66–213) written in 1915. For the 2nd edition he added a postscript of 1919 (pp. 214–59). The original papers were: 'The Herd Instinct and its Bearing on the Psychology of Civilised Man', *Sociological Review*, 1 (1908), 227–48; and 'Sociological Application of the Psychology of the Herd Instinct', *ibid.*, 2 (1909), 36–54. Graham Wallas's *Human Nature in Politics* also argued that psychology neglected biology.

83 Trotter has been said to be one of the first to treat human groups as biological phenomena in their own right, without using the suspect concept of 'group mind' beloved of Le Bon and McDougall: Harvey S. Greisman, 'Herd Instinct and the Foundation of Biosociology', *J. History Behavioral Sciences*, 15 (1979), 367–9. Greisman stresses Trotter's meliorism (unusual in those using cross-species comparisons), while Reba Soffer highlights his elitism: 'New Elitism: Social Psychology in Prewar England', *J. British Studies*, 8, 2 (1969), 111–40.

84 Tarde criticised Durkheim for imagining society as a 'collective self' independently of individuals composing it, and many crowd theorists fell into the same trap: Michael M. Davis, *Gabriel Tarde: An Essay in Sociological Theory* (New York, 1906), p. 98.

85 'To the gregarious species at war the only tolerable claim to any sort of superiority must be based on leadership. Any other affectation of superiority,

whether it be based on prescriptive right, on tradition, on custom, on wealth, on birth, or on mere age, arrogance or fussiness, and not on real functional value to the state, is ... an obstacle to true national unity' (p. 152).

86 Trotter was scathing about the Bernhardi doctrine of war as biological necessity: 'there is about it a confidence that the vital effects of war are simple and easy to define and a cheerful contempt for the considerable biological difficulties of the subject that remind one of the bracing military atmosphere'. However, a year of trench warfare made 'the syllogism a little less perfect, the new law of Nature not quite so absolute' (pp. 126–7).

87 Trotter alleged that the pseudo-biology of some Social Darwinisms had been undertaken 'less in the spirit of the scientific investigator than in that of the politician; the point of departure has been a political conviction and not a biological truth' (p. 100). It had contributed to the dogma that 'war is and always will be an inevitable necessity in human affairs as man is what is called a fighting animal' (pp. 125–6).

88 W. McDougall, *An Outline of Psychology* (London, 1923), pp. 154 n. 1, 432. For a popular account of current crowd theories, see Gilbert Murray, 'Herd Instinct and War', *Atlantic Monthly*, 115 (1915), 830–9; and for an eccentric effort to combine crowd and racial theory, Colonel F. N. Maude, 'National Psychology in the War', *The Quest* (January, 1917), 211–32 (Maude was author of *War and the World's Life*, London, 1907). For a critique of the instinct school, including Trotter, see Morris Ginsberg, *The Psychology of Society* (London, 1921), ch. 2: 'The real problems of sociology are left unsolved by the writers of the instinct school' (p. 21). For transatlantic developments, see H. Cravens, *American Scientists and the Heredity-Environment Controversy, 1900–1944* (Philadelphia, 1978).

89 For example, Davis, *Tarde* (1906), p. 89. Davis, a Columbia Ph.D., criticised Tarde's theory of 'imitation' as an 'illuminating half-truth'. Graham Wallas felt that terms like 'imitation' and 'suggestion' 'had no more precise meaning than the old bible-reader's "Mesopotamia"': 'Crowd Morality', *Hibbert Journal*, 15 (1915), 225.

90 Wallas, *The Great Society* (1914), pp. 123–44. Also Michael M. Davis, *Psychological Interpretations of Society* (London, 1909). A. L. Kroebner attacked Le Bon's genetic racism in 'The Superorganic', *American Anthropologist*, NS 19, 2 (1917), 184–7.

91 John T. MacCurdy, *The Psychology of War* (London, 1918), p. 31. In contrast to the various biological images of war as useful behaviour, MacCurdy typified a psychoanalytical inclination to brand war as a type of pathology – a case of humans unable to control themselves. He believed that science had made modern war 'almost a biological suicide', only to be avoided by psychological self-knowledge and some 'moral equivalents' (p. 2) or ultimately loyalty to the larger herd, humanity (pp. 32–3, 52).

92 Everett Dean Martin, *The Behavior of Crowds: A Psychological Study* (New York, London, 1920), pp. 108–112: 'As the crowd always shows an exaggerated ego-feeling similar to the paranoic's delusion of grandeur, and as in cases of paranoia this inner conflict is always "projected" in the form of delusions of persecution, may we not hold that the characteristic hostility of the crowd is also in some way a device for protecting this inflated self-appreciation from

injury?' Martin was a lecturer in social philosophy at the Cooper Union Forum, New York. Also on crowd psychology, see I. W. Howerth, 'The Great War and the Instinct of the Herd', *International J. Ethics*, 29 (1919), 174–87.
93 Nye, *Elite Theory*, p. 62.
94 MacCurdy, *Psychology of War*, pp. 51–2. Arthur Koestler later took up this theme. Total identification with the group made the individual perform 'comradely, altruistic, heroic actions to the point of self-sacrifice and at the same time behave with ruthless cruelty towards the enemy or victim of the group'. The self-assertive behaviour of the group was based upon the self-transcending behaviour of its members. The egotism of the group fed on the altruism of its members: *Ghost in the Machine*, p. 251.

6 THE SURVIVAL OF PEACE BIOLOGY

1 T. Dobzhansky, *Genetics and the Origin of Species* (3rd edn, New York, 1951), pp. 77–9; arguing for the use of 'adaptive value' instead of 'fitness'. See useful discussion in Diane B. Paul, 'The Selection of the "Survival of the Fittest"', *J. History of Biology*, 21, 3 (1988), 421–2.
2 Robert Munro, *From Darwinism to Kaiserism* (Glasgow, 1919), p. 49.
3 Theodore G. Chambers, 'Eugenics and the War', *Eugenics Review*, 6 (1914–15), 276–7 (lecture to Eugenics Educational Society, 8 October 1914). Chambers was a liberal civic reformer, a founder of Welwyn Garden City and a leader in the national savings movement. Important pioneering research in the area covered by this chapter has been done by my former research assistant Alexia Strong in early work for this project and in her unpublished doctoral thesis 'Darwinism and Social Reform' (University of Queensland, 1983). I am grateful to her for locating a number of sources used in this study.
4 Bernard Shaw, *Man and Superman* (London, 1903; reprinted, Penguin, 1962), p. 252.
5 E. Ray Lankester, *Nature and Man* (Oxford, London, 1905), p. 22 (Romanes lecture for 1905), also included as ch. 1 of Lankester's *The Kingdom of Man* (London, 1907).
6 *Nature and Man*, p. 11.
7 Lankester, 'Degeneration', lecture to British Association for Advancement of Science, Sheffield, August 1879; reprinted in his *The Advancement of Science: Occasional Essays and Addresses* (London, 1890), pp. 48–9, generally pp. 1–60. Natural selection (he said) acted to produce either homeostasis, elaboration of structure, or degeneration, i.e., diminishing complexity of structure, or retrogression from heterogeneity to homogeneity as an adaptation to less varied conditions of life. He speculated that highly elaborate human languages and civilisations had decayed, lost power and sophistication, under certain conditions. Modern Central Americans, Egyptians, Bushmen and Australian aborigines were probably degenerate descendants of civilised ancestors.
8 For his wartime opinion that human fighting had become 'unnatural', see Anon. [P. Chalmers Mitchell?], 'Sir Ray Lankester on the Darwinian Attitude to War', *Current Opinion*, 59 (1915), 333–4. Internal evidence suggests that Mitchell was the author.

9 George Nasmyth, *Social Progress and the Darwinian Theory: A Study of Force as a Factor in Human Relations* (London, New York, 1916), pp. 212, 301–2.
10 Beatrice Webb, *Diaries*, quoted M. J. Wiener, *Between Two Worlds: The Political Thought of Graham Wallas* (Oxford, 1971), p. 162.
11 Wallas was professor of political science at the London School of Economics, and on a number of government and expert committees, and Royal Commissions during the war: see Wiener, *Wallas*, ch. 7.
12 Koestler remarked of modern warfare: 'There is waiting ... There is grumbling and grousing, much preoccupation with sex, intermittent fear, and, above all, the fervent hope that it will soon be over ... but *hating* does not enter into the picture': *Ghost in the Machine*, p. 252. Pacifist theory tended to view war as an impersonal, mechanistic clash of organised pressure groups, or a confidence trick played upon citizens by politicians, generals and arms merchants, rather than as an extension of primal aggression in individuals. Censorship tended to prevent open disclosure of evidence in war diaries and letters that ordinary soldiers felt little primal enthusiasm for trench warfare (although there is also evidence that some preferred army life to their depressive existence at home).
13 Wallas, *Our Social Heritage* (London, 1921), p. 19.
14 Havelock Ellis, 'Evolution and War', in his *Essays in War-Time: Further Studies in the Task of Social Hygiene* (London, 1917; reprinted, New York, 1969), pp. 16, 19–21. Darwin's phrase about struggle being used in a metaphorical sense was repeated endlessly, almost litanically, by the peace school. Sir James Crichton-Browne echoed Ellis: he declared that by favoured races Darwin meant 'not those that are pugnacious and destructive, but those that are best suited to their varied environment ... So far was Darwin from applying to human groups the principle of the struggle for existence, as seen in plants and animals, that he condemned war and regarded it as anti-evolutionary and a sort of disease arresting healthy development': *Bernhardi and Creation: A New Theory of Evolution* (Glasgow, 1916), pp. 6, 12.
15 Lankester, *Nature and Man*, p. 55 n. 3. He thought that animal comparisons were tailored to the political biases of the observer. Chambers also denied that the fittest were the most warlike, or war the historically determined form of struggle: 'Eugenics and the War', 276–7.
16 'Darwinian Attitude to War', *Current Opinion*, 59 (1915), 333–4. Lankester thought it unlikely that war had had much selective effect upon mankind after the earliest times: 'Union and absorption were more usual results of the contact of primitive tribes than struggles to the death': *Nature and Man*, p. 23.
17 J. Arthur Thomson, 'Eugenics and War', *Eugenics Review*, 7 (1915), 1–14. Thomson feared the genetic legacy of the First World War: 'Let us not conceal the fact that war, *biologically regarded*, means wastage and a reversal of eugenic or rational selection.'
18 Nasmyth, *Social Progress*, p. 19. Subsequent references in text are to this source.
19 See Angell's introduction to *Social Progress*, p. v. Nasmyth (1882–1920) was a friend of Angell. Nasmyth's book is put in its American context in Bannister, *Social Darwinism*, ch. 12.
20 Konrad Lorenz, *On Aggression* (London, 1966). Lorenz argued that early humans did not need inhibitory mechanisms, since they lacked killing claws and

teeth. He blamed man's acquisition of tools and weapons for escalating the destructiveness of fighting. Nasmyth observed that 'when men massacre each other, it is said that they act like animals. This is a profound error; it is when men do *not* massacre each other that they are like animals' (p. 169). He approvingly quoted Lapouge (*Les sélections sociales*, Paris, 1896): 'Murder, and war which is assassination by wholesale, are human acts and not the atavistic legacies of far distant ancestors. It is with the progress of civilization that the art of killing has been developed' (quoted, p. 171).

21 For an interesting case-study of Germanophobia among scholars, see Charles E. Bailey, 'The British Protestant Theologians in the First World War: Germanophobia Unleashed', *Harvard Theological Review*, 77, 2 (1984), 195–221. Also Stuart Wallace, *War and the Image of Germany: British Academics, 1914–1918* (Edinburgh, 1988). For a powerful analysis of the genuine differences between Germanic and Anglo-Saxon culture, see John A. Moses, 'The "Ideas of 1914" in Germany and Australia: A Case of Conflicting Perceptions', *War and Society*, 9, 2 (1991), 61–82.

22 Crichton-Browne, *Bernhardi and Creation* (1916), pp. 6, 12 (based on an address to Browning Settlement, Walwirth, November 1915).

23 William Cecil Dampier Whetham, *The War and the Nation* (London, 1917), pp. 203–4, ch. 5 generally. Whetham accepted that early human warfare had parallels with animal fighting: the strong and skilful got the food, killed their enemies, possessed the females, while the 'fierce, warlike and well-disciplined tribe overcomes the timid, peaceful and unorganised and inherits the earth'. But when large armies came into being, qualities of combination and self-sacrifice 'acquire "survival value"', and thus, by heredity, become ingrained in the race'. Finally total war meant serious racial loss to all countries. See also Whetham, 'The War and the Race', *Quarterly Review*, 227 (1917), 17–38.

24 Munro, *From Darwinism to Kaiserism*, 24, 49, 91–2, 129.

25 Jacques Loeb, 'Biology and War', *Science*, 45, 1152 (1917), 73–76. The Columbia historian Carlton Hayes criticised both German and British social thought for applying a strictly biological hypothesis like evolution 'as a genuine law in the improper field of sociology': 'The War of Nations', *Political Science Quarterly*, 29 (1914), 702–5, quoted, Bannister, *Social Darwinism* p. 240. Bannister remarks that the indictment of Darwinised *Machtpolitik* was not without irony since American progressives invoked their own reading of Darwinism in defence 'of the Anglo-American spiritual struggle against *Kultur*' (p. 240).

26 V. L. Kellogg, *Headquarters Nights: A Record of Conversations and Experiences at the Headquarters of the German Army in France and Belgium* (Boston, 1917), p. 28, ch. 1 generally.

27 Raymond Pearl, 'Biology and War', *J. Washington Academy of Science*, 8 (1918), 341–60; reprinted, Pearl, *Studies in Human Biology* (Baltimore, 1924), pp. 534–49.

28 See, for example, J. M. Winter, 'Balliol's "Lost Generation" of the First World War', *Balliol College Records* (1975), 10–14; Reginald Pound, *The Lost Generation* (London, 1964). Trevor Wilson argues that the upper classes paid a disproportionately high price in terms of deaths in the firing line, volunteering more readily than their social inferiors, less prone to fail army medicals, leading

their men into action as officers: *Faces of War*, pp. 758–61. James Lindsay commented: 'many only sons have fallen, and many families have become extinct. The loss to literature, science, politics, and administration has been very grave. Poets, writers, artists, thinkers and statesmen – the Intelligentsia of the Nations – have fallen in large numbers': J. A. Lindsay, 'The Eugenic and Social Influence of the War', *Eugenics Review*, 10 (1918–19), 135.

29 National Birth-Rate Commission, *Report on the Declining Birth-Rate* (London, 1916), p. 43. The *Lancet* publicised La Torre's opinion that wars were generally dysgenic, slaying the young, healthy and robust: 'Italian View on Eugenics', *Lancet*, 2 (6 November 1915), 1038–9.

30 J. M. Winter, *The Great War and the British People* (Cambridge, Mass., 1986), p. 71, and ch. 3 generally. Winter had earlier estimated war-related deaths for Great Britain and Ireland, 1914–18, as 610, 114: see 'Some Aspects of the Demographic Consequences of the First World War in Britain', *Population Studies*, 30 (1976), 539–52, esp. Table 6, p. 547. Winter confirmed the conventional view of the time that war-related mortality was highest for young men, in their late teens and early twenties, mortality being greatest at age twenty (p. 545).

31 Sir Bernard Mallet, 'Vital Statistics as Affected by the War', *J. Royal Statistical Society*, 81, 1 (January 1918), 1–36.

32 Mallet, 'Vital Statistics'. The demographer Savorgnan calculated towards the war's end that Britain would lose about 9 per cent of its 9 million men of military age, and that it would take ten years to recoup this population loss at the normal rate of increase. Germany would lose 15 per cent of its 13 million and take twelve years to recoup, while France would lose 17 per cent of its 7.3 million and need sixty-six years to recoup. He condemned war as 'wholly dysgenic', killing the most efficient males and increasing infant mortality: F. Savorgnan, 'La Problème de la Population', *Scientia*, 1–3 (1918), 200–8.

33 A later study by Major Greenwood tried to play down the First World War's uniqueness in terms of casualties. He estimated that there were about 550,000 war losses in the fighting forces, a figure that rose by 300,000–370,000 with the inclusion of civilian deaths (with the disputable flu pandemic making up the highest figure). By comparison the wars of 1794–1815 (admittedly a much longer period) totalled about 322,000. He and others also noted that deaths from disease were low in 1914–18 compared with earlier conflicts: 1.0–5.3, non-battle to battle casualties in 1914–18; cf. 8–1 in the 1794–1815 wars: Major Greenwood, 'British Loss of Life in the Wars of 1794–1815 and in 1914–1918', *J. Royal Statistical Society*, 105, 1 (1942), 1–11.

34 Daniel Pick, *International Review of Psycho-Analysis*, 13 (1986), 498, reviewing Martin Stone, 'Shellshock and the Psychologists' in W. F. Bynum, R. Porter and M. Shepherd, eds., *The Anatomy of Madness*: *Essays in the History of Psychiatry* (London, New York, 1985), II, 242–71. As Pick says, it became increasingly difficult to explain shell-shock in older terms of degeneration theory and as the result of 'tainted heredity', given that officers were supposedly volunteers of quintessential nobility. Stone argues that shell-shock redefined 'the boundary of the pathological', and brought neuroses into 'the mainstream of mental medicine and economic life and set psychiatry's field of practice squarely within the social fabric of industrial society' (p. 266).

35 E. B. Poulton, 'Eugenic Problems After the Great War', *Eugenics Review*, 8 (1916), 36. Poulton was the author of *Charles Darwin and the Theory of Natural Selection* (London, 1896), and *Charles Darwin and the Origin of Species* (London, 1909).

36 G. W. Crile, *A Mechanistic View of War and Peace* (London, c. 1915), p. 42. Dr W. J. Robertson called war 'the most dysgenic of all dysgenic factors': preface to Adelyne More, *Uncontrolled Breeding* (New York, 1917), p. 7.

37 Mallet, 'Vital Statistics'. Mallet worried that, because of demographic weakening, the British Empire would be obliged to play a reduced role in peopling the great waste spaces of the world. The Harvard economic rationalist Thomas Nixon Carver predicted great changes in the world's emigration patterns as a result of the war, with an unwelcome influx of 'hyphenated' Americans, foreign migrants from Europe, into the US: 'The Probable Effect of the European War upon the Redistribution of Population', *Scientia*, 21 (1917), 144–51. For background see J. M. Winter, 'Fear of Population Decline in Western Europe', in R. Hiorns, edn, *Demographic Patterns in Developed Societies* (London, 1979).

38 C. H. Melville, 'Eugenics and Military Service', *Eugenics Review*, 2 (1910–11), 55.

39 Raymond Pearl, 'Biology and War', in his *Studies in Human Biology* (Baltimore, 1924), pp. 547–9.

40 Chambers, 'Eugenics and the War' (1914–15), 286.

41 G. R. Searle, *Eugenics and Politics in Britain, 1900–1914* (Leyden, 1976), pp. 36–8. Kipling idealised military service in his utopian story 'The Army of a Dream', first published in the right-wing *Morning Post* in June 1904. J. A. Lindsay asked whether it was self-evident that drill fostered good health, citing the anthropologist Sergi to the effect that military training could injure youths whose arterial and muscular systems had not yet matured: Lindsay, 'The Eugenic and Social Influences of the War', 133–34.

42 Anon, 'War and Eugenics', *Lancet*, 1 (27 February 1915), 450.

43 Chambers, 'Eugenics and the War'. Chambers was careful not to make dogmatic judgments about modern warfare, given that 'the consequences were so far-reaching and indeterminable'. War losses in the recent historical past (c. 1790–1880) were probably fewer than deaths by preventible disease and infant mortality. Chambers recognised that anaesthetics, antiseptics and nursing had revolutionised war conditions. He was shown to be correct in this, for it turned out that deaths from disease within the British army were dramatically lowered during the war. This progress was widely attributed to better army hygiene: see, for example, files of *Public Health* and *J. State Medicine*; C. W. Saleeby, 'Imperial Health and the Dysgenics of War', *J. State Medicine*, 25 (1917), 307–16; P. W. Bassett-Smith, 'Improvement in the Health of the Royal Navy during the Last Ten Years', *ibid.*, 23 (1915), 257–61; G. W. Goler, 'War: Some of its Effects upon the Health of the Military and Civil Population ...', *New York State J. of Medicine*, 18, 3 (1918), 113–17; F. Prinzing, *Epidemics Resulting from War* (Oxford, 1916).

44 Lothrop Stoddard, *The Revolt Against Civilization* (New York, 1923), pp. 120, 122. Stoddard thought that the racial losses of the war were as grave as the material losses.

45 J. A. Thomson, 'Eugenics and War', *Eugenics Review*, 7 (1915), 2–5. Losses would be hard to make up since Britain had over six million men aged 18–45, almost 14 per cent of the population. If, as seemed likely in 1915, an army of three million needed to be raised, every second man in this age group would be enlisted: 'If the fitter join the army in larger numbers and are thinned in larger proportions, war must be regarded as a dysgenic eliminator.'

46 Major Leonard Darwin, 'On the Statistical Enquiries Needed after the War in Connection with Eugenics', *J. Royal Statistical Society*, 79 (1916), 159–75. Leonard Darwin was president of the Eugenics Society, and this lecture was given to the Royal Statistical Society in February 1916.

47 He warned that Britain was in peril of 'slowly drifting down the hill of racial degradation and of never again occupying its past high position in the councils of the world'. Darwin's overall position was that ancient war had probably been eugenic, but that with the advance of firepower modern war had become a matter largely of numbers, organisation, wealth and alliances, rather than a test of genetic superiority: 'Statistical Enquiries'. See also Leonard Darwin, 'The Disabled Sailor and Soldier and the Future of Our Race', *Eugenics Review*, 9 (1917), 1–17; and his *The Need for Eugenic Reform* (London, 1926), esp. pp. 499–504.

48 Some further examples: Crichton-Browne, *Bernhardi and Creation* (1916), pp. 6, 12; W. B. Cannon, *Bodily Changes in Pain, Hunger, Fear and Rage* (New York, 1915; 2nd edn, 1929), pp. 377–92; Munro, *From Darwinism to Kaiserism*, pp. 81–92; Nasmyth, *Social Progress*, pp. 140–4, 282, *passim*; E. J. Smith, *Race Regeneration* (London, 1918), ch. 1; S. J. Holmes, 'The Decadence of Human Heredity', *Atlantic Monthly*, 114 (1914), 302–8; G. T. W. Patrick, 'The Psychology of War', *Popular Science Monthly*, 87 (1915), 155–68; W. R. Inge, 'Patriotism', *Quarterly Review*, 224 (1915), 77.

49 Whetham, *War and the Nation* (1917), p. 215, generally ch. 5. For a debate over war's effects upon stature, especially the alleged loss of stature in the French population due to the Napoleonic and later wars, see: Sir Hercules Read, 'Anthropology and War', *J. Royal Anthropological Institute*, 49 (1919), 12–19; H. H. O'Farrell, 'War and the Stature of the Population', *Eugenics Review*, 9 (1917–18), 218–22.

50 W. Trotter, *The Instincts of the Herd in Peace and War* (London, 1916; 2nd edn, 1919), pp. 126–9. The Fabians Graham Wallas and Havelock Ellis saw modern war as 'an act of biological retrogression': see Wallas, *Human Nature in Politics* (London, 1908), p. 291; Ellis, *Essays in War-Time* (London, 1916, chs. 2, 3 (which have a circumspect review of the debate), and his *Philosophy of Conflict* (London, 1919).

51 Harold Boag, 'Human Capital and the Cost of the War', *J. Royal Statistical Society*, 79 (1917), 7–17.

52 Giuseppi Sergi, 'Does War Lower the Birth Rate?', *Current History*, 5, 2 (1916), 272–3.

53 William S. Rossiter, 'Influence of the War Upon the Population', *North American Review*, 203 (1916), 700–10.

54 Walter H. Page, letter to Virginia, 1916, quoted Masterman, *England After War: A Study* (London, 1922), p. 2.

55 Rossiter, 'Influence of War', 710.

56 Augustin Hamon gave a dramatic post-war reckoning that conjured up not only possibilities of genetic and social upheaval, but also a revival of democratic commonality. Thirteen million dead in action, ten million dead of privation and epidemics, 150 million undernourished and ill – this spelt a recipe for racial decline in Europe. Hamon predicted a weakening in religion and a reversion to primitive cults, a rise in class prejudice, and the scientisation of society. Unfortunately the scientisation of war meant the impossibility of humanising it: Augustin Hamon, 'Le bilan de la guerre mondiale', *Scientia*, 7 (1919), 39–46. Thorstein Veblen also speculated on the breakdown of dynastic and capitalist hegemony and the rise of 'underbred classes' (said with irony) in *An Inquiry into the Nature of Peace* (New York, 1917), pp. 251, 257, ch. 6. See also Homer Folks, *Human Costs of the War* (New York, London, 1920), with its graphic account of post-war dislocation in Europe. Folks warned of a depleted white Europe facing a 'yellow and black peril' (pp. 309–11). Also Emma O. Lundberg, 'The Illegitimate Child and War Conditions', *American J. Physical Anthropology*, 1, 3 (1918), 338–52.

57 *Science Progress*, 9 (1914), 514–16. He also theorised that virile cultural periods followed great wars in history, as after the English Wars of the Roses, or the wars of Frederick the Great.

58 W. McDougall and Charles Hose, *The Pagan Tribes of Borneo* (London, 1912), I, ch. 10; also McDougall, *Introduction to Social Psychology* (London, 1908; 28th edn, London, 1946), p. 248.

59 E. B. Copeland, 'War Selection in the Philippines', *Scientific Monthly*, 3 (1916), 151–4. However the losers in the selective struggle had been the Moro people, who had degenerated after centuries of struggle, a point against war.

60 The Greek philosopher Hesiod (eighth century BC) lyricised about a Golden Age when men 'feasted gaily, undarkened by sufferings'. Even eastern thought reflected this mythology. A fourth century BC Chinese medical treatise described how men had lived to 100 in ancient times, 'but eventually the tranquil era came to an end, and as men turned more violent they became more vulnerable to noxious influences': quoted René Dubos, *Mirage of Health: Utopias, Progress and Biological Change* (London, 1960), p. 12.

61 Edward Carpenter, *Civilization: Its Causes and Cure* (London, 1889), pp. 8–9, 26–9, 45. Carpenter used an island metaphor to show how the modern family and art conserved 'in island-miniatures, as it were, the ancient communal humanity' that was being threatened, 'when the seas of individualism and greed covered the general face of the earth' (p. 48).

62 Havelock Ellis believed that war had no place among animals in nature, or in the life of early/primitive man: *Essays in War-Time*, chs. 3, 5.

63 William Johnson Sollas, *Ancient Hunters and Their Modern Representatives* (London, 1911; 2nd edn, 1915), pp. 87, 104–6, 116: 'Only in rare instances can a race of hunters contrive to co-exist with an agricultural people. When the hunting ground of a tribe is restricted owing to its partial occupation by the new arrivals, the tribe affected is compelled to infringe on the boundaries of its neighbours: this is to break the most sacred 'law of the Jungle' and inevitably leads to war: the pressure of one boundary is propagated to the next, the ancient state of equilibrium is profoundly disturbed, and inter-tribal feuds become increasingly frequent' (pp. 104–5). A comparative study of war by

Quincy Wright in 1942 found that collectors, lower hunters and lower agriculturalists were least warlike, while higher agriculturalists and pastoralists were the most warlike. However Wright denied that there had ever been a 'golden age' of peace, or an 'iron age' of war at any stage of human history: Philip Quincy Wright, *A Study of War* (Chicago, 1942; reprinted Chicago, 1965), pp. 34–6, ch. 6 generally.

64 L. T. Hobhouse, G. C. Wheeler and T. Ginsberg, *The Material Culture and Social Institutions of the Simpler Peoples* (London, 1915), p. 228, ch. 4 generally. Also A. C. Parker, 'The Peace Policy of the Iroquois', *Southern Workmen*, 40 (1911), 691–9; D. S. Jordan, 'War Selection in the Ancient World', *Scientific Monthly*, 1 (1915), 36–43.

65 W. J. Perry, 'The Peaceable Habits of Primitive Communities: An Anthropological Study of the Golden Age', *Hibbert Journal*, 16 (1917), 28–46; 'An Ethological Study of Warfare', *Manchester Literary and Philosophical Society Memoirs*, 61, 6 (1917), 1–16; *The Children of the Sun* (London, 1923); and *The Growth of Civilization* (London, 1924). Perry hypothesised that peaceful primitive peoples had acquired war from predynastic Egypt, where it was invented and then 'diffused' during the pyramid-building age. Diffusionists such as W. H. R. Rivers and G. Elliot Smith also held that warfare had been diffused from one or a small number of centres: See Rivers, *History and Ethnology* (London, 1922), Elliot Smith, *The Evolution of Man* (Oxford, 1924), *Culture: The Diffusion Controversy* (New York, 1927). See discussion in Wright, *Study of War*, p. 34ff., Appendix VI. For another view on the rarity of war in primitive cultures, see A. J. Todd, *Theories of Social Progress* (New York, 1918; reprinted 1922), pp. 294–5.

66 Nancy Stepan, '"Nature's Pruning Hook": War, Race and Evolution, 1914–18', in J. M. W. Bean, ed, *The Political Culture of Modern Britain* (London, 1987), pp. 132–8. I am indebted to this source for a thoughtful analysis of Keith's ideas, and for references to a number of Keith's less well-known works.

67 Stepan, 'Nature's Pruning Hook', p. 136: 'it took the experience of contemporary nationalistic struggle on a vast scale to make Keith's implicitly conflictual model of human evolution explicit – to make struggle between races seem, to Keith, an inevitable result of the tribal instinct for isolation and self-preservation'.

68 Arthur Keith (MD), 'War as a Factor in Racial Evolution', *St Thomas's Hospital Gazette*, 25 (1915), 153–62.

69 Other publications by Keith included: 'On Certain Factors Concerned in the Evolution of Human Races', *J. Royal Anthropological Institute*, 46 (1916), 10–34; 'The Differentiation of Mankind into Racial Types', *Nature*, 1104 (1919), 301–5; *The Place of Prejudice in Modern Civilization* (London, 1931); *Evolution and Ethics* (New York, 1946); *Darwin Revalued* (London, 1955), esp. ch. 21.

70 Roland Hugins, 'The Eugenic Judgment of War', *South Atlantic Quarterly*, 13, 4 (October 1914), 303–9. Hugins however accepted that war had often 'overplayed its role of leech', especially during the Thirty Years War and Napoleonic Wars. Hugins's ideas are interesting in reflecting the confused state of military thought at the outbreak of war. He shared the feeling of some

military experts that modern wars were less protracted and destructive than before: 'what the eugenist will most fear is not some great European war, some sudden, brief death-grapple between giants like England and Germany, but rather that class-struggle still prophesied by the extreme wing of the Marxian socialists' (p. 308). See also Hugins, 'Norman Angellism Under Fire', *Forum and Century*, 54 (1915), 155–64; 'Militant Minorities', *Atlantic Monthly*, 123 (1919), 701–05.

71 P. Chalmers Mitchell, *Evolution and the War* (London, 1915), p. 78.

72 Rossiter, 'Influence of the War' (1916), p. 709. Kellogg's view that mortality by gunfire was largely non-selective, but dysgenic because working upon an elite group, seemed borne out by the experience of the trenches: Kellogg, *Military Selection*, pp. 185–6, and ch. 4 above.

73 'Evolution and War', *Science Progress*, 9 (1914), 514–16.

74 A. G. Thacker, 'Some Eugenic Effects of War', *Science Progress*, 10 (1915), 73–80.

75 *Ibid.*

76 Lindsay, 'Influence of the War', 133–44. Lindsay, educated at Belfast, Paris and Vienna, and an expert on lung and heart disease, was very active in Belfast scientific and literary circles. See also his 'Case For and Against Eugenics', *Nineteenth Century*, 72, 5 (1912), 546–7.

77 Mitchell, *Evolution and the War*, pp. 72–80.

78 G. G. Coulton, *The Main Illusions of Pacificism* (London, 1916), pp. 112–13.

79 Ronald Campbell Macfie, 'Some of the Evolutionary Consequences of War', *Science Progress*, 12A, 45 (1917), 132–7. Neither sociology nor biology (he said) had adequately studied war's significance for human evolution, even though war had been in the world 'since the time of the tribolites, and though its importance in the evolution of animal types has long been a cardinal article in the creed of biologists'.

80 Jay Winter has assembled evidence that army conditions were a step up for recruits from the slums and factories of industrialised Britain, where mortality (especially infant) was high, comparable to third world conditions today. Winter claims that the 'purely demographic' losses of World War I were offset by demographic gains for the lower classes, achieved through improved wartime incomes and nutrition: Jay Winter, 'Army and Society: the Demographic Context' in Ian F. W. Beckett and K. Simpson, *A Nation in Arms: A Social Study of the British Army in the First World War* (Manchester, 1985), pp. 193–210; and his *The Great War and the British People*, (Cambridge, Mass., 1986) part II.

81 Macfie, 'Evolutionary Consequences of War'.

82 S. de Jastrzebski, 'War and the Balance of the Sexes', *Eugenics Review*, 10 (1918), 76–80. For Germany, Austria and Hungary the ratio of females to 1,000 males had risen from under 1,030 to about 1,200. Interestingly there was a marked rise in the proportion of male births in Britain during the war, although demographers were at a loss to explain this 'natural' tendency to redress the sex balance: see, for example, Mallet, 'Vital Statistics', 15. The proportion of male to female births for England and Wales, 1915–17, was 1,046 to 1,000, or eight above the average of the previous forty years.

83 'Since inheritance is strictly bi-sexual, nothing is completely lost to the race by

the slaughter of the males, but qualities are passed on to descendants, both male and female, by the sex which bears the burden of war in waiting and tears rather than in actual fighting. Even the loss in numbers is lessened in proportion as the women who might have married the dead soldiers marry others. Nor, indeed, can we look upon all the strong men who give up their life in battle as potential fathers': Hugins, 'Eugenic Judgment', 306.

84 Mitchell, *Evolution and the War*, p. 78.

85 Cited in P. Sorokin, *Contemporary Sociological Theories* (New York, London, 1928), p. 333. Edward Krehbiel, the Mennonite pacifist and scholar, put the unusual argument that wartime society tended to root out the unfit at home, when women denied sexual favours to cowards and feeble 'stay-at-homes' – are case where genetic defence was made of wartime persecution of those not contributing to the war effort: *Nationalism, War and Society* (New York, 1916), ch. 10. Krehbiel, a Chicago Ph.D., was a wartime member of the American Union Against Militarism.

86 Lindsay, 'Influences of the War', 136. Joseph H. Marcus also believed that the genetic damage caused by war losses would be rapidly made up. He deplored widespread misconceptions of a Lamarckian kind that mutilated soldiers would return home to breed defective offspring: 'Man After the War', *New York Medical Journal*, cited *Literary Digest*, 57 (6 April 1918), 34–5. See also Raymond Pearl and Roswell Johnson, below, on sexual selection.

87 Pearl, 'Biology and War' (1918), pp. 534–49.

88 For similar arguments see the anthropologist Ales Hrdlicka, 'The Effects of the War on the Race', *Art and Archaeology*, 7 (1918), 404–7: 'little if any permanent biological harm' had been done to the US by the war: 'blood price is paid for all human progress ... War is merely the most intensified part of the general struggle for existence and advance' (p. 407).

89 Roswell H. Johnson, 'Natural Selection in War', *J. of Heredity*, 6, 11 (1915), 546–8.

90 A. Chase, *The Legacy of Malthus* (New York, 1977), p. 115.

91 Johnson, 'Natural Selection in War', 546–8. Following quotes in text refer to this source.

92 *Ibid.* Johnson suggested that inter-group selection had occurred historically when a victorious army impregnated enemy women, but that this factor had lessened (he shared the age's optimism) with better army discipline and higher social ideals. Within groups, selection was adversely affected by hasty marriages and increased illegitimacy around training camps. Given the reduction of marriageable males at home in belligerent nations, it was necessary to compare the quality of surviving combatants and non-combatants. Whether a war had a good or harmful effect was a matter for empirical inquiry into particular wars.

93 See also R. H. Johnson and Paul Popenoe, *Applied Eugenics* (New York, 1918), ch. 16; and Popenoe, 'The Racial Value of Death', *Advocate of Peace* (Wash.), (1918), 175–6, arguing that war was dysgenic. This paper raised the ire of the young R. A. Fisher, who believed that the pre-war years in Britain were already 'very highly dysgenic', with the proliferation of the poor and controlled fertility of the rich and middle class. Peace, it seemed to Fisher, was likely to have worse genetic effects than any war: *Eugenics Review*, 8 (1916), 291–2. Also Krehbiel, *Nationalism, War and Society*, ch. 10, 'War and Biology', a curious syllabus of

theories on the eugenics of war. For a racial eugenic opinion see Anon., 'America's Fighting Stocks', *J. of Heredity*, 8, 10 (1917), 435–41: pleading that the American army be drawn from all racial groups to avoid heavy losses of Nordics.

94 For example, Winter, *The Great War and British People*, ch. 3.
95 J. B. S. Haldane, *Adventures of a Biologist* (New York, 1931), p. 151.
96 This point is made in R. J. Halliday, 'Darwinism, Biology and Race' (unpublished paper, University of Warwick, 1988).

7 NATURALISTIC FALLACIES AND NOBLE ENDS

1 See Greta Jones, *Social Darwinism and English Thought* (Sussex, 1980), pp. 2–3.
2 See Robert J. Richards, *Darwin and the Emergence of Evolutionary Theories of Mind and Behavior* (Chicago, London, 1987), pp. 323–4, ch. 4 and *passim* for a searching attack upon Moore's position, and a logical analysis of the 'naturalistic fallacy'; also his 'A Defense of Evolutionary Ethics', *Biology and Philosophy*, 1 (1986), 263–93.
3 James Bryce, 'War and Human Progress' (1916) in his *Essays and Addresses in War Time* (London, 1918), pp. 72–5. There was nothing in the animal world, Bryce said, like the wars of human tribes or states. In nature it was adaptation, not fighting, that was the key factor when one species superseded another.
4 I. W. Howerth, 'War and the Progress of Society', *Popular Science Monthly*, 87 (1915), 195–9. Howerth, who became an educationist at the University of California, saw war as dissociated from social progress, except in incidental ways: 'War, it may be said, belongs to the economy of nature and not to the economy of mind … [War] is perhaps the superlative example of social waste … Social intelligence … cannot countenance war' (p. 199). See also his 'War and Social Economy', *International J. Ethics*, 17 (1906–7), 70–8; *Work and Life* (New York, 1912), esp. ch. 5; 'War and the Survival of the Fittest', *Scientific Monthly*, 3 (1916), 488–97; 'The Great War and the Instinct of the Herd', *International J. Ethics*, 29 (1919), 174–87.
5 T. G. Chambers, 'Eugenics and the War', *Eugenics Review*, 6 (1914–15), 281.
6 Sir Charles Waldstein, *Aristodemocracy: from the Great War back to Moses, Christ and Plato* (London, 1916), pp. 1–7, 57–9, 147, 187–8, and *passim*. Borrowing the words of the French ambassador to the court of St James, Waldstein described the war as a relapse into barbarism, which had 'bedecked itself with the showy attributes of intellectual pedantry'. Waldstein changed his name to Walston during the war, and also wrote under the pseudonym of Gordon Seymour. His works include: *What Germany is Fighting For* (London, 1917), *Patriotism, National and International* (London, 1917), *The Next War: Wilsonism and Anti-Wilsonism* (Cambridge, 1918), *Eugenics, Civics, Ethics* (Cambridge, 1920).
7 F. A. E. Crew, 'A Biologist in a New Environment', *Eugenics Review*, 11 (1919–20), 119–23. Crew of course was unfair to Spencer, neglecting his pacifism. Crew's ideas are briefly discussed in N. Stepan, '"Nature's Pruning Hook": War, Race and Evolution, 1914–18', in J. M. W. Bean, ed, *The Political Culture of Modern Britain* (London, 1987), p. 142.
8 Benjamin Kidd, *The Science of Power* (London, New York, 1918). Kidd finished the first draft only days before the outbreak of war, which caused him

great angst. He studied anew the literature of militarism, and forced himself, despite desperate ill health, to rewrite the book. It was finished only weeks before his death in October 1916. However, as his son Franklin observed, his main themes were preserved: 'he saw in the war the dramatic climax of tendencies which he had divined'. See D. P. Crook, *Benjamin Kidd* (Cambridge, 1984), ch. 6.

9 Ralph Barton Perry, *The Present Conflict of Ideals* (New York, 1918), pp. 119–20, 127, 142. Following references in text to this edition. Bannister suggests that the term 'Social Darwinism' gained wider currency during the war years because of American denunciations, especially in the writings of Perry, Jordan, Nasmyth, Arthur James Todd, Carlton Hayes, and Lucius M. Bristol: *Social Darwinism*, pp. 240–41.

10 Perry quoted Brunetière: 'The morality which one can extract from the evolutionary doctrine, will always be a "refracted" morality, of which one must look elsewhere for the origin'. Perry observed that 'Socialism has certainly gone to sources other than scientific evolutionism for its ethical light' (p. 148).

11 Nobody, said Perry, could deny 'the importance and permanence of the social environment' (p. 133). See also J. H. Muirhead, *German Philosophy in Relation to the War* (London, 1917), p. 95; Graham Wallas, *Our Social Heritage* (London, 1921). A. L. Kroebner maintained that the 'attempt today to treat the social as organic, to understand civilization as hereditary, is ... essentially narrow minded': 'The Superorganic', *American Anthropologist*, NS 19, 2 (1917), 180, generally 163–213. Kroebner argued that the application of principles of organic development to the facts of cultural growth involved reasoning by analogy and dubious assumptions about similarities. These tended to predetermine mental attitudes 'with the result that when the evidence begins to accumulate which could prove or disprove the assumption based on analogy, this evidence is no longer viewed impartially and judiciously' (p. 164).

12 Frederick J. Teggart, *The Processes of History* (New Haven, London, 1918), esp. ch. 3. Maitland, Balfour and Jastrow were among the specific influences upon Teggart, who founded the Department of Social Institutions at Berkeley in 1919 and was highly respected for his work on the theory of history and the use of scientific method in research.

13 Albert G. Keller, *Through War to Peace* (New York, 1918), p. 134. Subsequent page references are to this source. Keller devised his theory of 'societal selection' in specific reaction against Weismann's stress on physical selection, with its depreciation of 'the cultural elements that are the hallmarks of human association': see R. C. Bannister, *Sociology and Scientism* (Chapel Hill, London, 1987), p. 101, and generally on Keller, pp. 101–6. Bannister discerns inconsistencies between Keller's 'speculative use of selectionist analogies' in the theory of cultural selection, and his residual 'Darwinian' inductionism, part legacy of Yale's prevalent Baconianism (p. 101).

14 'What we actually see in history is a progressive development of restriction on violence, both as between individuals and classes within the same society, and also as between societies. But the very prohibition of violence witnesses to the priority of violence' (p. 52).

15 Edwin Grant Conklin, 'Biology and Democracy', *Scribner's Magazine*, 65 (1919), 403, generally 403–12. Page references hereafter in text. Conklin

accused scientists and professional men of joining heartily 'in a crusade to force militarism, war and autocracy upon an unwilling world' (p. 403). Conklin (1863–1952) was a leader in embryological and cytological research, professor of biology at Princeton (1908–1933) and a popular science writer and speaker. His works included *Heredity and Environment in the Development of Men* (Princeton, 1915). The Minnesota sociologist Arthur James Todd also warned that humanity was threatened by violent doctrines spread by those 'hypnotized by doctrinaire science': *Theories of Social Progress* (New York, 1922; 1st edn, 1918), p. 292. Todd, like Nasmyth, Teggart and Keller, put Novicovian interpretations of war, depicting it as dysgenic and 'a debased form of the instinct to compete' (p. 293).

16 Among his early writings were: 'The Duration of Life', *Nature*, 37 (1888), 541–2; 'Professor Tyndall', *New Review*, 10, 56 (1894), 77–85; 'The Spencer–Weismann Controversy', *Nature*, 49 (1894), 373–4; 'Pasteur', *New Review*, 13, 78 (1895), 537–44; 'The Future of the Tropics', *North American Review*, 176 (1903), 711–18.

17 Peter Chalmers Mitchell, *My Fill of Days* (London, 1937), pp. 264, 383; also *My House in Malaga* (London, 1938). See also Sir Campbell Stuart, *The Secrets of Crewe House* (London, 1920); Henry Wickham Steed, *Through Thirty Years* (London, 1924), II, 221, 224, 242, 244–6. Mitchell wrote the article on propaganda for the 12th edition of the *Encyclopaedia Britannica*. He was awarded a CBE in 1918 and a knighthood in 1929.

18 Peter Chalmers Mitchell, *Evolution and the War* (London, 1915), pp. x, xxi, 107; also *My Fill of Days*, chs. 3, 6. He wrote *Materialism and Vitalism in Biology* (Oxford, 1930), warning against the rash interpretation of Idealism and vitalism by social prophets and politicians.

19 [Mitchell], 'A Biological View of Our Foreign Policy', *Saturday Review*, 82, 210 (1896), 118–20. He also forecast ultimate war between Europe's dominant power and the United States. Bernard Shaw noted the article with alarm and confronted Frank Harris over it. When Harris denied writing it, Shaw retorted that it was equally harmful whether written by Harris or the office boy: *My Fill of Days*, p. 65.

20 [Mitchell], 'A Word with Mr. Huxley', *National Review*, 21 (1893), 713–15. See ch. 2.

21 *Evolution and the War*, p. xxv. Following references in text are to this source.

22 Havelock Ellis, 'Evolution and War', in his *Essays in War-Time* (London, 1917), ch. 2. Mitchell may have underestimated the central role of struggle in Shelston's work, which stressed 'negative mechanisms – the war of all against all, and the self-elimination of species from their own habitat': J. R. Engel, *Sacred Sands: The Struggle for Community in the Indiana Dunes* (Middletown, Conn., 1983), p. 171, generally pp. 168–72. As Engels shows, Shelford was in a similar tradition to pioneer ecologist Frederick Clements who was influenced by Spencer's organismic philosophy, whereas most members of the Dunes movement were co-operationists in the tradition of another pioneer in animal ecology, Henry Chandler Cowles, reflecting the social democratic paradigm of the Chicago pragmatists (pp. 148–9). Mitchell wrote: 'I could adduce from the writings of Darwin himself, and from those of later naturalists, a thousand instances taken from the animal kingdom in which success has come about by

means analogous with the cultivation of all the peaceful arts, the raising of the intelligence, and the heightening of the emotions of love and pity' (*Evolution and the War*, p. 41).

23 He had nineteen years earlier translated and written an introduction to Oscar Hertwig, *The Biological Problem of Today: Preformation or Epigenesis? The Basis of Organic Development* (London, 1896), and had published a detailed abstract of Hertwig's work in *Natural Science* (1894) at a time of excitement over Weismann's theories. Hertwig was an epigenesist, opposed to Weismann's preformationism as a 'doctrine of determinants' (Hertwig, pp. 15, 139–40).

24 He had made an earlier statement of this case in 'The Making of Modern Races', *North American Review*, 179 (1904), 526–42.

25 Sir James Crichton-Browne, *Bernhardi and Creation: A New Theory of Evolution* (Glasgow, 1916), pp. 14, 17–18; Havelock Ellis, 'Evolution and War', p. 17; *Sociological Review*, 8, 3 (1915), 201; *New Statesman*, 5 (14 August 1915), 451; *Scientific American* (Supplement), 83, 2157 (5 May 1917), 274.

26 G. G. Coulton, *The Main Illusions of Pacificism* (Cambridge, 1916), pp. 112–13. See ch. 6 for Mitchell's critique of peace eugenics. The *Saturday Review* accused Mitchell of drifting into the 'danger-zone of pacifism' under the influence of dreamers like Tolstoy: 191 12 (29 May 1915), 556–7.

27 Bryce, *Essays in War Time*, pp. 72–3; *Times Literary Supplement*, 696 (20 May, 1915), 166: 'He [Mitchell] is constrained once again to defend Darwin against the Darwinians, and in the process shows that the whole study of natural selection has been divergent from the crude conception of natural war.'

28 Ross, *Science Progress*, 10 (1916), 183–4. *Nature* put a reservation: 'when the author expresses his belief that "nurture is inconceivably more important than nature", he is opposing complementary, not antithetic, factors': 95 (August, 1915), 695–96.

29 P. Chalmers Mitchell, *La Darwinisme et la guerre*, trans. M. Solovine, Lettre-préface de M. Emile Boutroux (Paris, 1916), pp. xiii, 168; Etienne Rabaud, 'Qu'est-ce que la biologie humaine', *La Revue Scientifique*, 55 (1917), 163–8; Joseph Grasset, 'La biologie humaine', *ibid.*, 55 (1917), 65–9. The book was also translated into Portuguese as *O Darwinismo e a guerra* (Rio Grande do Sul, Brasil, 1918).

30 Brian Mackenzie, 'Darwinism and Positivism as Methodological Influences on the Development of Psychology', *J. History of Behavioral Sciences*, 12 (1976), 330–7. Paradoxically, if Mackenzie is right, the revival of positivism was associated with the prestige of physics, for positivism flourished with the rise of a scientific methodology that 'stressed fact-finding and ... devalued theory' (p. 336).

31 *Evolution and the War*, pp. 93–4. For modern parallels to Mitchell's criticism of analogy in biology, see ch. 8.

8 CONCLUSION

1 E. O. Wilson, *On Human Nature* (New York, 1979; 1st edn, Cambridge, Mass., 1978), p. 101.

2 Colin Creighton and Martin Shaw, eds., *The Sociology of War and Peace* (London, 1987), p. 3.

3 Robert Munro, *From Darwinism to Kaiserism* (Glasgow, 1919), p. 49.
4 Robert C. Bannister, *Social Darwinism* (2nd edn, Philadelphia, 1988), new preface, p. xxix; also Howard Kaye, *The Social Meaning of Modern Biology* (New Haven, 1985), p. 157 and *passim*.
5 Wilson, *On Human Nature*, p. 119.
6 Ross, 'Evolution and War', *Science Progress*, 9 (1914), 516.
7 Wilson, *On Human Nature*, pp. 108, 119–124.
8 S. A. Barnett, 'The Reductionist Imperative and the Nature of Humanity' (unpub. paper, c. 1988), p. 1.
9 S. A. Barnett, 'Cooperation, Conflict, Crowding and Stress: An Essay on Method', *Interdisciplinary Science Reviews*, 4, 2 (1979), pp. 106, 125. Barnett had elaborated these themes in many works and broadcasts, including: 'Models and Morals: Biological Images of Man', in P. F. Brain and D. Benton, eds., *Multidisciplinary Approaches to Aggression Research* (Elsevier, 1981), ch. 33; 'Humanity and Natural Selection', *Ethology and Sociobiology*, 4 (1983), 35–51; and *Biology and Freedom* (Cambridge, 1988).
10 Marvin Bressler, 'Biological Determinism and Ideological Indeterminacy', in Elliott White, edn, *Sociobiology and Human Politics* (Lexington, Mass., Toronto, 1981), p. 185.
11 Barnett, *Biology and Freedom*, p. 24.
12 Stephen Jay Gould, *Ever Since Darwin* (Harmondsworth, 1987), p. 242.

APPENDIX: SOCIAL DARWINISM

1 In 1877 a symposium of British thinkers, ranging from Huxley to Dean Church, leaned to the conclusion that science had the potential to cause religious decline, which in turn could foreshadow a decline in social (but not necessarily individual) standards of behaviour. But the symposium also bravely declared that falsehood could not be tolerated just because it sustained moral standards: Owen Chadwick, *The Victorian Church* (London, 1966), pp. 121–2. Generally see John Durant, edn, *Darwinism and Divinity: Essays on Evolution and Religious Belief* (Oxford, New York, 1985).
2 Walter F. Cannon, 'The Bases of Darwin's Achievment: A Revaluation', *Victorian Studies*, 5 (1961), 109–32; Robert M. Young, 'The Impact of Darwin on Conventional Thought', in A. Symondson, edn, *The Victorian Crisis of Faith* (London, 1970), pp. 13–36; also his 'The Darwin Debate', *Marxism Today*, 26, 4 (1982), 20–2, and other papers; James R. Moore, *The Post-Darwinian Controversies: A Study of the Protestant Struggle to Come to Terms with Darwin in Great Britain and America* (Cambridge, 1979). Dov Ospovat gave support to the idea of residual elements of natural theology in Darwin's early theories in *The Development of Darwin's Theory* (Cambridge, 1981); see also N. C. Gillespie, *Charles Darwin and the Problem of Creation* (Chicago, London, 1979).
3 John Durant has observed that, by emphasising the immanence of God in nature and the gradual ascent of nature and humankind towards divinity, the modernists 'sustained a powerful synthesis of science, religion and the politics of "progressive social reform"': Durant, *Darwinism and Divinity*, p. 28.

4 Quoted Alec Vidler, *The Church in an Age of Revolution* (Harmondsworth, 1961), p. 121. Jim Moore also argues a case that Calvinism was more amenable to harsher selection theory than other sects, because Calvinism could accept apparent disorder in the universe as a divine order beyond human understanding: *Post-Darwinian Controversies* (1979).

5 Edward Manier, *The Young Darwin and His Cultural Circle* (Dordrecht, 1978); Thomas S. Kuhn, *The Structure of Scientific Revolutions* (Chicago, 2nd edn, 1970), pp. 171–2. Further discussion and bibliography in David Kohn, edn, *The Darwinian Heritage* (Princeton, 1985).

6 R. J. Halliday, 'God and Natural Selection', *History of European Ideas*, 2, 3 (1981), 237–46 (quote p. 245). Halliday contends that Marx 'always maintained a consistent and absolute distinction between man and animal, resting ultimately on his concept of species-being ... [and] he always regarded talk of the species man with great suspicion': 'Darwinism, Biology and Race', unpublished paper (University of Warwick, 1988), p. 6.

7 John Angus Campbell, 'Scientific Revolution and the Grammar of Culture: The Case of Darwin's *Origin*', *Quarterly Journal of Speech*, 72, 4 (1986), 351–76; also see Gillian Beer, *Darwin's Plots* (London, 1983).

8 Gertrude Himmelfarb, *Darwin and the Darwinian Revolution* (New York, 1959; reprinted New York, 1968), pp. 418–20, and generally ch. 19. (Himmelfarb, it should be said, discerned a wide range of Social Darwinisms.) Also Richard Hofstadter, *Social Darwinism in American Thought* (Philadelphia, 1944). On the Malthusian legacy for Darwinism see Robert M. Young, 'Malthus and the Evolutionists: The Common Context of Biological and Social Theory', *Past and Present*, 43, (1969), 109–45, a stance he has stoutly defended against persistent attack in numerous later writings.

9 Irwin G. Wylie, 'Social Darwinism and the Businessmen', *Proceedings of the American Philosophical Society*, 103 (1959), 629–35. On Spencer see J. D. Y. Peel, *Herbert Spencer: The Evolution of a Sociologist* (London, 1971), and Robert J. Richards, *Darwin and the Emergence of Evolutionary Theories of Mind and Behavior* (Chicago, London, 1987), chs. 6, 7. For historiographical discussion see James R. Moore, 'Socializing Darwinism: Historiography and the Fortunes of a Phrase', *Radical Science*, 20 (1986), 38–80; and Donald C. Bellomy, '"Social Darwinism" Revisited', in B. Bailyn, D. Fleming, S. Thernstrom, eds., *Perspectives in American History* (Cambridge, 1984), pp. 1–130.

10 Generally see Robert C. Bannister, *Social Darwinism: Science and Myth in Anglo-American Social Thought* (Philadelphia, 1979). The quotes are from his preface to the new edition (Philadelphia, 1988), pp. 1–2. For Bannister's revisionist views on Sumner see his foreword to R. C. Bannister, ed., *On Liberty, Society and Politics: The Essential Essays of William Graham Sumner* (Indianapolis, 1992). For another revisionist work see Howard L. Kaye, *The Social Meaning of Modern Biology* (New Haven, 1985).

11 Bannister, *Social Darwinism* (1979), p. 10.

12 For example, A. La Vergata, 'Images of Darwin: A Historiographical Overview', in Kohn, *The Darwinian Heritage* (Princeton, 1985), pp. 961–2. He speaks of 'an utterly over-simplified and misleading image of Darwin'.

13 John Durant, *British Journal for History of Science*, 15 (1982), 77. Also Peter

Bowler, 'The Social Implications of Evolutionism', in his *Evolution: The History of an Idea* (Berkeley, 1984), ch. 10: 'It is impossible to see social Darwinism as a simple and obvious application of the Darwinian theory to man. Links between biology and social thought could be established in many different ways, and in each case one aspect of the scientific theory was chosen to be stressed' (p. 267). Paul Weindling has criticised the excessive emphasis on natural selection: 'Schematic accounts of Social Darwinism as a proto-fascist ideology concentrate on natural selection, forgetting that this was only one biological concept from which laws of social development were derived': 'Theories of the Cell State in Imperial Germany', in C. Webster, edn, *Biology, Medicine and Society, 1840–1940* (Cambridge, 1981), p. 101.

14 D. P. Crook, *American Democracy in English Politics, 1815–50* (Oxford, 1965).

15 Douglas Lorimer argues, for instance, that racism intensified in the later nineteenth century as 'scientific' racial theory – compounded of many elements including Darwinism, anthropometry, brain topography, Galtonian statistics and genetic theory – was fostered by 'the external reality of expanding European domination over the globe', and by the fact that 'the presumptions and values of the professional middle class gave focus to the scientists' inquiries': Lorimer, 'Theoretical Racism in Later-Victorian Anthropology, 1870–1900', *Victorian Studies*, 32, 3 (1988), 405–30.

16 Robert J. Richards, 'Defense of Evolutionary Ethics', *Biology and Philosophy*, 1 (1986), 265–93.

17 On Social Darwinism as the product of an exploitative capitalist *système* based upon Malthusianism and classical economics, see the writings of Robert M. Young: for example, 'Darwinism *Is* Social' in Kohn, *Darwinian Heritage* (1985), pp. 609–40; *Darwin's Metaphor* (Cambridge, 1985).

Writings relevant to the discourse of Social Darwinism include:

R. J. Halliday, 'Social Darwinism: A Definition', *Victorian Studies*, 14, 4 (1971), 389–405.

J. A. Rogers, 'Darwinism and Social Darwinism', *J. History Ideas*, 33, 2 (1972), 265–80.

Harold Vanderpool, ed, *Darwin and Darwinism: Revolutionary Insights Concerning Man, Nature, Religion and Society* (Lexington, London, 1973).

Raymond Williams, 'Social Darwinism', in J. Benthall, edn, *The Limits of Human Nature* (London, 1973).

Ethel Tobach, 'Social Darwinism Rides Again', in Tobach *et al.*, eds., *The Four Horsemen: Racism, Sexism, Militarism and Social Darwinism* (New York, 1974).

Barry Barnes and Stephen Shapin, 'Darwin and Social Darwinism: Purity and History', in Barnes and Shapin, eds., *Natural Order: Historical Studies of Scientific Cultures* (Beverly Hills, London, 1979).

Norman E. Smith, 'W. G. Sumner as a Social Darwinist', *Pacific Historical Review*, 22 (1979), 32–47.

Greta Jones, *Social Darwinism and English Thought* (Sussex, 1980).

D. R. Oldroyd, *Darwinian Impacts* (Milton Keynes, 1980).

Michael Ruse, 'Social Darwinism: The Two Sources', *Albion*, 12 (1980), 23–36.

John C. Greene, 'Darwin as a Social Evolutionist', in Greene, *Science, Ideology and World View* (Berkeley, 1981).

Alfred Kelly, *The Descent of Darwin: The Popularization of Darwinism in Germany, 1860–1914* (Chapel Hill, 1981).

Paul Crook, 'Darwinism: The Political Implications', *History European Ideas*, 2, 1 (1981), 19–34.

Howard L. Kaye, 'The Myth of Social Darwinism', *Contemporary Sociology*, 11 (1982), 274–300.

Ted Benton, 'Social Darwinism and Socialist Darwinism in Germany, 1860 to 1900', *Revista di Filosophia*, 23 (1982), 79–121.

Linda L. Clark, *Social Darwinism in France* (University of Alabama, 1984).

Paul Crook, *Benjamin Kidd: Portrait of a Social Darwinist* (Cambridge, 1984).

Diane Paul, 'Eugenics and the Left', *Journal History Ideas*, 45 (1984), 567–90.

James R. Moore, 'Socializing Darwinism', *Radical Science*, 20 (1986), 38–80.

Paul Crook, 'Nature's Pruning Hook? War and Evolution, 1890–1918', *Australian J. Politics and History*, 33, 3 (1987), 237–52.

Diane Paul, 'The Selection of the "Survival of the Fittest"', *J. Hist. Biology*, 21, 3 (1988), 412–14.

Pauline Mazumdar, *Eugenics, Human Genetics and Human Failings: The Eugenics Society, its Sources and Critics in Britain* (London, New York, 1992).

Bibliography

Primary: pre-1945

BOOKS AND PAMPHLETS

Alexander, Samuel, *Moral Order and Progress*, London, 1889

Angell, James Rowland, *Psychology: An Introductory Study of the Structure and Function of Human Consciousness*, New York, 1904

Angell, Norman, *The Great Illusion*, London, 1910
Peace and the Plain Man, London, 1935

Anon, '*Militarism versus Feminism*, London, 1915

Atkinson, James Jasper, *Primal Law*, London, New York, 1903

Bachofen, Johann J., *Das Mutterrecht*, Stuttgart, 1861

Bagehot, Walter, *Physics and Politics: Or Thoughts on the Application of the Principles of 'Natural Selection' and 'Inheritance' to Political Society*, London, 1872, reprinted in *The Collected Works of Walter Bagehot*, edited by N. St John-Stevas, London, 1974

Baldwin, R. N. edn, *Kropotkin's Revolutionary Pamphlets*, New York, 1927; reprinted New York, 1970

Balfour, Arthur, J., *Decadence*, Cambridge, 1908

Bateson, William, *The Method and Scope of Genetics*, Cambridge, 1908

Beard, G. M., *American Nervousness: Its Causes and Consequences*, New York, 1881

Belloc, Hilaire, *A General Sketch of the European War: The Second Phase*, London, 1916

Bernard, Luther L., *Instinct: A Study in Social Psychology*, London, 1924

Bernhardi, General Friedrich von, *Germany and the Next War*, London, 1912
Britain as Germany's Vassal, translated by J. Ellis Barker, London, 1914

Bloch, Jean de, *The Future of War in its Technical, Economic and Political Relations*, translated by R. C. Long, Boston, 1902, reprinted Garland, New York, London, 1972

Bodart, Gaston, *Losses of Life in Modern Wars: Austria-Hungary, France*, Oxford, 1916

Bosanquet, Bernard, edn, *Aspects of the Social Problem*, London, 1895

Bovet, Pierre, *The Fighting Instinct*, translated by J. Y. T. Greig, London, 1923; from French edn, 1917

Bristol, L. M., *Social Adaptation*, London, 1915

Bryce, James, *The Relations of the Advanced and the Backward Races of Mankind*, Romanes Lecture, 1902, Oxford, 1903
  'War and Human Progress' (1916) in his *Essays and Addresses in War Time*, London, 1918
Burroughs, John, *Time and Change*, London, Cambridge, Mass., 1912
  The Light of Day, Boston and New York, 1915
  The Breath of Life, Boston and New York, 1915
C., T. B., *A War Policy for Greater Britain*, London, 1910
Campbell, Harry, *The Biological Aspects of Warfare*, London, 1918
Cannon, W. B., *Bodily Changes in Pain, Hunger, Fear and Rage: An Account of Research into the Function of Emotional Excitement*, New York, London, 2nd edn, 1919; 1st edn, 1915
  'Neural Organisation for Emotional Expression', in Martin L. Reymert, ed., *Feelings and Emotions: The Wittenberg Symposium* (*Worcester, Mass.*, 1928).
Carpenter, Edward, *Civilization: Its Causes and Cure*,London, 1889
Carpenter, William B., *Principles of Mental Physiology*, London, 1874
Carr, H. Wildon, *The Survival Value of Play*, University of Colorado, 1902
Carter, John, *Man is War*, Indianapolis, 1926
Chatterton-Hill, G., *Heredity and Selection in Sociology*, London, 1907
Chesterton, G. K., *Orthodoxy*, London, 1909
  The Thing, London, 1929
Chittenden, Hiram M., *War or Peace: A Present Duty and a Future Hope*, London, n.d., c. 1911
Clayton, I. M., *The Shadow on the Universe, or the Physical Results of War*, London, 1915
Clouston, Sir Thomas Smith, *The Hygiene of Mind*, London, 1906
Coker, F. W., *Organismic Theories of the State*, New York, 1910
Comte, Auguste, *The Positive Philosophy*, translated by Harriet Martineau, New York, 1853
Conklin, Edwin Grant, *Heredity and Environment in the Development of Men*, Princeton, 1915
Constantin, André, *Rôle sociologique de la guerre*, Paris, 1907
Conway, Sir Martin, *The Crowd in Peace and War*, London, 1915
Coulton, G. G., *The Main Illusions of Pacifism*, Cambridge, 1916
Cowdry, Edmund V., *Human Biology and Racial Welfare*, New York, 1930
Crackanthorpe, Montague Hughes, (M. H. Cookson), *Population and Progress*, London, 1907
Cramb, J. A., *The Origins and Destiny of Imperial Britain*, London, 1915
Crichton-Browne, Sir James, *Bernhardi and Creation: A New Theory of Evolution*, Glasgow, 1916
Crile, George Washington, *A Mechanistic View of War and Peace*, edited by Amy F. Rowland, New York, 1915
  The Origin and Nature of the Emotions: Miscellaneous Papers, Philadelphia, London, 1915
Crozier, J. B., *Religion of the Future*, London, 1880
  Civilisation and Progress (*London*, 1885).
Darwin, Charles, *Journal of Charles Darwin, Naturalist to the Beagle*, London, 1839

The Origin of Species by Means of Natural Selection or the Preservation of Favoured Races in the Struggle for Life, London, 1859

The Variations of Animals and Plants under Domestication, London, 1868

The Descent of Man, London, 1871

Expression of the Emotions in Man and Animals, London, 1872

Autobiography, in Sir Francis Darwin, *Life and Letters of C. Darwin*, vol. I, London, 1887, pp. 26–107

Early and Unpublished Notebooks, in H. E. Gruber, *Darwin on Man*, London, 1974

Natural Selection: Being the Second Part of his Big Species Book Written from 1856 to 1858, edited by R. C. Stauffer, Cambridge, 1975

Darwin, Erasmus, *The Temple of Nature*, London, 1803

Darwin, Leonard, *The Need for Eugenic Reform*, London, 1926

Davenport, Charles, *Heredity in Relation to Eugenics*, New York, 1911

Davis, Michael M., *Gabriel Tarde. An Essay in Sociological Theory*, New York, 1906

Psychological Interpretations of Society, London, 1909

De Vries, Hugo, *Die Mutationstheorie*, 2 vols., Leipzig, 1901–3, translated as *The Mutation Theory*, London, 1910

Demolins, Edmond, *Anglo Saxon Superiority: To What it is Due*, translated from the 10th French edn, London, 1898

Boer or English: Who are in the Right?, trans. London, 1900

Dewey, John, 'The Influence of Darwin on Philosophy', Columbia lecture 1909, in P. Appleman, edn, *Darwin: A Norton Critical Edition*, New York, 1970

Drever, James, *Instinct in Man*, Cambridge, 1917

Driver, C. H., 'Walter Bagehot and the Social Psychologists', in F. J. C. Hearnshaw, ed, *The Social and Political Ideas of Some Representative Thinkers of the Victorian Age*, London, 1933, reprinted, 1967

Drummond, Henry, *Natural Law in the Spiritual World*, London, 1883

The Ascent of Man, London, 1894

Ellis, Havelock, *Studies in the Psychology of Sex*, 7 vols., Philadelphia, 1897–1928

The Task of Social Hygiene, London, 1912

Essays in War-Time: Further Studies in the Task of Social Hygiene, London, 1917

The Philosophy of Conflict and Other Essays in War-Time, London, 1919

Ellwood, Charles A., *Sociology in its Psychological Aspects*, London, 1913

Ewart, John S., *The Roots and Causes of the Wars* (1914–1918), 2 vols., London, 1925

Ferrero, Guglielmo, *Militarism*, London, 1902, translated and revised from *Il Militarismo*, Italy, 1898, reprinted Garland, London, 1972

Folks, Homer, *Human Costs of the War*, New York, London, 1920

Freud, Sigmund, 'Thoughts for the Times on War and Death', in *Imago*, 1915, reprinted in John Strachey, ed, *Standard Edition of Complete Works of Freud*, vol. XIV, London, 1957

Fuller, J. F. C., *The Reformation of War*, London, 1923

The Dragon's Teeth: A Study of War and Peace, London, 1932

Galton, Francis, *Hereditary Genius*, London, 1869

English Men of Science, London, 1874

Essays in Eugenics, London, 1909

Giddings, Franklin H., *Principles of Sociology*, New York and London, 1896
Democracy and Empire, New York, 1900

Ginsberg, Morris, *The Psychology of Society*, London, 1921

Gooch, G. P., *History of Our Time*, London, 1911

Gordin, A. L. and V. L. *Pan-anarchist Manifesto*, Moscow, 1918

Grane, W. L., *The Passing of War*, London, 1912

Grant, John E., *The Problem of War and its Solution*, London, 1922

Gumplowicz, Ludwig, *Outlines of Sociology*, translation of *Grundriss der Sociologie*, Vienna, 1877, edited by I. L. Horowitz, New York, 1963

Haeckel, Ernst, H. P. A., *The History of Creation*, trans. London, 1876, 1st edn,
1868
Die Welträthsel [*The Riddle of the Universe*], Stuttgart, 1899

Haldane, J. B. S., *Adventures of a Biologist*, New York, 1931

Hall, G. Stanley, *Adolescence*, 2 vols., New York, 1904
Youth, New York, 1907

Hamilton-Grace, R. S., *Finance and War*, London, 1910

Harvey, Charles H., *The Biology of British Politics*, London, New York, 1904

Haycraft, John Berry, *Darwinism and Race Progress*, London, 1895

Headley, F. W., *Darwinism and Modern Socialism*, London, 1909

Hegel, G. W. F., *Philosophy of Right*, Berlin, 1821; trans., New York, Oxford, 1952

Heron, David, *On the Relation of Fertility in Man to Social Status, etc.*, London,
1906

Hertwig, Oscar, *The Biological Problem of Today: Preformation or Epigenesis? The
Basis of Organic Development*, London, 1906 (introduction by P. Chalmers
Mitchell)

Hobhouse, L. T., *Mind in Evolution*, London, 1901
The World in Conflict, London, 1915

Hobhouse, L. T., Wheeler, G. C. and Ginsberg, T., *The Material Culture and
Social Institutions of the Simpler Peoples*, London, 1915

Hobson, John A., *The Psychology of Jingoism*, London, 1901
The New Protectionism, New York, 1916
Democracy After the War, London, 1917
Forced Labour, London, 1917

Hofstadter, Richard, *Social Darwinism in American Thought*, Philadelphia, 1944

Holmes, John Haynes, *New Wars for Old*, New York, 1916

Holmes, Samuel Jackson, *Human Genetics and its Social Import*, New York,
London, 1936

Howerth, I. W., *World and Life*, New York, 1912

Huxley, T. H., *Man's Place in Nature*, London, 1863
'Administrative Nihilism', 1871; reprinted in *Collected Essays*, vol. I, London,
1896, pp. 251–89

Huxley, T. H., 'Science and Morals', 1886; reprinted in *Collected Essays*, vol. IX,
pp. 117–46
'The Struggle for Existence in Human Society', 1888; reprinted in *Collected
Essays*, vol. IX, pp. 195–236
'*Social Diseases and Worse Remedies*', London, 1891; reprinted in *Collected
Essays*, vol. IX, pp. 188–334

Evolution and Ethics, New York, 1902

Inge, William Ralph, *Outspoken Essays*, London, 1919

James, William, *Principles of Psychology*, 2 vols., London, 1890
   The Will to Believe, New York, 1897
   Memories and Studies, Cambridge Mass., 1911
   'Robert Gould Shaw Oration', Boston, 1897, reprinted in *Essays in Religion and Morality*, Cambridge, Mass. and London, 1882

Jane, L. C., *Nations at War*, London, 1914

Jastrow, Joseph, *The Subconscious*, London, 1906

Johnson, R. H. and Popenoe, Paul, *Applied Eugenics*, New York, 1918

Jones, F. Wood, *Arboreal Man*, London, 1926

Jordan, David Starr, *The Human Harvest. A Study of the Decay of Races Through the Survival of the Unfit*, Boston, 1907, reprinted and introduced by Roland C. Marshall, Garland, New York, London, 1972
   War and Waste, New York, 1914, reprinted Garland, 1972

Jordan, David Starr, and Jordan, Harvey Ernest, *War's Aftermath: A Preliminary Study of the Eugenics of War as Illustrated by the Civil War of the United States*, Boston, New York, 1914

Keith, Arthur, *The Place of Prejudice in Modern Civilization*, London, 1931

Keller, Albert G., *Through War to Peace*, New York, 1918

Kellogg, Vernon L., *Beyond War: A Chapter in the Natural History of Man*, New York, 1912
   'Eugenics and Militarism', in *Problems in Eugenics: Papers to the First International Eugenics Congress*, London, 1912, pp. 220–31
   Military Selection and Race Deterioration, edited by H. Westergaard, Oxford, 1916, published under the auspices of Carnegie Endowment for International Peace
   Headquarters Nights: A Record of Conversations and Experiences at the Headquarters of the German Army in France and Belgium, Boston, 1917

Kidd, Benjamin, *Social Evolution*, London, New York, 1894
   Control of the Tropics, London, New York, 1898
   Two Principal Laws of Sociology, 2 vols., London, 1907–8
   The Science of Power, London, New York, 1918

Kipling, Rudyard, 'The Mark of the Beast', in *Life's Handicap*, London, 1908

Knox, Robert, *The Races of Men: a Fragment*, London, 1850–62

Krehbiel, Edward, *Nationalism, War and Society*, New York, 1916

Kropotkin, Peter, *Fields, Factories, and Workshops*, London, 1899
   Mutual Aid: A Factor of Evolution, London, 1902
   Modern Science and Anarchism, Philadelphia, 1903
   Ethics: Origin and Development, trans., London, 1924, 1st edn, Moscow, 1922

Lane, Fred T., *The Violet Flame*, 1899, reprinted New York, 1975

Lankester, E. Ray, 'Degeneration', lecture to British Association for Advancement of Science, Sheffield, August 1879, reprinted in his *The Advancement of Science: Occasional Essays and Addresses*, London, 1890
   The Advancement of Science: Occasional Essays and Addresses, London, 1890
   Nature and Man, Oxford, London, 1905, Romanes lecture for 1905, also included as chapter 1 of Lankester's *The Kingdom of Man*, London, 1907
   The Kingdom of Man, London, 1907

Lapouge, George Vacher de, *Social Selections*, London, 1896, translation of *Les selections sociales*, Paris, 1896
  The Aryan and His Social Role, London, 1899, translation of *L'Aryan, son role social*, Paris, 1899
  Race et milieu social, Paris, 1909
Le Bon, Gustave, *La psychologie des foules*, Paris, 1895, translated into English as *The Crowd*, London, 1896
Lea, Homer, *The Valor of Ignorance*, New York, 1909
  The Day of the Saxon, New York and London, 1912
Lee, Gerald Stanley, *The Voice of the Machines: An Introduction to the Twentieth Century*, New York, 1906
  Crowds; a Moving-Picture of Democracy, New York, London, 1913
  We: A Confession of Faith for the American People During and After the War, London, New York, 1916
Letourneau, C., *Property: Its Origins and Development*, London, 1892
Lilley, W. S., *An Invisible Kingdom: Being Some Chapters in Ethics*, London, 1919
London, Jack, *Martin Eden*, New York, 1909
Lubbock, Sir John, *Prehistoric Times*, London, 1865
  Ants, Bees and Wasps, London, 1872
Lull, Richard Swann, *Organic Evolution: A Text-Book*, New York, 1917
Lydstrom, G. F., *The Diseases of Society*, Philadelphia, 1904
MacBride, Ernest W., *An Introduction to the Study of Heredity*, London, 1924
MacCurdy, John T., *The Psychology of War*, London, 1918
Maine, Sir Henry, *Ancient Law*, London, 1861
Malthus, Thomas Robert, *An Essay on the Principle of Population*, London, 1798; 6th edn, 1826
  Principles of Political Economy, London, 1820
Marshall, Henry Rutgers, *Instinct and Reason*, New York, London, 1898
  War and the Ideal of Peace, London, 916
Martin, Everett Dean, *The Behavior of Crowds: A Psychological Study*, New York, London, 1920
Marx, Karl and Engels, Friedrick, *Selected Correspondence 1846–1859*, Moscow, London, 1953
Masterman, Charles F. G., *The Condition of England*, London, 1909
  England After War: A Study, London, 1922
Masterman, Charles F. G. edn, *The Heart of the Empire: Discussions of Problems of Modern City Life in England*, London, 1901
Maude, Colonel F. N., *War and the World's Life*, London, 1907
Maudsley, Henry, *Physiology and Pathology of the Mind*, London, 1867
  Body and Mind, London, 1870
  Organic to Human: Psychological And Sociological, London, 1916
Maurice, Colonel F., *War*, London, 1891
McDougall, William, *Introduction to Social Psychology*, London, 1908
  The Group Mind, New York, 1920
  An Outline of Psychology, London, 1923
  Janus: The Conquest of War. A Psychological Inquiry, London, 1927
McDougall, William and Hose, Charles, *The Pagan Tribes of Borneo*, London, 1912
McKim, W. Duncan, *Heredity and Human Progress*, London, 1900

McLennan, John F., *Primitive Marriage*, London, 1865
   Studies in Ancient History, London, 1886
Mitchell, Peter Chalmers, *Evolution and the War*, London, 1915
   La Darwinisme et la guerre, translated by M. Solovine, Lettre-préface de M.
      Emile Boutroux, Paris, 1916. Translated into Portuguese as *O Darwinismo e a
      guerra*, Rio Grand do Sul, Brasil, 1918
   Materialism and Vitalism in Biology, Oxford, 1930
   My Fill of Days, London, 1937
   My House in Malaga, London, 1938
More, Adelyne, *Uncontrolled Breeding or Fecundity Versus Civilization*, New York,
   1917
Morgan, Conwy Lloyd, *Introduction to Comparative Psychology*, London, 1894
   Habit and Instinct, London, New York, 1896
   Instinct and Experience, London, 1912
Morgan, Lewis H., *Ancient Society*, New York, 1877
Muirhead, J. H., *German Philosophy in Relation to the War*, London, 1917
Munro, Robert, *From Darwinism to Kaiserism*, Glasgow, 1919
Nasmyth, George, *Social Progress and the Darwinian Theory*: *A Study of Force as
   a Factor in Human Relations*, London, New York, 1916
National Birth-Rate Commission, *Report on The Declining Birth-Rate*, London,
   1916
Newland, C. Bingham, *What is Instinct?*, London, 1916
Nicolai, G. F., *The Biology of War*, translated from the German, New York, 1919
Nietzsche, Friedrich, *Twilight of the Idols*, London, 1896
   Thus Spake Zarathustra, London, 1900
   The Will to Power, 2 vols., Edinburgh and London, 1909, 1910
Novicow, Jacques, *La Fédération de l'Europe*, Paris, 1901, reprinted, Garland, New
      York, London, 1971, with an introduction by Sandi Cooper
   Méchanisme et limites de l'association humaine, Paris, 1912
   War and Its Alleged Benefits, trans. London, 1912. Introduction by Norman
      Angell
Park, Robert E., *Masse and Publikum* [The Crowd and the Public], Bern, 1904,
   trans. Chicago, 1972
Patrick, George Thomas White, *The Psychology of Social Reconstruction*, Boston,
   New York, 1920
Pearson, Karl, *The Grammar of Science*, London, 1892
   The Chances of Death and other Studies in Evolution, London, New York, 1897
   National Life from the Standpoint of Science, London, 1900
   The Problem of Practical Eugenics, London, 1909
   Darwinism, Medical Progress and Eugenics, London, 1912
   Social Problems: *Their Treatment, Past, Present and Future*, London, 1912
Perris, G. H., *A Short History of War and Peace*, London, 1911
Perry, Ralph Barton, *The Present Conflict of Ideals*, New York, 1918
Perry, W. J., *The Children of the Sun*, London, 1923
   The Growth of Civilization, London, 1924
Petrie, W. M. Flinders, *The Revolutions of Civilisation*, London, New York, 1911
Poulton, E. B., *Charles Darwin and the Theory of Natural Selection*, London, 1896
   Charles Darwin and the Origin of Species, London, 1909

Prinzing, F., *Epidemics Resulting from War*, Oxford, 1916

Punnett, R. C., *Mendelism*, London, 1905

Ratzenhofer, Gustav, *Die Sociologische Erkenntnis*, Leipzig, 1898
Soziologie, Leipzig, 1907

Read, Carveth, *The Metaphysics of Nature*, London, 1905
Natural and Social Morals, London, 1909
The Origin of Man and of His Superstitions, Cambridge, 1920

Reclus, Elie, *Primitive Folk: Studies in Comparative Ethnology*, translated from the French, London [?], 1891

Redgrove, H. S., *Indictment of War*, London, 1919

Reich, Emil, *Graeco-Roman Institutions from an Anti-evolutionist Point of View*, Oxford, 1890

Reid, G. Archdall, *Alcoholism: A Study in Heredity*, London, 1901

Rentoul, Robert Reid, *Race Culture: or Race Suicide?*, London, New York, 1906

Report of Proceedings: Problems in Eugenics, Papers to the First International Eugenics Congress, London, 1912

Ribot, Théodule, *The Psychology of the Emotions*, translated from the French, London, 1897

Richet, Charles, *Peace and War*, translated from the French, London, 1906

Ritchie, David G., *Darwinism and Politics*, London, 1889; 2nd edn, 1891 (with additional essays on 'Human Evolution')
Studies in Political and Social Ethics, London, 1902
Philosophical Studies, edited and with a memoir by R. Latta, London, 1905

Rivers, William H. R., *Instinct and the Unconscious: A Contribution to a Biological Theory of the Psycho-Neuroses*, Cambridge, 1920
History and Ethnology, London, 1922

Roberts, Morley, *Bio-Politics*, London, 1938

Robertson, John M. *et al.*, *Essays Towards Peace*, London, 1913

Romanes, George J., *Mental Evolution in Animals, etc*, London, 1883

Ross, Captain Charles, *Representative Government and War*, London, 1903

Rossi, Pascal, *Les suggesteurs et la foule*, Paris, 1904
Sociologie e psicologia collectiva, Rome, 1904

Routledge, Robert, *Discoveries and Inventions of the Nineteenth Century*, London, 1876

Santayana, George, 'The Intellectual Temper of the Age', 1913, N. Henfrey, ed, *Selected Critical Writings of George Santayana*, Cambridge, 1968
Soliloquies, New York, 1922

Schiller, F. C. S., *Social Decay and Eugenical Reform*, London, 1932

Seillière, E., *The German Doctrine of Conquest: A French View*, London, 1914

Shaw, Bernard, *Man and Superman*, London, 1903

Sherrington, Charles S., *The Integrative Action of the Nervous System*, New Haven, 1906, reprinted London, 1911

Sighele, Scipio, *Psychologie des sectes*, Paris, 1898
La Foule criminelle, Paris, 1910

Slaughter, J. W., *The Adolescent*, London, 1912

Small, Albion, *General Sociology*, Chicago, 1905

Smith, E. J., *Race Regeneration*, London, 1918

Smith, Grafton Elliot, *The Evolution of Man*, Oxford, 1924

Culture: The Diffusion Controversy, New York, 1927

Sollas, B. William Johnson, *Ancient Hunters and Their Modern Representatives*, London, 1911

Sorokin, P., *Contemporary Sociological Theories*, New York, London, 1928

Spencer, Herbert, *Social Statics*, London, 1851

    Principles of Psychology, London, 1855

    First Principles, London, 1862

    The Study of Sociology, London, 1873

    The Principles of Sociology, 3 vols., London, 1876–96

    Facts and Comments, London, 1902

Stanley, Hiram H., *Studies in the Evolutionary Psychology of Feeling*, London, New York, 1895

Stead, W. T., 'A Russian Cobden', chapter 5 of his *United States of Europe*, London, 1899

Steed, Henry Wickham, *Through Thirty Years*, London, 1924

Steinmetz, S. R., *Der Krieg als Soziologisches Problem*, Amsterdam 1899

    Die Philosophie des Krieges, Leipzig, 1907

Stephen, Leslie, *The Science of Ethics*, London, 1882

Stoddard, Lothrop, *The Revolt Against Civilization*, New York, 1923

Strachey, John St Loe, *A New Way of Life*, London, 1909

Strong, Josiah, *Expansion Under New World-Conditions*, New York, 1900

Stuart, Sir Campbell, *The Secrets of Crewe House*, London, 1920

Sumner, William Graham, *Folkways: a Study of the Sociological Importance of Usages, Customs, Mores and Morals*, Boston, 1907

    War and Other Essays, edited by A. G. Keller, New Haven, 1911

Sutherland, Alexander, *Origin and Growth of the Moral Instinct*, London, 1898

Talbot, Eugene S., *Degeneracy*, London, 1898

Talbot, Edward S., *The War and Conscience*, London, 1914

Teggart, Frederick J., *The Processes of History*, New Haven, London, 1918

Thomson, J. Arthur, *Heredity*, London, 1909

Thorndike, Edward, *Educational Psychology: Briefer Course*, New York, 1914

Todd, Arthur J., *Theories of Social Progress*, New York, 1918

Trotter, Wilfred, *The Instincts of the Herd in Peace and War*, London, 1916, 2nd edn, 1919

Tylor, E. B., *Primitive Culture*, London, 1871

Veblen, Thorstein, *An Inquiry into the Nature of Peace*, New York, 1917

    The Instinct of Workmanship, New York, 1924

Waldstein, Sir Charles, *Aristodemocracy: from the Great War back to Moses, Christ and Plato*, London, 1916

    Patriotism, National and International, London, 1917

    What Germany is Fighting For, London, 1917

    The Next War: Wilsonism and Anti-Wilsonism, Cambridge, 1918

    Eugenics, Civics, Ethics, Cambridge, 1920

Wallace, Alfred Russel, 'The Origin of Human Races and the Antiquity of Man Deduced from the theory of "Natural Selection"', *Anthropological Review: Journal of the Anthropological Society of London*, 2 (1864), clviii–clxxxvii; reprinted (with changes) in Wallace, *Contributions to the Theory of Natural Selection*, London, 1870, essay 9

'Polynesians and their Migrations', *Quarterly Journal of Science* (April 1867); reprinted in *Studies: Scientific and Social*, vol. I, London, 1900, pp. 399–415

The Malay Archipelago, London, 1869

Contributions to the Theory of Natural Selection, London, 1870

Darwinism (London, 1889)

'Human Selection', *Fortnightly Review*, 48 NS (1890), 325–37; reprinted in *Studies: Scientific and Social*, vol. I, pp. 509–26

'Human Progress, Past and Future', *Arena* (January 1892); reprinted in *Studies: Scientific and Social*, vol. II, pp. 493–508

The Wonderful Century: Its Successes and Failures, London, 1898

'The Causes of War and the Remedies', *L'Humanité Nouvelle* (May 1899); reprinted in *Studies: Scientific and Social*, vol. II, pp. 384–93

Studies: Scientific and Social, 2 vols., London, 1900

Wallas, Graham, *Human Nature in Politics*, London, 1908

The Great Society, London, 1914

Our Social Heritage, London, 1921

Walsh, W., *The Moral Damage of War*, London, 1902

Ward, Lester Frank, *Dynamic Sociology*, 2 vols, New York, 1883

The Psychic Factors of Civilization, Boston, 1893

Pure Sociology, New York, 1903

Watson, John B., *Behavior*, New York, 1914

Webb, Sidney and Beatrice, *The Decay of Capitalist Civilization*, London, 1923

Weismann, August, *Studies in the Theory of Descent*, trans., London, 1882

Essays upon Heredity and Kindred Biological Problems, Oxford, trans., 1888

The Germ Plasm: A Theory of Heredity, trans., New York, 1893

Wells, H. G., *Anticipations of the Reaction of Mechanical and Scientific Progress upon Human Life and Thought*, London, 1901

'The Collapse of Civilisation', *Works of H. G. Wells*, vol. xx, New York, 1924–7

The Croquet Player, London, 1936

Wheeler, William Morton, *Ants: Their Structure Development and Behavior*, New York, 1910

Emergent Evolution and the Social, London, 1927

Whetham, William Cecil Dampier, *The War and the Nation*, London, 1917

White, Arnold, *Efficiency and Empire*, London, 1901, reprinted Harvester, 1973, introduction by G. R. Searle

Wilkinson, Spencer, *War and Policy*, London, 1910

Wilm, E. C., *The Theories of Instinct: A Study in the History of Psychology*, New Haven, London, 1925

Wilson, Albert, *Unfinished Man: A Scientific Analysis of the Psychopath or Human Degenerate*, London, 1910

Woodhull Martin, Victoria C., *The Rapid Multiplication of the Unfit*, London, 1891

Woods, F. A., and Baltzly, A., *Is War Diminishing?*, Boston, 1915

Wright, Philip Quincey, *A Study of War*, Chicago, 1942

Wundt, Wilhelm, *Lectures on Human and Animal Psychology*, trans. from 2nd German edition by J. E. Creighton and E. B. Titchener, London, New York, 1894

Wyatt, Harold Frazer and Horton Smith, L. G. H., *The Passing of the Great Fleet*, London, 1909

Britain's Imminent Danger, London, 1912
Yeats-Brown, F., *Dogs of War*, London, 1934
Yerkes, Robert M., *The Dancing Mouse*, New York, 1907
    Introduction to Psychology, New York, 1911
    The Mental Life of Monkeys and Apes, New York, 1916
    Almost Human, New York, London, 1925.

ARTICLES

Acher, R. A., 'Spontaneous Constructions and Primitive Activities of Children
    Analogous to Those of Primitive Man', *American Journal of Psychology*, 21
    (1910), 114–50
Allen, Grant, 'The New Theory of Heredity', *Review of Reviews*, 1 (1890), 537–8
Anon, "America's Fighting Stocks", *Journal of Heredity*, 8, 10 (1917), 435–41
Anon, 'The Evolution of John Burroughs', *Current Opinion*, 70 (1921), 666–7
Anon, 'The Intellectual Charm of War', *Spectator*, 58 (25 April 1885), 542–3
Aston, George, '"Military" and "Militarist"', *Nineteenth Century*, 86 (1919),
    631–9
Barnes, Harry E., 'The Struggle of Races and Social Groups as a Factor in the
    Development of Political and Social Institutions: An Exposition and Critique
    of the Sociological System of Ludwig Gumplowicz', *Journal of Race
    Development*, 9 (1919), 394–419
    'A Sociological Criticism of War and Militarism: An Analysis of the Doctrines
    of Jacques Novicow', *Journal of International Relations*, 12, 2 (1921), 238–65
Basevi, Major W. H. F., 'The Great Transition', *Journal of the Royal United
    Service Institution*, NS 59, 438 (1914), 419–20
Bassett-Smith, P. W., 'Improvement in the Health of the Royal Navy during the
    Last Ten Years', *Journal of State Medicine*, 23 (1915), 257–61
Battine, Cecil, 'What is Militarism?', *Fortnightly Review*, 111 (1919), 375–86
Bloch, Jean de, 'Wars of the Future', *Contemporary Review*, 80 (1901), 305–32
Blyth, Estelle, 'On the Use of War', *United Service Magazine*, NS 44, 997 (1911),
    247–51
Boag, Harold, 'Human Capital and the Cost of the War', *Journal of the Royal
    Statistical Society*, 79 (1917), 7–17
Boulger, Demetrius, 'The Peace of Europe', *United Services Magazine*, 44, 995
    (1911), 1
Bradbury, Harriet B., 'War as a Necessity of Evolution', *The Arena*, 21 (1899),
    94–6
Bridge, C. F., 'War as Medicine', *Hibbert Journal* 16 (October 1917), 47–54
Bryce, James, 'War and Human Progress', *Atlantic Monthly* 118 (1916), 301–15
Bullard, Arthur, 'Arms and the Instincts', *Harper's Magazine* 144 (1922), 167–74
Burroughs, John, 'The Arrival of the Fit', *North American Review*, 201 (1915),
    197–201
Cannon, Walter Bradford, 'The Interrelationships of Emotions as Suggested by
    Recent Physiological Researches', *American J. Psychology*, 25 (1914) 256–82
Carliol, J. W., 'The Inner Meaning of the War', *Nineteenth Century*, 76 (1914),
    730–36
Carr, H. Wildon, 'Instinct and Intelligence', *British Journal of Psychology*, 3
    (1910), 230–6

Carver, Thomas Nixon, 'The Probable Effects of the European War upon the Redistribution of Population', *Scientia*, 21 (1917), 144–51

Case, Clarence Marsh, 'Instinctive and Cultural Factors in Group Conflicts', *American Journal of Sociology* 28, 1 (1922), 1–20

Chambers, Theodore G., 'Darwinian Attitude to the War', *Current Opinion*, 59 (1915), 333–34

'Eugenics and the War', *Eugenics Review*, 6 (1914–15), 271–90

Cole, Leon J., 'Biological Philosophy and the War', *Scientific Monthly* 8 (1919), 247–57

Conklin, Edwin Grant, 'Biology and Democracy', *Scribner's Magazine*, 65 (1919), 403–12

Copeland, E. B., 'War Selection in the Philippines', *Scientific Monthly*, 3 (1916), 151–4

Coulton, G. G., 'War and the Breed', *Eugenics Review*, 7 (1915–16), 287–92

Crew, F. A. E., 'A Biologist in a New Environment', *Eugenics Review*, 11 (1919–20), 119–23

Darwin, Leonard, 'On the Statistical Enquiries Needed after the War in Connection with Eugenics', *Journal of the Royal Statistical Society*, 79 (1916), 159–75

'The Disabled Sailor and Soldier and the Future of Our Race', *Eugenics Review*, 9 (1917), 1–17

Davenport, C. B. and Love, A. G., 'Defects Found in Drafted Men', *Scientific Monthly*, 10, (1920), 5–25, 125–41

Dean, James Camden, 'War and Nature', *Forum and Century*, 57 (1917), 365–70

Dewey, John, 'On Understanding the Mind of Germany', *Atlantic Monthly*, 117 (1916), 251–62

Dickie, Robert M., 'War and Survival of the Fittest', *Scientific American*, 75 (4 January 1913), 3

Dunlap, Knight, 'Are There Any Instincts?', *Journal of Abnormal Psychology*, 14 (1919), 307–11

Durant, Will, 'The Biology of War', *The Dial*, 66 (25 January 1919), 84–5

Ellis, Havelock, 'The German Spirit', *Atlantic Monthly*, 115 (1915), 551–9

Ellwood, Charles A., 'The Instinctive Element in Human Society', *Popular Science Monthly* (March 1912), 263–72

Fisher, R. A., 'Some Hopes of a Eugenist', *Eugenics Review*, 4 (1912–13), 26–38

'Positive Eugenics', *Eugenics Review*, 9 (1917–18), 206–12

Goler, G. W., 'War: Some of its Effects upon the Health of the Military and Civil Population...', *New York State Journal of Medicine*, 18, 3 (1918), 113–17

Grasset, Joseph, 'La biologie humaine', *La Revue Scientifique*, 55 (1917), 65–9

Greenwood, Major, 'British Loss of Life in the Wars of 1794–1815 and in 1914–1918', *Journal of the Royal Statistical Society*, 105, 1 (1942), 1–11

Gumplowicz, Ludwig, 'An Austrian Appreciation of Lester F. Ward', *American Journal of Sociology*, 10 (1904–5), 643–53

Hall, A. D., 'National Ideals: English and German', *Edinburgh Review*, 452 (1915), 290–308

Hall, G. Stanley, 'A Study of Anger', *American Journal of Psychology*, 10 (1899), 516–91

'A Synthetic Study of Fear', *American Journal of Psychology*, 25, 2, (1914), 149–200, and 25, 3 (1914), 321–92

'Recreation and Reversion', *Pedagogical Seminary*, 22 (1915), 510–20

'Psychology and War', *Journal of Heredity*, 8 (1917), 442–47

Hamon, Augustin, 'Le bilan de la guerre mondiale', *Scientia*, 7 (1919), 39–46

Hapgood, Norman, 'Bernhardi and the United States', *Harpers Weekly*, 59 (1914), 367–8

Hart, R. C., 'A Vindication of War', *Nineteenth Century*, 70 (1911), 226–39

Hayes, Carlton, 'The War of Nations', *Political Science Quarterly*, 29 (1914), 687–707

Hobson, John A., 'The Scientific Basis of Imperialism', *Political Science Quarterly*, 17 (1902), 460–89

Holmes, Samuel Jackson, 'The Decadence of Human Heredity', *Atlantic Monthly*, 114 (1914), 302–8

Howard, William Lee, 'The Psychology of War', *New York Medical Journal*, 101 (1915), 15–18

Howerth, I. W., 'War and Social Economy', *International Journal of Ethics*, 17 (1906–7), 70–8

'War and the Progress of Society', *Popular Science Monthly*, 87 (1915), 195–99

'War and Survival of the Fittest', *Scientific Monthly*, 3 (1916), 488–97

'The Great War and the Instinct of the Herd', *International Journal of Ethics*, 29 (1919), 174–87

Hrdlicka, Ales, 'The Effects of the War on the Race', *Art and Archaeology*, 7 (1918), 404–7

Hugins, Roland, 'The Eugenic Judgement of War', *South Atlantic Quarterly*, 13, 4 (October 1914), 303–9

'Norman Angellism Under Fire', *Forum and Century*, 54 (1915), 155–64

'Militant Minorities', *Atlantic Monthly*, 123 (1919), 701–5

Huxley, T. H., 'Mr Darwin's Critics', *Contemporary Review*, 18 (1871), 443–76

Inge, William Ralph, 'Patriotism', *Quarterly Review*, 224 (1915), 71–93

Jacks, L. P., 'Human Nature and the War', *Current History*, 5 (1916), 113–15

'Arms and Men: A Study in Habit', *Hibbert Journal*, 17 (1919), 21–8

James, Edwin, D., 'The Malthusian Doctrine and War', *Scientific Monthly*, 2 (1916), 260–71

Jastrzebski, S. de, 'War and the Balance of the Sexes', *Eugenics Review*, 10 (1918), 76–80

Jefferson, Charles Edward, 'The Delusion of Militarism', *Atlantic Monthly*, 103 (1909), 379–88

Jensen, Johannes V., 'Darwinism and the War', *Living Age*, 3, 18 (1923), 257–77

Johnson, George E., 'The Fighting Instinct: Its Place in Life', *Survey*, 25 (4 December 1915), 243–8

Johnson, Roswell H., 'Natural Selection in War', *Journal of Heredity*, 6, 11 (1915), 546–8

Jordan, David Starr, 'War and Manhood', *Eugenics Review*, 2 (1910), 95–109

'The Eugenics of War', *Eugenics Review*, 5 (1913), 197–213

'War Selection in the Ancient World', *Scientific Monthly*, 1 (1915), 36–43

'War Selection in Western Europe', *Popular Science Monthly*, 87 (1915), 143–54

'The Repair of Human Wastage', *Independent*, 89 (1917), 179–80

'Social Darwinism', *The Public* (30 March 1918), 400–1

'War and Genetic Values', *Journal of Heredity*, 10 (1919), 223–5

Keene, Colonel A., 'War and How to Meet It: The Views of Some Great British Thinkers', *Hibbert Journal*, 13 (1914–15), 765–80

Keith, Arthur, 'War as a Factor in Racial Evolution', *St Thomas's Hospital Gazette*, 25 (1915), 153–62

'On Certain Factors Concerned in the Evolution of Human Races', *Journal of the Royal Anthropological Institute*, 46 (1916), 10–34

'The Differentiation of Mankind into Racial Types', *Nature*, 1104 (1919), 301–5

Kellogg, Vernon L., 'Eugenics and Militarism', *Atlantic Monthly*, 112 (1913), 99–108

'The Bionomics of War: Race Modification by Military Selection', *Journal of Social Hygiene*, 1 (1914), 44–52

'War for Evolution's Sake', *Unpopular Review*, 10 (1918), 146–59

'War and Human Evolution: Germanized', *North American Review*, 207 (1918), 364–9

'Race and Americanization', *Yale Review*, NS 10 (1921), 729–40

Kessler, Charles, 'Le pacifisme', *Le Correspondent*, 221 (1905), 855–64

Kidd, Benjamin, 'Darwin's Successor at Home', *Review of Reviews*, 2, 12 (1890), 647–50

'Darwinism', *Encyclopedia of Religion and Ethics*, Edinburgh, New York (1911), vol. IV, 402–5

Kipling, Rudyard, 'The Army of a Dream', *Morning Post* (June 1904)

Kroebner, A. L., 'The Superorganic', *American Anthropologist*, NS 19, 2 (1917), 163–213

La Torre F., 'Italian View on Eugenics', *Lancet*, 2 (6 November 1915), 1038–9

Laski, Harold J., 'The Scope of Eugenics', *Westminster Review*, 174 (1910), 25–34

Lindsay, J. A., 'The Case for and against Eugenics', *Nineteenth Century*, 72, 5 (1912), 546–57

'The Eugenic and Social Influence of the War', *Eugenics Review*, 10, (1918–19), 133–44

Loeb, Jacques, 'Biology and War', *Science*, 45, 1152 (1917), 73–6

Long, R. E. C., 'Jean de Bloch', *Fortnightly Review*, 321 (1902), 228–36

Love, Lt.-Col. Albert G., 'A Comparison of White and Colored Troops in Respect to Incidence of Disease', *Proceedings of the National Academy of Sciences*, 5 (1919), 58–67

Luce, S. B. (Rear-Admiral, US), 'The Benefits of War', *North American Review*, 153 (1891), 672–83

Lundberg, Emma O., 'The Illegitimate Child and War Conditions', *American Journal of Physical Anthropology*, 1, 3 (1918), 338–52

Macfie, Ronald Campbell, 'Some of the Evolutionary Consequences of War', *Science Progress*, 12A, 45 (1917), 132–7

Mahan, A. T. (Rear-Admiral, US), 'The Place of Force in International Relations', *North American Review*, 195 (1912), 28–39

Mallet, Sir Bernard, 'Vital Statistics as Affected by the War', *Journal of the Royal Statistical Society*, 81, 1 (January 1918), 1–36

Mallock, W. H., 'General von Bernhardi on the Moral Logic of War', *Nineteenth Century*, 76 (1914), 1360–76

Marcus, Joseph H., 'Man After the War', *New York Medical Journal*, cited *Literary Digest*, 57 (6 April 1918), 34–5

Marshall, H. Rutgers, 'The Relation of Instinct and Intelligence', *British Journal of Psychology*, 5 (1912), 247–66
    'The Pacifist at War', *Atlantic Monthly*, 121 (1918), 665–7
Maude, Colonel F. N., 'National Psychology in the War', *The Quest* (January 1917), 211–32
McDougall, William, 'Instinct and Intelligence', *British Journal of Psychology*, 3 (1910), 250–66
Mead, Edwin D., 'Jean de Bloch and the "Future of War"', *New England Magazine*, 28 (1903), 298–309
Mead, Margaret, 'Warfare is only an Invention – Not a Biological Necessity', *Asia*, 40 (1940), 402–5
Melville, C. H., 'Eugenics and Military Service', *Eugenics Review*, 2 (1910–11), 53–60
Miller, Joseph Dana, 'Militarism or Manhood', *The Arena*, 24 (1900), 379–92
Mitchell, Peter Chalmers, 'The Duration of Life', *Nature*, 37 (1888), 541–2
    [?], 'A Word with Mr. Huxley', *National Review*, 21 (1893), 713–15. [attributed in *Poole's Index*, vol. 4, p. 190.]
    'Professor Tyndall', *New Review*, 10, 56 (1894), 77–85
    'The Spencer-Weismann Controversy', *Nature*, 49 (1894), 373–4
    'Pasteur', *New Review*, 13, 78 (1895), 537–44
    [?], pseudonym of 'A Biologist', 'A Biological View of Our Foreign Policy', *Saturday Review*, 82, 210 (1896), 118–20 [attribution in Mitchell, *My Fill of Days*, London (1937), p. 59].
    'The Future of the Tropics', *North American Review*, 176 (1903), 711–18
    'The Making of Modern Races', *North American Review*, 179 (1904), 526–42
    [?], 'Sir Ray Lankester on the Darwinian Attitude to War', *Current Opinion*, 59 (1915), 333–4
Mivart, St George, 'Evolution in Professor Huxley', *Nineteenth Century*, 34 (1893), 198–211
Morgan, Conwy Lloyd, 'Some Definitions of Instinct', *Natural Science*, 7 (1895), 321–9
    'Instinct and Intelligence', *British Journal of Psychology*, 3 (1910), 219–29
Morgan, J. H., 'Treitschke', *Nineteenth Century*, 76 (1914), 776–81
Mügge, M., 'Eugenics and the Superman: A Racial Science and a Racial Religion', *Eugenics Review*, 1 (1909–10), 184–93
Mumford, Alfred A., 'Physical Degeneration of the British Race', *Fortnightly Review*, 76 (1904), 324–64
Murray, Gilbert, 'Herd Instinct and War', *Atlantic Monthly*, 115 (1915), 830–9
Myers, Charles S., 'Instinct and Intelligence', *British Journal of Psychology*, 3 (1910), 209–18
O'Farrell, M. M., 'War and the Stature of the Population', *Eugenics Review*, 9 (1917–18), 218–22
Palmer, General John McAuley, 'The Insurance of Peace', *Scribner's Magazine*, 51 (1912), 186–91
Parker, A. C., 'The Peace Policy of the Iroquois', *Southern Workmen*, 40 (1911), 691–9
Patrick, George Thomas White, 'The Psychology of War', *Popular Science Monthly*, 87 (1915), 155–68

Pearl, Raymond, 'Biology and War', *Journal of Washington Academy of Science*, 8 (1918), 341–60; reprinted Pearl, *Studies in Human Biology* (Baltimore, 1924), 534–49

Perry, W. J., 'The Peaceable Habits of Primitive Communities: An Anthropological Study of the Golden Age', *Hibbert Journal*, 16 (1917), 28–46
   'An Ethological Study of Warfare', *Manchester Literary and Philosophical Society Memoirs*, 61, 6 (1917), 1–16

Popenoe, Paul, 'The Racial Value of Death', *Advocate of Peace* (Washington) (1918), 175–6

Poulton, E. B., 'Eugenic Problems After the Great War', *Eugenics Review*, 8 (1916), 34–49

Rabaud, Etienne, 'Qu'est-ce que la biologie humaine', *La Revue Scientifique*, 55 (1917), 163–68

Ratzenhofer, Gustav, 'The Problems of Sociology', *American Journal of Sociology*, 10 (1904–5), 177–88

Read, Sir Hercules, 'Anthropology and War', *Journal of the Royal Anthropological Institute*, 49 (1919), 12–19

Read, Carveth, 'On the Differentiation of Man from the Anthropoids', *Man* (November 1914), 181–6

Reid, G. Archdall, 'The Biological Foundation of Society', *Sociological Papers*, 3 (1906), 3–52

Richardson, A. M., 'The Professional Classes, the War, and the Birth-Rate', *Nineteenth Century*, 77 (1915), 603–8

Ritchie, D. G., 'Social Evolution', *International Journal of Ethics*, 6 (1895–6), 165–81
   'Darwinism and Politics', *Fortnightly Review*, 86 (1909), 519–32

Romanes, George J., 'The Darwinian Theory of Instinct', *Nineteenth Century*, 16, 91 (1884), 434–50

Rosenblatt, Alfred, 'The Civilizing Influences of War', *Current History*, 5 (1916), 103–5

Ross, Sir Ronald, 'Evolution and War', *Science Progress*, 9 (1914), 514–16 (paraphrased by G. Taylor-Loban).

Rossiter, William S., 'Influence of the War upon the Population', *North American Review*, 203 (1916), 700–10

Russell, Bertrand, 'The Ethics of War', *International Journal of Ethics*, 25 (1915), 127–42

Saleeby, C. W., 'Imperial Health and the Dysgenics of War', *Journal of State Medicine*, 25 (1917), 307–16

Savorgnan, F., 'La problème de la population', *Scientia*, 1–3 (1918), 200–8

Sergi, Giuseppi, 'Does War Lower the Birth Rate?', *Current History*, 5 (1916), 272–3

Shadwell, A., 'German War Literature', *Edinburgh Review*, 222 (1915), 22–40

Shaler, N. S., 'The Natural History of Warfare', *North American Review*, 162 (1896), 328–40

Skrine, F. M., 'War and German Universities', *Journal of the Royal United Service Institution*, 60, 439 (1915), 469–75

Smith, G. Elliot, 'Notes Upon the Natural Subdivision of the Cerebral Hemisphere', *Journal of Anatomy and Physiology*, London, 35 (1901), 431–54

'The Morphology of the Occipital Region of the Cerebral Hemisphere in Man and the Apes', *Anatomischer Anzeiger*, 24 (1904), 436–51

'The Term "Archipallium" – a Disclaimer', *Anatomischer Anzeiger*, 35 (1910), 429–30

Smith, Munroe, 'The German Theory of Warfare', *North American Review*, 206 (1917), 394–405

Spearman, Charles, 'The Heredity of Abilities', *Eugenics Review*, 6 (1914–15), 219–37

Spencer, Herbert, 'A Theory of Population, Deduced from the General Law of Animal Fertility', *Westminster Review*, 57 (1852), 468–501

'Theories of Primitive Marriage', *Popular Science Monthly*, 10 (1876), 272–85

'On Justice', *Nineteenth Century*, 27 (1890), 435–48, 608–20

Stead, William T., 'Character Sketch: The Late M. Jean de Bloch', *Review of Reviews*, 25 (15 February 1902), 136–42

Stephen, Leslie, 'Ethics and the Struggle for Existence', *Contemporary Review*, 64 (1893), 157–70

Stevenson, J. J., 'Is This a Degenerate Age?', *Popular Science Monthly*, 60 (1902), 481–94

Stout, G. F., 'Instinct and Intelligence', *British Journal of Psychology*, 3 (1910), 237–49

Sutherland, Alexander, 'The Natural Decline of Warfare', *Nineteenth Century*, 45 (1899), 570–8

Taylor, G. R. Stirling, "Horrors" in Peace Time – and Their Commercial Exploiters', *Nineteenth Century and After*, 93 (1923), 633–41

Thacker, A. G., 'Some Eugenic Effects of War', *Science Progress*, 10 (1915), 73–80

Thomson, J. Arthur, 'The Sociological Appeal to Biology', *Sociological Papers*, 3 (1906), 157–96

'Eugenics and War', *Eugenics Review*, 7 (1915), 1–14

Tredgold, A. F., 'The Problem of Degeneracy', *Quarterly Review*, 228 (1917), 31–50

Trotter, Wilfred, 'The Herd Instinct and its Bearing on the Psychology of Civilized Man', *Sociological Review*, 1 (1908), 227–48

'Sociological Application of the Psychology of the Herd Instinct', *Sociological Review*, 2 (1909), 36–54

Ulmann, Heinrich, 'Heinrich Von Treitschke and War', *Living Age*, 307 (1920), 130–5

Villard, Oswald Garrison, 'Militarism and Democracy in Germany', *Scribner's Magazine*, 57 (1915), 245–51

Wallace, Alfred Russel, 'The Future of Civilisation', *Nature*, 49 (12 April 1894).

'Evolution and Character', *Fortnightly Review*, vol. 82 NS (1908), 1–24

Wallas, Graham, 'Crowd Morality', *Hibbert Journal*, 15 (1915), 224–8

Ward, Lester F., 'Evolution of Social Structures', *American Journal of Sociology*, 10 (1904–5), 589–605

'Social and Biological Struggles', *American Journal of Sociology*, 13, (1907), 289–99

'Eugenics, Euthenics, and Eudemics', *American Journal of Sociology*, 18 (1913), 737–54

Warren, Howard C., 'A Classification of Reflexes, Instincts and Emotional Phenomena', *Psychological Review*, 26, 3 (1919), 197–203

Watson, John, 'German Philosophy and the War', *Queen's Quarterly*, 23 (1916), 365–79

Webb, Sidney, 'Eugenics and the Poor Law: The Minority Report', *Eugenics Review*, 2 (1910–11), 233–7

Wells, D. Collin, 'Social Darwinism', *American Journal of Sociology*, 12 (1907), 695–716

Westermarck, Edward, 'The Essence of Revenge', *Mind* NS 27 (1898), 289–310

Whetham, William Cecil Dampier, 'The War and the Race', *Quarterly Review*, 227 (1917), 17–38

Whittaker, Herman, 'Weismannism and its Relation to Socialism', *International Socialist Review*, 1, 9 (1901), 513–23

Wyatt, Harold Frazer, 'War as the Supreme Test of National Value', *Nineteenth Century*, 45 (1899), 216–25

 'God's Test by War', *Nineteenth Century*, 76 (September, 1914), 489–510; originally published *ibid.* (April 1911)

Yerkes, Robert M., 'The Heredity of Savageness and Wildness in Rats', *Journal of Animal Behavior*, 3 (1913), 286–96.

Yerkes, Robert M., and Bloomfield, Daniel, 'Do Kittens Instinctively Kill Mice?', *Psychological Bulletin*, 7, 8 (1910), 253–63

Secondary (post-1945)

BOOKS AND PAMPHLETS

Adams, Mark B., *The Wellborn Science*: *Eugenics in Germany, France, Brazil and Russia*, New York, Oxford, 1990

Aho, James Alfred, *German Realpolitik and American Sociology*: *An Inquiry into the Sources and Political Significance of the Sociology of Conflict*, London, 1975

Allett, John, *New Liberalism*: *The Political Economy of J. A. Hobson*, Toronto, London, 1981

Appleman, P., edn, *Darwin*: *A Norton Critical Edition*, New York, 1970

Ardrey, C. Robert, *The Hunting Hypothesis*, New York, 1976

Avrich, Paul, *The Anarchists in the Russian Revolution*, London, 1973

Bannister, Robert C., *Social Darwinism*: *Science and Myth*, Philadelphia, 1979
 Sociology and Scientism: *The American Quest for Objectivity*, 1800–1940, Chapel Hill, London, 1987
 Social Darwinism: *Science and Myth in Anglo-American Social Thought*, revised edition, Philadelphia, 1988

Barnes, B. and Shapin, S., eds., *Natural Order*: *Historical Studies of Scientific Cultures*, Beverly Hills, 1979, esp. ch. 5, Barnes and Shapin, 'Darwin and Social Darwinism; Purity and History'

Barnett, S. A., 'Models and Morals: Biological Images of Man' in *Multidisciplinary Approaches to Aggression Research*, edited by P. F. Brian and D. Benton, Elsevier, 1981
 Biology and Freedom, Cambridge, 1988

Barraclough, Geoffrey, *An Introduction to Contemporary History*, Harmondsworth, 1964

Beckett, Ian F. W., 'The Nation in Arms, 1914–18', in *A Nation in Arms: A Social Study of the British Army in the First World War*, edited by I. F. W. Beckett and K. Simpson, Manchester, 1985, pp. 1–7

Beer, Gavin de, *Charles Darwin*, London, 1963

Beer, Gillian, *Darwin's Plots: Evolutionary Narrative in Darwin, George Eliot and Nineteenth Century Fiction*, London, 1983

'Darwin's Reading and the Fictions of Development', in *The Darwinian Heritage*, edited by David Kohn, Princeton, 1985, pp. 543–88

Bellomy, Donald C., 'Social Darwinism Revisited', in *Perspectives in American History*, edited by B. Bailyn, D. Fleming and S. Thernstrom, new series, vol. I, Cambridge, 1984

Berger, Martin, *Engels, Armies and Revolution: The Revolutionary Tactics of Classical Marxism*, Hamden, Conn., 1977

Best, Geoffrey, 'Militarism and the Victorian Public School', in *The Victorian Public School*, edited by B. Simon and I. Bradley, London, 1975

Biddiss, Michael D., *The Age of the Masses*, Harmondsworth, 1977

Blacker, C. P., *Eugenics: Galton and After*, London, 1952

Blainey, Geoffrey, *The Causes of War*, London, 1973

Boakes, Robert, *From Darwin to Behaviourism*, Cambridge, 1984

Bock, Kenneth, *Human Nature and History: A Response to Sociobiology*, New York, 1980

Bowler, Peter J., *The Eclipse of Darwinism: Anti-Darwinian Evolution Theories in the Decades around 1900*, Baltimore, London, 1983

Theories of Human Evolution: A Century of Debate, 1844–1944, Baltimore, London, 1986

Bramson, Leon, *The Political Context of Sociology*, Princeton, 1961

Bramson, Leon, and Goethals, George W., eds., *War: Studies From Psychology, Sociology, Anthropology*, New York, London, 1964

Bressler, Marvin, 'Biological Determinism and Ideological Indeterminacy', in *Sociobiology and Human Politics*, edited by Elliott White, Lexington, Mass., Toronto, 1981, pp. 181–92

Bridgwater, Patrick, *Nietzsche in Anglosaxony*, Leicester, 1972

Bryant, Christopher, G. A., *Positivism in Social Theory and Research*, London, 1985

Burrow, John, Introduction to Charles Darwin, *The Origin of Species*, Harmondsworth, 1969, pp. 11–48

'Bagehot and the Nature of Political Understanding', in *That Noble Science of Politics: A Study in Nineteenth-Century Intellectual History*, edited by S. Collini, D. Winch and J. Burrow, Cambridge, 1983, pp. 161–82

Bush, Stephen G., *The Temperature of History: Phases of Science and Culture in the Nineteenth Century*, New York, 1978

Chase, A., *The Legacy of Malthus*, New York, 1977

Chickering, Roger, *Imperial Germany and World Without War: The Peace Movement and German Society*, 1892–1914, Princeton, 1975

Clark, Linda L., *Social Darwinism in France*, Alabama, 1984

Clarke, I. F., *Voices Prophesying War*, 1863–1984, London, 1966

Colinvaux, Paul, *The Fates of Nations: A Biological Theory of History*, New York, 1980

Cravens, H., *American Scientists and the Heredity-Environment Controversy*, 1900–1944, Philadelphia, 1978

Creighton, Colin and Shaw, Martin, eds., *The Sociology of War and Peace*, London, 1987

Crook, David Paul, *Benjamin Kidd: Portrait of a Social Darwinist*, Cambridge, 1984

Dickson, Lovat, *H. G. Wells*, Harmondsworth, 1972

Dobzhansky, T., *Genetics and the Origin of Species*, New York, 1937

Dubos, René, *Mirage of Health: Utopias, Progress and Biological Change*, London, 1960

Durant, John, *Darwinism and Divinity*, Oxford, New York, 1985

Eksteins, Modris, *Rites of Spring: The Great War and the Birth of the Modern Age*, Boston, 1989

Engel, J. R., *Sacred Sands: The Struggle for Community in the Indiana Dunes*, Middletown, Conn., 1983

English, Peter C., *Shock, Physiological Surgery, and George Washington Crile: Medical Innovation in the Progressive Era*, Westport, London, 1980

Fichman, M. F., *Alfred Russel Wallace*, Boston, 1981

Fischer, Fritz, *War of Illusions: German Policies from 1911 to 1914*, trans., Marion Jackson, London, 1975

Fletcher, R., *Instinct in Man*, London, 1957

Freeden, Michael, *The New Liberalism: An Ideology of Social Reform (Oxford, 1978)*

edn, *J. A. Hobson: A Reader*, London, 1988

Fromm, Erich, *The Anatomy of Human Destructiveness*, New York, 1973

Gasman, D., *The Scientific Origins of National Socialism: Social Darwinism in Ernst Haeckel and the German Monist League*, London, New York, 1921

Ghiselin, M. T., *The Triumph of the Darwinian Method*, Berkeley, 1969

Gillispie, C. C., *The Edge of Objectivity*, Princeton, 1960

Gilman, R., *Decadence*, London, 1979

Gilman, S. and C., and Edwards J., eds., *Degeneration*, New York, 1985

Givens, R. D. and Nettleship, M. A., *Discussions on War and Human Aggressiveness*, The Hague, 1976

Glick, T. F. edn, *The Comparative Reception of Darwinism*, Austin, 1974

Gould, Stephen Jay, *Ever Since Darwin*, Harmondsworth, 1980

Greene, John C., *Science, Ideology and World View*, Berkeley, London, 1981

Gruber, Howard E., *Darwin on Man: a Psychological Study of Scientific Creativity; together with Darwin's Early and Unpublished Notebooks*, transcribed and annotated by Paul Barrett; foreword by Jean Piaget, London, 1974

Haller, J. S., *Outcasts from Evolution: Scientific Attitudes of Racial Inferiority*, 1859–1900, New York, 1971

Haller, Mark, *Eugenics: Hereditarian Attitudes in American Thought*, Rutgers, 1963

Halliday, R. J., *John Stuart Mill*, London, 1976

Harvey, Joy, 'Evolutionism Transformed: Positivists and Materialists in the *Société D'Anthropologie De Paris* from Second Empire to Third Republic', in *The Wider Domain of Evolutionary Thought*, edited by D. Oldroyd and I. Langham, Dordrecht, London, Boston, 1983, pp. 289–310

Hays, Alice N., comp., *David Starr Jordan: A Bibliography of His Writings*, 1871–1931, Stanford, London, 1952

Heidbreder, Edna, 'William McDougall and Social Psychology', in Mary Henle, et. al., *Historical Conceptions of Psychology*, New York, 1973, pp. 267–75

Henfrey, N. ed, *Selected Critical Writings of George Santayana*, Cambridge, 1968

Hodge, M. J. S., and Kohn, D., 'The Immediate Origins of Natural Selection', in *The Darwinian Heritage*, edited by David Kohn, Princeton, 1985, pp. 185–206

Holborn, Hajo, ed, *Republic to Reich: The Making of the Nazi Revolution*, New York, 1972

Horowitz, I. L., *The Idea of War and Peace in Contemporary Philosophy*, New York, 1957

Howard, Michael, *War and the Liberal Conscience*, London, 1978

Hyman, S. E., *The Tangled Bank: Darwin, Marx, Frazer and Freud as Imaginative Writers*, New York, 1962

Hynes, Samuel, *The Edwardian Turn of Mind*, Princeton, 1968
  A War Imagined: The First World War and English Culture, London, 1990

Jones, Greta, *Social Darwinism and English Thought*, Sussex, 1980

Jordanova, L. J. edn, *Languages of Nature: Critical Essays on Science and Literature*, London, 1986

Kaye, Howard, *The Social Meaning of Modern Biology*, New Haven, 1985

Keith, Sir Arthur, *Evolution and Ethics*, New York, 1946 (published in Britain as *Essays on Human Evolution*, London, 1946).
  Darwin Revalued, London, 1955

Kelly, Alfred, *The Descent of Darwin: The Popularization of Darwinism in Germany*, 1860–1914, Chapel Hill, 1981

Kemp, Peter, *H. G. Wells and the Culminating Age*, London, 1982

Kevles, Daniel J., *In the Name of Eugenics: Genetics and the Uses of Human Heredity*, New York, 1985

Koestler, Arthur, *The Ghost in the Machine*, London, 1967
  Problems of Life, New York, 1978

Kohn, David, ed, *The Darwinian Heritage*, Princeton, 1985

La Vergata, Antonello, 'Images of Darwin: A Historiographical Overview', in *The Darwinian Heritage*, edited by David Kohn, Princeton, 1985, pp. 901–72

Lorenz, Konrad, *On Aggression*, London, 1966

Ludmerer, Kenneth, *Genetics and American Society*, Baltimore, 1972

MacKenzie, Donald A., 'Sociobiologies in Competition: the Biometrician-Mendelian Debate', in Charles Webster ed, *Biology, Medicine and Society*, 1840–1940, Cambridge, 1981, pp. 243–88

Mackenzie, N. and J., *The Time Traveller*, London, 1973

MacLean, Paul D., *The Triune Brain in Evolution*, New York, 1990

Manier, Edward, *The Young Darwin and His Cultural Circle*, Dordrecht, 1978

Marrin, A., *The Last Crusade: The Church of England in the First World War*, Durham, NC, 1974
  Sir Norman Angell, Boston, 1979

Martindale, D., *The Nature and Types of Sociological Theory*, London, 1961

Mazumdar, Pauline, *Eugenics, Human Genetics and Human Failings: The Eugenics Society, its Sources and Critics in Britain*, London, New York, 1992

McNeil, E. B., *The Nature of Human Conflict*, New Jersey, 1965

Midgley, Mary, *Beast and Man*, New York, 1978
Miller, J. B. D., *Norman Angell and the Futility of War: Peace and the Public Mind*, London, 1986
Morton, Peter, *The Vital Science: Biology and the Literary Imagination*, 1860–1900, London, 1984
Nagel, Gunter, *Georges Vacher de Lapouge*, Freiburg, 1975
Nef, John U., *War and Human Progress*, Cambridge, Mass., 1952
Nye, Robert A., *The Origins of Crowd Psychology: Gustave Le Bon and the Crisis of Mass Democracy in the Third Republic*, London, 1975
   The Anti-Democratic Sources of Elite Theory: Pareto, Mosca, Michels, London, 1977
   Crime, Madness and Politics in Modern France: The Medical Concept of National Decline, Princeton, 1984
Oldroyd, D. and Langham, I., eds., *The Wider Domain of Evolutionary Thought*, Dordrecht, London, Boston, 1983
Ospovat, Don, *The Development of Darwin's Theory: Natural History, Natural Theology, and Natural Selection, 1838–1859*, Cambridge, 1981
Paradis, James G., *T. H. Huxley: Man's Place in Nature*, Lincoln and London, 1979
Peel, J. D. Y., *Herbert Spencer: The Evolution of a Sociologist*, London, 1971
Pick, Daniel, *Faces of Degeneration: A European Disorder, c.1848-c. 1918*, Cambridge, 1989
Pound, Reginald, *The Lost Generation*, London, 1964
Powell, Walter W. and Robbins, R., eds., *Conflict and Consensus*, London, 1984
Reed, J. R., *The Natural History of H. G. Wells*, London, 1982
Richards, Robert J., *Darwin and the Emergence of Evolutionary Theories of Mind and Behavior*, Chicago, London, 1987
Ritter, Gerhard, *The Sword and the Scepter: The Problem of Militarism in Germany*, translated by Coral Gables, Florida, 1970
Ritvo, Harriet, *The Animal Estate: The English and Other Creatures in the Victorian Age*, Cambridge, Mass., London, 1987
Rose, Jonathon, *The Edwardian Temper*, Athens, Ohio, London, 1986
Ruse, Michael, *Sociobiology: Sense or Nonsense?*, Dordrecht, London, Boston, 1979
Schweber, Silvan S., 'The Wider British Context in Darwin's Theorizing', in *The Darwinian Heritage*, edited by David Kohn, Princeton, 1985, pp. 35–70
Searle, G. R., *Eugenics and Politics in Britain, 1900–1914*, Leyden, 1976
Silberner, E., *The Problem of War in Nineteenth Century Economic Thought*, trans. Princeton, 1946
Singer, J. D. and Small, Melvin, *The Wages of War, 1816–1965: A Statistical Handbook*, New York, 1972
Smith, A. D., *The Ethnic Origins of Nations*, Oxford, 1986
Smith, Woodruff, D., *The Ideological Origins of Nazi Imperialism*, New York, Oxford, 1986
Somit, Albert, *Biology and Politics: Recent Explorations*, Paris, 1976
Spengler, Oswald, *The Decline of the West*, 2 vols, New York, 1947
Standley, A. R., *Auguste Comte*, Boston, 1981
Stepan, Nancy, '"Nature's Pruning Hook": War, Race and Evolution, 1914–18',

in *The Political Culture of Modern Britain*, edited by J. M. W. Bean, London, 1987, pp. 129–48

Stocking, George W. Jr, *Victorian Anthropology*, London, 1987

Stromberg, Roland, *Redemption by War: The Intellectuals and* 1914, Kansas, 1982

Teich, M. and Young, R. M., eds., *Changing Perspectives in the History of Science*, London, 1973

Thomas, Keith, *Man and the Natural World: Changing Attitudes in England* 1500–1800, London, 1983

Tiger, Lionel and Fox, Robin, *The Imperial Animal*, New York, 1971

Toback, Ethel, 'Social Darwinism Rides Again', in *The Four Horsemen: Racism, Sexism, Militarism and Social Darwinism*, edited by E. Tobach *et al.*, New York, 1974, pp. 99–123

Travers, T. H. E., 'Future Warfare: H. G. Wells and British Military Theory, 1895–1916', in *War and Society: A Yearbook of Military History*, edited by Brian Bond and Ian Roy, London, n.d., pp. 67–87

Turner, F. M., *Between Science and Religion*, New Haven, 1974

Van Den Dungen, P., edn, and introd., *A Bibliography of the Pacifist Writings of Jean de Bloch*, London, 1977

Vanderpool, Harold Y., edn, *Darwin and Darwinism; Revolutionary Insights Concerning Man, Nature, Religion, and Society*, Lexington, London, 1973

Vincent, A., and Plant, R., *Philosophy, Politics and Citizenship: The Life and Thought of the British Idealists*, New York, 1985

Vogeler, Martha, S., *Frederick Harrison: The Vocations of a Positivist*, Oxford, 1984

Von Bertalanffy, Ludwig, *Problems of Life*, New York, 1978

Wallace, Stuart, *War and the Image of Germany: British Academics, 1914–1918*, Edinburgh, 1988

Webster, Charles, ed, *Biology, Medicine and Society, 1840–1940*, Cambridge, 1981

Weindling, Paul, 'Theories of the Cell State in Imperial Germany', in *Biology, Medicine and Society, 1840–1940*, edited by Charles Webster, Cambridge, 1981, pp. 99–155

'Darwinism in Germany', in *The Darwinian Heritage*, edited by David Kohn, Princeton, 1985, pp. 683–730

Health, Race and German Politics between National Unification and Nazism, 1870–1945, Cambridge, 1989

Weiner, M. J., *Between Two Worlds: The Political Thought of Graham Wallas*, Oxford, 1971

Wertham, Frederick, *A Sign for Cain*, New York, 1966

Westbrook, Perry D., *John Burroughs*, New York, 1974

Williams, Raymond, 'Social Darwinism', in *The Limits of Human Nature*, edited by J. Benthall, London, 1973, pp. 115–30

Wilson, Edward O., *Sociobiology: The New Synthesis*, Cambridge, Mass., 1975
On Human Nature, Cambridge, Mass., 1978

Wilson, Trevor, *The Myriad Faces of War: Britain and the Great War, 1914–1918*, Cambridge, 1986

Wiltshire, D., *Social and Political Thought of Herbert Spencer*, Oxford, 1978

Winter, Jay M., 'Fear of Population Decline in Western Europe', in *Demographic*

Patterns in Developed Societies, edited by R. Hiorns, London, 1979, pp. 193–210

Winter, Jay M., 'Army and Society: The Demographic Context', in *A Nation in Arms: A Social Study of the British Army in the First World War*, edited by Ian F. W. Beckett and K. Simpson, Manchester, 1985, pp. 193–210

The Great War and the British People, Cambridge, Mass., 1986

Worster, Donald, *Nature's Economy: A History of Ecological Ideas*, Cambridge, 1985 (1st edn, San Francisco, 1977)

Wright, T. R., *The Religion of Humanity: The Impact of Comtean Positivism on Victorian Britain*, Cambridge, 1986

Young, Robert M., 'The Historiographical and Ideological Contexts of the Nineteenth Century Debate on Man's Place in Nature', in *Changing Perspectives in the History of Science*, edited by M. Teich, and R. M. Young, London, 1973, pp. 344–438

Darwin's Metaphor: Nature's Place in Victorian Culture, Cambridge, 1985

'Darwinism *Is* Social', in *The Darwinian Heritage*, edited by David Kohn, Princeton, 1985, pp. 609–40.

ARTICLES

Anderson, O., 'The Growth of Christian Militarism in Mid-Victorian Britain', *English Historical Review*, 86 (1971), 46–72

Avineri, S., 'The Problem of War in Hegel's Thought', *Journal of the History of Ideas*, 22, 4 (1961), 463–74

Bailey, Charles E., 'The British Protestant Theologians in the First World War: Germanophobia Unleashed', *Harvard Theological Review*, 77, 2 (1984), 195–221

Barnett, S. A., 'Cooperation, Conflict, Crowding and Stress: An Essay on Method', *Interdisciplinary Science Reviews*, 4, 2 (1979), 106–31

'Humanity and Natural Selection', *Ethology and Sociobiology*, 4 (1983), 35–51

Beach, Frank A., 'The Descent of Instinct', *Psychological Review*, 62, 6 (1955), 401–10

Beer, C. G., 'Darwin, Instinct and Ethology', *Journal of the History of the Behaviorial Sciences*, 19 (1983), 68–80

Benton, Ted, 'Social Darwinism and Socialist Darwinism in Germany: 1860 to 1900', *Rivista Di Filosofia*, 23 (1982), 79–121

Bowler, Peter J., 'Malthus, Darwin and the Concept of Struggle', *Journal of the History of Ideas*, 37, 4 (1976), 631–50

'Hugo de Vries and T. H. Morgan: The Mutation Theory and the Spirit of Darwinism', *Annals of Science*, 35 (1978), 55–73

Burnham, J. C., 'Instinct Theory and the German Reaction to Weismannism', *Journal of the History of Biology*, 5, 2 (1972), 321–26

Churchill, F. B., 'August Weismann and a Break from Tradition', *Journal of the History of Biology*, 1, 1 (1968), 91–112

Collini, Stefan, 'Sociology and Idealism in Britain, 1888–1920', *Archives Euro-péenes de Soziologie*, 19 (1978), 3–50

Cravens, Hamilton, 'The Abandonment of Evolutionary Social Theory in

America: The Impact of Academic Professionalization upon American Sociological Theory', *American Studies*, 12, 2 (1971), 5–20

Crook, D. P., 'Was Benjamin Kidd a Racist?', *Ethnic and Racial Studies*, 2, 2 (1979), 213–21

'Darwinism: the Political Implications', *History of European Ideas*, 2, 1 (1981), 19–34

'Darwin on War and Aggression', *Australian Journal of Politics and History*, 29, 2 (1983), 344–53

'Nature's Pruning Hook? War and Evolution, 1890–1918: A Response to Nancy Stepan', *Australian Journal of Politics and History*, 33, 3 (1987), 237–52

'Man the Fighting Animal: Belligerent Images of Humankind in the Anglo-American World, 1914–18', *Australasian Journal of American Studies*, 8, 2 (1989), 25–39

'Peter Chalmers Mitchell and Anti-War Evolutionism in Britain during the Great War', *Journal of History of Biology*, 22, 2 (1989), 325–56

'War as Genetic Disaster? The World War I Debate over the Eugenics of Warfare', *War and Society*, 8, 1 (1990), 47–70

Davies, James, D. 'Violence and Aggression: Innate or Not?', *Western Political Quarterly*, 23 (1970), 611–23

Edgerton, David, 'Liberal Militarism and the British State', *New Left Review*, 185 (1991), 138–69

Farrall, L. A., 'Controversy and Conflict in Science: A Case Study. The English Biometric School and Mendel's Laws', *Social Studies of Science*, 5 (1975), 269–301

Feuer, Lewis, S., 'Marx and Engels as Sociobiologists', *Survey*, 23, 4 (1977–8), 109–36

Field, A. J., 'Malthus's Methodological and Macroeconomic Thought', *History of European Ideas*, 4, 2 (1983), 135–49

Freeden, M., 'J. A. Hobson as a New Liberal Theorist', *Journal of the History of Ideas*, 34 (1973), 421–43

Freeman, Derek, 'The Evolutionary Theories of Charles Darwin and Herbert Spencer', *Current Anthropology*, 15, 3 (1974), 211–37

Gale, Barry, 'Darwin and the Concept of a Struggle for Existence', *Isis*, 63, (1972), 321–44

Ginneken, Jaap van, 'The 1895 Debate on the Origins of Crowd Psychology', *Journal of the History of the Behaviorial Sciences*, 2 (1985), 375–82

Goode, John, 'Gissing, Morris and English Socialism', *Victorian Studies*, 12, 2 (1968), 200–26

Greene, John C., 'Darwin as a Social Evolutionist', *Journal of the History of Biology*, 10, 1 (1977), 1–27

Greisman, Harvey S., 'Herd Instinct and the Foundation of Biosociology', *Journal of the History of the Behavioral Sciences*, 15 (1979), 357–69

Haines, Barbara, 'The Inter-Relations Between Social, Biological, and Medical Thought, 1750–1850: Saint-Simon and Comte', *British Journal for the History of Science*, 11 (1978), 19–35

Halliday, R. J., 'Social Darwinism: A Definition', *Victorian Studies*, 14, 4 (1971), 389–405

'God and Natural Selection', *History of European Ideas*, 2, 3 (1981), 237–46

'Darwinism, Biology and Race', unpublished paper, University of Warwick (1988)

Hamilton, W. D., 'The Genetical Evolution of Social Behavior', *Journal of Theoretical Biology*, 7 (1964), 1–51

Hammond, Michael, 'Anthropology as a Weapon of Social Combat in Late Nineteenth Century France', *Journal of the History of the Behavioral Sciences*, 16 (1980), 118–32

Helfand, Michael S., 'T. H. Huxley's "Evolution and Ethics": The Politics of Evolution and the Evolution of Politics', *Victorian Studies*, 20, 2 (1977), 159–78

Herbert, Sandra, 'Darwin, Malthus and Selection', *Journal of the History of Biology*, 4 (1971), 209–17

Kara, Karel, 'On the Marxist Theory of War and Peace', *Journal of Peace Research*, 5 (1968), 1–27

Kaye, Howard, L., 'The Myth of Social Darwinism', *Contemporary Sociology*, 11 (1982), 274–75

Kennedy, T. C., 'Homer Lea and the Peace Makers', *The Historian*, 45 (1983), 473–96

Kevles, D. J., 'Genetics in the U. S. and Great Britain', *Isis*, 71 (1980), 441–55

Kottler, M. J., 'A. R. Wallace, the Origin of Man, and Spiritualism', *Isis*, 65 (1974), 145–92

'Hugo de Vries and the Rediscovery of Mendel's Laws', *Annals of Science*, 36 (1979), 517–38

Krantz, David L, and Allen, David, 'The Rise and Fall of McDougall's Instinct Theory', *Journal of the History of the Behavioral Sciences*, 3 (1967), 326–38

Levin, S. M., 'Malthus and the Idea of Progress', *Journal of the History of Ideas*, 27 (1966), 92–108

Lorimer, Douglas, 'Theoretical Racism in Late-Victorian Anthropology, 1870–1900', *Victorian Studies*, 31, 3 (1988), 405–30

Ludmerer, Kenneth, 'American Geneticists and the Eugenics Movement, 1905–1935', *Journal of the History of Biology*, 2, 2 (1969), 337–63

MacKenzie, Brian, 'Darwinism and Positivism as Methodological Influences on the Development of Psychology', *Journal of the History of Behavioral Sciences*, 12 (1976), 330–7

MacKenzie, Donald, A., 'Eugenics in Britain', *Social Studies of Science*, 6 (1976), 499–532

'Karl Pearson and the Professional Middle Class', *Annals of Science*, 36 (1979), 125–43

MacLean, Paul D., 'Man and his Animal Brains', *Modern Medicine* (Chicago), 32 (1964), 95–106

Mallan, John P., 'Roosevelt, Brooks Adams and Lea: The Warrior Critique of the Business Civilization', *American Quarterly*, 8, 3 (1956), 216–30

Mayer, Jean, 'Walter Bradford Cannon – A Biographical Sketch', *Journal of Nutrition*, 87 (1965), 3–8

Mayr, Ernst, 'The Recent Historiography of Genetics', *Journal of the History of Biology*, 6, 1 (1973), 125–54

'Weismann and Evolution', *Journal of the History of Biology*, 18, 3 (1985), 295–329

Miller, Jonathan, 'Crowds and Power', *International Review of Psycho-Analysis*, 10 (1983), 253–64

Moore, James R., 'Creation and the Problem of Charles Darwin', *British Journal for the History of Science*, 14 (1981), 189–200
  'Socializing Darwinism', *Radical Science*, 20 (1986), 38–80

Moses, John A., 'The "Ideas of 1914" in Germany and Australia: A Case of Conflicting Perceptions', *War and Society*, 9, 2 (1991), 61–82

Muller, D. R., 'Josiah Strong and American Nationalism: A Re-evaluation', *Journal of American History*, 53 (1966–7), 487–503

Nelson, Alvin, F., 'Lester Ward's Conception of the Nature of Science', *Journal of the History of Science*, 33 (1972), 633–38

Norton, B., 'The Biometric Defense of Darwinism', *Journal of the History of Biology*, 6 (1973), 283–316

Paul, Diane B., 'Eugenics and the Left', *Journal of the History of Ideas*, 45 (1984), 567–90
  'The Selection of the "Survival of the Fittest"', *Journal of the History of Biology*, 21, 3 (1988), 411–24

Pick, Daniel, 'The Faces of Anarchy', *History Workshop*, 21 (1986), 70–3

Rambo, L. R., 'Ethics, Evolution and the Psychology of William James', *Journal of the History of the Behavioral Sciences*, 116 (1980), 50–7

Richards, Robert J., 'A Defense of Evolutionary Ethics', *Biology and Philosophy*, 1 (1986), 263–93

Rogers, J. A., 'Darwinism and Social Darwinism', *Journal of the History of Ideas*, 33, 2 (1972), 265–80

Ruse, Michael, 'Charles Darwin's Theory of Evolution: An Analysis', *Journal of the History of Biology*, 8, 2 (1975), 219–41
  'Social Darwinism: The Two Sources', *Albion*, 12 (1980), 23–36

Schneider, William, 'Toward the Improvement of the Human Race: The History of Eugenics in France', *Journal of Modern History*, 54, 2 (1982), 268–91

Schweber, Silvan S., 'Darwin and the Political Economists: Divergence of Character', *Journal of the History of Biology*, 13 (1980), 95–289

Semmel, B., 'Karl Pearson: Socialist and Darwinist', *British Journal of Sociology*, 9, 2 (1958), 111–25

Smith, Roger, 'A. R. Wallace: Philosophy of Nature and Man', *British Journal of Science*, 6, 2 (1972), 179–99

Soffer, Reba N., 'New Elitism: Social Psychology in Prewar England', *Journal of British Studies*, 8, 2 (1969), 111–40
  'Why Do Disciplines Fail? The Strange Case of British Sociology', *English Historical Review*, 385 (1982), 767–802

Soloway, Richard, 'Counting the Degenerates: The Statistics of Race Deterioration in Edwardian England', *Journal of Contemporary History*, 17, 1 (1982), 137–64

Spall, R. F. Jr, 'Free Trade, Foreign Relations, and the Anti-Corn-Law League', *International History Review*, 10, 3 (1988), 405–32

Spring, D., 'Walter Bagehot and Deference', *American Historical Review*, 81, 3 (1976), 524–31

Stein, Arthur A., 'Conflict and Cohesion: A Review of the Literature', *Journal of Conflict Resolution*, 20, 1 (1976), 143–72

Stromberg, R. N., 'The Intellectuals and the Coming of War in 1914', *Journal of European Studies*, 3 (1973), 109–22

Strong, Alexia, 'Darwinism and Social Reform', Ph.D. dissertation, University of Queensland (1983)

Summers, Anne, 'Militarism in Britain before the Great War', *History Workshop*, 2 (1976), 104–23

Supina, P. D., 'The Norman Angell Peace Campaign in Germany', *Journal of Peace Research*, 9 (1974), 161–4

Thatcher, D. S., 'Nietzsche, Bagehot and the Morality of Custom', *Victorian Newsletter*, 62 (1982), 7–13

Weinroth, Howard, 'Norman Angell and *The Great Illusion*: An Episode in Pre-1914 Pacifism', *Historical Journal*, 17, 3 (1974), 551–74

Westwater, Martha, 'The Victorian Nightmare of Evolution: Charles Darwin and Walter Bagehot', *Victorian Newsletter*, 64 (1983), 9–13

Westwater, S. A. M., 'Walter Bagehot: A Reassessment', *Antioch Review*, 35 (1977), 39–49

Winter, Jay M., 'Balliol's "Lost Generation" of the First World War', *Balliol College Records* (1975), 10–14

'Some Aspects of the Demographic Consequences of the First World War in Britain', *Population Studies*, 30 (1976), 539–52

Young, Robert M., 'Malthus and the Evolutionists: The Common Context of Biological and Social Theory', *Past and Present*, 43 (1969), 109–41.

Index